The Essential
Good Food Guide

The Essential Good Food Guide

The Complete Resource for Buying and Using
Whole Grains and Specialty Flours, Heirloom Fruits and Vegetables,
Meat and Poultry, Seafood, and More

MARGARET M. WITTENBERG

Photography by Jennifer Martiné

TEN SPEED PRESS
Berkeley

Published in the United States by Ten Speed Press, an imprint of
the Crown Publishing Group, a division of Random House, Inc., New York.
www.crownpublishing.com
www.tenspeed.com

Ten Speed Press and the Ten Speed Press colophon are
registered trademarks of Random House, Inc.

Previous editions of this work were published as *Good Food: The Complete Guide to
Eating Well* by The Crossing Press, Freedom, California, in 1995, and as *New Good Food:
Essential Ingredients for Cooking and Eating Well* by Ten Speed Press, in Berkeley,
California, in 2007.

Instructions on page 67 courtesy of the Carolina Gold Rice Foundation

Library of Congress Cataloging-in-Publication Data is on file with the publisher

ISBN 978-1-60774-434-4
eBook ISBN 978-1-60774-435-1

Printed in China
Cover and text design by Sarah Adelman

10 9 8 7 6 5 4 3 2 1

Third Edition

Contents

Introduction

~

I am an intuitive cook. Put a variety of foods in front of me and I can visualize how they might fit together, enhancing one another in terms of flavors, textures, and presentation. Although some of my knack is likely innate, much of it I developed through experience, by cooking, observing, listening, and reading. In the process, I have learned a lot about different foods, their history, how they are grown or produced, their nutritional attributes, and the best methods for cooking them. I've also learned a lot about how various foods affect one's overall well-being. Writing this book, then, has stirred up a lot of memories for me. Each food I describe evokes the time and place when I first tried or heard about it, and all the circumstances surrounding that experience.

Nourishing My Interests

My mother's extraordinary cooking served as a backdrop to sharing the day's happenings at meals with my parents and five siblings. Sunday breakfasts were my father's realm. Inspired by my parents' talents, I tried my own hand at cooking, following recipes from my beloved *Better Homes and Gardens Junior Cook Book* and also improvising on my own.

My interest in cooking reached a new level when, for a 4-H Club meeting food demonstration project, I was assigned the task of highlighting the visual differences between two cakes, one made with baking powder and the other without. That a food could change so dramatically by adding or deleting just one ingredient was utterly fascinating to me, igniting what would be a lifelong enthusiasm for food science and the interactions between foods and various ingredients.

When I met my husband, Terry, in 1974, we realized immediately that we shared an interest in food. Starting with a visit to a local natural foods co-op, Terry introduced me to many new foods, as well as to familiar ones that, to me, were largely unrecognizable in their raw forms. Take dried beans, for example. Although I had eaten plenty of navy bean soup and pork and beans while growing up, that had been the extent of my bean repertoire—and they were purchased precooked in cans. While I knew I had a lot to learn, the beautiful, earthy colors and various shapes of uncooked beans intrigued me, as did the many bins of whole grains, nuts, and seeds. I knew I was hooked.

Terry was also the catalyst for my fascination with the nutritional aspects of food. Because he's an avid long-distance cyclist, often logging more than ten thousand miles a year, using food as a source of functional fuel has been just as important to him as the sensual pleasure of eating. While hiking, Pilates, running, weights, and dance have also figured into the picture for one or both of us throughout the years, finding the best food choices for recovery from the long miles of cycling along with maintaining overall vitality has been the biggest challenge—and greatest reward—of eating a good food diet.

Fortunately for me, my love of food turned into a career. The start of more than three decades of professional connection with food began with Sunseed Natural Foods, a small natural foods store Terry and I opened in West Bend, Wisconsin, during the fall of 1977. Along with the challenges of introducing natural foods to a small, conservative Midwestern town, we also had to learn the realities of running a business. We thrived on the experience, which also got us connected with our community. We sold beef, maple syrup, fresh eggs, and fresh vegetables from a local organic farmer. And we also enjoyed a wide variety of fresh culinary herbs and unique vegetables, like kohlrabi and Jerusalem artichokes, that we bought from organic gardeners at our small town's farmers' market. From teaching cooking classes to helping customers in the aisles, for us it was all about sharing the great flavors, fun, and health benefits of cooking with natural foods. It also laid a good foundation for what was to come.

After selling our store at the end of 1980, Terry and I happened by the first Whole Foods Market in Austin, Texas, just four months after the store had opened for business. We were hired in January 1981 as two of the company's original twenty-five team members, sharing in the excitement of being part of a new concept in grocery stores—a

one-stop shop where all the food was natural and minimally processed. In the early years, beyond working in many different areas within the store, I taught cooking classes, developed recipes, conducted food information trainings, and wrote the company's food-focused publication. The remainder of my thirty-plus years with the company have included food product and policy research along with coordinating the company's quality standards program.

Meanwhile, in the mid-1980s, I also had a one-year part-time stint as the principal cook of the East West Macrobiotic Center in Austin, Texas, where I honed my cooking skills, learning about balancing elements within a meal and the very real effects food has on body, mind, and spirit. In addition to teaching cooking classes, my main role was to create and cook a wide variety of seasonal and ethnic-focused menus for up to fifty guests for the lunches and one hundred for the monthly Friday night dinners the East West Center offered (along with the occasional Sunday brunches). There I mastered the art of cooking greens and sea vegetables, as well as using seasonings and condiments to make dishes sizzle with flavor.

For further inspiration, in the intervening years I took as many classes as I could from many of my esteemed natural foods cooking teachers, including Annemarie Colbin, Mary Estella, Susan Jane Cheney, Meredith McCarty, Carole Goodman Price, and many others who traveled through the Austin area. One of these classes spurred my interest in whole grain sourdough baking. In 1992, I started my beloved whole wheat sourdough starter and a couple years later a rye starter; both are still going strong from weekly feedings and regular use to make amazing sourdough breads, breadsticks, and muffins.

My interest in heirloom fruits, vegetables, beans, and grains also began to flourish during this time; I experimented with any new variety I could get my hands on. While on a trip to London, England, in 2003, I discovered the extraordinary

Borough Market, London's oldest fruit and vegetable market—still trading at the same location since 1755. While I had been to all types of farmers' markets in the United States, never had I seen in one place such artistry, craftsmanship, and simple beauty celebrating good food. Since then I have returned to Borough Market several times, and have been to many other markets around the world, each with its own special flavor. And, at each one I have enjoyed watching the people as much as encountering the food; these experiences underscore for me the universal hunger for eating good food using whole food ingredients to make both traditional and contemporary dishes as well as our appetite for exploring foods not yet experienced.

Truly, throughout my life I've had the good fortune to meet a number of extraordinary people—farmers and producers, home and professional cooks and chefs, scientists, food experts and food lovers worldwide—all of whom have contributed to the constant expansion of my knowledge and deep appreciation of food—its extraordinary flavors and what it takes to produce it. Continued access to good food and good health requires everyone's commitment to working in concert with nature and each other. Not only does this involve protecting the health of the land through continual restoration of the soil, conservation practices, and the avoidance of toxic chemicals, but also a commitment to the sustainable wild capture or farming of seafood, and the welfare of food producing animals from birth through slaughter. Without a doubt: when it comes to ecological sustainability and the opportunity for eating well, we humans are intrinsically connected to every element within the universe, including our fellow creatures.

The Intrinsic Value of Whole Foods

Every day, discoveries are being made that underscore the truth that keeping foods whole, not processed or fractionated, is vital to our overall health and well-being. Increasingly, we are learning that isolated nutrients don't always have the same health benefits as the whole foods from which they were derived. And beyond the familiar vitamins and minerals most of us know about, whole plant foods, including herbs and spices, contain an almost bewildering array of healthful compounds known as phytonutrients or phytochemicals (*phyto* means "plant"). Pigments, flavor components, and aromatic qualities that we once thought were primarily of benefit to plants—helping them either to better flourish or to protect themselves—have turned out to be powerful antioxidants that can help moderate damage to our own cells. Phytonutrients have also been found to enhance our immune response, help repair DNA damage from toxic exposures, and enhance cell to cell communication. Unlike protein, fat, vitamins, and minerals, the vast array of phytonutrients may not be essential for keeping us alive, but their positive effects on health, such as helping prevent cancer and reducing inflammation are unmistakable and certainly make living life that much more enjoyable.

Some of the most studied phytonutrients may sound familiar:

- **Carotenes**, including alpha- and beta-carotenes, beta-cryptoxanthin, lutein, lycopene, and zeaxanthin as found in red, orange, and yellow vegetables and fruits
- **Polyphenols,** including flavonoids (anthocyanins, catechins, flavanones, and isoflavones) and nonflavonoids (ellagic acid, coumarins, tannins, and lignans) as found in a wide variety of fruits, vegetables, beans, nuts, whole grains, tea, culinary herbs and spices, dark chocolate, and red wine

- **Isothiocyanates** and **indoles,** as found in cruciferous vegetables such as cabbage, broccoli, arugula, chard, kale, bok choy, collard greens, cauliflower, rutabaga, turnips, radishes, watercress, and brussels sprouts

Scientific studies have repeatedly shown the powerful positive effects of eating a good diet, starting from the maternal nutrition we receive while still in the womb and continuing through all stages of life, including our senior years. Eating a good, nutritious diet high in phytonutrients, maintaining a healthy weight, and getting sufficient exercise are essential for reducing the incidence of myriad chronic noncommunicable heath conditions such as cardiovascular disease, hypertension, stroke, diabetes, cancer, dental diseases, and osteoporosis.

And a good diet is not a numbers game involving basing one's diet choices on how high or low a food is in fat, cholesterol, sodium, and the like. Food manufacturers can process food in a variety of ways to make it look good on a nutrition facts label, but that doesn't mean the food within the package is inherently nutritious or even good for you. The lowest rates of coronary heart disease, certain types of cancers, and other diet-related chronic diseases have been found in cultures where the everyday diet is based primarily on whole foods. This diet is high in fruits, vegetables, whole grains, whole grain breads and pastas, beans, nuts and seeds, and includes some unrefined healthy oils. It has low amounts of eggs, red meat, fish, poultry, and dairy products in the form of cheese and yogurt. Not only is eating such a diet the most nutritious—remember that phytonutrients are present only in whole plant foods—it is also the most delicious—which helps motivate us to maintain such a diet. The trick is to know all the fabulous good food possibilities available in every category of food.

And that is exactly what this book is all about. Rather than being about what foods to avoid and why, it is an introduction to or a reminder of *what good food is and what to do with it.* It is a weaving together of descriptions, cooking suggestions, and

Dried beans

just enough history, food science, and nutrition to give a glimpse of the wonders each food has to offer. It is an appreciation of food for its possibilities: its bringing together of people to the table, its melding of cultures, its nourishment of body and soul, its celebration of the people and plants that make it all happen, and, of course, its extraordinary flavors.

Each chapter focuses on specific foods and related ideas that I personally have found to be essential to an intuitive style of wholesome, delicious cooking. You'll experience an abundant world of food within these pages, which I hope will serve as a catalyst for the development of your own natural connection to foods. Your path of discovery will bring you not only sheer enjoyment but also better health and well-being.

Now, it's time to turn the page and get out your fork. Explore and enjoy the possibilities!

Fruits and Vegetables

Fruits and vegetables represent one of our closest links to nature—and to life itself. Who doesn't have a sense of wonder that a tiny seed can grow into an entire plant that we can then harvest and eat? Who doesn't marvel at the transformation of small flowers into crisp apples or succulent pears as the season progresses? Fruits and vegetables don't merely appease our pangs of hunger or provide needed nutrients; they nourish us on many levels.

Beyond the joy of harvesting vegetables from my own garden, when I'm in a well-stocked produce department or farmers' market with a wide variety of produce in all sizes, shapes, flavors, and colors, I genuinely want to eat my way through it, and it takes all the restraint I can muster to hold myself back. Fortunately, we all have many opportunities to buy fruits and vegetables, stimulating our thrill of discovery, and with the diversity available no one meal ever needs to be the same.

Science has corroborated what we instinctively know: eating plenty of fruits and vegetables is the primary key to overall health and well-being. More specifically, in large part thanks to their high levels of phytonutrients, fruits and vegetables can help reduce the risk of many diseases and disorders, including heart disease, stroke, cancer, and age-related eye diseases such as macular degeneration and cataracts. Both fruits and vegetables are equally essential in the diet, with each making valuable and unique contributions to health that cannot be completely replaced by the other. While variety is essential (given that no one plant has every nutrient ever needed to enhance one's health), some been shown to be superstars within their categories, again owing largely to their phytonutrient content, the mysteries of which science is continuing to unearth. Among fruits, berries of all types appear to rank highest. In vegetables, dark leafy greens, especially those of the cruciferous family, are tops. It makes sense to include some berries and dark greens nearly every day to take advantage of their beneficial effects, not to mention their terrific flavors.

Produce Labeling

Whether you're buying fruits and vegetables from a grocery store, farmers' market, or farmer, specific terms are used—often on labels or stickers—to convey how the product was produced or other special attributes. While some of the language on labels may reflect the producer's claims, many represent adherence to specific standards, especially in regard to special methods of production—"organic," for example, has a very specific legal meaning in regard to environmental stewardship and the use of toxic or environmentally persistent agricultural chemicals.

Since fruits and vegetables account for the majority of pesticide residues in our foods, access to production method information is important to know. Continual exposure to residues from synthetic highly toxic pesticides in our foods are linked to a variety of health problems for farm workers and their families, include nerve damage, cancer, and birth defects; the chemicals also have a gravely adverse effect on and long-term persistence in wildlife and the environment at large. Pesticide residues in our food pose risks to fetuses, infants, and children, who are most vulnerable to their effects. Lower IQ levels in children have been linked to pesticide exposure in early pregnancy when the child's brain is developing; so have premature births and lower birth weights. Consuming food treated with certain synthetic pesticides like organophosphates while pregnant may also increase the unborn child's risk of autism, attention–deficit/hyperactivity disorder (ADHD), allergies, obesity, diabetes, reproductive problems, and some forms of cancer.

Production claims are best verified by a qualified inspector not personally affiliated with the producer or a company for whom a farmer may grow products; this process is called independent third party auditing. In most cases, the name or seal of the auditing group is listed on the label. These inspectors, hired by a private auditing company, governmental agency, or standards-creating organization, are trained and qualified to objectively evaluate the producer's compliance with the standards represented by the label.

BIODYNAMIC

Biodynamic farming, an agricultural method in which the farm is managed as a self-contained, living organism, integrates soil health and nutrient management, not only in conjunction with raising crops and livestock, but also within the context of the subtle rhythms and energies of nature. Biodynamic agricultural methods are based on lectures presented in 1924 by Rudolf Steiner, an Austrian scientist who believed farming should be done with both an understanding of its practical, scientific aspects and a spiritual appreciation of nature.

Biodynamic farming is similar to organic agriculture in many regards. It focuses on building and maintaining soil quality by rotating crops, using cover crops, and composting. And like organic farming, it doesn't make use of genetically engineered seeds or crops, sewage sludge as compost, or toxic pesticides, herbicides, or fungicides. However, biodynamic farming is different than organic agriculture because of its metaphysical underpinnings, which manifest in specific practices used to enhance vital life forces and subtle energetic frequencies on the farm. Planting and harvesting are planned according to certain lunar and astrological cycles, and specific soil treatments are made in a precise manner from minerals, plants, or animal manure extracts and applied to compost in extremely diluted amounts. Research has affirmed that the quality of soil on biodynamic farms is indeed superior, and it may be that food quality and overall nutrition of products from such farms are enhanced in ways the standard nutritional analysis, which is focused on vitamin and mineral content, cannot gauge.

Food and products that have been certified by qualified, independent auditors as meeting the rigorous requirements of biodynamic farming are labeled with the Demeter International trademark. As biodynamic standards include those required by organic standards, many biodynamic products are doubly certified as organic, too.

ECOLOGICALLY OR SUSTAINABLY GROWN

A wide range of labels refer to a product's having been **ecologically** or **sustainably grown** in one way or another. Standards for some of these methods prohibit specific pesticides and the use of genetically modified seeds. Other standards may be crop-specific or region-specific. Still others may require producers to monitor and document performance measures related to management of wildlife habitat, the soil's organic matter potential, water conservation, and irrigation efficiency to enhance ecosystem health. Other metrics may include overall energy use efficiency, or whether fertilizers, herbicides, or pesticides have been applied, and if so how much. Look for details about the particular requirements of any given label and, for extra assurance that label claims were met, the name or seal of an independent auditing company on the label itself.

Biointensive integrated pest management (IPM) is a more enhanced and defined approach within the ecologically grown arena. Its focus is on proactive management of pests and beneficial organisms within an ecological context. The over-arching intent is to prevent pest infestations before they happen by monitoring crops closely and treating pests only as needed and using only the amount and duration of treatment needed to get the job done.

This style of farming requires a thorough understanding of insects and microbes, both beneficial and potentially destructive varieties, and their interactions with other organisms and the environment. It also requires commitment to close monitoring and record keeping. Skill is required to determine which methods to use to prevent or treat pests in the most ecological, integrated manner and restore and enhance natural balances in the ecosystem. These include using appropriate pest-resistant and disease-resistant cultivars, crop rotation, creation of habitats that attract beneficial organisms, use of companion crops that draw insects away from the main crop, and physical barriers against pests, along with measures to increase overall biological diversity within the farm system and to develop and maintain healthy soil.

Natural biological pest control is a central approach of biointensive IPM. Insects, bacteria, fungi, viruses, birds, and bats may be natural enemies to a particular pest, and their presence may be encouraged. Pest-specific synthetic sex pheromones may also be used to reduce insect populations; these work to confuse male insects, disrupting the mating cycle. Mechanical and physical controls such as soil solarization, floating row covers, and insect vacuums can also be utilized. Pesticides are employed as a last resort, with attention on choosing reduced risk pesticides that are the least toxic to humans and the ecosystem.

FAIR TRADE

The term **fair trade** refers to a program of ethical trading practices that aims to help producers from developing countries have better equity in overall trading conditions when gaining access to markets and long-term trading relationships in the developed world. It also encompasses the guarantee of fair prices, better wages, and safe, equitable working conditions.

There are a variety of fair trade–focused labeling and certification programs available, each with its own logo to identify products that are grown and produced according to its particular fair trade standards and criteria. For example, some fair trade programs certify only small-scale farming operations that belong to farmer cooperatives, while others allow independent producers and larger estate operations to be audited and verified as fair trade operations. Other features may include a particular program's requirement for sustainable agriculture methods and responsible environmental practices, access for the community to development funds to improve living conditions and provide needed services, access to tools and training, and adherence to product quality standards. To better understand specific fair trade program claims, check out its details on the program's website or product literature, paying special attention on how the fair trade claim is being verified.

HEIRLOOM

Like family heirlooms—valued possessions passed down from generation to generation—**heirloom** fruits and vegetables are treasured varieties that are often symbols of regional pride and living connections to the past. In general, an heirloom plant is a variety that has been known through historical documentation or folk history for at least fifty years, although most in this category have a legacy of far more than one hundred years. Most are grown through open pollination, which means their seeds are set naturally, often helped by wind, rain, and insects. One benefit of heirlooms is that seeds produced by open pollination can be used to grow a new generation of plants, which is not the case with hybrids, which are either sterile or don't breed.

Many heirloom varieties grown in the United States originated from seeds brought by immigrants. Subsequent decades and centuries of adaptation and natural selection have resulted in one-of-a-kind fruit and vegetables varieties, many of which thrive only in certain regions. That's why their names are often as interesting as their characteristics: some are known by the name of the family, farm, or locale where they're grown, while others are tagged with colorful names that attempt to describe flavor or appearance.

Unusual shapes and sizes, flavors that range from familiar to complex and unique, curious colors, and mottled facades—all are typical hallmarks of heirloom fruits and vegetables that allow us to celebrate diversity in a world all too often focused on the homogenous. By keeping a wide array of plants in circulation, heirloom varieties also help protect the biodiversity that is so vital to the health of our planet and the resilience of our food supply. What's more, many heirloom varieties demonstrate exceptional tolerance to adverse weather and pests.

If you were to compare the amounts of basic vitamins and minerals in heirloom varieties and their modern counterparts, they might look much the same. However, the distinctive colors and flavors of some heirloom foods hint at the presence of unique phytonutrients that may not be as available or plentiful in hybrids. Contemporary hybrids have been developed by deliberately crossing two or more varieties to achieve traits such as uniformity, prolonged shelf life, higher yield, or specific flavors or cooking properties.

Heirloom varieties of fruits and vegetables—apples, pears, tomatoes, potatoes, zucchini, and green beans, to name a few—are widely available in many parts of the country. Explore the world of these interesting and flavorful alternatives. Because many of them grow better in small-production systems or certain areas, buying them locally is often the way to go.

LOCALLY GROWN

There is no single definition of **locally grown**. The claim might be based on how many miles or hours away a farm is from the market, or it could be considered in terms of state or regional production. Whatever the criteria, a focus on locally grown produce has the potential to provide fruits and vegetables that are much fresher and, therefore, more flavorful and nutritious; produce shipped from far outside the local area may already be several days old by the time it arrives in a market. Buying locally grown produce also increases your opportunity to enjoy the flavors, shapes, sizes, and textures of varieties that are unique to the area. Knowing that a person within your community produced a particular product adds a personal level to the experience, including appreciation of the effort and commitment the farmer took to grow it. Still, it's important to remember that locally grown produce isn't necessarily grown without agricultural chemicals. Look into a local producer's growing methods, which may be reflected in a certified organic label or through statements listed on a custom label or sign. Better yet, ask the farmer directly.

ORGANICALLY GROWN

Organic agriculture is a system of production based on enhancing the health of the soil in order to produce crops in a way that fosters the health and harmony of the ecosystem, including the people and animals within it. The universality of the organic label adds to its value; it signifies the only agricultural production claim that is recognized and accessible worldwide. The International Federation of Organic Agriculture Movements (IFOAM), an international umbrella organization for agencies supporting organic agriculture, helps maintain harmony and commitment to four overarching philosophical principles: 1) sustaining the health of soil, plant, animal, and planet as indivisible; 2) emulating and helping to sustain living ecological systems and cycles; 3) building relationships among people and their connection with other living things to ensure equity, respect, and stewardship; and 4) managing processes in a precautionary and responsible manner to protect the health and well-being of current and future generations and the environment.

An organic plan is a key element of and requirement for organic certification; it outlines the details of the farmer's production, preparation, handling, and management practices. Certain cultivation practices, such as rotating crops, planting cover crops, and composting, are used to help support soil fertility. Methods that support and enhance biodiversity within the agricultural landscape are also emphasized, including recycling of nutrients, protection of habitat for wildlife and beneficial insects, conservation of soil and water, and protection of soil and water quality. Pests, weeds, and diseases are managed primarily through physical, mechanical, and biological controls, many of them similar to those used in biointensive integrated pest management programs. However, in organic farming, neither pesticides that persist within the environment nor toxic chemicals in general are allowed. In the event that more support is needed for a particular crop, only biological, botanical, or specific approved low-risk substances may be used; these are quickly broken down by oxygen and sunlight.

In addition, fruits and vegetables certified as organic must be grown on land that has gone through a transition time (in the United States and Canada, three years; in the European Union (EU), two years for annuals and three years for perennials) in which no prohibited substances are applied to it prior to harvest of the crop. Organic certification farm audits are conducted by sanctioned or accredited companies that are qualified to conduct rigorous reviews of records and thorough on-site inspections of the farm.

Organic Standards

Development and maintenance of organic standards also includes a system for appointed committees with governmental oversight to review materials, policy, and procedures reviews. For example, in the United States, a list of substances allowed or prohibited in organic farming, production, and processing is reviewed by the National Organic Standards Board (NOSB), whose fifteen appointed members represent various stakeholders. All products are evaluated for their effects on human health and their short-term and long-term effects on the environment, taking into consideration toxicity and mode of action, availability of gentler alternatives, chances of environmental contamination (during manufacture, use, and disposal), potential for interactions with other substances, and overall compatibility with a system of sustainable agriculture. Recommendations of the NOSB are taken under advisement, with final policy decisions made by the Secretary of the United States Department of Agriculture.

Many countries have recognition agreements and equivalency agreements among one another to ensure the products that enter their respective countries labeled as organic have authenticity. **Recognition agreements** allow a foreign government to accredit certifying agents in its country to be able to certify organic products and facilities to meet or exceed the organic regulations in another country so those products can then be imported for sale. **Equivalency agreements** between countries indicate that while some differences between organic standards may exist, not only do those differing standards meet the same objectives and principles assuring conformity, but that common organic principles exist for defining and ensuring the organic label. These include biologically based production practices; cycling of resources; no toxic/harmful substances used—or, any that are have low impact on the environment; traceability from farm to market; continuous improvement; similar organizational, policy, and procedural quality management system requirements; and effective accountability and enforcement. The result is that a product certified as organic by either one of the equivalency partner countries would be able to be sold, labeled, and represented as organic by both countries. For example, in 2012, the United States and the European Union (EU) member states signed an equivalency agreement; the United States and the EU each have separate equivalency agreements with Canada.

Nutritional Benefits of Organics

Science has begun to confirm many of the health and nutrition benefits of eating organically produced food. For example, consuming organic foods is an excellent way to avoid exposure to organophosphate pesticides. Widely used in conventional agriculture, these pesticides have been associated with increased risk of negative neurological effects in infants and children. Studies of dietary interventions have shown dramatic reductions in organophosphate metabolites within children's bodies when they were switched to a diet consisting primarily of organic foods.

Another benefit of organic farming is the enhanced levels of nutrients found in organics. Among the many studies demonstrating this point, one that came out in 2008 that was based on a review of all peer-reviewed studies since 1980 comparing the nutrient levels between organic and conventional foods revealed organic's nutritional premium in eleven key nutrients: vitamins A, C, and E; potassium; phosphorus; total protein; nitrates (lower levels are desired); and four measures of antioxidants (total phenolics, total antioxidant capacity, quercetin,

and a flavonoid called kaempferol). Studies making direct comparisons of antioxidant levels in organic versus conventionally raised crops, using the same plant varieties, on similar soils, and under the same weather conditions, have shown that organic farming methods contribute to increased antioxidant concentrations in fruits and vegetables on average by 30 percent. In essence, what organic advocates had intuitively believed about these practices' benefits to both people and place is now being corroborated by science.

Prohibition of Genetic Engineering

Organic standards worldwide also prohibit the use of genetically engineered seeds or ingredients (also known as genetically modified organisms, GMOs, GE, or GM) in the growth and production of organic foods, which makes buying organic a simple way to avoid foods intentionally produced through this technology. Genetic engineering (GE) is the manipulation of an organism's genes by eliminating or rearranging specific genes or by introducing genetic elements from other organisms into an organism (including across species boundaries) in order to create traits in plants and animals that do not occur in nature and could not be developed by natural means. In contrast to the agroecological systems approach and classical plant breeding techniques, genetic engineering has shown its major limitations, potentially risking the overall health of the environment.

Whether it refers to an organic or a nonorganic food, a "GMO-free" claim is, unfortunately, not achievable for crops grown in countries where genetically engineered seeds are available to grow and sell for foods intended for human consumption due to potential sources of unintentional contamination. These include pollen drift, seed impurity, or commingling of GMO and non-GMO foods during transportation or manufacture.

Still, when looking for non-GMO foods, several options exist. Buying certified organic products is always your best bet. And, when it comes to nonorganic products, the simplest is to look for products that do not contain ingredients derived from crops that have governmental approval to be grown as crops from genetically engineered seed and used in products for human consumption. Regulations within the European Union and many other countries require labeling for all foods in which the presence of GMO material is 0.9 percent or more of the product's total weight. And in North America, which lacks governmental GMO labeling requirements, another option is the Non-GMO Project Verified label, which indicates a product has been independently confirmed as produced according to best practices and procedures to avoid the intentional use of GMO ingredients.

PESTICIDE-RELATED DESIGNATIONS

When produce is designated as having **"no detectable pesticide residues,"** this means a representative sample has been tested in a laboratory to determine how much or how many pesticides remain on the produce after harvest. Results are based on the specific level of detection deemed possible for a specific pesticide. Frequency of testing and testing methods are important questions to have answered from any company making this claim. Fruits and vegetables raised using conventional agricultural methods are generally most likely to be evaluated for such labeling. Like the "pesticide-free" claim (below), this label lacks any guarantee of or commitment to sustainable agricultural practices.

Typically, **pesticide-free** is simply a self-affirmed producer claim that no synthetic chemical pesticides were used to grow the fruit or vegetable. Be aware that such a declaration does not mean the produce was organically grown, or that the crop was grown using any other ecologically friendly methods than no pesticides. As this claim is not independently evaluated and the avoidance of harmful synthetic pesticide use is only one factor within the context of sustainable agriculture, this label lacks depth.

Exploring Fruits and Vegetables

The easiest way to experience the diversity of fruits and vegetables and take advantage of the wide range of vitamins, minerals, and phytonutrients they contain is to include selections from all the color groups in your diet each day (see pages 20 to 22) and eat them in a variety of forms.

FRESH AND FROZEN

It's important to eat both raw and cooked fruits and vegetables. Because some phytonutrients and vitamins, such as vitamin C and folic acid, are heat sensitive, including raw fruits and vegetables preserves these in your diet. On the other hand, certain nutritional components of some vegetables, such as tomatoes and carrots, are more bioavailable after cooking. Using only a minimal amount of cooking water will help retain nutrients.

While fresh produce is usually optimal in terms of nutrition, sometimes frozen fruits and vegetables are more nutritious than fresh ones, depending on the length of time since a fresh product was harvested and the conditions under which it was transported and stored. If packed without any additives, including sweeteners, canned products can be healthful options, too.

JUICED AND DRIED

Although juices can be a good way to consume fruits and vegetables, they usually lack the fiber and phytonutrients found in the foods' whole forms. And because juices are low in fiber, their concentrated sugars will be absorbed very rapidly (depending on the amount of juice consumed, its dilution, and whether it's drunk as part of a meal or as a single beverage). Moderation, as always, is the key. Reading labels is particularly important when shopping for juice. Be sure to buy only 100 percent fruit juice with no added sweeteners.

Another way to enjoy fruit and vegetables is in their dried or dehydrated state. Grapes become raisins, some plums become prunes, and other fruits reveal sides of themselves that are merely hinted

Dried gogi berries

The texture of dried fruit can be made softer by steaming or cooking in a small amount of water for a few minutes or by soaking in water for a few hours or overnight. These methods can help plump dried fruit nearly to its original size, and as a side benefit, the soaking water can be used as a cooking liquid or sweet beverage. Soaking the fruit can also reduce our tendency to overeat dried fruit, which, although it's a healthful food, does contain concentrated sugars. The high sugar content of dried fruits acts as a preservative, so refrigeration of dried fruits is not necessary, though they will keep much longer if refrigerated. Store them in airtight jars or plastic containers to keep them from absorbing moisture and attracting insects. Occasionally, the natural sugars in the fruit will solidify, forming crystals on the surface of the fruit, particularly prunes and figs; this is harmless.

Dried vegetables can be eaten as a good alternative to typical salty snacks. They can also be used as you would fresh vegetables: put them in boiling water for at least 5 minutes to allow their concentrated flavor to awaken and add them to soups, stews, sauces, casseroles, omelets, breads, and pizza toppings. Similar to dried fruits, store dried vegetables in airtight jars or plastic containers.

Fruits and vegetables can also be freeze-dried, a process in which the fresh product is first flash frozen in a special vacuum chamber that causes the water in the food to change directly to a gas, thus preserving the cell structure of the food without compromising vitamins, nutrients, color, or aroma. Low levels of heat also help make a freeze-dried food's taste, texture, appearance, and aroma more like its fresh state than it would be if simply dried.

Like their dehydrated counterparts, freeze-dried fruits and vegetables can be eaten directly out of hand as a snack or added to salads, yogurt, smoothies, granola, or cold cereal and used as a substitute for dried fruit in any recipe. Because they are highly moisture sensitive, they rehydrate quickly when exposed to cold or hot water. Accordingly, if you want them to retain their texture, add them in

at when they're consumed fresh. Besides concentrating flavors and sugar content, dehydration also concentrates a fruit's nutrients, making it very high in fiber, potassium, and phytonutrients, including carotenoids and other antioxidants. On the other hand, as with cooking, the heat (albeit low) used during the dehydration process can lower levels of heat-sensitive nutrients, such as vitamin C.

Even though most dried fruits are very sweet, some are sprayed with a honey or sugar solution to keep the fruit soft, balance out acidity, and prevent the dried fruit from turning brown. Sulfur dioxide, sodium sulfite, sodium and potassium bisulfite, and sodium and potassium metabisulfite are sometimes used to prevent discoloration and help retain moisture in dried fruit and vegetables. However, any products preserved with sulfites should be avoided, as they are known to cause reactions in sensitive individuals. Fortunately, dried fruits and vegetables processed without sulfites are readily available. Even though some of them may be more leathery or chewy in texture and less vibrant in color, their flavor is not affected.

toward the end of the cooking process, for example, in oatmeal and other types of porridge or soups, stews, and other savory recipes. No refrigeration is needed to store freeze-dried fruits and vegetables, but moisture-proof containers are a must.

Fruit and Vegetable Storage and Food Safety Tips

When you store them, keep fruits and vegetables separate, as the ethylene gas produced by some fruits can make certain vegetables taste bitter. However, you can also put that ethylene gas to work to help fruit ripen more quickly. Just place underripe bananas, peaches, plums, nectarines, or apricots in a loosely closed paper sack or a ripening bowl made expressly for that purpose. Within a day or two, some of the fruit's starch will convert to its sweeter form—sugar. Refrigerate fruit after it is fully ripened to slow further ripening. Bananas don't play by the same rules; they turn black when refrigerated. Instead, peel and freeze any extra ripe bananas and use them as a flavorful thickener for smoothies.

Some raw vegetables, including whole tomatoes, potatoes, and sweet potatoes, should also never be refrigerated, as cold temperatures can adversely affect their flavor and texture. Winter squash need not be refrigerated, either. However, fresh-cut produce should always be sold and stored refrigerated. Likewise, all perishable fresh fruit and vegetables and fresh-pressed juices should be kept at temperatures below 40°F and away from raw meat, poultry, and seafood. Mushrooms should be stored in the refrigerator in paper bags, not plastic. Remove any green tops from root vegetables to prevent moisture from being drawn up and out of the roots.

Treat fresh basil and cilantro like flowers, placing their long stems in water, changing the water daily, and keeping at a cool room temperature for up to a couple of days. Store other fresh herbs in the refrigerator loosely within perforated or partially open plastic bags to provide air flow; insert a paper towel to absorb excess moisture.

Because berries are very perishable, keep them dry, washing them only right before eating rather than before storing in the refrigerator. It's important to thoroughly wash or rinse all produce before eating, including fruits or vegetables that will be peeled, even if they're organically grown. Firm produce should be scrubbed with a vegetable brush. Damaged or bruised portions of fruits and vegetables should be cut away and discarded before cooking or eating them. Bagged produce can be used without further washing, although it's safest to rinse it thoroughly just prior to use.

Fruits

Oranges, apples, grapes, berries, and bananas—we love them all, but sometimes it's great to venture out a bit and try something new. If some of those listed below are already familiar to you, perhaps consider including them a bit more frequently in your diet. If you haven't tried them, do so! Not only will incorporating these fruits supply a different spectrum of nutrients from the usual fruit brigade, but since each features unique shapes, textures, colors, and flavors, adding them is just plain fun.

ASIAN PEAR

Also known as apple pears, Asian pears have the juicy, sweet flavor of a pear and the crispness and shape of an apple. Not a hybrid, this fruit was brought to the United States by Chinese prospectors during the California Gold Rush. Since Asian pears are picked ripe, they are ready to eat when purchased. Unlike other fruits, they store well for several months when refrigerated. Their refreshing flavor and texture are best appreciated when they are eaten out of hand or added to fruit salads thinly sliced, cut into small chunks, or coarsely grated. While Asian pears can be stewed or baked, they take longer to cook than other varieties of pears, and they will remain slightly firm (although bursting with flavor).

BUDDHA'S HAND CITRON

A canary-yellow fruit sporting gnarled, fingerlike sections is definitely hard to miss. Sniff the fruit and what to do with it suddenly becomes very clear; its highly fragrant rind—some say it is redolent of violets, some say a combination of kumquats and tangerines—is a prized flavoring for savory foods, fruit preserves, and desserts. Unlike other citrus, the Buddha's hand citron (also known as a fingered citron) has no juice, pulp, nor seeds—just a solid white pith (albedo) beneath the outer skin; the skin contains the fruit's flavor oils. Remove the zest either with a citrus zesting tool or the very fine side of a grater and use as you would in any sweet or savory recipes that call for lemon or lime zest; its distinctive flavor can completely transform the dish. Also unique is the fact that the inner white pith of the Buddha's hand is not bitter, which means that beyond using the zest, whole pieces of the fruit can be cut off and sliced longitudinally with a vegetable peeler and strewn over a dish while cooking. Considered to be one of the most ancient citrus known to humans, the Buddha's hand originated in India and China; it grows on a small evergreen tree in frost-free areas, including parts of China, Japan, and California, with its peak season in late fall to early winter. Choose bright yellow, fragrant fruit without blemishes and mold. Buddha's hand citrons can be stored at room temperature for up to two weeks or, when refrigerated, up to four weeks.

CARAMBOLA

Not only is carambola (also known as starfruit) delicious, but when it's cut horizontally, its slices look like a five-pointed star, making anyone who uses it in sweet or savory dishes look like a garnishing genius. Yellow when ripe, beneath the somewhat waxy though edible skin is translucent flesh that can be sweet, very tart, or a combination of both. The texture of carambola is slightly crisp, making it an excellent contrast element in fruit salads composed of soft fruits. It is also terrific simply eaten out of hand or served with seafood, cooked grains, or vegetables.

CHERIMOYA

Although its rough, green pine cone–like notched exterior may not look too inviting, cherimoya (also known as custard apple) is truly a treat. Its unique, delicious flavor can be described as a combination of strawberry, banana, and pineapple. Add in its custardlike texture and it is easy to see why cherimoyas should be on everyone's "must-try" list. Quite high in vitamin C, cherimoyas are also special due to their delicate nature in production. Not only must female cherimoya flowers be hand-pollinated to produce fruit, but because cherimoyas are so fragile, they must be harvested and sorted by hand. When ripe, their skin turns brownish green and yields to light pressure. Half or quarter a cherimoya and eat it right out of its own "cup," or peel it and cut it into chunks and add to fruit salads or smoothies, first discarding its large black seeds. If you're not eating immediately, drizzle the cut fruit with orange juice or dip it in lemon water to retain its color. And don't bother cooking cherimoya; the flavor dissipates with heat.

Cherimoya

The Colors and Peak Seasons for Fruits and Vegetables

GREEN

Fruits	Spring	Summer	Fall	Winter
Apples, Granny Smith	x	x	x	x
Avocados	x	x	x	x
Grapes, green (Thompson or Perlette)	x	x	x	x
Honeydew			x	x
Kiwifruit	x	x	x	x
Limes	x	x	x	x
Pears, Anjou	x		x	x
Pears, Comice			x	x
Pears, Packham	x	x		

Vegetables	Spring	Summer	Fall	Winter
Artichokes	x		x	
Arugula	x	x	x	x
Asparagus	x			
Beans, green		x		
Beet greens		x	x	
Bok choy	x	x	x	x
Broccoflower			x	x
Broccoli	x		x	x
Broccoli raab	x		x	x
Broccoli romanesco			x	x
Brussels sprouts				x
Cabbage, Chinese	x	x	x	x
Cabbage, green	x	x	x	x
Celery	x	x	x	x
Chayote squash	x		x	x
Chives	x	x	x	x
Collard greens	x		x	x
Cucumbers		x		
Dandelion greens	x			
Endive, curly	x			x
Herbs, all fresh	x	x	x	x
Kale			x	x
Leeks	x		x	x

GREEN (cont.)

Vegetables (cont.)	Spring	Summer	Fall	Winter
Lettuce, all	x	x	x	x
Mâche	x	x	x	x
Mizuna	x	x	x	x
Mustard greens	x			x
Okra		x		
Onions, green	x	x	x	x
Parsley	x	x	x	x
Peas, fresh	x			
Peas, snow	x	x		
Peas, sugar snap	x	x		
Peppers, green bell	x	x		
Sorrel		x	x	
Spinach	x	x	x	x
Sprouts, alfalfa and sunflower	x	x	x	x
Swiss chard, green		x	x	
Tomatillos	x	x	x	x
Turnip greens	x		x	x
Watercress	x	x	x	x
Zucchini	x	x		

YELLOW and ORANGE

Fruits	Spring	Summer	Fall	Winter
Apricots, dried	x	x	x	x
Apricots, fresh	x	x		
Bananas, red	x	x	x	x
Cantaloupe		x	x	
Carambola (star fruit)		x	x	x
Figs, Calimyrna, dried	x	x	x	x
Figs, Calimyrna, fresh		x		
Grapefruit	x			x
Kumquats	x			x
Lemons	x	x		
Lemons, Meyer			x	x
Mangoes	x	x	x	x

YELLOW and ORANGE *(cont.)*

Fruits *(cont.)*	Spring	Summer	Fall	Winter
Nectarines	x	x		
Oranges	x		x	x
Papayas	x	x	x	x
Peaches	x	x		
Pears, Bartlett			x	x
Persimmons			x	x
Pineapple	x	x		
Quince			x	x
Tamarind	x	x		
Tangelos				x
Tangerines	x			x
Ugli fruit	x			x

Vegetables	Spring	Summer	Fall	Winter
Carrots	x		x	x
Corn		x	x	
Mushrooms, chanterelle	x	x	x	
Onions, yellow	x	x	x	
Peppers, yellow bell		x	x	
Potatoes, fingerling	x		x	x
Potatoes, Yellow Finn		x	x	
Potatoes, Yukon gold		x	x	
Rutabagas	x		x	x
Summer squash, yellow	x	x		
Sweet potatoes			x	x
Sweet potatoes, Japanese	x		x	x
Tomatoes, yellow		x	x	
Winter squash			x	x
Yams			x	x
Zucchini, golden	x	x		

RED

Fruits	Spring	Summer	Fall	Winter
Apples	x		x	x
Blood oranges	x		x	x
Cherries		x		

RED *(cont.)*

Fruits *(cont.)*	Spring	Summer	Fall	Winter
Cranberries			x	x
Grapefruit, pink or red	x			x
Grapes, red (Flame, Tokay)	x	x	x	x
Guava, red-fleshed	x			x
Pears, Red Bartlett			x	x
Plums, El Dorado, Laroda		x	x	
Pomegranates			x	x
Raspberries	x	x		
Strawberries	x	x		
Watermelon		x		

Vegetables	Spring	Summer	Fall	Winter
Beets		x	x	
Onions, red	x	x		
Peppers, red bell		x		
Potatoes, red			x	
Radicchio				x
Radishes	x			
Rhubarb	x	x		
Tomatoes		x	x	

WHITE

Fruits	Spring	Summer	Fall	Winter
Bananas	x	x	x	x
Dates, dried	x	x	x	x
Dates, fresh		x		
Figs, brown Turkey	x			x
Lychees		x	x	
Nectarines, white	x	x		
Peaches, Babcock	x	x		
Pears, Bosc	x		x	x
Plantains	x	x	x	x

Vegetables	Spring	Summer	Fall	Winter
Burdock	x	x	x	x
Cauliflower			x	x
Celery root	x		x	x

THE ESSENTIAL GOOD FOOD GUIDE

WHITE *(cont.)*

Vegetables *(cont.)*	Spring	Summer	Fall	Winter
Corn, white		x	x	
Daikon			x	x
Endive, Belgian	x			x
Fennel bulb	x		x	x
Garlic	x	x	x	x
Ginger	x	x	x	
Jerusalem artichokes			x	x
Jicama	x		x	x
Kohlrabi		x		
Lotus root		x	x	x
Mushrooms, beech	x	x	x	x
Mushrooms, button	x	x	x	x
Mushrooms, crimini	x	x	x	x
Mushrooms, enoki	x	x	x	x
Mushrooms, portobello	x	x	x	x
Mushrooms, shiitake	x	x	x	x
Onions		x	x	x
Parsley root				x
Parsnips			x	x
Potatoes, new	x	x		
Potatoes, russet	x		x	x
Shallots	x			
Sprouts, mung bean	x	x	x	x
Taro root	x	x	x	x
Turnips	x		x	x

BLUE or PURPLE

Fruits	Spring	Summer	Fall	Winter
Blackberries		x	x	
Black currants		x		
Blueberries		x	x	
Elderberries		x	x	
Figs, black Mission, dried	x	x	x	x
Figs, black Mission, fresh	x	x	x	
Grapes, purple (Ribier)	x	x	x	x
Passion fruit		x	x	x
Plums		x		
Prunes	x	x	x	x
Raisins	x	x	x	x
Vegetables				
Cabbage, red or purple	x	x	x	x
Carrots, purple	x	x	x	x
Eggplant		x	x	
Mushrooms, black trumpet			x	x
Mushrooms, morel	x			
Potatoes, purple			x	
Salsify, black			x	x

Kumquats

KUMQUAT

Kumquats look like miniature, oblong oranges but that's where the similarity stops. Remarkably, kumquats aren't even classified as citrus; they are in their own genus, *Fortunella*, named after the man who introduced them into Europe in the mid-1880s. One of the more apparent distinctions between kumquats and oranges is that both the skin and the flesh of kumquats can be consumed, with the sweet skin providing a delicious contrast to the pulp's tart flavor. Eat kumquats whole, discarding the seeds, or chop or thinly slice them and add to fruit salads or use as a flavorful garnish for any dish that would be enhanced by their color and flavor. To use kumquats as an ingredient when baking muffins, first blanch them in boiling water for about thirty seconds, dip in ice water to stop the cooking process, let dry, and then chop or slice before adding to the recipe. Their high pectin content also makes them a perfect addition to preserves and marmalade.

PERSIMMON

Although there is a type of persimmon tree native to the United States, the two varieties most often available commercially—Hachiya and Fuyu—are from a species originating in Eastern Asia. The Hachiya persimmon has a bright orange color and is slightly pointed in shape. The Fuyu is also bright orange but flatter, shaped much like a tomato. Both have a very sweet flavor with spicy undertones. They are also very high in vitamins C and A. Although Hachiya persimmons are best eaten when they are very soft, like jelly in a bag, Fuyu persimmons may also be eaten when firm. Both types can be consumed raw, including the skin, or use a spoon to scoop the flesh out of the skin, working over a bowl to catch the juicy pulp. Pureed, they can be used in pies, muffins, cakes, and custards.

POMEGRANATE

Inside the hard, red, leathery rind of the pomegranate lie many seeds surrounded by translucent seed sacs (arils) bursting with ruby red, juicy, sweet yet tart pulp. Recognition of the pomegranate's high polyphenol antioxidant phytonutrient content, high vitamin C, and high fiber (from the crunchy white seeds within each aril) has boosted interest in pomegranates, making them fairly easy to find in most markets from October through January. Pomegranates are picked when already ripe, so primarily look for fruits without blemishes, cracks, or soft spots. Larger ones that feel heavy are best, as these contain the plumpest, juiciest kernels.

Whole pomegranates can last a week or so at room temperature or up to three months in the refrigerator if wrapped individually in paper bags and stored in the compartment with the lowest humidity. The great burst of flavor, crunchy texture, and beautiful red color from the pomegranate arils will liven up virtually any dish—it doesn't get any simpler or more luscious than this. Use them to top hot and cold cereals, fruit- or vegetable-based salads, cooked winter squash, grain or pasta salads, guacamole, and soups. Or simply add them to smoothies or blended dressings.

Pomegranate

While seeded pomegranate can often be found ready to eat in the produce cooler in many grocery stores, it really is very easy, and usually less expensive, to seed a pomegranate yourself. The average pomegranate will yield about three-quarter cup of seeds. One of the quicker and tidier ways to extract the seeds is to place a washed pomegranate in a large bowl. Add about four inches of water to the bowl. Working within the bowl, cut off the top crown and then score the pomegranate skin lengthwise into quarters. Gently separate each section in the water, revealing the seeds within an ivory colored, bitter-tasting membrane (the pith). Loosen the seeds from the pith. The pith will float while the fruit sinks to the bottom, making it easy to remove. Discard the pith along with the pomegranate skin. Strain the juicy arils from the water and use or store.

Refrigerate the arils and use within three to five days. Or quick-freeze them in a single layer on a baking sheet to ensure they freeze separately rather than in a clump, then store in the freezer in airtight freezer bags or containers for up to six months; use immediately after thawing.

Pomegranates are also known for their delicious juice, which can be enjoyed simply as a beverage or used as an ingredient in many recipes. Although pomegranate juice is readily available, a more entertaining way to enjoy it is to extract the juice directly from the fruit through a straw. Just roll the whole pomegranate on a hard surface to break up the fruit's juicy arils until the obvious cracking sounds of the arils bursting cease. Then pierce the fruit, insert a straw, and enjoy, lightly pressing the fruit to help extract the juice. Each pomegranate yields, on average, about half a cup of juice.

TAMARIND

At first glance, with its fuzzy brown pods ranging from two to eight inches in length, tamarinds look like anything but a fruit. And yet, within the pods are seeds that are surrounded by a sticky pulp with a tart flavor reminiscent of apricots and dates. Although the pulp can be eaten raw, it is generally used in marinades or to flavor chutneys and curries. When sweetened and mixed with water, it makes a refreshing drink. Tamarind can be used when the pods are green or when they're brown and brittle. Crack and peel the pods to access the pulp. To make tamarind concentrate, soak the pulp from six tamarind pods in one cup of hot water for two hours. Then strain the pulp, pressing it to extract as much of the flavorful juice as possible. Use the concentrate to flavor grains, beans, and vegetables, or dilute and sweeten it for a beverage.

Leafy and Cruciferous Greens

The greens category encompasses a wide variety of leafy vegetables, from delicate to hardy. Lettuces, including the soft butterhead varieties, the many types of tender loose leaf lettuces, crisply textured romaine, and crunchy iceberg, comprise the most widely used leafy greens, gracing salad bowls and sandwiches alike. Many of the hardier greens, including bok choy, broccoli raab, collard greens, kale, and mustard greens are also classified as cruciferous vegetables (members of the cabbage family), which are particularly known as a rich source of vitamins, minerals, and, most notably, unique phytochemicals that can help boost the immune system and even lower one's risk of cancer. Although they can be eaten raw, these hearty greens are often steamed, braised, or sautéed. The nutrients in all greens are best absorbed when they're served or cooked with nuts or a small amount of oil. Beyond the more familiar varieties, there are many other interesting greens available that are great to add to your repertoire.

ARUGULA

Also known as rocket, arugula has tender, dark green, jagged leaves and a somewhat bitter flavor. It adds a zesty accent to salads and serves as a very worthy substitute for lettuce in sandwiches and wraps. Sauté onions and mushrooms, then add and briefly sauté arugula and chopped fresh tomatoes and toss the whole lot with just-cooked pasta—glorious.

BOK CHOY

Bok choy has soft, dark green leaves with long, thick, white stalks in a loose head—it is a kind of cabbage. Best known for its use in stir-fries, bok choy has a sweet, slightly milky flavor and remains crisp even when cooked to a tender stage. It can also be cooked in soup or simply steamed. Because the stalks require a longer cooking time, cut the green leaves from the white stalks and trim and slice the stalks; add the stalks first, then stir in the leaves during the last few minutes of preparation to prevent overcooking. Since baby bok choy is picked when less mature, it is much more delicate than regular bok choy and requires much less cooking time. Its miniature size also provides the opportunity to enjoy it at its best: the head kept intact and steamed whole. Baby bok choy is also delicious raw in salads.

BROCCOLI RAAB

Broccoli raab (also known as broccoli rabe or rapini) looks more like kale or turnip greens than broccoli. As it turns out, turnip is, indeed, its closest relative.

"Bitter with pizzazz" is perhaps the best way to describe its flavor, which provides a special spark when combined with other foods. Braise or simmer broccoli raab, watching closely not to overcook the leaves.

CHARD

Chard is unmistakable with its big green leaves and deeply veined and ribbed stalks, which, depending on the variety, can be deep red, yellow, orange, white, or pink/white striped. When steamed, braised, boiled, or sautéed, chard's texture is reminiscent of spinach, although more earthy in flavor, ranging from mild to robust. Red chard has moderately puckered leaves with deep red veining, ribs, and stalks. Green chard's leaves are somewhat ruffled with creamy white veining, ribs, and stalks. And no need to discard the stalks; they can be eaten, too. Just cut on the diagonal into ½ inch pieces and cook a few minutes before adding the leaves to the pot. Rainbow chard lives up to its name through the variety of coloring found in the veining, ribs, and stalks of individual smoothly textured or puckered leaves. In preparation to cook chard, trim leaves from stalks and thick ribs and cut into strips or coarsely chop.

COLLARD GREENS

Collards have leathery gray-green leaves. For optimal flavor and tenderness, buy them during fall and winter and choose a bunch with small to medium leaves. Very small leaves can be eaten raw in salads. Trim stems from larger leaves before cooking. Steam, braise with onions, or sauté in a fragrant cooking oil and serve topped with a flaky finishing salt.

DANDELION GREENS

These are bitter and have deeply notched leaves. While young leaves can be used in salads as an accent, older, larger leaves are best braised or cooked in stews. There are basically two distinct types of dandelion greens, although they can be used interchangeably in recipes if the specific type designated for a recipe is not available. *Taraxacum officinale*, the familiar leaves of wild dandelion that grows on lawns, is the same variety that is also cultivated and sold in produce markets, most often in springtime. On the other hand, *Cichorium intybus*—also known as Italian dandelion, catalogna-type chicory, or dandelion chicory—is actually a type of chicory that looks like common dandelion leaves but is larger and darker green.

ENDIVE

Endive is also called chicory; it has curly, frilly, coarse leaves with dark green edges and pale yellow stems. Use it raw in salads for a bitter accent or cook it briefly for a milder flavor.

Belgian endive is another type of endive, which looks like a cigar made from pale yellow leaves. Its bitter flavor contrasts nicely with milder lettuces in a salad. For a delicious side dish, braise in vegetable or chicken broth for five to ten minutes, until tender. **Escarole**, another member of the endive family, has broad, firm, flat leaves and a slightly bitter taste. Use it raw in salads or cook it briefly to mellow the bitter flavor.

GREEN CAULIFLOWERS

Broccoflower's name incorrectly implies it's a deliberate cross between broccoli and cauliflower, but it is not—it's a green cauliflower. Originating in Italy, it has a milder flavor than cauliflower and a hint of green vegetable flavor. Steam broccoflower whole for a special treat, cooking only until just tender to maintain its pleasant flavor. **Broccoli romanesco**, another type of green cauliflower, has a beautiful shape and form, with swirled geometric patterns of turrets or cones over the surface of its head. Its flavor, which matches its exotic look and texture, is lighter and nuttier than that of broccoflower or white varieties of cauliflower. Steam broccoli romanesco in chunks or whole until just tender, making sure to avoid overcooking.

KALE

Kale has dark green or, depending on the variety, even red or bluish-black leaves that are either puckered or curled and plumelike leaves. While small "baby" kale leaves can be simply chopped and added raw to salads, used as an ingredient in green smoothies, or steamed or sautéed, larger leaves should first be prepped by cutting the leaves from their tough stems. This can be done without a knife by placing the thumb and next finger on opposite sides of the stem at the bottom of the leaf, then zipping them down the stem to magically separate the leaves from the stem. Kale has a subtle cabbagelike flavor; braising it with a little liquid helps to tenderize tougher leaves. It is especially good sautéed with olive oil or sesame oil or braised with onions and mushrooms. There are several varieties of kale, including **Tuscan** or **Lacinato kale**, also known as dinosaur kale for its puckered leaves, and **Russian red kale**, which looks like large oak leaves. While all varieties of kale are chewy, each has a different texture, and any of them can range from quite tender to very fibrous, depending on their age when picked or sold.

MÂCHE

Also known as corn salad or lamb's lettuce, mâche is an exquisite lettuce with small, soft, tender, rounded leaves, generally sold with its rootlets still attached. Its flavor has a faint floral essence, making salads and sandwiches made with mâche seem like a delicacy, whether it's used as the sole type of lettuce or as an accent amid other varieties.

MIZUNA

This is a dark leafy green with serrated leaves and a pungent, exotic flavor that adds a nice accent when mixed with other greens in a salad. It is also good briefly steamed or braised.

MUSTARD GREENS

These have curly edges, a texture that's more tender, albeit more chewy, than that of collard greens, and a spicy, peppery, sometimes pungent flavor. Steam,

Mustard Greens

Radiccio

braise, or sauté them. Small raw mustard green leaves can be added judiciously to salads to add a flavor kick.

RADICCHIO

Radicchio looks like a small ruby red cabbage with thick, white-veined leaves. Slightly bitter, it provides an interesting flavor and color contrast in salads. It can also be cooked like other cabbages: steamed, braised, or stir-fried. It is especially good cut into wedges and grilled with olive oil, herbs, and a splash of tamari or shoyu.

SORREL

Sorrel has a sour lemony flavor and bright green color, and resembles young spinach leaves. Use it sparingly in salads, cooked vegetable medleys, and soups.

Fresh Herbs

Fresh herbs are valued for their exceptional flavors, textures, and shapes, which can make even the simplest salad or sandwich a delicious, stylish masterpiece. They're also a rich source of nutrients. Even when used as a garnish, they can make an irreplaceable contribution to a dish: a whole sprig or chopped leaves arranged on an entrée or as an accent on a plate can help whet the appetite and create a harmonious mood. Herbs are generally easy to raise, and because many of them can be grown in pots, even someone without a garden or backyard can have a personal culinary herb garden.

As a general rule, use three times as much fresh herb as dried. Except for the more hardy herbs such as rosemary, thyme, and winter savory, fresh herbs should be added only during the last ten to fifteen minutes of cooking—just long enough to lose their volatile oils without losing flavor or becoming bitter. Sometimes it's best to add especially tender herbs,

27

such as cilantro and chervil, at the very end of the cooking time, when you turn off the heat. On the other hand, when you're making dips, herb butters, and cheese spreads, fresh herbs should be added several hours before serving to allow the flavor to fully develop.

While basil, chives, cilantro, dill, oregano, parsley, rosemary, and sage will always remain cherished favorites, I encourage you to explore the fresh herbs described below.

CHERVIL

An herb with lacy, green, fernlike leaves, chervil has a delicate flavor and fragrance reminiscent of anise and parsley. Although it is most frequently found dried in traditional mixtures like fines herbes, it is delicious in its own right, finely minced or used as sprigs (like parsley), in salads or as a garnish. Also try it adding it to soups, potato dishes, cooked beans, and egg dishes just before serving.

CURRY LEAVES

These are small, soft-textured, shiny, pointed leaves with a mild, lemony, bitter taste and spicy, citrus-like aroma. They grow on a tree native to India and Sri Lanka, where they contribute their distinctive flavor to curries and other dishes. Look for them sold fresh and still on the branch, detach the leaves right before using them. Typically used as whole leaves, they are traditionally fried briefly in butter or oil before being added to a dish, allowing them to start releasing their aroma and flavors. Unlike bay leaves, curry leaves are edible, although some diners choose to set them aside rather eat them.

FENNEL

Fennel root is a marvelous vegetable; the plant also has feathery bluish green leaves with a mild aniselike flavor and fragrance, which can be used as an herb. Mince the leaves and sprinkle them sparingly on salads or use them to garnish soups, beans, cabbage, fish, egg dishes, and rice. Fennel leaves are also delicious when added to gently heating

oil to add dimension to a vegetable sauté. (**Fennel seeds**, while they are not a fresh herb, are equally important as a seasoning; I always add them to spaghetti sauce and even include a few when preparing oatmeal.)

KAFFIR LIME LEAVES

These are dark green, glossy, fragrant leaves from a Southeast Asian tree that also produces a small, wrinkled, green citrus fruit. An essential ingredient in Thai soups, stir-fries, and curries, kaffir lime leaves have a refreshing and unique lemonlike flavor and aroma. The leaves are very distinctive, as they grow in doubles, with one leaf connecting directly to the end of another. Use kaffir lime leaves whole when making soups and curries (but, as with bay leaves, don't eat them whole), or finely shred them to add to salads or sprinkle over curries.

LEMONGRASS

Lemongrass has long, fibrous stalks with a decidedly lemony flavor, which is so characteristic of soups, stir-fries, and noodle dishes from Thailand and Southeast Asia. When it's intended as an ingredient within a dish, only the tender inner stalk is minced. To use as a flavoring agent, cut a large piece from the whole stalk that will be easy to remove once the dish is cooked.

MINT

Mint is available in many varieties beyond the familiar peppermint and spearmint, several with names that suggest their heavenly scents and flavors. Use **chocolate mint** in tea (two tablespoons fresh mint per cup of hot water) or as a garnish on desserts, or just rub the leaf between your thumb and index finger to enjoy its marvelous aroma. **Pineapple mint**, which has just a hint of pineapple taste, also makes a wonderful tea and works well as a garnish for sweet beverages, fruit salads, and desserts. Finely chopped, it's a delicious addition to cooked rice or other grains; stir it in just before serving. **Ginger mint**, another must-try fruity-flavored variety, is delicious in salads or when stirred into steamed carrots or cooked rice just before serving.

RAU RAM

This herb, also known as Vietnamese coriander, has narrow, pointed leaves with a spicy taste and aroma similar to those of lemon and cilantro (coriander). Commonly served with Vietnamese spring rolls, rau ram is also used fresh in salads or as a garnish for many foods in Vietnam, Malaysia, and Singapore.

SUMMER SAVORY

This herb has small, narrow, grayish green leaves with a peppery flavor and aroma. It's similar to winter savory but milder. Best used fresh, summer savory is most celebrated as a seasoning for cooked beans, but it's also very good in salads, served with cheeses, and cooked in soups, sauces, and poultry dishes, as well as with sweet vegetables like carrots, winter squash, or parsnips.

TARRAGON

Tarragon has narrow, delicate, grayish green leaves that are at their best when used fresh. The preferred variety, French tarragon, has an assertive but sweet flavor and an aroma reminiscent of anise and fennel. It's a familiar component in culinary blends such as herbes de Provence, fines herbes, and bouquet garni, and sprigs of tarragon are often used to flavor vinegar. On its own, it's a good seasoning for beans, vegetables, sauces, poultry, eggs, and fish dishes, but use a light hand when adding it.

THAI SWEET BASIL

This is an Asian variety of basil with dark green leaves, thick purple stems, and an anise scent and flavor, making it quite different from typical Italian basil varieties. Add it to soups, curries, and stir-fries, or use it whole or shredded as a garnish.

THYME

Thyme is an all-purpose herb that, like mint, is available in a wide range of flavors. Some have a lem-ony taste; others, a hint of orange or caraway. Use all varieties in salads, as a garnish, or cooked with vegetables, especially sautéed or grilled mushrooms, as well as in soups and stews and to season poultry, meat, or fish dishes.

Edible Flowers

Although it may seem unusual to eat a salad that contains flowers we normally admire in gardens or arrange in vases, when you think about it, it's no stranger than eating leaves such as lettuce, or other flowers like broccoli and cauliflower. Beyond providing flavor and color, edible flowers add drama to salads, soups, entrées, and desserts. As they are eaten in such minute amounts, they are nutritionally negligible in terms of the standard vitamins and minerals framework. Nevertheless, they supply a range of beneficial phytonutrients. And, beyond that, the beauty and sense of adventure they contribute to a meal can lift the spirits and make a significant contribution to overall well-being.

However, it is very important to eat only those flowers known to be nontoxic. Never experiment; always make sure you can identify the flower as one that is safe to eat. When purchasing edible flowers, only buy those grown specifically for consumption. Avoid flowers from florists and, in many cases, even wildflowers, which may have been treated with pesticides, herbicides, or fungicides. Ideally, grow your own organically. Home gardeners growing any kind of squash, both summer and winter varieties (and particularly zucchini), will have a ready source of squash blossoms as the plants produce new squash. They are best gathered in the morning before the sun causes them to wilt. It's best to harvest the female blossoms, which have an immature squash at their base. Male flowers end at the stem and are needed for pollination, to ensure a steady stream of vegetables for the rest of the season.

Since edible flowers are very delicate, wash them by gently immersing them in a bowl of water to remove any dirt and insects, then let them dry on a towel. Use edible flowers raw in salads, on sandwiches, or as a colorful garnish on pasta, cooked rice and other grains, or really on any other dish in the meal. Go easy; only a few petals are needed per portion. Although only the petals of some flowers should be eaten, other flowers, such as violets, nasturtiums, and Johnny-jump-ups, can be eaten in their entirety, including the stems and leaves.

Many heartier flowers, such as squash blossoms, calendula, chive blossoms, and chrysanthemums, can be cooked, too. Add them to creamy soups or sauces, omelets, scrambled eggs, or mashed and sautéed tofu, or sauté them with any vegetable. Squash blossoms are substantial enough that they can be stuffed with cheese or other savoring fillings and baked; for this purpose, be sure to keep the stem on the blossom so it will retain its shape.

Common edible flowers include: **begonias** (sweet, lemony); **borage** (cucumberlike); **calendula** (slightly tangy, bitter); **chive blossoms** (like mild sweet onions); **chrysanthemums** (mildly to strongly bitter); **geraniums** (lemony); **German chamomile** (applelike); **Johnny-jump-ups** and **pansies** (mild, lettucelike); **lavender** (strong, lemony, perfumelike); **marigolds** (lemony, tangy); **nasturtiums** (sweet, mustardlike); **rose petals** (strong, fragrant); **scarlet runner beans** (sweet bean/pea taste); **squash blossoms** (sweet, nectarlike); **tulip petals** (sweet, lettucelike); and **violets** (sweet, floral).

Sprouts

Sprouts are the very young shoots from the germinated seeds of vegetables, beans, or grains. Almost any seed, bean, or grain will sprout. Red clover, alfalfa, cabbage, radish, sunflower, and buckwheat seeds will sprout into leafy greens. Starchy beans and grains can also grow edible shoots and roots.

Sprouts have long been hailed as a good source of vitamin C, fiber, folic acid, and phytonutrients. Sprouting beans and grains can also improve their digestibility. However, as with other vegetables, each day after harvest brings reductions in nutrient levels, so they should be used as soon after purchase or, if growing them at home, as soon after they are ready to eat as possible.

As the conditions that promote sprouting of the seeds, including temperature and humidity, can increase the potential for growth of pathogens (including salmonella, listeria, and *E. coli*, it is very important to buy sprouts only from certified growers who follow stringent food safety standards for growing and handling sprouts and use only sanitized, uncontaminated seeds. Improper handling of sprouts after they are purchased can also be an issue. They should be kept cold—at temperatures no higher than 40°F—at all times, whether purchased from the produce section or from a salad bar. Because children, pregnant women, the elderly, and persons with compromised immune systems are most vulnerable to the health risks of contamination, they are advised to avoid eating all raw sprouts. Thoroughly cooking sprouts can help reduce the risks, and although some sprouts are so delicate that they are intended to be eaten raw, all bean and grain sprouts can and should be cooked.

You can also grow sprouts at home, but again, it's important to use sanitized seeds, exceptionally clean equipment, and proper sprouting procedures to ensure the best quality and, most critical of all, food safety. Equipment can be as simple as a sterile wide-mouth glass jar covered with a piece of cheesecloth affixed with a rubber band, or as elaborate as sprouting devices with multiple vessels or trays. Screw-on plastic or stainless steel screen lids that fit on wide-mouth quart jars are also available.

The amount of seed needed depends on the size of the seed. For small seeds, such as alfalfa, use one tablespoon of seeds to grow a volume of sprouts that will fill a quart jar. For beans and other large seeds, you may need to use as much as ¼ cup. To initiate the sprouting process, soak the seeds in cool water, generally for eight to twelve hours, depending on the type of seed. After soaking, rinse and drain them thoroughly a couple times or more per day. Most sprouts will be ready to eat within two

Fresh and Dried Peppers from Mild to Very Hot

Fresh Peppers	Relative Heat	Appearance	Flavor	Suggested Use
Bell pepper	0	Green, red, yellow, orange, purple, or white; rounded, cubic shape; about 4 inches long, 3 inches wide, but size varies widely.	Very mild. Green: vegetable-like flavor. Red, orange, and yellow: sweet. Purple and white: less sweet than red.	Raw in salads, stir-fried, stuffed, roasted, grilled, and cooked in sauces and stews.
Pimento	1	Dark red, smooth, heart-shaped, 3 to 4 inches long, 2 to 3 inches wide.	Sweet and succulent.	Raw in salads, dips, spreads. Cooked in vegetable and pasta dishes, stuffed with cheese, and roasted. Pickled.
Hungarian cherry	1 to 3	Deep red, round, about 1¾ inches in diameter.	Mild, medium sweetness.	In salads and pickled.
Anaheim	2 to 3	Related to New Mexico pepper. Green, red when ripe, about 6 inches long, 2 inches in diameter, tapered.	Mild. Green has vegetable-like flavor. Red is sweeter.	Generally used cooked or roasted. Leave whole and stuff with cheese. Dice or cut into strips and add to cornbread batter, omelets, stews, dips, and sauces.
Poblano	3	Dark green or reddish brown when ripe, 4 inches long and 3 inches in diameter, tapered, thick fleshed and shiny surface gloss.	Deep, rich, green bell pepper-like flavor	Best roasted or cooked. A favorite for chiles rellenos and in sauces, moles, and stews.
New Mexico	red: 2 to 4; green: 3 to 5	Related to Anaheim peppers. Green, red when ripe, and sometimes brown, orange, or yellow.	Red is sweeter; green has a vegetable-like flavor.	Use like Anaheim peppers.
Hungarian wax	3 to 4	Yellow, 6 inches long and 1½ inches wide, tapered, waxy surface texture.	Mild to medium heat; subtle, slightly lemony flavor.	Salads, soups, stews, dips, and pickled.
Jalapeño	5.5	Green, red when ripe, 2 to 3 inches long and 1½ inches in diameter.	Green: slightly bitter, vegetable-like flavor. Red: sweet.	Raw: diced as a topping and in nachos and dips. Cooked in salsas, stews, and sauces. Roasted, pickled, and stuffed with cheese.
Serrano	7	Green, red when ripe, 2 to 3 inches long and ¾ inch diameter.	Clean, biting heat, pleasant acidity. Red is sweeter.	Raw: a favorite for making salsa, pico de gallo, and guacamole. Pickled or roasted.

Fresh Peppers (cont.)	Relative Heat	Appearance	Flavor	Suggested Use
Thai	7 to 8	Green, red when ripe, thin, 1½ inches long, ¼ inch in diameter, thin wall, tapered.	Grassy, vegetable-like flavor. Green are hotter than red.	Sauces and Thai and Southeast Asian cooking. Red provide a decorative accent.
Rocotillo	7 to 8	Related to habanero and Scotch bonnet. Orange-yellow or red, rounded with vertical furrows, 1 inch long, 1½ inches in diameter.	Very hot, mildly fruity.	Ceviche and salsas and pickled.
Scotch bonnet	9 to 10	Close cousin to habanero and rocotillo. Light yellow, orange, or red, 1½ inches long and in diameter, some furrows.	Very hot, fruity, smoky.	Jamaican jerk sauce, Caribbean curries, and used in condiment sauces.
Habanero	10	Green, orange, or red, lantern-shaped, 2 inches long, 1½ inches in diameter.	Very hot; tropical fruit and apricot tones in flavor and aroma.	Salsas, chutneys, marinades, and sauces.

Dried Peppers	Relative Heat	Appearance	Flavor	Suggested Use
Hungarian cherry	1 to 3	Dark red, round and wrinkled, 2 inches long and in diameter.	Lightly fruity and peppery.	Stews and sauces.
Guajillo	2 to 4	Orangish red to brown, 5 inches long, 1 inch wide, tapered.	Notes of green tea, pine, tannins, and berry.	Salsas, sauces, soups, and stews.
New Mexico	red: 2 to 4; green: 3 to 5	Olive to dark green or bright red; 5 inches long, 1 inch wide.	Red: dried cherry, earthy. Green: light, smoky, fruity, with herbal undertones.	Red: sold as crushed flakes and ground; also decoratively in ristras. Green: beef jerky seasoning, soups, and stews.
Ancho	3 to 5	The dried form of poblano peppers. Large, flat, mahogany-colored, wrinkled, 4 inches long, 3 inches wide at the "shoulders."	Sweet, faintly reminiscent of raisins and coffee.	Widely used in Mexican cuisine, including mole and adobo. Often sold as ristras (many anchos strung together) and hung in the kitchen for easy access.
Pasilla	3 to 5	Very dark brown, wrinkled, about 5 to 6 inches long, 1 inch wide, tapered.	Mild; flavor similar to Spanish meaning of its name: "little raisin."	Sauces, including mole.

Dried Peppers (cont.)	Relative Heat	Appearance	Flavor	Suggested Use
Cascabel	4	Reddish to brown, round, smooth, 1½ inches in diameter. Rattles when shaken.	Rich, smoky, woodsy.	Salsas, stews, soups, and sauces.
Pepperoncini	5	Orangish red, 2 inches long, ½ inch wide, tapered and curved.	Sweet.	Southern European seafood dishes and tomato sauces.
Chipotle	5 to 6	The dried, smoked form of jalapeño pepper. Brown, ridged, 2 to 4 inches long, 1 inch wide.	Subtle heat, smoky, sweet, slightly chocolatey.	Mexican and Southwestern cooking; sauces, salsas, soups, and cooked in adobo.
De árbol	7.5	Brick red, 2 inches long, ¼ inch wide.	Hot, tannic, smoky, grassy.	Sauces, soups, and stews.
Serrano seco	7.5	Dried form of serrano pepper. Orangish red, 2 inches long, ½ inch wide, tapered.	Very hot, fruity.	Sauces.
Cayenne	8	Red, crinkled, 2 to 4 inches long, ½ inch wide.	Very hot, tart, smoky.	Sauces, soups, and seasoning; African and Cajun cooking.
Pequín	8.5	Orangish red, ¾ inch long, ¼ inch wide.	Very hot, sweet, smoky, with citrus and nutty tones.	Salsas, soups, and vinegars.
Habanero	10	Yellow-orange, lantern-shaped, 1½ to 2 inches long, 1 inch wide.	Very hot, tropical fruit flavor.	Sauces.

Relative heat data from Mark Miller's *The Great Chile Book*. Berkeley, CA: Ten Speed Press, 1991.

to six days, depending on the type of seed and the ambient temperature. Sprouts should be stored in a clean, perforated container that allows air circulation or loosely packed in a plastic bag; they should keep for three to seven days.

Fresh and Dried Peppers

There is a type of pepper for everyone. Sweet peppers, like bell peppers and pimentos, are a mild haven for those averse to heat. They can be served raw, cooked, or roasted, and used like many other vegetables as a side dish or flavorful adjunct to a recipe. Hot peppers, on the other hand, more frequently referred as chiles, are generally used for flavoring, to provide depth, character, and extra pizzazz to foods, rather than standing on their own.

Paradoxically, chile peppers can also help cool us off, which explains why they are so commonly used in the cuisines originating in hot climates. Spicy food makes us sweat, and the sweat's evaporation cools the skin. And then there is the stimulant effect of hot peppers. Capsaicin, a natural chemical component found in the seeds and the whitish ribs within the pepper and the source of peppers' "heat," triggers the brain to produce endorphins, transforming the painful burning sensation into pleasure.

Judging the heat of chile peppers is done in a variety of ways. The simplest is by just looking at the size: the smaller the chile, the higher the heat. The more scientific way is with the Scoville scale. In 1912, pharmacologist Wilbur Scoville created his scale for rating the heat of chiles by measuring the number of grams of water required to cancel the heat of 1 gram of chile. The scale ranges from 0 Scoville units for green and red bell peppers and sweet banana peppers to as much as 500,000 units for red habanero peppers, and even higher for a few obscure varieties like the Moruga Scorpion, a native of Trinidad that can be as hot as 2 million units. However, as chiles grown on the same plant can vary in their heat, the Scoville units claimed for one type of pepper are best understood as approximate.

That's all well and good, but how do you tame the heat? Cooking, roasting, drying, or freezing won't do the trick. The answer is to remove some or all of the seeds and inner membranes inside the chiles, which is where most of the capsaicin lies. At the table, drinking milk or eating yogurt, sour cream, rice, or bread can help provide a welcome cooling sensation.

Chiles are available fresh, freshly roasted, dried, and dried and roasted or smoked, and each form provides distinctive flavors. Take jalapeños, for example: these medium-hot chiles are slightly bitter when dark green but become more sweet if left to ripen until red. Ripe jalapeño peppers that are dried and smoked, called chipotle peppers, are known for their rich, slightly chocolaty flavor.

Roast fresh peppers in a 450°F oven for four to five minutes (turning them a time or two) or campfire style, using a grilling fork about four inches above a gas flame, until the skin turns black. Place them in a covered pot to steam and cool. Then peel them and remove the stems, seeds, and all or part of the inner membranes, as desired, before proceeding with your recipe.

Always use caution when working with hot chiles. To avoid potential burning, protect your hands by wearing rubber gloves, and be sure not to touch your eyes, any part of your face, or any sensitive skin at any time when working with chiles, either fresh or dried. Afterward, wash your hands thoroughly with soap and warm water to ensure all traces of capsaicin are removed.

Because peppers readily cross-pollinate, there are hundreds of varieties of chile peppers. Check out some of the more commonly available fresh and dried varieties listed in the chart to whet your appetite for exploring the rest.

Mushrooms

Wild, cultivated, fresh, or dried, mushrooms are both center-stage performers and potent flavor enhancers that can accentuate and bring together all of the flavors in a dish. While a few cultivated varieties such as white button, crimini, portobello, and enoki can be eaten raw, most wild varieties should be cooked to ensure food safety. Indeed, cooking all mushrooms in some way is prudent. Most mushrooms taste better when sautéed, grilled, or baked, and many are also more easily digested and even more nutritious once they're cooked.

Nutrient-wise, mushrooms are notable for their mineral content, especially potassium, copper, and selenium, and they're a good source of certain B vitamins. Recently, knowledge about their powerful phytonutrient potential has also begun to emerge. In Asia, varieties such as shiitake, oyster, maitake, and enoki have long been valued for their immune-enhancing properties, but even common white button mushrooms and criminis contain healthful antioxidants that help protect our bodies against cancer and other diseases.

Choose only whole and dry mushrooms with spongy, firm, plump caps. Certain varieties of cultivated mushrooms, such as beech and enoki, will be sold as a clump with their stems still attached to the growing medium.

Unlike most other vegetables, mushrooms should be stored in the refrigerator in paper bags rather than plastic. It is best to transfer mushrooms purchased in shrink-wrapped or vacuum-sealed containers into a paper bag, with the exception of delicate beech and enoki mushrooms, which can be refrigerated in the containers they came in.

To clean fresh mushrooms, wipe them with a damp cloth or soft vegetable brush, using minimal water to prevent loss of nutrients and a change in texture. Some mushrooms, such as chanterelles and morels, may need to be briefly rinsed in running water to remove dirt embedded within crevices.

To reconstitute dried mushrooms, pour hot water over them to cover and let them soak for about thirty minutes. The flavorful soaking liquid is wonderful in soups or sauces. Strain it through a paper coffee filter to remove any grit. Much of the flavor of dried mushrooms will be lost to the liquid, but when chopped or sliced, the reconstituted mushroom provides a chewy texture to dishes. Risotto and tomato sauce, in particular, benefit from the addition of dried mushrooms, especially porcini.

ABALONE

These are related to the oyster mushroom and, true to their name, look like the abalone shellfish both in terms of shape and ivory white color; they also have thin golden lines on their surface. The mushroom should always be eaten cooked; it's often used in stir-fries, curries, and stews. Its dense, plump, meaty flesh has a silky texture, while the flavor is a combination of mild, earthy, and buttery. When buying abalone mushrooms, be sure to avoid those that may have a sour odor, choosing only those that have a pleasant aroma.

BEECH (HON-SHIMEJI)

These are a cultivated variety that grows in clusters. Each small mushroom has a one- to two-inch stem and sports a small cap. Brown varieties may be referred to as brown clamshell mushrooms, while white types are sometimes called alba or white clamshell mushrooms. They have a somewhat crunchy texture and a flavor that's mild, nutty, and rather herbaceous. Individual mushrooms should be separated from the thick base before cooking. They can then be sautéed, stir-fried, braised, or roasted in the oven. They require a much shorter cooking time than most other mushrooms.

BLACK TRUMPET

Black trumpet mushrooms look somewhat like petunias but are gray to black in color. A member of the chanterelle family, they have an aromatic, smoky, earthy, almost cheeselike flavor. They are available both fresh and dried and are particularly good with rice dishes; they provide an intriguing dramatic accent when added to or served with lighter colored foods. Always clean black trumpet mushrooms very well before preparation.

BLUEFOOT

Bluefoots are the cultivated variety of blewits. Both varieties are dense-fleshed and whitish, with a blue tint throughout. When cooked, their flavor is deep and earthy, and unlike many mushrooms, they remain firm, becoming tender but not watery. As such, they can add a lot of texture and body to a dish. Cook them like any other mushroom—sauté, roast, or braise—alone or in a dish.

CHANTERELLE

Chanterelles are a beautiful trumpet-shaped forest mushroom, and grow widely throughout western North America. Gold in color, chanterelles have a light, delicate, almost fruity or apricot-like flavor and aroma and a texture that's slightly chewy and dry but meaty. Use chanterelles quickly after purchase.

They are expensive, but you owe it to yourself to experience, at least once, their incredible flavor. They can be sautéed or braised, or combine both techniques, first sautéing, and then braising. They make a wonderful addition to pastas, sauces, soups, or virtually any savory dish. Dried chanterelles are available, but they are not nearly as tasty as fresh.

CRIMINI

Also known as Italian brown mushrooms, criminis are closely related to the common button mushroom. In fact, they are variants of the same species, *Agaricus bisporus*, but criminis are much richer in flavor and meatier in texture, primarily due to their lower moisture content. Use them as you would white button mushrooms, raw or cooked.

ENOKI

These are mild-flavored, creamy white mushrooms with long slender stems and very small round caps. Originally grown on the stumps of the enoki tree in the mountains of Japan, enoki mushrooms are now commercially produced on a growing medium of moist sawdust and rice bran packed into plastic containers. Their crisp, tender texture makes them a delicious raw addition to salads. If using them in a stir-fry or other cooked dish, stir them in just before serving to preserve their exceptional texture.

HEDGEHOG

Hedgehog mushrooms are wild orange-gold mushrooms with a cap that has a depression in the middle. They are characterized by tiny spindles on the underside of the cap. Their wonderful flavor and dry texture is reminiscent of chanterelles, for which they can be substituted. Braise, roast, or sauté them, and because they're a bit dry, cover the pan so they can simmer in their own juices.

LOBSTER

These mushrooms are known for their distinctive red exterior color, which gives some understanding of the origin of its name, but it turns out that lobster mushrooms really aren't mushrooms at all but, rather a fungus living on a couple of species of mushrooms (*Russula* and *Lactarius* genera), both of which, ironically, would otherwise be unpalatable. Still, they are prepared as if they were mushrooms, primarily providing color and a firm, meaty texture to dishes. The lobster's natural flavor is mild, but it readily absorbs flavor from other foods it's cooked with. The red exterior and white interior colors of the lobster mushroom remain present in its dried form.

MAITAKE

Also known as hen-of-the-woods, maitake are a smoky brown color and look somewhat like a head of curly lettuce or perhaps—with a little imagination and a nod to its nickname—feathers. Maitake can grow to immense sizes—over fifty pounds! Its texture, when cooked, is tender but firm, and its flavor is somewhat earthy and nutty. Cut maitake as you would a cauliflower, breaking it into wedges or clumps and cleaning them thoroughly before cooking—a task more critical for wild varieties than cultivated. Indigenous to both North America and Japan, it is very good in Japanese-inspired soups and dishes. Although it's best braised, stewed, or cooked in a sauce, it can also be roasted. Or sauté it with onions, covering the pan for a few minutes in the middle of the process to allow the mushroom to become tender and absorb juices and flavors.

MATSUTAKE

With a name meaning "pine mushroom," this highly prized wild mushroom grows primarily under pine or fir trees the Pacific Northwest, gathered in the fall and winter. It is white or brown in color with a firm, short broad stem. With its meaty texture, powerful and distinctive piney aroma, and earthy, subtly smoky, spicy flavor, it is best prepared simply roasted, steamed, or grilled. It has a special affinity with Japanese cuisine. Store for up to a couple of days in a basket in a single layer, covered with a towel. Matsutakes are also available dried.

MORELS

Morels, which look like elongated sponges or honeycombs with stems, can be yellow, brown, or black. Gathered from woodland areas during the spring, particularly within recently burned forests, morels have a deep, earthy, nutty, smoky flavor and a crisp, chewy texture that is terrific with creamy sauces, pasta, rice dishes, fish, or poultry. For optimal flavor

Oyster mushrooms

and texture, use them quickly after purchase. Dried morels are also available.

OYSTER

These are fan-shaped mushrooms that grow on the trunks and limbs of trees. True to their name, these mildly flavored mushrooms look somewhat like oyster shells. Lightly sauté them and add to sauces, soups, pasta, and rice. **French horn** (or king trumpet) mushrooms are a particularly large variety of oyster mushrooms. Long and conical in shape, French horns have a thick, meaty texture and a taste reminiscent of sweet, buttery, nutty-flavored porcini. They are delicious sautéed, braised, or roasted.

POM-POM

Also called bear's head or lion's mane, pom-poms look like small heads of cauliflower with a slightly furry texture. Their delicate flavor is enhanced when baked whole or sliced and sautéed.

PORCINI

Also known as king boletes or cèpes, porcini are woodland mushrooms gathered during late summer to late fall. Light brown in color with flat, very large caps and chunky stems, they are prized for their rich, meaty, nutty, assertive flavor. Instead of gills underneath the cap, as found in many other mushrooms, this variety of mushroom has a spongy layer consisting of pores and tubelike crevices. Grill the caps, or slice them and braise or sauté for adding to sauces or pasta and grain dishes. Dried porcinis are also highly valued.

PORTOBELLO

These mushrooms are very flavorful, meaty-textured, dark brown Italian mushrooms whose broad flat caps range from three to eight inches in diameter. Unlike their cousins, criminis and common button mushrooms, which are picked while their gills are still enclosed, portobello mushrooms are picked when their gills are fully exposed. Sometimes referred to as "vegetarian steak," portobellos are exceptional when marinated and grilled. They can also be sliced and sautéed with olive oil or butter and seasonings such as tamari or rosemary. Serve the slices with a thick piece of crusty bread or as a side dish.

SHIITAKE

Shiitakes have a woodsy, almost smoky flavor and meatlike texture, making them a favorite in both Asian and Western dishes. They are named from their origins in Japan, where they're grown on the wood of the shii tree; in other parts of the world they are grown on wood from other varieties of oak. Just a few shiitakes will impart a delicious flavor to soups, stews, stir-fries, and pasta dishes. Because they have a tendency to dry out and burn easily, for maximum flavor and meatiness, keep the caps whole or cut them in bite-size chunks rather than slicing them. When cooking, first lightly sauté them, then simmer in a little liquid until dry. Eat the caps only, and use the tough, woody stems for stock. Herbs and spices such as rosemary, thyme, and ginger are exceptional with shiitakes, as is a splash of tamari added during cooking. Dried shiitakes are also available.

STRAW

These mushrooms are typically sold dried, canned, or in jars, and only rarely fresh as a thumb-size mushroom with a thick, bulbous white stem and a drooping yellow or brown cap. Their interesting name relates less to their appearance than to the fact that their traditional growing medium was the straw that remains from growing rice. Use straw mushrooms in stir-fries and soups.

WHITE BUTTON

These are the white, mild-flavored mushrooms commonly sold in supermarkets. Although this species of mushroom, *Agaricus bisporus*, has been commercially cultivated since 1650 in France, the white variety to which we are so accustomed was unknown until its discovery by a Pennsylvania farmer in 1926. Button mushrooms are harvested when the gills on the underside of the cap are tightly enclosed. However, they are most flavorful when they are allowed to "ripen" within a paper bag in the refrigerator until their gills are exposed. While white button mushrooms can be eaten raw, sautéing, steaming, or baking will enhance their flavor.

WOOD EAR

Wood ear mushrooms are grown on logs and are indeed shaped like ears when fresh. Firm yet gelatinous, wood ear mushrooms add an interesting texture to stir-fries, pasta, and rice dishes. Dried wood ear mushrooms are also available.

Roots and Tubers

Roots and tubers are hearty vegetables that impart a grounding, comforting quality to meals, in keeping with their belowground origins. Carrots are the most ubiquitous, but many other roots of all shapes, sizes, and colors deserve equal attention.

Some are quite surprising, changing character and flavor significantly depending on whether they're left raw or cooked to different levels of tenderness. In general, roasting will provide the most depth and concentration of flavor to any root or tuber. For a special treat, roast a medley of root vegetables with rosemary and a splash of oil and tamari. Daikon, rutabagas, and turnips are also classified among the supernutritious cruciferous vegetables.

BURDOCK

Most familiar in Japanese cuisine, burdock is a long, slender root vegetable with an earthy flavor that is a perfect complement to sweet-tasting vegetables such as carrots, winter squash, and onions. To prepare burdock, scrub it but don't peel it. As it can be somewhat tough, burdock often is simmered for ten minutes before adding other vegetables. In addition to cutting burdock into slices, try shaving it with a knife, as if you were manually sharpening a pencil.

CELERY ROOT

Also known as celeriac, celery root is a tough, knobby root derived from a different variety of celery than the one raised for its stalks. Since its rough-textured skin is difficult to clean, it is generally peeled before use. It has a subtle celery flavor and can be steamed or braised, and tastes especially good when cooked with other root vegetables, or it can be added to soups. It can also be grated and used raw as a component or basis for a salad with a creamy salad dressing. If using it raw, tenderize the grated root by adding 1½ teaspoons of salt and 1½ teaspoons of lemon juice or vinegar per pound of celery root. Refrigerate for 30 minutes, rinse thoroughly, and use a towel or paper towel to squeeze out any excess moisture. Then add a salad dressing and marinate for an additional 2 hours.

CHIOGGA BEETS

Chiogga beets, also known as candy cane beets, have red and white concentric rings that are exposed when the beets are sliced horizontally. Pre-

Daikon

are a brown-skinned tuber that can be cooked like potatoes—sautéed, boiled, baked, or simmered in soups. They can also be eaten raw in salads or used as a substitute for water chestnuts.

JICAMA

Jicama is the light brown root of a plant native to Central America. It can be sautéed, boiled, or used raw in salads or for dips. Because the skin is tough, it must be peeled before use. When raw, it has a texture similar to that of an apple and a refreshing, somewhat sweet flavor. It stays crisp when cooked.

LOTUS ROOT

The mild-flavored, ivory-fleshed underwater stem of a water lily, lotus root looks like lengths of sausage on the outside. Inside, several tunnels run the length of the root and form an attractive pattern when the root is sliced crosswise. Soak lotus root in lemon juice and water after cutting to avoid discoloration. It can be baked, steamed, boiled, or added to soups and vegetable dishes both for flavor and for its visual interest.

PARSLEY ROOT

This root looks similar to a parsnip but tastes like a cross between celery root, parsley, and carrot. Cook as you would parsnips. The extra bonus is the opportunity to use the leaves at the top of the root as a fresh herb; taste it first, though—depending on the crop, the flavor may be like mild Italian parsley or it may be bitter tasting.

PARSNIPS

Parsnips look like beige-colored carrots—and are indeed related to carrots—but they have a quite different flavor. Usually cooked rather than eaten raw, their distinctive sweet and nutty flavor complements bean dishes, soups, hearty stews, and curries.

RUTABAGA

Rutabagas have yellowish-brown skin turning purple around the ridged crown, yellow or golden flesh,

pare similarly to other beets. Steam or bake the whole root with one inch of the stem still attached and the root end intact. Once the beet is tender, its tougher outer skin will slip off easily. Then slice or cube and serve alone as a side dish or in a salad, or cook into borscht, a traditional Russian beet-based soup finished with a dollop of yogurt, crème fraîche, sour cream, or a creamy tofu-based spread.

DAIKON

A long, cucumber-shaped white radish native to Asia, daikon is actually a member of the cabbage family. Used raw, it has a hot, spicy flavor that's a nice addition to salads, or it can be grated and served on its own as a delicious condiment for fried or oily foods. When cooked in soups or stews or alone, daikon becomes surprisingly sweet.

JERUSALEM ARTICHOKES

Also known as sunchokes, Jerusalem artichokes bear no resemblance to artichokes. Rather, they and a rounded, albeit irregular shape. Thought to be an accidental cross of turnips with wild cabbage that likely occurred in central Europe in the seventeenth century, they are also known as swedes (short for "Swedish turnip," due to their popularity in Scandinavia) and, in Scotland, as neeps (perhaps a derivation of "new turnips"). When eaten raw, they have a sharp-sweet flavor, but their marvelous nutty, sweet, mildly peppery flavor emerges when cooked, growing sweeter and more complex the longer they're cooked.

To prepare, scrub rutabagas well, cut off the top and bottom, and peel the tough skin with a knife prior to cutting into desired shapes for eating raw or for cooking. An extra bonus when braising, steaming, or adding rutabaga to soups and stews is the vegetable's delicious sweet broth. Be sure to reserve it for use in sauces and soups or as part of the liquid for cooking grains, or just drink it as you would a vegetable juice. It's really that good. Rutabagas can also be steamed and pureed or mashed alone or in concert with potatoes. And they are fantastic when roasted for about 45 minutes in a 400°F oven with a splash of oil and tamari shoyu, either solo or along with other vegetables. This preparation allows the root's natural sweetness to caramelize.

Taro Root

Taro is a vegetable most familiar to people living in Japan, Egypt, and Syria, and in New Zealand, Hawaii, and other islands in the Pacific Ocean. Technically a corm, not a root, it resembles a hairy potato and can indeed be cooked like a potato—baked, steamed, boiled, or used in soup. It generally can't be eaten raw because of bitter, irritating compounds in the sap. The tough skin should be removed; this is most easily accomplished after cooking. If you're determined to peel raw taro and you have sensitive skin, wear rubber gloves.

Squash

Squashes can be divided into two main categories: summer and winter, denoting the time of year each is at its peak in flavor. They also differ in thickness of skin, density of flesh, and relative water content.

SUMMER SQUASH

As any home gardener knows, summer squash are prolific warm-weather crops, and as a result, they have found their way into a variety of recipes, from basic salads, vegetable side dishes, and fritters to muffins, cookies, cakes, and even cobblers. It's a good thing this sometimes overabundant vegetable is so versatile. Many varieties have been developed over the years, in a wide range of shapes and colors.

Chayote, once a principal food of the Aztecs and Mayas, is a summer squash with a pale green rind, a flavor somewhat similar to cucumber, and a fibrous texture like that of winter squash. Chayote can be steamed or baked; try it stuffed. If peeled, it can be eaten raw in salads or sautéed. **Armenian cucumbers** are long and coiled, with ridged skin and crisp, pale flesh. Although sliced cucumbers are delicious raw, they can also be cooked as you would any other summer squash. **Pattypan squash** are yellow or a very pale green, round, and about two to four inches in diameter, and have scalloped edges. Smaller pattypans are more tender and are delicious steamed whole; larger ones can be sliced or quartered before steaming, sautéing, or baking. **Scallopini squash**, shaped like pattypan squash but with a dark green color like a classic zucchini, are the result of a cross between the two. Prepare them just like pattypan squash.

WINTER SQUASH

Winter squash (more correctly designated fall and early winter squash) have hard rinds, are sweeter in flavor than summer varieties, and contain high levels of beta-carotene, as evidenced by the color of their flesh—usually yellow to orange. Most types of winter squash can be steamed, braised, or baked.

Acorn squash is somewhat stringy and also has one of the mildest and least sweet flavors of all the winter squash. As such, it serves as an excellent backdrop, ready to be accented with other seasonings or a flavorful stuffing. Its outer skin is ridged, somewhat thick, and typically dark green, although it sometimes has splashes of orange, and other color varieties do exist. Cut it in half or in wedges and steam, or bake with a splash of oil, a favorite seasoning, and salt or tamari.

Banana squash is a very large, pink to orange banana-shaped squash that can grow to immense sizes—larger than a small child! As such, it is often sold precut into smaller, more reasonably sized pieces. It can be steamed or baked, resulting in a mildly sweet and fruity flavor. Blue-gray, thick-skinned **blue hubbard squash** can also be quite large in size, which is one reason it is sometimes stuffed with a bread or rice dressing and baked, similarly to a stuffed turkey. Its flavor is sweet and its pulp has a dry texture. **Golden hubbard squash** is a smaller variety of hubbard squash with orange skin and sweet flesh. It is delicious baked or steamed, and each half is the perfect size for an individual portion.

Buttercup squash (not to be confused with butternut squash, below) looks like a dark green globe with a light green crown. It has a dry, smooth pulp and a very sweet flavor reminiscent of a dry-textured sweet potato. Bake, braise, or steam and season with a splash of oil and tamari. The very popular **butternut squash** is a light brown, bottle-shaped squash with a sweet, fruity flavor. A favorite squash to use when making soup, it's also a welcome addition to stews, and can be baked or steamed.

Delicata squash is an elongated, thin-skinned squash. Its skin is usually yellow or beige, with green stripes. Best when baked, it is moist and has a very mild, sweet flavor.

Golden nugget squash is a small, round squash with a very thick, hard orange skin and a sweet, nutty flavor. Cut it in half before baking or steaming. **Kabocha squash**, with its dark green skin and pumpkin shape, is the sweetest of all the squashes

Winter squash

and has a delicious, smooth and dense pulp. Baked, braised, or steamed, it's perfectly complemented by sautéed and braised kale cooked with onions and seasoned with tamari. **Red kuri squash** is a medium to large reddish or golden squash with sweet, golden flesh and a high ratio of seeds. Cut in half, or into wedges or chunks, and bake or steam. **Spaghetti squash**, as its name implies, can be a vegetable substitute for spaghetti. Cut this yellow-skinned, oblong squash in half and bake or steam until tender, and then use a fork to separate the fibers into mildly sweet "noodles."

Pumpkins are available in two basic types: the less flavorful jack-o'-lantern variety and the sugar pumpkin, which is used for cooking and baking. Pumpkins are not as sweet as other winter squashes and generally need additional sweetening, particularly when they're used in pies or sweet breads. Still, they can be cooked and used as you would any other type of winter squash.

Grains, Flour, and Bread

_ℒ_

"What grain would you like for dinner?" It's a frequent question at my house. For many people, however, the concept of grain starts and ends with rice. Not until you've experienced the extensive variety of grains from around the world does the question of which grain to choose for a meal even begin to make sense. Because my husband and I have been exploring the world of whole foods for decades, our answer could range from a specific variety of rice, such as Bhutanese red rice, to quinoa, Kamut, millet, or farro. Then again, it could be bulgur, spelt, wild rice, barley, or something made with rye. My husband may choose corn while I might go for steel-cut oats.

Fortunately, there's rising interest in the wide variety of grains used in traditional cuisines, in part due to their excellent health benefits. This has propelled grains from humble fare to trendy and almost exalted status. Quinoa, for example, is as commonly featured in recipes in the food sections of newspapers as it is on restaurant menus.

When it comes down to it, the extraordinary flavors and pleasing textures of grains clinch the deal. And because several kinds of grains can be cooked in less than half an hour, they can easily be incorporated into a busy lifestyle.

Whole Grains

What is a whole grain? It's simply this: a whole grain contains all of the components that are naturally present in the seed of a cereal grass plant, and thus contains all its inherent nutrients. And because grains are designed to support the growth of the seed when it sprouts, they're a rich (and compact) source of nutrition for us, too. Some of the foods we typically think of as grains are actually the seeds of plants other than cereal grasses: buckwheat and quinoa, for example. However, these are very similar to grains from cereal grasses, both functionally and nutritionally, so for most ordinary purposes they share the grains category.

There are three major structural components of a whole grain: the bran, the germ, and the endosperm. The **bran**, the outer covering of the grain, contains the highest concentration of fiber and is also rich in B vitamins, trace minerals, and potent antioxidants, including lignans. The role of bran is to protect the contents of the seed prior to germination. From a human perspective, it's useful too, helping preserve the quality and nutrients of whole grains during storage. The **germ** is the life force of the grain: the small part of the seed that sprouts to form a new plant. It contains vitamin E, trace minerals, unsaturated fats, B vitamins, minerals, and protein—all the nutrients needed to get the sprout going during its initial growth phase. The **endosperm**, the largest part of the seed, consists of starchy carbohydrates, protein, and small amounts of vitamins and minerals, stored as fuel to nourish the sprouted grain during its early growth.

There is a lot to be said about the extraordinary benefits of whole grains and the foundational role they play in a healthy diet. Their complement of fiber, vitamins, minerals, and health-promoting phytonutrients has been shown to help reduce cholesterol levels, improve intestinal health, stabilize blood sugar levels, and decrease the incidence of heart disease, diabetes, and some forms of cancer. Eating whole grains can also help reduce the risk of diabetes, obesity, and stroke.

Whole grains in their intact seed form are the most nourishing option. However, grains that are processed in ways that preserve most or all of the major components—bran, germ, and endosperm—are still considered whole grain products. This includes grains that are cracked, rolled, ground, flaked, extruded (as with pasta), or minimally pearled (removing only a tough, inedible outer hull).

In contrast, refined grains (and refined carbohydrates) are grains that have been processed to remove the bran, the germ, or both, leaving primarily the starchy endosperm. Refining results in a significant loss of valuable dietary fiber, as well as vitamins, minerals, antioxidants, lignans, phytosterols, and a wide variety of other phytonutrients, compounds found in plants that are critical for optimal health.

Refining was once a difficult and costly process, and as a result, products made with white flour were primarily consumed by the upper classes. During the Industrial Revolution, new machinery made it more economical to produce white flour, so items like white bread became more affordable. For a long time thereafter, many regarded them as superior because they were a symbol of privilege. There are other reasons for the prevalence of refined grain products, and as is often the case, a big one is that it's beneficial for manufacturers. Because the germ contains more oils, which can go rancid, whole grain products generally have a shorter shelf life. There's at least one nutritional benefit to refining: bran contains phytic acid, which can bind with minerals and prevent them from being absorbed in the body. However, this is primarily a concern among populations whose diets are low in minerals, or who consume bran in excessive amounts.

Overall, the health benefits of whole grains greatly outweigh any benefits of refined grains. Recognizing this, many manufacturers add nutrients back into their flours to replace those lost during processing. However, this is no panacea. Generally, only five of the missing vitamins and minerals are replaced, leaving refined grains deficient in many important nutrients and, of course, fiber.

There is no question that whole grains are significantly more nutritious and flavorful and the way to go, and that you should aim for them most if not all the time. Still, they represent a new venture for many. And, even for those more familiar with whole grains, not having time is an often-used justification for not serving them more.

In fact, it's very easy to incorporate more whole grains into your diet. Breakfast is a good place to start—in part because that's one meal where we do tend to eat more whole grains. They've long been at the top of the list as a good, satisfying choice for supplying sustained energy throughout the morning. Even if you have a busy schedule, it doesn't take long to make a delicious hot cereal from any type of whole grain, perhaps with some fresh or dried fruit.

Quick Cooking Grains

Check out these whole grain and lightly milled grain varieties that take only ten to thirty minutes to prepare, making them a cinch to fit within a busy schedule. While 100 percent whole grain remains the best option, the lightly milled grains included below have just a bit of the top bran layer removed while retaining their natural color, letting them cook quicker while preserving much of their original whole grain nutrition.

10 minutes or less
Couscous, whole wheat

15 minutes or less
Oats, rolled
Quinoa

20 minutes or less
Buckwheat
Rice, Bhutanese red
Rice, kalijira brown
Rice, Madagascar pink (lightly milled)
Teff
Wheat, bulgur
Wheat, cracked
Roasted green wheat (farike)

25 minutes or less
Einkorn
Rice, Ifugao Diket sticky (lightly milled)
Rice, Kalinga Jekot sticky (lightly milled)
Rice, Kalinga Unoy (lightly milled)
Rice, Mountain Violet sticky (lightly milled)
Rice, sprouted brown
Rice, Tinawon Fancy (lightly milled)
Rice, Tinawon white (lightly milled)
Rice, Ulikan Red (lightly milled)

30 minutes or less
Amaranth
Corn grits, whole
Grano (lightly milled)
Millet
Oats, steel-cut
Rice, Black Forbidden
Rice, brown Mekong Flower

Rolled, coarsely cracked, or finely ground grains all cook in less than twenty minutes. Or you can let whole grains cook overnight in a slow cooker. When choosing dry ready-to-eat cereals, your best choices are shredded whole grain cereals, muesli, granola made without oil, or low-fat granola that's only lightly sweetened.

When it comes to lunch and dinner, any type of grain can be topped with stir-fried or grilled vegetables. Or serve grains as a side dish alongside beans, tofu, tempeh, meat, or poultry. They are a wonderful basis for casseroles, croquettes, salads, and stuffing. Or you can simply add them to soups to lend a chewy texture and act as a thickening agent.

Buying and Storing Whole Grains

Look for plump, unbroken grains with uniform size and color. Whether you're buying packaged or bulk grains, you'll be assured of the best quality and freshest flavor if you buy them from businesses that specialize in selling grains and know how to store them properly. They're also likely to have a faster turnover, so their products are likely to be fresher. While buying grains in bulk is usually less expensive, make sure the bins are tightly covered and constructed to allow for easy rotation of the bulk goods.

Grain pests such as weevils and mealworm moths can be avoided at home by storing grains in clean, airtight containers—plastic and paper bags don't qualify. Instead, use glass jars or rigid plastic containers with good seals. Whole grains are best stored at a cool room temperature (below 70°F), and will generally keep for up to six months. Warmer conditions will significantly reduce shelf life. If you have room in your refrigerator, that's a good option, too. Since refined grains such as white rice and white flour lack the natural oils found in the bran and germ, they can be stored at room temperature much longer, often up to a year.

Cooking Whole Grains

Though the amount will vary depending on appetites and what else is being served, one cup of uncooked whole grain typically yields enough cooked grain to serve two to four people.

All whole grains should be rinsed prior to cooking to remove any dirt and dust. For best results, place the grain in its cooking pot, add approximately twice the amount of cool water, then swish the grain to allow the debris to rise to the top. Carefully pour off most of the water to remove the grit, then repeat the process one or two more times to ensure that all the dirt is washed away.

Depending on the type of grain and the cooking method, preparation time can be as little as ten minutes or as long as several hours. Although refined grains generally cook more quickly than do their whole versions, there are many whole grains that require only minimal cooking time. Even hearty whole grains that typically need longer cooking can be prepared more quickly if cooked in a pressure cooker or soaked for several hours before cooking. Or a slow cooker can also do all the work while you sleep or while you're away from home. Although cooking on the stovetop in a saucepan using the absorption method is the most familiar way of preparing grains, other cooking methods bring out unique qualities, flavors, and textures.

ABSORPTION METHOD

Depending on the amount of water added, the texture of grain cooked in a saucepan can range from somewhat dry and dense to moist and even soupy. To use the absorption method, bring the liquid to a boil in the pot, then add the grain and a pinch of salt. Occasionally, a recipe will specify that the grain, liquid, and salt be combined in the pot first and then brought to a boil together. Either way, allow the liquid to return to a boil, then cover, lower the heat, and simmer gently until the grain is tender and the liquid is absorbed. To prevent a sticky texture, avoid stirring or removing the lid during cooking. Let the pot stand, undisturbed, for 5 to 10 minutes before fluffing with a fork to separate the grains.

Toasting the grain in a dry skillet over medium heat before cooking enhances flavor and provides a light and fluffy texture. In contrast, sautéing the grain in a bit of oil or butter before cooking results in a fluffier texture with more separate, individual grains; this method is often used when making pilafs. With either method, stir constantly until the grain is slightly browned and fragrant, being careful not to burn it. Then add the toasted grain (and just a pinch of salt, if using) to boiling water and cook as above.

PRESSURE-COOKING

Long gone are the days of pressure cookers prone to blowing their lid—and the cooker's contents. Newer pressure cookers incorporate built-in safety mechanisms and are extremely easy to use. In addition to reducing cooking time, they also help retain the distinctiveness of each grain while creating a softer texture and sweeter taste. Even quick-cooking grains, including millet, quinoa, and white rice, can be pressure-cooked for variety in texture.

In general, use ½ cup less water per cup of dry grain than required for the absorption method unless a softer consistency is desired. Add the water, rinsed grain, salt, and any herbs or spices to the pressure cooker and bring to full pressure, then lower the heat to medium-low. A heat diffuser or flame tamer is optional, but it can help distribute heat evenly and prevent scorching or burning. Pressure-cooking typically shaves 5 to 10 minutes off time required to cook the grain using the absorption method. At the end of that time, remove the pressure cooker from the heat and let the pressure come down naturally. If you're pressed for time, place the pressure cooker in the sink and run cold water over the lid until the pressure comes down. Either way, allow the grain to rest, undisturbed, in the unopened pressure cooker for 5 to 10 minutes before serving.

SLOW-COOKING

A slow cooker makes it effortless to prepare hot cereal and long-cooking whole grains such as wheat, Kamut, oat groats, and corn. All you have to do is add the ingredients—water, grains, salt, and other seasonings you wish—then plug in the slow cooker, put on the lid, and cook at low heat. Eight hours later, you'll have the basis for a great meal ready to eat. If you're planning on a cooked grain for dinner and you'll be away from home longer than 8 hours, you can cook the grain in the slow cooker overnight, refrigerate it the next morning, and then warm it up that evening. If you use the high setting, the grains will be ready in half the time—3½ to 4 hours.

The amount of water needed depends on the final texture desired. To make pilafs in a slow cooker, only use hearty kinds of whole grains, and use 3½ to 4 cups of water per cup of grain. Parboiled or converted rice and rice varieties specifically used to make risotto are the only kinds of white rice suitable for cooking in a slow cooker. For hot breakfast cereals, the proportion of water to grain is typically 4 to 5 cups of water per cup of grain. A thin, soupy rice porridge called congee in China and kayu in Japan, traditionally served at breakfast and sometimes other meals, is an ideal, easily digested, nourishing, and even centering way to start the day. This hot breakfast cereal is made by slow-cooking rice or any other whole grain with a bit of salt, using approximately six times as much water as grain. It's easily made in a slow cooker; cook at low heat for

4 to 8 hours. Other ingredients can be added, as well, such as walnuts or almonds, raisins or dates, fennel or cinnamon, or even vegetables, such as fresh ginger, carrots, sweet potatoes, leeks, or celery.

USING A RICE COOKER

An automatic rice cooker is specifically designed for steaming rice. It shuts off automatically when it senses the water has been absorbed and keeps the rice warm until you're ready to eat. The original rice cookers were made for cooking medium and short-grain white rice, but most of them are now adaptable to cooking other types of rice, including brown rice, as well as other whole grains. The current machines vary in complexity. Some just have a basic on-off switch, whereas others are multipurpose machines that use advanced technology to automatically adjust the cooking time depending on the weight of rice put into the machine. Some also include options like a programmable timer to start the cooking process while you're away or a special lower-temperature porridge cycle to prepare hot cereals, polenta, and risotto.

BAKING

Cooking grains in a covered baking dish in the oven is a handy method when all the burners on your stove are in use. To prepare grain for baking, first sauté it in 1 tablespoon of oil or butter per cup of grain, making sure all of the grains are evenly coated with the oil. Although this step is optional, it enhances the flavor of the grain and helps prevent it from drying out. Then combine the grain, any desired seasonings, and water in a baking dish, using the same amount of water as you would for that grain with the stovetop absorption method. Cover tightly with a lid or foil and bake at 350°F until the water is absorbed and the grain is tender. Most grains require longer cooking time when baked than they do when using the stovetop absorption method, usually about one-third longer. For example, white rice will be done in about 30 minutes and brown rice will take about 1 hour.

SPROUTED GRAINS

When whole grains are sprouted, protein and vitamin content increases, and minerals are made more available and easier to absorb thanks to the sprouting process breaking down phytic acid, a natural substance found in the bran layers of whole grains that can otherwise reduce absorption. Some of the carbohydrates are also converted into more easily digested simple sugars. Consequently, grain sprouts can taste quite sweet.

Grains are generally germinated until the tiny sprouts that appear are no longer than the length of the seed. The longer the sprout, the more alpha-amylase, an enzyme that breaks down some of the complex starches in flour into sugar, will be developed. Larger grains, such as wheat, rye, barley, and spelt, begin to develop into grass when grown longer than three days. The grass can then be processed into a beverage using a specialized wheatgrass juicer.

Grain sprouts and grass will keep for about a week in the refrigerator but must be kept at all times at temperatures no higher than 40°F. Buy them only be from certified growers who follow stringent food safety standards for growing and handling sprouts and use only sanitized, uncontaminated seeds. Due to potential food safety issues with fresh sprouts—especially for children, pregnant women, the elderly, and persons with compromised immune systems—fresh grain sprouts should always be cooked. When steamed, they can be used like hot breakfast cereal. For lunch or dinner, try them in a stir-fry or sautéed in oil or butter. Cooked sprouts can be added to soups and salads.

Drying sprouts gives them an even sweeter flavor, which is not a surprise given that dried and ground sprouted barley is also known as barley malt. Very low temperature drying, around 125°F, will retain the enzymatic activity of grain sprouts that were grown long enough (about the length of the grain) to develop alpha-amylase enzyme, creating what is referred to as diastatic malt. Due their high level of enzymatic activity, grain sprouts dried into diastatic malt should be used sparingly when making bread—only about ¼ teaspoon per loaf—as too much can make sticky-textured loaves. Higher drying temperatures, between 140°F and 160°F, will inactivate the enzyme in the sprouts. The result, known as nondiastatic malt, is used in baked goods to contribute a sweet flavor and darker color.

PRESOAKING

Some cooks like to soak their grain for many hours before preparation to initiate the germination process (that is, start the grain sprouting) and/or to reduce cooking time. Typically, the soaking liquid is discarded and replaced with fresh water for cooking if the soaking process is longer than twelve hours. For specific cooking reduction times, see individual grain listings on pages 49 to 86.

Sprouted (sometimes called germinated) and dehydrated grains, such as quinoa, whole grain brown rice, and lightly milled brown rice (in which some of the bran layer is removed for more of a white rice texture) are commercially available packaged and in bulk, ready to use in the same way as regular unsprouted grains. When cooked, they have a really delicious, sweeter, slightly nutty flavor and a softer, less chewy texture. While the cooking process itself essentially remains the same for sprouted quinoa, when it comes to sprouted brown rice, most recipes call for less water and half the time you'd typically use when cooking regular brown rice: 1 cup of sprouted brown rice to 1¾ cups of water, cooking for 25 minutes after the rice and water come to a boil and then letting it sit covered for about 10 minutes after cooking.

SEASONING

Add dried herbs and spices at the start of the cooking process. Due to their delicacy, fresh herbs should be added only during the last few minutes of cooking or right before serving. Another way to season grains is to cook them with liquids other than water, such as vegetable or meat broth or diluted fruit or vegetable juice.

Although optional, adding a pinch of salt per cup of grain during cooking deepens the flavor and boosts the grain's natural sweetness. It can also reduce the tendency to add excessive salt or salty condiments at the table, adjusting for what could have been accomplished during the cooking process with a lighter hand.

Gluten and Wheat Intolerance and Allergies

Grains are categorized in two primary ways: the presence or absence of gluten, the protein complex that affects the texture of baked goods and helps give bread the structure to rise; and whether or not the grain is wheat.

While the search for gluten-free grains can simply be due to an interest in exploring a wide variety of tastes and textures, some individuals must avoid all grains that contain gluten, specifically the gliadin fractions found in wheat (other gluten-containing grains include Kamut, spelt, farro, einkorn, rye, barley, and triticale). Strict avoidance of gluten-containing grains is a lifelong obligation for individuals with celiac disease or dermatitis herpetiformis. **Celiac disease**, also known as gluten intolerance, is a hereditary disorder in which the body responds to gluten by damaging the lining of the small intestine, which blocks the body's ability to absorb nutrients from food. While symptoms will vary, they can include difficulty gaining or losing weight, fatigue, bloating, abdominal pain, diarrhea, constipation, and anorexia. **Dermatitis herpetiformis** is another form of celiac disease that manifests in severely itchy, even blistering skin, usually on the elbows, knees, and buttocks.

Wheat allergy and wheat intolerance are entirely different conditions from gluten intolerance, and from each other. A **wheat allergy** is a condition in which eating even a small amount of wheat can trigger the body's immune system to produce immunoglobulin E (IgE), which causes the release of histamine. Swelling, inflammation, nausea, diarrhea, and other symptoms may occur as a reaction,

including hives or even life-threatening anaphylactic shock. A wheat allergy requires strict lifelong avoidance of wheat and triticale, a grain that is a hybrid of wheat and rye. Although Kamut, spelt, farro, and einkorn are related to wheat, their gluten components are unique. Still, any experimentation with these grains for anyone with a wheat allergy should always be done under the guidance of a health care professional.

In contrast, **wheat intolerance** is a condition in which the body does not adequately digest wheat, although the reaction remains a metabolic disorder and does not involve the immune system. Symptoms are milder, although not particularly comfortable, and include bloating, flatulence, cramping, diarrhea, rashes, and fatigue. Some individuals with wheat intolerance may still be able to eat wheat occasionally or in small servings.

Gluten-Free Grains

Amaranth	Quinoa
Buckwheat	Rice
Corn	Sorghum
Job's Tears	Teff
Millet	Wild rice
Oats*	

*Although oats don't contain gluten, in North America they are often listed as inappropriate for gluten-free diets out of concern that they could have been grown or processed in the vicinity of wheat. Some companies market oats guaranteed to be grown on dedicated oat-growing farms, processed in a gluten-free facility, and tested to ensure its purity.

Heirloom Grains

Heirloom grain varieties are those that have been known through historical documentation or folk history for at least fifty years, although most have a history far more than a century old, sometimes more than a thousand years. All are open pollinated, meaning that the plants produce seed that is true to the parent plant. Cross-pollination between varieties of the same species can occur, as well, naturally creating new unintentional hybrids. Such plants that survive the environment in which they are grown, including drought resistance, pests, and disease, likewise reproduce strong plants, allowing for natural adaptation and variation. Open pollination also allows the opportunity to farmers and gardeners to save and plant the seeds of plants whose flavors, textures, size, colors, and other traits they appreciate and want to keep producing, which has been the source of some of the heirloom crops we see today.

In contrast, hybrid grains are those that have been purposely cultivated for specific traits through a deliberate crossing of two distinct parent plant varieties from the same species, whether for pest resistance, disease resistance, flavor or color attributes, baking or cooking properties, or for easier production and harvest. While hybrid varieties are very beneficial in that they provide valuable food options, the importance of preserving genetic diversity with heirloom grains cannot be overemphasized. Unlike open-pollinated varieties, saved seed from the first generation hybrid plant will not generate plants like the parent. Production of new seed to create the same hybrid variety needs to come from plants that have been deliberately crossed each time.

Beyond their resilience within a specific environment, heirloom varieties are most known for their extraordinary variety of flavors, colors, and cooking properties—which is both invigorating and inspiring. For instance, one could eat a different variety of rice each night for months without repeating. What's more, heirloom varieties help ensure we are exposed to nutritional diversity, each providing its own set of basic nutrients and phytonutrients—components that science may never fully detect and yet by which our health is greatly enhanced. And, then there is the sheer pleasure in knowing and respecting the history these heirloom grains represent, not only of a time and place, but of the people who used them as well. As you explore the many grains in this section, you'll have a chance to meet and experience some of these heirloom grains.

AMARANTH

Gluten free

Sometimes referred to as "the grain of the future," amaranth is actually a rediscovered ancient Aztec crop that was first domesticated in Mexico around 2000 BCE—and it's harvested from a broad-leaved plant, not a cereal grass. Although difficult to plant and harvest, amaranth is naturally resistant to weeds and can grow in poor soil and dry conditions, making it a promising crop for otherwise unproductive areas. It is also a high-yield crop, with each plant producing up to half a million tiny seeds, about the size of poppy seeds.

Amaranth is high in fiber and rich in calcium, iron, and phosphorus. It is especially notable for its high concentration of lysine, the amino acid usually found in only limited amounts in grains. This extra lysine gives it a better amino acid profile than any other grain except quinoa.

Varieties and Cooking Guidelines

Types of amaranth range from purple-black to buff yellow in color. The golden variety is most commonly available, with black amaranth more limited in supply and the unique red dye amaranth heirloom variety of the Pueblo peoples even harder to find. Different colors of amaranth also have different textures when cooked. While buff-colored amaranth thickens like cornmeal as it cooks, the seeds of black amaranth remain more separate.

With its nutty, mildly spicy flavor, whole amaranth is delicious whether eaten on its own, cooked with other grains for a breakfast cereal or pilaf, or used to make an alternative version of thick polenta. Or try adding a small amount of amaranth to stews and soups to make them heartier and thicker. For extra crunch and variety in cookies, muffins, pancakes, and quick breads, use raw amaranth as a substitute for poppy seeds in the batter. Amaranth also blends well with brown rice, buckwheat, or millet, making for an interesting texture and a better nutritional profile. Use one part amaranth to three parts other grains and cook according to the predominant grain's instructions.

To prepare amaranth as a side dish, use one part amaranth to two parts liquid and cook for 15 to 20 minutes. When making a hot breakfast cereal, go with one part amaranth to three to four parts liquid and simmer for 20 to 30 minutes. In either case, the method is the same: bring the amaranth and water to a boil, add a pinch of salt per cup of amaranth, then lower the heat, cover, and simmer. Plain cooked amaranth congeals as it cools, so eat it immediately or keep it warm until ready to serve.

Amaranth can also be popped; the result looks like a miniature version of popcorn. Since it turns rancid quickly, prepare only as much as you'll use immediately. In addition to being a great snack, popped amaranth can be sprinkled on top of cereal, used as a substitute for bread crumbs, or added to soups, stews, and cakes for additional flavor and texture. To prepare popped amaranth, heat a wok or deep, heavy skillet until very hot. Start with just 1 tablespoon of amaranth and move the seeds constantly with tongs or a heat-resistant spatula to prevent them from burning. Transfer the popped amaranth into a bowl, and if more is desired, add another tablespoon of amaranth to the skillet and continue stirring until each grain has popped and expanded. Each tablespoon of whole amaranth makes ¼ cup of popped amaranth.

Amaranth Flavor Enhancers Onions, garlic, parsley, walnuts, almonds, lemon, and olive oil. Sweet flavor enhancers include apples, apple juice, raisins, and orange peel.

BARLEY
Contains gluten

As one of the first grains cultivated for food, for both humans and animals, barley is an old soul. After falling out of favor because it was perceived as peasant fare, it has recently become popular again because of its beta-glucans, a form of soluble fiber. When beta-glucans (and all forms of soluble fiber) mix with liquids in the digestive tract, they develop a gelatinous consistency that can bind with fatty substances and remove them from the body, thus helping to reduce low-density lipoprotein (also known as LDL or "bad cholesterol") and total cholesterol. Fortunately, the beta-glucans are found throughout the entire barley kernel, so even pearled barley provides this benefit. And because soluble fiber helps slow the release of sugars into the bloodstream, eating barley with other foods helps moderate blood sugar levels and provide steady, sustained fuel for the body.

Varieties and Cooking Guidelines

When it comes to flavor and texture, barley is well known for its role in making hearty soups and stews. But that is just a hint of what barley can bring to a menu. It is also excellent as a hot breakfast cereal or as a basis for warming pilafs or cooling summer salads. Since barley readily absorbs flavors, it's a chameleon among grains, reflecting the flavors of other ingredients it's cooked with: water, broth, or fruit juices used as the cooking liquid; seasonings such as herbs and spices; dried fruits or sun-dried tomatoes; or flavorful culinary oils, salad dressings, and marinades.

Two main types of barley are grown. The most common, **covered barley**, refers to barley that grows with an inedible hull that adheres tightly to the grain. **Hullless barley** varieties do have a hull, but it is only loosely attached to the grain and generally falls off during harvesting.

The tightly attached tough outer husk of covered barley varieties must be mechanically removed for the grain to be cooked and eaten. The process, known as pearling, is comparable to sanding. The term *pearled* is very fitting, as barley looks very much like a small pearl when all of the husk and bran layers are removed. Use this as a visual guide when buying barley: the browner the barley, the less it has been pearled.

Whole barley has only the hull removed, leaving the bran in place. This form has the most fiber, protein, vitamins, and minerals, making it the most nutritious, but it also requires the longest cooking time.

Whole barley will cook more quickly if it's presoaked for 2 to 6 hours. To retain nutrients, soak it in its cooking water, using 3 cups of water per cup of barley. If the ambient temperature is warm (above 75°F), soak it in the refrigerator.

- For the absorption method, use 3 cups of water per cup of barley. Bring the barley and its soaking water to a boil, then lower the heat, cover, and simmer until tender, about 1 hour if presoaked or about 1½ to 2 hours if not.
- To pressure-cook, use 3 cups of water per cup of barley and cook at pressure for 35 minutes if presoaked or 45 minutes if not.
- To slow-cook, use 4 cups of water per cup of barley and cook on the high setting for 3½ to 4 hours or on low for 7 to 8 hours.

Pearled barley is hulled barley with its outer layers further removed. It is classified as coarse pearl, medium pearl, or fine pearl, depending on much of the bran is removed. Coarse pearled barley, also known as Scotch barley or pot barley, is pearled only a little more than whole barley. It is less chewy than whole grain barley. Medium pearled is the variety most commonly available. It's pearled just until the grains are white. It is slightly less chewy than coarse pearled barley. Fine pearled, being the most pearled, is the whitest, smallest, most tender, and least nutritious form.

For the absorption method, use 3 cups of water per cup of pearled barley. Combine the water and barley, bring to a boil, then lower the heat, cover, and simmer until tender. Coarse pearled will take approximately 60 minutes, medium pearled about 50 minutes, and fine pearled about 35 to 40 minutes.

From top center: (1) Amaranth, (2) einkorn, (3) spelt, (4) toasted green wheat frikeh, (5) emmer farro, (6) Kamut khorasan wheat, (7) grano, (8) teff, (9) sorghum

To pressure-cook coarse or medium pearled barley, use 2 to 2½ cups of water per cup of barley and cook at pressure for 35 minutes. Don't pressure-cook fine pearled barley, as it's more likely to plug up the pressure vent.

Medium or coarse pearled barley can also be used to make a risotto-like dish. It's prepared similarly to traditional risotto but isn't as creamy. Just substitute pearled barley for Arborio rice in your favorite risotto recipe, and use 4 cups of hot broth per cup of barley, adding the hot broth ½ cup at a time while cooking over medium heat. Unlike rice risotto, barley risotto needs to be stirred only frequently rather than constantly, sparing you for other tasks. Allow up to 1 hour for the cooking process to ensure the barley is tender.

In hullless varieties of barley, the hull is only loosely connected to the kernel, so pearling isn't necessary. Hullless varieties of barley, and any products made from them, are the most flavorful and the most nutritious, containing the highest amounts of beta-glucan fiber.

Whole hullless barley will cook more quickly if it's presoaked for 2 to 6 hours. To retain nutrients, soak it in its cooking water, using 3 cups of water per cup of barley. If the ambient temperature is warm (above 75°F), soak it in the refrigerator.

- For the absorption method, use 3 cups of water per cup of barley. Bring the barley and its soaking water to a boil, then lower the heat, cover, and simmer until tender, about 50 minutes if presoaked or 90 minutes if not.
- To pressure-cook, use 3 cups of water per cup of barley and cook at pressure for 35 minutes if presoaked or 45 minutes if not.
- To slow-cook, use 4 cups of water per cup of barley and cook on the high setting for 3½ to 4 hours or on low for 7 to 8 hours.

Black barley is an heirloom variety of hullless barley that originated in Ethiopia. It has a beautiful black, shiny appearance after cooking, making it a good grain to use as a contrast to other grains in pilafs or stuffing. **Purple buffalo barley** is an heirloom variety that originated in Tibet. Although as with any hullless variety, its cooking time is long unless presoaked, its delicious, sweet flavor and unusual purple color add a new twist to any recipe that calls for barley.

Other Forms of Barley

Barley flakes are produced from barley kernels that have been rolled flat and dried. Use them as you would oatmeal, in cookies, breads, and casseroles, or as a thickening agent in soups and stews. To make a hot cereal, add 1 cup of barley flakes and a pinch of salt to 3 cups of boiling water, then lower the heat, cover, and simmer until the water is absorbed, about 25 minutes. **Barley grits** are made from barley kernels cracked into tiny pieces, which reduces cooking time to about 20 minutes. Use barley grits as a hot cereal or to thicken soup.

Barley Flavor Enhancers Onions, mushrooms, parsley, thyme, garlic, chives, cilantro, basil, dill, peas, and especially miso, tamari shoyu, and black olives.

BUCKWHEAT
Gluten free

Despite its name, buckwheat isn't related to wheat, and in fact, it isn't even truly a grain. Rather than being produced by a cereal grass, it is the seeds of a plant related to rhubarb that was brought to the United States by Dutch and German settlers. The name buckwheat is a variation on its Dutch name, *bockweit* and the German *buchweizen* (beechwheat). Both of those names arose because the three-cornered buckwheat kernels resemble the triangular nuts of the beechnut tree, and because buckwheat has nutritional qualities similar to those of wheat. Buckwheat is rarely grown with agricultural chemicals. Fertilizer tends to encourage too much leaf growth, and pesticides harm or kill the bees needed for pollination.

Because it contains all of the essential amino acids, including lysine, in proportions close to those that are ideal, buckwheat can almost be considered a complete protein. It also contains good amounts of calcium, iron, and B vitamins.

Varieties and Cooking Guidelines

Though the hard, black hulls of buckwheat may be retained when buckwheat is ground into flour, they must be removed to make whole forms of buckwheat edible. Hulled whole buckwheat kernels, known as **buckwheat groats**, are white and have a mild flavor and soft texture, making them a nice accompaniment to delicately flavored foods.

To cook buckwheat groats using the absorption method, use 2 cups of water and a pinch of salt per cup of buckwheat. Bring the water to a boil, stir in the buckwheat and salt, then lower the heat, cover, and simmer until tender, about 15 to 20 minutes. For a nuttier flavor, toast the buckwheat groats before cooking, either dry-roasting them or sautéing them in butter or oil, stirring constantly for 2 to 3 minutes. Buckwheat groats don't require or benefit from the egg treatment described below for kasha. Potatoes serve as a great companion to buckwheat.

To make anyone an instant fan of buckwheat, sauté 1 cup of uncooked buckwheat with an onion in olive oil or butter for 5 minutes, then add 2 cups of boiling water, along with a couple of cubed potatoes, celery sliced on the diagonal, and ½ teaspoon of thyme. Bring to a boil, cover, then lower the heat and simmer for 20 minutes. Although fantastic without it, you could even serve this pilaf topped with a sprinkling of Parmesan cheese. It is a good side dish for fish or tofu, or for a quick and easy take on knishes, wrap some of the pilaf in a tortilla.

To make a buckwheat version of polenta, combine 1½ cups of buckwheat groats, plain or toasted, with 4 cups of water. Bring to a boil, then lower the heat, cover, and simmer until the buckwheat becomes very thick, about 25 minutes. Spoon the cooked buckwheat into an oiled baking dish in an even layer, then allow it to cool. Cut it into strips, slices, or cubes and serve with your favorite sauce. For an interesting breakfast dish, warm the polenta in a skillet and serve with maple syrup, applesauce, or apple butter.

Buckwheat croquettes are another way to serve cooked buckwheat groats. Cook 1 cup of buckwheat groats, then mix in 2 tablespoons of flour as soon as you turn off the heat, stirring until thoroughly combined. Allow the mixture to cool just until it is easy to handle, then form it into patties or golf ball shapes. Bake the croquettes on an oiled baking sheet at 375°F for 20 minutes. These are delicious with either savory or sweet accompaniments; try them with your favorite sauce or topped with nut butter and maple syrup.

Kasha is simply white buckwheat that has been pretoasted, giving it an assertive flavor and drier texture when cooked. Traditional foods such as kasha varnishkes (kasha mixed with bowtie pasta), stuffed cabbage rolls, and dumplings are based on kasha. To prepare kasha the traditional way, coat 1 cup of kasha with one beaten egg, allowing any excess egg to drain off as you transfer the mixture to a saucepan (use a slotted spoon). Over medium heat, stir the kasha constantly until toasted. The egg coating seals each individual buckwheat groat, preventing the kasha from becoming mushy. Once the kasha is toasted, add 2 cups of boiling water and a pinch of salt. Lower the heat, cover, and simmer until the water is absorbed, about 15 to 20 minutes.

Buckwheat grits, sometimes called cream of buckwheat, are a finely ground form of untoasted white buckwheat. They cook in just 10 to 12 minutes, making a delicious, very digestible hot cereal with a texture similar to that of wheat farina. To cook ½ cup of buckwheat grits, bring 2½ cups of water to a boil. For optimal flavor, add a pinch of salt and the grits, then lower the heat, cover, and simmer for 10 to 12 minutes. Truth be told, this is one of the favorite breakfasts at my house. Not only is it really delicious, it's very easy to incorporate within a typical morning routine. We cook it with large flame raisins and serve it with homemade almond milk, garnished with thick dried coconut flakes and a couple whole almonds for extra texture. Yum!

Buckwheat Flavor Enhancers Onions, parsley, sage, poultry seasoning, garlic, red bell peppers, roasted walnuts, thyme, mushrooms, black pepper, and especially potatoes. Sweet flavor enhancers include maple syrup, honey, roasted walnuts, almond butter, and raisins.

CORN

Gluten free

Corn is one of the few grains native to the Western hemisphere. It's also the source of appreciable amounts of antioxidant phytonutrients, including the carotenoids (especially lutein and zeaxanthin) in yellow corn and anthocyanins in blue corn. In its whole, dried form, complete with the bran and germ, corn is also a good source of B vitamins, vitamin C, potassium, and fiber. However, unless the corn is pretreated with an alkaline substance, a diet that relies too heavily on corn can cause significant nutritional deficiencies. Besides being low in two essential amino acids, tryptophan and lysine, most of its niacin is bound by another molecule, making it unavailable to the body.

In the past, entire regions and cultures with a corn-based diet, including areas of the southern United States, South America, and Africa, suffered devastating epidemics of pellagra, a serious disease resulting from niacin deficiency. Fortunately, many native cultures traditionally cooked whole corn with various alkaline substances, such as slaked lime (calcium hydroxide created from the thermal decomposition of materials such as limestone), wood ashes (potassium hydroxide), or lye (sodium hydroxide). Today, slaked lime (sometimes sold as "cal") is most often used. Not only does this alka-linizing treatment, known as nixtamalization, help remove the corn's tough outer hull for easier eating and processing, it also improves the amino acid bal-ance, liberates the bound niacin, and, when slaked lime is used, provides bonus calcium.

The distinctive slightly sour flavor of corn tor-tillas, corn chips, hominy, and masa harina are a result of their manufacture from alkali-treated corn.

Varieties and Cooking Guidelines

Eating fresh corn as a vegetable is a relatively new practice, requiring the development of varieties of "sweet corn," in which the sugars in the kernel don't turn into starch as the corn matures. Corn grown for its use as a grain is divided into three types: popcorn, dent corn, and flint corn.

Popcorn, which is probably the most widely consumed whole grain form of corn, is a specific variety of corn that has a hard outer protein layer protecting the inner starch layers and a moisture content between 11 and 14 percent, factors that combine to make it especially poppable. When sub-jected to high heat, pressure builds up in the interior starch layers until the protein layer explodes. Yellow popcorn, with its corny flavor and crunchy, firm texture, pops up the most, expanding up to forty times its original size. In contrast, white popcorn

has a slightly sweet taste, is crisp yet tender, and expands up to thirty-five times its original size.

Store dry popcorn in a tightly sealed jar or plastic container, preferably in the refrigerator, to retain the moisture inside the kernels. Just ¼ cup of pop-corn kernels will yield about 8 cups of popped corn. With 2 grams of fiber and only 69 calories in 3 cups of popcorn, it can be a very nutritious whole grain snack if popped using a good-quality, nonhydro-genated oil specifically designated for high-heat applications, or, better yet, popped in an air popper without oil and served without butter or even salt. If plain popcorn isn't enough for you, dust it with any of your favorite seasonings such as garlic granules, cayenne pepper, paprika, basil, cinnamon, ginger, granulated sea vegetables, or nutritional yeast.

True to its name, **dent corn** has hard, smooth sides and a soft inner core of starch that collapses during drying, causing a dent at the top. Either yel-low or white in color, dent corn is also frequently referred to as "field corn" to distinguish it from sweet corn. Higher in soft starch than flint corn, dent corn is easier to mill and makes exceptional corn grits and cornmeal. Hominy, also known as posole, can also be made with dent corn, with exceptional results from heirloom varieties known for their unique flavors and textures. Among the best of these are Hickory King, with its full, pearly white or yellow kernels, and Carolina Gourdseed White, celebrated for its classic floral aroma and luxurious creamy consistency.

Flint corn has a hard outer shell and kernels in a wide variety of beautiful colors and was for decades considered among the public primarily as a decora-tive item, often referred to as "Indian corn." Now blue and red corn are popular in food items like tortillas and chips. However, flint corn has a long history of use as a staple food among native peo-ples in the southwestern United States, Mexico, and Central and South America. It has a hard, starchy interior (though not actually as hard as flint!)—so much so that it is gritty rather than powdery when ground. It is a prime type of corn for making hominy, and its meal is also prized for polenta and corn breads and corn cakes of all types. The grain's color varieties accentuate its beneficial phytonutrient elements and its excellent flavors. For example, blue and red corn are higher in protein, iron, potassium, and zinc than typical yellow or white varieties of dent corn, and they are also known for their sweet, nutlike flavor. Treasured heirloom flint corn varieties have begun to re-emerge, allowing us to share in and respect the best from cultures long past. Chapalote corn, an ancient variety, is distinguished by its smoky coffee-colored kernels, of which a third on the ear are flinty, with the rest of its kernels more like ornamental popcorn. Tuscarora White corn is valued for its large ears and large white kernels, along with its exceptional flavor and texture that makes for unsurpassed cornmeal, roasted corn flour, and, of course, hominy.

Hominy, also known as posole (or samp when coarsely ground), is whole dent or flint corn that has been treated with an alkaline agent. When cooked, the whole kernels are very chewy and have a slightly sweet, slightly sour flavor that, surprisingly, is not very cornlike. Hominy is used whole in soups and stews or as a side dish, or it may be ground to make fresh masa. Slaking corn with lime at home to make hominy takes about two and a half hours, but the flavor is significantly better than that of canned, precooked whole hominy. However, there is a time-saving alternative: buy dried corn labeled "posole," which means it has already been slaked with lime, had its hulls removed, and then been dried again. After soaking the dried posole for 6 to 8 hours or overnight, all you need to do is the final cooking step. The posole is done when the kernels have bloomed open and become soft.

- To cook posole using the absorption method, put the dried posole in a pot and add water to cover. Bring to a boil, then lower the heat, cover, and simmer until tender, about 3 to 4 hours.
- To pressure-cook, put the dried posole in the pressure cooker and add water to cover.

Cook at pressure for 1 hour and then simmer for an additional hour.
- To slow-cook, use 6 cups of water per cup of posole. Cook on the high setting for 1 hour and then on the low setting for 9 to 12 hours.

Hominy grits, made by grinding dried hominy, are available in coarse, medium, or fine grind. Most often served as a hot cereal or simple side dish in Southern-style cooking, they can also be used as the basis for soufflés and puddings. To cook hominy grits, use four parts water to one part grits. Bring the water to a boil, then gradually pour in the grits, whisking all the while. Lower the heat, cover, and simmer for 25 to 30 minutes. Quick-cooking grits are very finely ground and will cook in 5 minutes. **Masa**, also called nixtamal, is dough made from ground, freshly cooked hominy. It's typically used to make tamales, tortillas, and dumplings, but it can also be served like mashed potatoes, topped with butter or cheese. When dried and finely ground, it is called **masa harina**. **Corn grits** are made by coarsely grinding whole or degerminated corn. Look for stone-ground whole corn grits, processed to retain the bran and germ. Unlike true hominy grits, corn grits are not processed with lime. To cook corn grits, use four parts salted water to one part grits. Bring the water to a boil, then slowly pour in the grits, whisking all the while. Lower the heat, cover, and simmer for 25 to 30 minutes.

Corn Flavor Enhancers Onions, chives, tomatoes, cilantro, cumin, cheese, garlic, hot and sweet peppers, oregano, epazote, chili powder, and parsley.

EINKORN
Contains gluten

Known as the first cultivated form of wheat, as well as one of the first grains raised for food, einkorn (*Triticum monococcum*) has roots going back about ten thousand years ago. It is distinguished by its unusual diploid genetic structure, which has fourteen chromosomes, in contrast with the hexaploid forty-two chromosome structure of spelt and modern varieties of wheat. Also known in Italy as *farro piccolo, einkorn* is German for "single grain," which points to the single row of spikelets that emerges in the head of the wheat and from which the kernels develops. When compared to kernels found in other varieties of both heirloom and modern wheat, einkorn is distinctly thinner.

Current interest in heirloom grains and their unique nutritional attributes—which has the merit of supporting and protecting agricultural genetic diversity—has distinguished einkorn as a grain to explore and enjoy. When compared to modern varieties of wheat, einkorn is very high in protein and the carotenes, especially lutein and zeaxanthin, which accounts for the brownish-orange color of the grain. What's more, whole einkorn cooks in only 20 to 25 minutes, making it one of the few quick-cooking whole grains available. It's also delicious, with a flavor that is slightly sweet, complex, and nutty and a cooked texture similar to cracked wheat.

Although pockets of einkorn production have been maintained over the centuries, cultivation had been limited due to its lower yield and because, like farro and spelt, the kernels of einkorn do not thresh free of the tightly attached husk, which makes processing more difficult. Starting with the cultivation of farro, the availability of other grains with divergent protein and starch structures more adaptable for other types of cooking and baking, also contributed to einkorn's loss of prominence.

Although einkorn contains gluten, because it's genetically different from modern wheat, it's possible that some wheat-sensitive individuals may better tolerate einkorn. Still, anyone with gluten intolerance and severe allergies or sensitivity to wheat should always consult with a medical professional and be evaluated carefully before trying any new grain.

Varieties and Cooking Guidelines

Use einkorn as you would whole farro or cracked wheat in soups, stews, salads or serve it as a cereal at breakfast or at dinner instead of rice or other grains.

For the absorption method, use 2 cups of water per cup of einkorn. Bring the water and the einkorn to a boil, lower the heat, cover, and simmer until tender, about 20 to 25 minutes. Remove from the heat and let stand, covered, for 10 minutes before serving.

Alternatively, when cooking einkorn for use in salads or whenever more separate, slightly less chewy grains are desired, use 3 cups of water per cup of einkorn. Bring the water and the einkorn to a boil, lower the heat, cover, and simmer until tender, about 20 to 25 minutes. Remove from the heat and let stand, covered, for 10 minutes and then drain through a strainer. You can retain the cooking liquid to use as stock.

Einkorn Flavor Enhancers Celery, onion, leeks, oregano, parsley, garlic, rosemary, thyme, mushrooms, olives, and red bell peppers.

FARRO

Contains gluten

Farro and spelt are often confused with one another or considered to be the same; "farro" has also been used as a general term to refer to einkorn, emmer, and spelt (these are the three hulled wheat species that retain their husks during harvest); each is actually a different species. "Farro" is in fact another name for emmer; in Italy it's known as *farro medio.*

Whatever you decide to call it, farro is an unhybridized, ancient type of wheat that was common throughout Europe, northern Africa, and the Near East well before the early days of the Roman Empire. It is claimed to be the grain that fueled the Roman legions. Farro ultimately fell from favor as other types of wheat were developed that had higher yields and were easier to produce, such as durum wheat. Like spelt and hulled barley, farro has a tough outer hull that must be removed prior to cooking or further processing. Still, its cultivation survived in Ethiopia and some areas of northern and central Italy, especially Tuscany, Umbria, and areas around Rome. In fact, farro grown in the mountainous Garfagnana area of Tuscany is an IGP (Indicazione geografica protetta) product, with its geographic identity protected by law to ensure that the common variety that has adapted to the local climate and terrain throughout the centuries is safeguarded, with proscribed agronomic practices for its organic production. After languishing in obscurity for centuries, it is becoming popular once again.

Farro has a chewy texture and delicious flavor reminiscent of a cross between wheat and barley. The whole grain has a shape and color similar to that of short-grain brown rice, but is a bit darker. Nutritionally, it is rich in fiber, magnesium, vitamins A and E, and various B vitamins.

Because farro is distinct from modern hybridized wheat and is lower in gluten, some individuals who are sensitive to common wheat can better tolerate it. Nonetheless, as it is in the same general tetraploid class of wheat as modern-day durum wheat, farro contains gliadin, the element within gluten that is considered the most problematic to gluten-intolerant individuals, so anyone with gluten intolerance and severe allergies or sensitivity to wheat should always consult with a medical professional and be evaluated carefully before trying any new grain.

Varieties and Cooking Guidelines

In Italy, where farro continued to be grown and appreciated after its popularity waned elsewhere, the grain is often made into a risotto-like dish called farrotto. It is also added to soups and stews for thickening and texture, with the added bonus of making the final dish especially delicious, since farro captures the flavors of foods it's cooked with. In salads, it adds both a complementary chewy texture and a satisfying depth of flavor.

Whole farro takes a long time to cook—2 to 3 hours. However, you can reduce that time to about an hour by presoaking the grain for 6 to 12 hours. When adding presoaked farro to soups or stews, add it 1 hour before the soup or stew will be done. To retain nutrients, cook the farro in its soaking water, using 3 cups of water per cup of farro. If the ambient temperature is warm (above 75°F), soak it in the refrigerator.

- For the absorption method, bring the farro and its soaking water to a boil, then lower the heat, cover, and simmer until tender, about 50 to 60 minutes.
- To pressure-cook, use 3 cups of water per cup of farro and, if time permits, soak for 30 minutes before cooking at pressure for 45 minutes.
- To slow-cook, use 4 to 5 cups of water per cup of farro and cook on the high setting for 3½ hours or on low for 8 hours.

To make farrotto, use 5 cups of hot broth per cup of farro and cook as you would regular risotto. However, farrotto requires 1 hour of stirring and cooking time to achieve a tender, slightly chewy texture, rather than the 20 minutes it takes with Arborio and similar Italian types of rice. You can shorten that time to about 25 minutes by using semipearled farro, in which case only about 4 cups of hot broth will be needed. **Semipearled farro** has been slightly pearled to reduce cooking time to 20 minutes or less without presoaking. For the absorption method, use 2 cups of water per cup of semipearled farro. **Cracked farro**, made by coarsely cracking whole farro, cooks in about 30 minutes with no presoaking. Use 3 cups of water per cup of cracked farro. Use it as a hot cereal for breakfast, in pilafs, or in salads such as tabbouleh.

Farro Flavor Enhancers Basil, garlic, rosemary, thyme, mushrooms, olives, and red bell peppers.

FARIKE
SEE ROASTED GREEN WHEAT (PAGE 84)

GRANO
Contains gluten

Durum wheat is typically used to make pasta and semolina flour, but for many centuries, before pasta was even on the menu, durum wheat was eaten as a grain in the Apulia region in Italy and in Sicily. In fact, its name, *grano*, is the Italian word for "grain." Grano is specially selected whole durum wheat, lightly pearled to remove the thick outer casing.

With only a small amount of the bran sacrificed in the process, grano remains a very nutritious grain, especially in comparison to pasta, which is typically derived from durum wheat that is further refined.

Cooking Guidelines

Golden in color like semolina flour, grano tastes like pasta and is cooked like pasta, albeit for a bit longer. Traditional recipes featured the pleasant chewiness of grano in soups, pilafs, and entrées, but it's also a natural served cold in salads, where it provides added flavor, texture, and nutrition. When cooked with extra water, grano also makes a delicious hot breakfast cereal.

To cook grano, use 8 cups of water per cup of grano. Bring the water to a boil, salt it as you would for pasta, then add the grano. After it returns to a boil, lower the heat to medium and cook, stirring frequently, until the grano is tender but still chewy, about 35 minutes. Then, just as with cooking pasta, drain the grano and serve it with a sauce or as an accompaniment to meat, seafood, tofu, tempeh, or beans.

Grano can also be cooked in soups such as minestrone. Use 1 cup of grano for 2 quarts of soup, allowing at least 30 minutes of cooking after the grano is added. For a hot breakfast cereal, use a proportion of 4 cups of water per cup of grano. Bring to a boil, then lower the heat, cover, and, ideally, simmer for about 4 hours so it will become soft and creamy. Alternatively, a delicious, chewy version can be ready within 2 hours.

Grano Flavor Enhancers Onions, chives, dill, mushrooms, black pepper, garlic, curry powder, parsley, cilantro, and mint.

JOB'S TEARS
Gluten free

Also known as hatomugi and adlay, Job's Tears is a grain with a teardrop shape that somewhat resembles barley. Sometimes it is said to be a type of barley, but the two are in different genera. The seed of a wild grass cultivated for over four thousand years in China, it has been used extensively in traditional Chinese medicine. It's also often used in macrobiotic cooking, wherein it has a reputation for being strengthening to the body. Since only the outer husk is removed, it serves as a good source of dietary fiber. Its pleasant nutlike flavor permeates any dish in which it is cooked.

Cooking Guidelines

Job's Tears are generally cooked along with other grains or in soups or stews. For a good balance of flavor and texture, stick to no more than 25 percent when combining Job's Tears with other grains, allowing for the proportional use of 2 cups of water to each cup of Job's Tears, depending on the quantity being prepared. Cook until all the grains are tender, typically about 10 minutes longer than the primary grain would require. Job's Tears can also be cooked and eaten on their own.

- For the absorption method, use 2 cups of water per cup of Job's Tears. Bring the water to a boil, stir in the grain, then lower the heat, cover, and simmer until tender, about 50 to 60 minutes.
- To pressure-cook, use 2 cups of water per cup of Job's Tears and cook at pressure for 45 minutes.
- To slow-cook, use 4 cups of water per cup of Job's Tears and cook on the low setting for 6 to 8 hours.

Job's Tears Flavor Enhancers Ginger, parsley, onions, and chives.

KAMUT KHORASAN WHEAT
Contains gluten

"Kamut" is a registered trademark used by Kamut International to market, protect, and preserve the genetic purity of an ancient variety of landrace wheat called khorasan wheat. Although its place of origin remains unclear, the name Kamut (a word referring to wheat found in an Egyptian hieroglyphic dictionary) was chosen as a nod to the fact that the kernels of khorasan wheat that piqued renewed interest in the grain had been found in Egypt. Remnants of a more active cultivation of the variety survived, even though it had been an obscure grain known and used only by a few.

As is the story with many heirloom varieties that went out of favor for commercial growing, khorasan wheat has lower yields and is harder to grow than modern hybrids. But its rewards are significant. Kamut's flavor is noticeably rich, sweet, nutty, almost buttery tasting and the texture of the cooked whole grain is naturally firm and pleasantly chewy, adding appreciably to its versatility as an ingredient in pilafs, cold salads, and for texture in soups, stews, and chilis. The grains also have an unusual humpback shape and are noticably larger than a typical kernel of wheat—nearly two or three times as large—and with an amber color similar to that of semolina. Kamut is also much higher than modern wheats in protein (ranging from 12 to 18 percent), minerals (including selenium, known for its antioxidant activity, zinc, and magnesium), fatty acids, and vitamins B and E.

By virtue of the criteria in its trademark registration for using the name, Kamut also has the distinction of always being grown according to certified organic standards. This great grain's increasing popularity is reflected in an expanding variety of food products made with Kamut, including bulgur, couscous, flakes, pasta, and ready-to-eat cereals; it is also the basis for a nondairy beverage and beer. It also makes exceptionally good pasta.

Kamut, though it contains gluten, is distinct from modern-day wheat, and some individuals otherwise sensitive to common wheat find they can better tolerate Kamut and products made with it. However, anyone with gluten intolerance and severe allergies or sensitivity to wheat should always consult with a medical professional and be evaluated carefully before trying any new grain.

Varieties and Cooking Guidelines

Whether hot or cold, whole Kamut makes a terrific breakfast cereal. With a texture and shape similar to pine nuts (although larger in size), cooked whole Kamut is also excellent in baked goods, salads, cereals, and pilafs. It serves as a good addition to soups, stews, and chilis, providing both texture and thickening. Or cooked kernels can be added to pancakes and muffins, where it will enhance both flavor and texture. For an appealing textural contrast for side dishes and grain-based salads, combine cooked Kamut with rice, barley, or quinoa.

Whole Kamut takes 1½ to 2 hours to cook, but presoaking will shorten that time. No matter which of the following cooking methods you use, the proportion of water called for in the recipe is purposely greater than needed, in order to enhance and maintain the suppleness of the cooked grain. In fact, leftover cooked Kamut is best stored in the refrigerator submerged in its own cooking liquid to help keep it hydrated and soft. Excess liquid can be reserved for broth.

- For quicker cooking, presoak whole Kamut for 6 to 12 hours or overnight. To retain nutrients, cook it in its soaking water, using 3 cups of water per cup of Kamut. If the ambient temperature is warm (above 75°F), soak it in the refrigerator.

- To cook on the stove, use 3 cups of water per cup of Kamut. Bring the Kamut and its soaking water to a boil, then lower the heat, cover, and simmer until the grains are plumped and a few have burst, about 1 hour if presoaked and 1½ to 2 hours if not.

- To pressure-cook, use 3 cups of water per cup of Kamut and cook at pressure for 35 minutes if presoaked, or 45 minutes if not.

- For slow-cooking, presoaking is optional. Use 4 cups of water per cup of Kamut and cook on the high setting for 3½ to 4 hours or on low for 7 to 8 hours.

Kamut bulgur is cooked similarly to its wheat-based counterpart. Use 2 cups of water per cup of Kamut bulgur. Bring the water to a boil, stir in the bulgur, then lower the heat, cover, and simmer for 25 minutes. Remove it from the heat and allow it to stand, covered, for another 10 minutes before serving or using in a recipe. **Kamut couscous** is also cooked similarly to its wheat-based counterpart. Use 1½ cups of water or broth per cup of Kamut couscous. Bring the water to a boil, then stir in the couscous, lower the heat, cover, and simmer for 5 minutes. Remove from the heat and allow it to stand, covered, for another 5 minutes. Stir to fluff before serving or using in a recipe. **Kamut flakes** are made like oatmeal. Whole Kamut is steamed, dried, then flattened between rollers. Use them as you would oatmeal in cookies, other baked goods, and casseroles. For hot breakfast cereal, use 2 cups of water per cup of Kamut flakes. Bring the water to a boil, stir in the Kamut flakes, then lower the heat, cover, and simmer for 15 to 18 minutes. It's especially delicious when cooked with vanilla extract and dried apples and served topped with roasted pecans.

Kamut Flavor Enhancers Onions, garlic, parsley, basil, black pepper, mushrooms, raisins, and lemon.

MILLET
Gluten free

Its delicious, delicate flavor and soft, cohesive texture make millet perfect for basic side dishes, stuffing, burgers, and casseroles. Although this quick-cooking grain is most often associated with birdseed in the United States, it's a sacred grain in China, where it has a long history of use; it is a staple crop for about one-third of the world's population. The word *millet* is actually applied to at least five different species of varying colors and palatability. The species of millet used in the United States is yellow proso millet, and the tiny grain is always hulled or pearled, but the bran remains intact. In addition to being a good source of dietary iron, millet is also rich in lysine, making it a higher-quality protein than most grains. It is also very alkaline, making it easy to digest and a soothing comfort food.

Varieties and Cooking Guidelines

Try adding a couple of tablespoons of uncooked millet to breads and baked goods for a nutlike crunch, or stir some uncooked millet into stews and soups about 20 minutes before the end of cooking to provide body. To enhance millet's nutty flavor and ensure the grains cook up light and dry, toast it in a dry skillet, stirring constantly, for 3 to 4 minutes before rinsing it and cooking it. However, untoasted millet is equally good; it just has a milder flavor and softer texture.

- For the absorption method, use 2 cups of water per cup of millet. Combine the water and millet, bring to a boil, then lower the heat, cover, and simmer for 15 minutes. Remove from the heat and let stand, covered, for 20 minutes before fluffing.

- To pressure-cook, use 2 cups of water per cup of millet and cook at pressure for 10 to 15 minutes.

- To slow-cook, use 4 cups of water and cook on the low setting for 6 to 8 hours. For a hot breakfast cereal, consider replacing some of the water with juice, and add some fresh or dried fruit.

For a softer texture, similar to mashed potatoes, cook using the absorption method and increase the water to 3 or even 3½ cups per cup of millet. Simmer, covered, until the water is absorbed, about 45 minutes to an hour. Adding 1 cup of coarsely chopped cauliflower per cup of millet enhances the flavor and texture. Or, for a rich, creamy hot breakfast cereal, use 5 cups of water or a combination of water and apple juice per cup of millet and cook using the absorption method.

For a savory vegetable stew with millet, use 3 cups of water or broth per cup of millet and add any chopped vegetables and seasonings you wish. Bring to a boil, reduce the heat, and simmer for 45 minutes. To use it as you would polenta, press still-warm cooked millet into an oiled baking dish. Allow it to cool, then cut it into squares or strips. You can also press warm millet into oiled muffin cups to make millet timbales. Leftover millet splashed with your favorite dressing is an exceptional basis for a grain and vegetable salad.

Millet Flavor Enhancers Curry powder, chili powder, orange, rosemary, onion, chives, parsley, black pepper, bay leaf, thyme, garlic, ginger, toasted walnuts, and toasted pecans.

OATS
Gluten free
Of all the grains, oats are the ultimate comfort food, bringing soothing warmth whether cooked into a bowl of steaming hot oatmeal, a chewy raisin-studded oatmeal cookie, or a hearty pilaf made from steel-cut oats or whole oat groats. Processing oats is a two-step operation: first the outer hull is removed to expose the inner kernel, called the groat, and then the groats are steamed to inactivate enzymes that would otherwise cause them to go rancid very quickly. Thanks to this process, oats have a shelf life of up to one year when stored at a moderate room temperature, and even longer if kept in cooler conditions. The steaming also partially cooks the oats and enhances their nutty flavor. From there, the groats may be left whole, rolled into thick old-fashioned flakes, or chopped into small, coarse pieces, called steel-cut oats. Steel-cut oats can also be made into flakes, yielding the small, thin flakes of quick-cooking oatmeal or the even smaller and thinner flakes of instant oatmeal.

Besides having great flavor and texture, oats have extensive nutritional benefits. Because only the outer, indigestible husk is removed during processing, leaving the bran and germ intact, all forms of oats are considered to be whole grain, no matter what size or shape they're processed into. In addition, all forms of oats contain beta-glucan, the viscous soluble fiber that helps lower both total cholesterol and LDL or bad cholesterol. Their beta-glucan content means that oats, like barley, digest more slowly, which helps stabilize blood sugar levels and keeps you going longer, feeling more satisfied and energized. This type of fiber is also responsible for the smooth, thick texture of cooked oats and their moistening and tenderizing effect in baked goods.

While still fairly low in fat, oats contain more fats than most grains, mostly in the form of unsaturated fat, and particularly linoleic acid. This essential fatty acid plays an important role in the synthesis of prostaglandins, hormonelike compounds that help regulate vital body functions, including supporting a strong nervous system and healthy skin. Oats are also a good source of vitamin E, including tocotrienols, a component of vitamin E that helps reduce serum cholesterol by preventing the synthesis of cholesterol in the liver.

Oats are gluten free and studies have shown that oats do not trigger the symptoms associated with grains that contain gluten. In North America, they are often listed as being inappropriate for a gluten-free diet, but this is only out of concern that they may be contaminated by wheat during harvest and processing. To provide extra assurance, some companies market oats guaranteed to be grown on dedicated oat-growing farms, processed in a gluten-free facility, and tested to ensure purity.

Varieties and Cooking Guidelines
Oat groats have only their inedible outer chaff removed, so they have the most full-bodied flavor and provide the most nutrition. They make an exceptionally hearty breakfast cereal. Because they retain their shape and have a soft but chewy texture when cooked, they can also be served in place of rice or used as the basis for pilafs and stuffings. For any of the methods below, you can make a sweet dish by adding a bit of cinnamon and some raisins or other dried fruit during cooking. For a savory twist, add chopped onion, celery, salt to taste, and a sprinkling of your favorite herb.

- For the absorption method, use 3 cups of water per cup of oat groats. Combine the water and oats, bring to a boil, then lower the heat, cover, and simmer until tender, about 90 minutes, adding more water if necessary.
- To pressure-cook, use 3 cups of water per cup of oats and cook at pressure for 30 minutes.
- To slow-cook, use 4 cups of water per cup of oats and cook on the low setting for 8 to 12 hours.

Steel-cut oats, also known as Scotch oats, Scottish oats, or Irish oats, are oat groats that have been cut into small, coarse pieces. As a result, cooking time is reduced to 20 to 30 minutes, and you can further reduce that time to 10 to 15 minutes by soaking the oats in their cooking water overnight; you may need to increase the amount of water a bit. Another way to reduce the cooking time to about 15 minutes is to toast steel-cut oats in a pan over medium heat for 3 minutes before cooking. Because steel-cut oats have virtually all of the flavor and chewy texture of oat groats, they make a remarkable hot cereal, a great base for a pilaf, or a flavorful addition to breads. They can even be used to make an oat-based risotto: first sauté a small onion in 2 to 3 teaspoons of oil. Then stir in 1 cup of steel-cut oats and continue to stir and sauté for 5 minutes. Add ½ cup of hot broth, stirring constantly until the liquid is absorbed, then add another ½ cup of broth and continue in the same manner until you've added 3 cups of broth and the dish has the rich, creamy texture and slightly al dente quality of traditional risotto.

- For the absorption method, use 2 to 2½ cups of water per cup of steel-cut oats. For hot cereal, increase the water to 3 cups. Bring the water to a boil and stir in the oats, then lower the heat, cover, and simmer until tender—about 15 minutes if the oats were presoaked or toasted and about 20 to 30 minutes otherwise.
- Pressure-cooking isn't recommended because of the tendency for steel-cut oats to plug up the steam vent.
- To slow-cook, use 4 cups of water per cup of oats and cook on the low setting for 7 to 8 hours.

Rolled oats or oat flakes are the largest, thickest, and most flavorful kind of "oatmeal." While they require more cooking time than any other type of oatmeal, it's 15 minutes, tops, making them a quick and easy way to get more whole grains in your diet. In baking, they can be added to breads, cookies, and muffins, or add them to pancakes or casseroles for extra flavor, texture, and nutrition. Rolled oats also make a delicious creamy base for dairy-free soups. Just add a small amount while the soup is cooking—about ¼ cup of oats per 3 cups of broth. In most recipes, rolled oats and quick-cooking oatmeal are interchangeable, though you may need to add a bit more water when substituting rolled oats for quick-cooking oatmeal.

- To cook rolled oats in the traditional way, use 2 cups of water per cup of oats. Combine the water and oats, bring to a boil, then lower the heat, partially cover the pot with a lid, and simmer for 10 to 15 minutes. However, some people swear by adding the rolled oats to boiling water, preferring its chewier, less creamy texture.
- Pressure-cooking isn't recommended because the rolled oats could clog the steam vent.
- To slow-cook, use 2½ cups of water per cup of oats and cook on the low setting for 8 hours.

Quick-cooking oatmeal is about half the thickness of oat flakes and smaller, making a flake that can cook in just 5 minutes. Their texture doesn't stand up as well to cooking as that of regular rolled oats, making oatmeal cookies that are less chewy, for example. And because the flakes are smaller and sliced more thinly, they're digested more quickly and, consequently, are less effective at keeping hunger at bay as long as the thicker rolled oats. **Instant oatmeal**, an extremely thin form of oat flakes, cook in a snap. Just pour boiling water over them, let stand for 1 minute, and they're ready. Although convenient, they are the least flavorful. And because they are the most processed, they have a higher glycemic index value. This means their starch is converted into sugar and released into the bloodstream more quickly; as a result, you're likely to get hungry sooner than if you eat a thicker form of oatmeal. Also, most of the instant oatmeal sold is highly sweetened—and laden with artificial flavorings—making it more like a very sweet snack than a healthful, satisfying breakfast. Instead of reaching for a presweetened variety, choose plain instant oatmeal and add your own fresh or dried fruit or, better yet, use quick-cooking oatmeal or rolled oats. Instant oatmeal cannot be substituted for rolled oats or quick-cooking oatmeal in recipes.

Oat bran is the outer covering of hulled oat groats. It has a light color and texture and a pleasant oat flavor when cooked. It can be added to muffins, hot cereals, breads, casseroles, and soups for its beneficial soluble fiber and its tenderizing and moistening effects. As the health benefits of oat bran are a function of its forming gels or viscous solutions in water, oat bran should be cooked with plenty of water or added as an ingredient within food that will be cooked rather than simply sprinkled on foods. Oat bran can be cooked up into a delicious hot cereal that is ready to eat in just a few minutes. For one serving, slowly pour $1/3$ cup of oat bran into 1 cup of boiling water, stirring all the while, then add a pinch of salt if you wish, lower the heat, and simmer for a total of 2 minutes.

Oat Flavor Enhancers Dried fruits, cinnamon, fennel seed, honey, and maple syrup. Savory flavor enhancers include sage, Parmesan cheese, dill, nutmeg, parsley, and celery.

QUINOA
Gluten free

Quinoa has been cultivated for several thousand years in the high Andes of Peru, Bolivia, Ecuador, and Chile, as were potatoes. Because both can be cultivated at high altitudes, they were critical elements in the native diet. Although prepared as a grain, quinoa is actually the small dried seed of a plant in the same botanical family as beets and spinach. The seed is disk-shaped with a white band around its outside edges. During cooking, this band becomes more visually apparent, retaining its curved shape—and also giving quinoa its slightly crunchy texture. Quinoa is very quick cooking and versatile; within only 15 minutes, it can be transformed into an outstanding entree or side dish, a hot breakfast cereal, or even a dessert.

Flowering quinoa

Quinoa is the Spanish spelling for the name of the grain in the indigenous Quechua language in the Andes, which translates to "mother grain"—a fitting name, not only because quinoa was a source of sustenance in the harsh, cold, dry climate, but also because of its amazing nutritional profile. Unlike most grains, quinoa is considered a complete protein, containing all the essential amino acids in a nearly perfect balance. Combining quinoa with other grains or beans can help compensate for any amino acids they lack or are low in. Quinoa is also a good source of fiber and, compared to other grains, a relatively good source of iron, magnesium, calcium, vitamin A, and vitamin E. It is easily digested, but it has a relatively low glycemic index value, meaning its sugars are released into the bloodstream slowly, allowing it to provide sustained energy over many hours.

Quinoa seeds are coated with saponins, a bitter, inedible substance that serves to repel insects. This is removed after harvest either by soaking the seeds or through a mechanical polishing process. As with the pearling process for barley, mechanical polishing also removes some of the grain's dietary fiber and nutritional value; the extent depends on how much polishing the grain receives. Although saponin-free hybrid varieties of quinoa have been developed, they are more vulnerable to insects and thus more likely to be grown with pesticides.

Most quinoa is imported from South America, but cultivation has been attempted in higher-elevation areas of the United States, such as Colorado. Over the many centuries of its use and cultivation, many different varieties evolved, and they vary in color and richness of flavor. While the seeds can be black, purple, orange, red, pink, or white, most of the commonly available quinoa is either light tan or dark red. The tan version has a delicate nutty flavor when cooked, while red quinoa tastes somewhat like roasted walnuts and is crunchier in texture. Black quinoa has a crunchier texture and a more pronounced flavor.

Varieties and Cooking Guidelines

Although most commercial quinoa has been pre-washed or mechanically processed to remove the bitter-tasting saponins on its seed coat, play it safe and always rinse quinoa thoroughly, until the water runs clear, before cooking. Quinoa is so small that it can slip through the mesh of many strainers. To help with this, and to help remove the sticks and debris sometimes found in quinoa, wash it in a bowl rather than rinsing it in a strainer under a faucet. Put the quinoa in a bowl, cover with water, then swish it around to help the debris float to the top. Carefully pour off the water and debris, then repeat the process two more times.

Neither pressure-cooking nor slow-cooking is recommended. To cook quinoa using the absorption method, use 2 cups of water or broth per cup of quinoa. Combine the quinoa, water, and any seasonings in a pot, bring to a boil, then lower the heat to medium, cover, and cook for 15 minutes. For a richer flavor, toast quinoa in a dry or oiled skilled

before cooking. To use quinoa to thicken soup, add a small amount of uncooked quinoa during the last 15 minutes of cooking. For a unique breakfast or dessert, cook leftover plain quinoa with a bit of apple juice, dried fruit, nuts, and vanilla.

For more variety in color, flavor, and texture, combine equal amounts of tan and red quinoa, or try cooking quinoa with grains that have a similar cooking time and grain-to-water proportion, such as millet, white basmati rice, bulgur, and buckwheat. Leftover quinoa is an excellent basis for a quick main dish salad. Just add chopped vegetables, a cooked protein source (beans, tofu, tempeh, or chicken), fresh herbs if available, and your favorite salad dressing. This is a light but nutritious meal that can keep you going for hours.

Quinoa Flavor Enhancers Curry powder, onions, chives, parsley, cilantro, cumin, coriander, and orange.

RICE
Gluten free

More than forty thousand varieties of rice are grown throughout the world, including countless heirloom varieties that have been grown for centuries in obscure places, adapting to the environment and the surrounding culture. While only a small percentage of these types are commercially available, interest in ethnic cooking and heirloom varieties has introduced us to the wide array of colors, flavors, and textures of rice—and shattered the common belief that there are only two main types of rice: white and brown.

When it comes to nutrition, the clear winners are whole grain varieties, easily distinguished by their medium to dark colors, including brown, red, purple, and black. With only its inedible hull removed, whole grain rice is a good source of fiber, vitamin E, and trace minerals. However, when it's milled into white rice by machines that remove the bran layer and germ, leaving only the starchy endosperm, nutrient levels decrease significantly. In an effort to try to replace at least some, but certainly not all, of the nutrients lost

From top: (1) Black Forbidden Rice (medium-grain),
(2) short-grain brown rice, (3) Thai red rice (long-grain)

during processing, several brands of white rice have thiamin, niacin, folic acid, and iron added as a coating. This is why cooking instructions on packages of enriched rice discourage rinsing before cooking.

Varieties and Cooking Guidelines

The primary differences among the various types of rice can be attributed to the predominant type of starch found in the grain, and specifically the proportion of amylose to amylopectin. Amylose, the straight-chained starch characteristic of long-grain rice, expands when cooked to form drier, firmer, more separate grains of rice. In contrast, amylopectin, the branched-chain starch in short-grain rice, absorbs more moisture, which helps generate moister, softer, clingy grains. Medium-grain rice occupies the middle ground in terms of amylose and amylopectin content and consequently cooks up with some properties of both, but is unique in its ability to develop a creamy texture. Let's explore

just a few of the many varieties of rice within each of these broad categories.

Long-Grain Rice

Long-grain rice has slender grains that are four to five times longer than their width. Due to its relatively high proportion of amylose, its grains cook up light, fluffy, and separate. Since it becomes hard when it's cold, it is typically used for rice-based dishes that will be served warm: as a simple side dish, as a pilaf, or to be served with stir-fries and curries. Beyond the familiar brown and white, there are many aromatic varieties, each with its own unique flavor and qualities.

While the absorption method is the most common way to cook long-grain rice, its firmness allows it to be pressure-cooked if a moist, slightly sticky texture is desired. Thai black sticky rice is an exception. It is best cooked in a special steaming apparatus. Slow-cooking is only suitable for parboiled or converted white rice.

Long-grain brown rice adds plenty of fiber and nutrition, and a distinctively nutty flavor, to any dish. Unlike white rice, which depends on seasonings or a flavorful accompaniment to make up for its blandness, brown rice can easily stand on its own. Long-grain brown rice can be presoaked for several hours before preparing, cutting cooking time to about 35 minutes. To retain nutrients, cook them in their soaking water. If the ambient temperature is warm (above 75°F), place the soaking rice in the refrigerator until ready to cook.

- For the absorption method, use 2¼ cups of water per cup of long-grain brown rice. Combine the water and rice, bring to a boil, then lower the heat, cover, and simmer for 45 minutes. Don't peek until the rice is completely done.
- For variety, cook equal parts of brown rice with barley or with presoaked and drained Kamut, farro, wheat, or spelt, using 2½ cups of water per cup of mixed grains, and proceeding as for the absorption method.

- To pressure-cook, use 2 cups of water per cup of rice and cook at pressure for 40 to 50 minutes. Experiment with cooking times to find the texture you most prefer.

Parboiled or **converted rice** is the result of a process in which unhulled brown rice is soaked in water and then steamed and dried before it is milled. As a result, nutrients from the bran and germ are driven into the center of the grain, making it a more nutritious type of white rice. Flavor and texture are both impacted by the process. Parboiled rice has a mild nutty flavor and a texture that is less clingy and has more separate grains than that of ordinary white rice. Although this process has been used in Pakistan and India for more than two thousand years, it wasn't until World War II that parboiled rice was introduced in the United States. The US military recognized it as a relatively nutritious option with a long shelf life, and also appreciated its resilience in food service applications, such as standing up for long periods in steam tables.

- For the absorption method, use 2 cups of water per cup of rice. Combine the water and rice, bring to a boil, then lower the heat, cover, and simmer for 20 to 25 minutes.
- To slow-cook, use 2 cups of water per cup of rice and cook on the high setting for 1½ hours or on low for 2½ hours.

Long-grain white rice, or polished white rice, which is milled to remove its bran and germ without first being steamed, has a dry, fluffy texture and a mild, plain flavor. To cook using the absorption method, use 1½ to 1¾ cups of water per cup of rice. Bring the water to a boil, stir in the rice, then lower the heat, cover, and simmer for 15 minutes. **Long-grain instant white rice** is partially cooked and dried, creating a porous structure that allows for rapid rehydration. Although it's quick, the flavor, texture, and nutritional value suffer a great deal in the process. Instant white rice is often enriched.

Thai black sticky rice, also known as black sticky rice or black glutinous rice, is a whole grain, long-grain rice that looks similar to wild rice. Although its name implies otherwise, it is a whole grain with its bran layers retained, and it doesn't stick together when cooked. While there are many savory side dish recipes that use Thai black sticky rice, in Thailand this variety of rice is traditionally used for snacks or desserts. Its purplish black color readily discolors anything cooked with it. Therefore, if you are combining it with other grains in a mixed pilaf, it should be cooked separately so that each grain retains its distinctive color. The best way to prepare Thai black sticky rice is to soak the rice in water for 6 to 12 hours, then drain it and steam it in a woven bamboo steamer or Thai sticky rice steaming basket over a pot of boiling water until tender, about 45 minutes.

Basmati rice is an aromatic rice with a wonderful flavor and aroma, as suggested by its name, which means "fragrant." Authentic basmati rice is only grown in northern India and Pakistan, where naturally cool conditions contribute to its exceptional qualities. After harvest, basmati rice is aged for at least a year to develop its flavor and decrease its moisture content so it will cook more evenly. A distinctive characteristic of basmati rice is that it doubles in length during cooking. Although it's usually sold in its white form, with the bran and germ removed, brown basmati is also available. As with other varieties of brown rice, brown basmati takes almost three times as long to cook and has a chewier texture and nuttier flavor. Rinse either variety of basmati rice several times prior to cooking to release excess starch, which would otherwise make for very sticky rice.

- To cook white basmati rice, use 1½ cups of water per cup of rice. To help retain some of the natural components within the grain that are responsible for its nutty, floral aroma, presoak basmati in its cooking water for 20 to 30 minutes after rinsing. Bring the rice and its soaking water to a boil, then lower the heat, cover, and simmer for 15 minutes. Remove from the heat and let stand, covered, for 10 minutes before fluffing.

- White basmati is a perfect grain to cook with other grains with a short cooking time, such as millet, quinoa, bulgur, and buckwheat. Use less water based on the proportion of white rice to other grains, since white basmati requires ½ cup less water per cup of grain than these other grains.
- To cook brown basmati rice, use 2 cups of water per cup of rice. It can be presoaked and cooked as described for white basmati or simply cooked without the presoak step. The cooking time for brown basmati is 45 to 50 minutes, whether on the stove or in a pressure cooker.

Carolina Gold rice is an heirloom long-grain rice that had its heyday in the Carolina Territory during the 1800s. Considered the benchmark of high quality long-grain rice in the nineteenth century and noted for the beautiful gold color of its husk while in the fields and for the excellent quality, delicate flavor, floral aroma, and unique texture of its grains, Carolina Gold rice was exported worldwide. New varieties that were easier to grow and had other desired properties superseded Carolina Gold rice in the 1930s. However, it was resurrected from near extinction in the 1980s, with small production in North and South Carolina, Georgia, Arkansas, and Texas. Its resurrection was possible as seed for Carolina Gold rice had been archived since 1902 in a United States Department of Agriculture seed collection facility.

While technically classified as long-grain, Carolina Gold rice was crossbred with medium-grain rice shortly after 1800. This accounts for its unique starch structure, which gives it either the drier, separate grains that are a long-grain rice hallmark; the moister, clingy, somewhat sticky texture of short-grain rice; or the creamier texture typically found in medium-grain rice—all depending upon how it is cooked. To preserve the grain's unique flavor, it is recommended to store Carolina Gold rice in the freezer.

Carolina Gold rice can be cooked in many ways, including the simple absorption method, which yields a soft, delicately textured rice. While the instructions for making fluffy, individual-grained Carolina Gold rice may at first read seem a bit daunting and a tad unusual, they are really very easy and give great results. To bring out its medium- and short-grain properties, cooking instructions are similar to those for preparing white rice varieties in those categories.

- For the absorption method, use 2 cups of water per cup of Carolina Gold rice. Combine the water and rice, bring to a boil, then lower the heat, cover, and simmer for 15 minutes. Immediately fluff the rice with a fork and serve.
- For 3 cups of fluffy, separate grain texture, place 1 cup of Carolina Gold rice in a bowl and cover with cold water. Soak for 1 hour and then drain through a fine-mesh strainer and rinse. Set aside. Heat the oven to 200°F. Fill a large bowl halfway with water and ice cubes and set aside. Bring 4 cups of water to a boil in a heavy-bottomed saucepan. Add the rice, stir once, cover, and return to a boil. As soon as the water boils, uncover the pot and reduce the heat. Simmer gently, stirring occasionally, until the rice is just tender, about 5 minutes. Drain through a fine-mesh strainer. Turn the rice immediately into the ice water and swirl with your fingers to chill the rice. Drain well. Spread the rice out evenly on a rimmed sheet pan. Dry in the oven, turning gently from time to time, for 10 minutes. Season with ½ teaspoon of salt and, if desired, 2 teaspoons of butter, and return to the oven until the rice is hot and the butter melted, about 5 minutes more. Serve immediately.
- For a creamy risotto effect, use 3½ cups of hot broth per cup of Carolina Gold rice, adding the broth slowly and stirring it in until creamy and al dente.

Jasmine rice, an aromatic rice named after the sweet-perfumed jasmine flower, is traditionally grown in Thailand, where the climate and soil are perfect for creating this fragrant rice. Jasmine rice is known for its soft, slightly sticky texture; unlike other long-grain rice, it doesn't harden when it cools. That's because it has a high percentage of amylopectin rather than amylase starch. This also means that its sugars are released into the bloodstream more quickly, so it doesn't provide as much sustained energy as other long-grain varieties do. Although delicately flavored white jasmine is rice is more familiar, its brown counterpart is equally delicious, with bonus nutty undertones.

To distinguish authentic jasmine rice from Thailand from varieties grown in other parts of the world, Thailand's Department of Foreign Trade developed an authenticity certificate for use on packaging. Look for a round seal with an image of rice grains and rice plants that includes the statement "Thai Hom Mali Rice—Originated in Thailand—Department of Foreign Trade." In contrast, jasmine rice grown in the United States has a different flavor and aroma profile—more like that of popcorn.

- To cook white jasmine rice, use one of several methods. Although steaming jasmine rice in an Asian-style stacked steamer is often recommended (both to deal with its slightly sticky texture and to better retain its fragrance), an effective way to cook it using the absorption method is to presoak it as described for basmati rice, using 1¾ cups of water per cup of rice. Bring the soaked rice and its water to a boil, then lower the heat, cover, and simmer for 15 minutes. For best results and to prevent the rice from sticking to the pot, allow it to stand, covered, for 15 minutes before fluffing.

- For a quicker version, use 1½ cups of water per cup of white jasmine rice. Combine the water and rice, bring to a boil, lower the heat, cover, and simmer for 20 minutes. Remove from the heat and let stand, covered, for a few minutes before fluffing.

- To cook brown jasmine rice, use 2 cups of water per cup of rice. Combine the water and rice, bring to a boil, lower the heat, cover, and simmer for 45 minutes. Remove from the heat and let stand, covered, for a few minutes before fluffing.

Kalijira rice, an heirloom variety of aromatic long-grain rice grown in Bangladesh and India (where they call it Gobindavog), is traditionally used for certain holidays and religious festivals. It has a wonderful and delicate aroma, taste, and texture, and looks like a miniature version of basmati rice. Look for both white and brown kalijira; the whole grain version has a nuttier flavor, although it still remains delicate.

- To cook white kalijira rice, use 1½ cups of water per cup of rice. Combine the rice and water in a pot and bring to a boil. Lower the heat, cover, and simmer for 10 minutes. Remove from the heat and let stand, covered, for a couple of minutes before fluffing.

- To cook brown kalijira rice, use 1¾ cups of water per cup of rice. Combine the rice and water in a pot and bring to a boil. Lower the heat, cover, and simmer for 20 to 25 minutes. Remove from the heat and let stand, covered, for a couple of minutes before fluffing.

Madagascar pink rice is a quick-cooking, reddish brown Malagasy rice variety. When cooked, it has a lovely pink color; a subtly sweet flavor faintly reminiscent of cinnamon, cloves, and nutmeg; and moist, tender, separate grains. Lightly milled to retain 66 percent of its bran layer, Madagascar pink rice cooks in only 20 minutes. Serve as a simple side dish and great color accent to any meal, as a pilaf, as the basis for a stir-fry, in a salad, or in desserts.

Also known as "Dista's rice," it is grown in the Lac Alaotra region of Madagascar, which is the country's rice basket. The rice gets its name from the farmer, Jean Baptiste Rakotomandimby, nicknamed Dista, who noticed a couple of unusual looking grains lodged in a bag he had purchased from the market to store his harvested rice—illustrating how a unique heirloom can be rediscovered by chance and perhaps saved from extinction. This rice is grown according to the System of Rice Intensification (SRI), a sustainable farming method that began in Madagascar to help small-scale farmers improve their rice yields and incomes by conserving water, seeds, and land while at the same time growing more rice.

To cook Madagascar pink rice, use 1¾ cups of water per cup of rice. Combine the water and rice, bring to a boil, then lower the heat, cover, and simmer for 20 minutes. Remove from the heat and let stand, covered, for 5 minutes, and then fluff and serve.

Mekong Flower rice is the brand name of a Cambodian jasmine aromatic rice variety called Phka Malis, which means "fragrant flower," aptly describing its delicate floral aroma. It is grown in the Tramak district in southern Cambodia by members of the Damrei Romeal Organic Producers Federation, a cooperative of small family farmers who use a sustainable farming growing method called System of Rice Intensification (SRI), which enables them to use less water while harvesting more rice from their traditional varieties with less seed and land—and all without agrochemicals. The SRI process may also contribute to the enhanced flavor and aromatic qualities of this rice. In contrast to conventional growing methods in which farmers keep their fields continuously flooded, these farmers drain their paddies periodically, creating mild water stress, a conditional response in rice that researchers link to an increase in the aromatic compounds in rice.

Mekong Flower rice is available both as white, in which the grain's bran and germ are removed, and brown, in which these are left intact. Both are delicious and have a soft, slightly sticky texture, with the white rice more delicate in texture and flavor. The whole grain version is more fragrant, nuttier in flavor, and more nutritious. Quick to cook, white Mekong Flower rice is ready in 20 minutes and the brown whole grain version needs only 30 minutes to cook, significantly shorter than most brown jasmine rice varieties.

- To cook white Mekong Flower rice, use 1½ cups of water per cup of rice. Combine the water and rice bring to a boil, lower the heat, cover, and simmer for 20 minutes. Remove from the heat and let stand, covered, for a few minutes before fluffing.
- To cook brown Mekong Flower rice, use 1¾ cups of water per cup of rice. Combine the water and rice, bring to a boil, lower the heat, cover, and simmer for 30 minutes. Remove from the heat and let stand, covered, for a few minutes before fluffing.

Texmati is a trademarked rice developed to provide a less expensive, albeit less aromatic, alternative to basmati that could be grown in the United States. It's a variation of a strain developed by crossbreeding basmati rice with long-grain American rice. As its name implies, Texmati is grown primarily in Texas. While similar to basmati, Texmati rice is milder in flavor, making it a more all-purpose type of aromatic rice. Although it's most widely marketed in its refined, white form, as with basmati, a whole grain brown version is also available. It has a richer, nuttier flavor and is more nutritious.

- To cook white Texmati, use 1¾ cups of water per cup of rice. Combine the water and rice, bring to a boil, then lower the heat, cover, and simmer for 15 minutes. Remove from the heat and let stand, covered, for 5 to 10 minutes before fluffing.
- To cook brown Texmati, use 2 cups of water per cup of rice. Combine the water and rice, bring to a boil, then lower the heat, cover, and simmer for 50 minutes or pressure-cook for 40 minutes. Remove from the heat and let stand, covered, for 5 to 10 minutes before fluffing.

Thai red rice, also known as Khao Deng, is a whole grain rice from Thailand derived from an ancient red rice variety. Its delicious nutty, complex flavor, and beautiful natural red bran layer makes for a striking contrast at meals. Not only that, its deep color also flags its naturally elevated phytonutrient content.

To cook, use 1½ cups of water per cup of rice. Combine the water and rice, bring to a boil, then lower the heat, cover, and simmer for 30 minutes. Remove from the heat and let stand, covered, for 5 minutes before fluffing.

Ulikan Red is a long-grained, rustic red-colored rice; it is one of the Cordillera heirloom rice varieties (see below in Medium-Grain Rice) grown in the ancient, hand-carved stone and earthen rice terraces in Kalinga Province in the northern Philippine island of Luzon. (The same variety is also grown in Hungduan, Ifugao Province, where the variety is called Mini-angan.)

In Kalinga Province, it is admired as a flavorful grain that strengthens the body; this idea may have some basis in the fact that it has a rich phytonutrient content and that it is only lightly milled, retaining much of the whole grain nutrition. Its beautiful color (which is retained throughout the cooking process) and its unique texture and mild flavor make Ulikan Red a perfect complement to any component of a meal—whether sweet or savory. And it is quick to cook. Ulikan Red's grains are thicker than other long-grain rice varieties, looking more like those of a medium-grain type of rice, and its texture is slightly sticky when cooked.

To cook, use 1½ cups of water per cup of rice. Rinse thoroughly, two or three times, in cold water. Combine the water and rice (and salt, if desired), bring to a boil, lower the heat, just partially cover, and simmer 20 to 25 minutes. When done, fluff immediately and let stand for a few minutes before serving.

Wild pecan rice is closely related to Texmati rice. Although it neither contains pecans nor is related to wild rice, it does have a very nutty flavor and aroma. Grown in Louisiana, wild pecan rice is only lightly milled, leaving it with 80 percent of the bran and a pleasing amber color. To cook wild pecan rice, use 1¾ cups of water per cup of rice. Combine the water and rice, bring to a boil, then lower the heat, cover, and simmer for 15 minutes. Remove from the heat and let stand, covered, for 5 to 10 minutes before fluffing.

Medium-Grain Rice

Medium-grain rice is two to three times as long as it is wide. Because it has less amylose and more amylopectin, it cooks up slightly soft and sticky, with a creamy texture when certain preparation techniques are used, but it also retains some of the individual separateness of the grains that long-grain rice does. This explains its use in risotto, paella, and rice pudding. And because it has less amylose, medium-grain rice doesn't become hard as it cools, making it the best choice for rice salads.

The absorption method is the most common way to cook medium-grain rice, but a pressure cooker may also be used. For pressure-cooking, use the same proportion of water to rice, and experiment with the cooking time to determine what amount of time yields the texture you prefer. If pressure-cooked for the same amount of time as required for the absorption method, the texture will be softer; or try cooking it for 10 minutes less time, for a firmer, chewier texture. Although part of the experience

Clockwise, from top: (1) Bhutanese red rice, (2) Black Forbidden Rice, (3) Tinawon white rice, (4) Tinawon Fancy rice, (5) Bomba paella rice from Valencia, (6) Paella rice from Valencia, (7) Kalinga Unoy rice

of preparing risotto is watching the rice transform as you stir in small amounts of broth, it can also be prepared less dramatically in a pressure cooker with similar results.

Many strains of rice either originating in Asia or complementary to Asian-based fare are included in this category, as are many varieties used in Italian and Spanish cuisines. Because there are so many varieties of rice for risotto and paella, we'll explore them separately at the end of this section.

Be aware that sometimes varieties of rice in the medium-grain category are classified as short-grain, since some countries use only a two-tiered, long-grain (**indica** variety) and short-grain (**japonica** variety) classification system.

And then there is the unique medium-grain category of **tropical japonica rice**, formerly known as javanica, a subspecies of japonica rice that was originally found in only three places in the world: the rice terraces of the Philippines, certain remote areas of Indonesia, and the mountains of Madagascar. The grains are large, long, and thick, with cooked textures from the varieties of rice within this category ranging from firm and dense to chewy to sticky, similar to the span seen when comparing medium- and short-grain rice.

Bhutanese red rice is an heirloom rice grown for thousands of years at 8,000 feet in rice paddies on the steep mountainsides in the Paro Valley of the Kingdom of Bhutan. It is irrigated with Himalayan glacial-melt waters rich in trace minerals. It is the only 100 percent whole grain rice that cooks in only 20 minutes. With a texture that is both chewy and soft, it is also exceptionally flavorful—nutty, mushroomy, and earthy—far surpassing in complexity the flavor of most whole grain rice varieties. It is delicious whether used as a side dish providing color and textural contrast to other elements within the meal, in a pilaf, as the foundation for a stir-fry, in salads, or stuffed into vegetables or poultry. (Note: Rice often marketed as Himalayan red rice is not the same variety as Bhutanese red rice. Instead it is typically a long-grain rice from Thailand.)

To cook Bhutanese red rice, use 1½ cups of water per cup of rice. Combine the water and rice, bring to a boil, then lower the heat, cover, and simmer for 20 minutes. Remove from the heat and let stand, covered, for 5 minutes before fluffing and serving.

Black Forbidden Rice is a trademarked rice that originated from China; it takes its name from the fact that only the ruling class was considered worthy to eat it. This whole grain rice has a somewhat sweet, roasted nutty flavor and a dark purple color when cooked—a pigment that contributes to the grain's complement of the antioxidant phytonutrient anthocyanin. Its grains remain separate after cooking, making it a good choice for rice salads and pilafs. It is delicious and striking on its own, especially when paired with white or red protein foods such as halibut, tofu, or salmon, but it also makes for a nice color contrast when combined with other cooked varieties of rice. Cook them separately to ensure that the unique color of each variety is retained. To cook Black Forbidden Rice, use 1¾ cups of water per cup of rice. Combine the water and rice, bring to a boil, then lower the heat, cover, and simmer for 30 minutes. Remove from heat and let stand, covered, for 5 minutes.

Calrose rice, an all-purpose medium-grain white rice, accounts for about 85 percent of the rice grown in California. With its soft, slightly clingy texture and mild flavor, it can be used as an everyday rice or in Asian or Mediterranean cuisine. To cook Calrose rice, use 1½ cups of water per cup of rice. Combine the water and rice, bring to a boil, then lower the heat, cover, and simmer for 12 to 15 minutes. Remove from the heat and let stand, covered, for 5 to 10 minutes before fluffing.

Camargue red rice hails from the Camargue region of Provence, located along the Rhône River, which has the distinction of being the northernmost area where rice is grown in Europe. Snowmelt from the Alps supplies the water used to flood the fields. Camargue red rice is a hybrid of the area's native red rice and a short-grain rice variety. Its delicious nutty flavor and texture may seem similar to those of Bhutanese red rice, but its color is deeper and the grains are oval shaped and somewhat longer. It's delicious in pilafs and salads, or when prepared simply by mixing in some freshly chopped thyme or oregano and a splash of olive oil once it's cooked. To cook Camargue red rice, use 2½ cups of water per cup of rice. Combine the water and rice, bring to a boil, then lower the heat, cover, and simmer for 40 minutes. Remove from the heat and let stand, covered, for 10 minutes before fluffing.

Cordillera Heirloom Rices The rugged, mountainous Cordillera region in the northern part of Luzon Island in the Philippines is one of the three areas in the world in which the unique tropical japonica subspecies of rice is found, a slow-growing, cold-tolerant variety that grows at high altitude. Designated as a World Heritage Site in 1995 by the United Nations Educational, Scientific, and Cultural Organization (UNESCO), the rice terraces are an engineering masterpiece that have been in place for over two thousand years. Here farmers have followed the contours of the steep mountainsides, carving stone and earthen terraces that are irrigated with water from the rainforests situated above them. Due to the steep angle of the terraces, all work is done by hand and all the harvested rice is tied in bundles and laid out to dry.

Although there are more than three hundred traditional heirloom rice varieties in the provinces of Ifugao and Kalinga and the Mountain Province, several of these aromatic rice varieties have been singled out as exceptional for their distinctive red, pink, purple, and naturally white pigments, large-size grains, and unusual range of textural variety. And, remarkably, their cooking time is only 20 to 25 minutes; they are lightly milled, though they retain much of their whole grain nutrition.

All varieties from the Philippines have the same general cooking instructions. Use 1½ cups of water per cup of rice. Rinse thoroughly, two or three times, in cold water. Combine the water and rice (and salt, if desired), bring to a boil, lower the heat, just partially cover, and simmer for 20 to 25 minutes.

When done, fluff immediately and let stand for a few minutes before serving. Sticky rice varieties can also be presoaked for 30 minutes prior to cooking if an even stickier texture is desired, first draining the soaking water and adding fresh water when starting the cooking process.

Ifugao Diket sticky rice has rusty red, dark purple, and white variegated kernels that cook up medium purple in color. Grown in the Ifugao Province, where the name for sticky rice is *diket*, its fat, sticky grains are traditionally served in festive desserts. Ifugao Diket rice is equally good for making whole grain salads and both its flavor and color pair nicely with avocado slices or guacamole.

Kalinga Jekot sticky rice is a rusty red- or mauve-colored glutinous rice with a great, nutty flavor, plump kernels, and a chewy, slightly sticky texture. Grown in the Kalinga Province, where the term for sticky rice is *jekot*, this is a very versatile rice that can be used for desserts and sweet snacks but is also very appropriate for savory dishes, such as stir-fries and casseroles, and as a striking visual and textural accompaniment to any meal.

Kalinga Unoy rice has a mild flavor, a subtle, nutty aroma, and a firm texture, serving as a perfect complement to more boldly flavored entrées in a meal. While technically known as the Chong-ak variety and grown on the mountain terraces throughout the three provinces, in the Kalinga Province this rusty-colored rice variety is called Unoy. It is highly regarded by people in the area as a safeguard against illnesses, perhaps a nod to its phytonutrient content associated with its natural color. Unoy rice is traditionally served at very special occasions such as weddings and family reunions, especially during the Pusipus celebration, the gathering of relatives before a sick or elderly family member dies. Bundles of unthreshed Unoy rice are also displayed at the feet of the dead to symbolize his or her wealth in rice fields and harvest.

Mountain Violet sticky rice is a glutinous variety of rice that is a striking violet color when dry and cooks up into very dark purple, nearly black kernels, somewhat resembling Thai black sticky rice although significantly more plump in size. Grown in the remote terraces of Barlig, Mountain Province, and locally known as Ominio, this very delicious, nutty tasting rice is the most highly prized sticky rice grown in the remote terraces of northern Luzon in the Philippines. While traditionally used for desserts and for making rice wine, it is equally good as a side dish accented by any of the colorful bell peppers or carrots, or in salads or soups where its color, flavor, and texture would make a fun contrast.

Tinawon Fancy rice has white and brown variegated kernels that, when cooked, turn slightly pink and brown. It is grown in the mountain terraces in the Ifugao Province, where the name *Tinawon* means "once a year," a reference to its harvesting cycle. With its mild flavor and popcornlike aroma, Tinawon Fancy is especially distinguished by its very large and puffy looking cooked grains, which make a dramatic presence on the plate. Respected as a symbol of Ifugao identity and cultural integrity, Tinawon Fancy is considered a precious gift from the Ifugao god of the skyworld to nourish one's body, mind, and spirit. Traditionally, it is served during weddings, celebrations, and family gatherings.

Tinawon white rice has kernels that resemble Italian Arborio rice, complete with the amylose-rich pearl, accounting for its often referred to as "the mother of all Arborio types." Naturally white in color, this unpolished rice from the Ifugao Province has a particularly delicious, mild nutty flavor and a sturdy, dense texture. A must-try.

Italian Risotto Rice

Risotto is a celebrated Italian rice dish made using a method that defies all the usual rules for cooking rice. Hot liquid is added to the rice in small increments, the pot is never covered, the rice is stirred constantly, and more liquid is used than normal—usually 3½ cups of hot broth or other liquid per cup of rice. The result is rice that is infused with flavor and an unusual and pleasing texture that combines a rich, creamy consistency and an al dente firmness.

Risotto can be the highlight of a meal or an extraordinary accompaniment to the main course.

Successful results depend not only on technique but also on using the proper type of rice. Arborio rice is most commonly used to make risotto, but three other varieties of medium-grain rice are also recommended: Vialone Nano, Baldo, and especially Carnaroli. All of these, and any other variety of rice suitable for risotto, are derived from the japonica family of rice, which is distinguished by a low percentage of amylose, allowing for the al dente texture within each grain of rice in the finished risotto. Japonica rice varieties also have a high percentage of amylopectin, which is responsible for the creamy texture. Both types of starch are actually visually apparent in the grains. Within the translucent amylopectin that makes up the bulk of the kernel, you can see an amylose-rich "pearl" in the middle of the kernel.

Recipes for risotto are created based on using polished white rice rather than brown whole grain versions. The best quality risotto results from using rice aged in the husk up to a year before being hulled and polished. Because drying reduces the moisture content of the rice, the longer it's dried, the more broth it can absorb, yielding a more flavorful risotto. For optimal flavor and freshness, look for rice that is vacuum-packed.

Although since 1992 Italian law has not required packaging to state the grade of rice, rice used for risotto is still often described or marketed according to its grade. These grades are not a gauge of quality; they're simply used to differentiate the rice according to size and rate of absorption. This information helps you determine which rice is best for a particular application. Three primary grades of Italian rice are used for making risotto: *superfino*, *fino*, and *semifino*. *Superfino*, considered to be best, has the largest, most pearly white grains. It is longer and more tapered than round. Arborio, Baldo, and Carnaroli are three *superfino* varieties to choose from when making risotto, and each brings a unique quality to the dish. *Fino* is the next best grade; its grains are somewhat shorter and rounder than *superfino*. *Semifino*, which is yet rounder and shorter in length, is the least preferred for risotto. A fourth grade of Italian rice, *originario* (or *comune* grade), is used for making desserts and dishes that will be cooked for a long time, such as soups and baked rice casseroles made with sauces—applications where using a rice with high absorbency works well to capture flavors.

Arborio is the most commonly used *superfino* rice in the United States, but it has less amylose and therefore absorbs less liquid than Baldo or Carnaroli do, making it somewhat more starchy and sticky. Beyond risotto, Arborio rice makes a good rice pudding. **Baldo**, a long, slim, golden-colored *superfino* rice, is a good choice for rice salads, rice pudding, and risotto. It has less amylose than do Vialone Nano and Carnaroli and therefore cooks up softer, much like Arborio. **Carnaroli**, a *superfino* rice, has the highest amylose content of any risotto rice, which allows it to absorb the most liquid while still having firm, distinct grains and a creamy but not sticky texture. Accordingly, many chefs consider it to be the rice of choice when making risotto. **Vialone nano**, a *semifino* rice, is grown in the northeastern part of Italy. This hybrid of traditional Vialone rice and a smaller Nano (dwarf) variety is a favorite for traditional Venetian rice dishes and soups. In risotto, it provides a good amount of starch, creating a creamy but wavy consistency—a characteristic of a well-made risotto in which the rice and sauce move as one rather than as separate layers when tossed in the pan. With almost as much amylose as Carnaroli, it cooks up firmer than Arborio. Since it can absorb twice its own weight in liquid, it also absorbs flavors particularly well.

Although rice from Italy usually springs to mind when choosing rice for risotto, American Arborio rice is also available. The flavor is good, but the results aren't as creamy. Whatever variety of rice you use to make risotto, don't rinse it before cooking, as this will wash away some of the rice's amylopectin layer and cause the rice's internal starch to release

too soon, disrupting the gradual cooking process needed to coax out the creaminess. Cooking risotto is a process that never ceases to be amazing as, seemingly in an instant, the separate, translucent kernels of rice become creamy—something everyone needs to experience at least once.

- If you are not making risotto, medium-grain Italian rices can be prepared as you would any white rice, albeit with a bit longer cooking time. To cook, use 1½ cups of water per cup of rice. Combine the water and rice, bring to a boil, then lower the heat, cover, and simmer for 20 minutes. Remove from the heat and let stand, covered, for a few minutes before fluffing.

- Medium-grain Italian rice varieties are also good in rice-based salads. Try mixing them with tomatoes, olives, fresh herbs, and pesto or your favorite salad dressing. To cook any of these types of rice for salad, use 4 cups of water per cup of rice. Bring the water to a boil, then stir in the rice, lower the heat, and cook uncovered until the rice is firm but tender, about 15 minutes. Drain the rice and spread it on a clean kitchen towel to cool.

Spanish or Paella Rice

While Italian rice brings to mind risotto, rice from Spain conjures up visions of paella, a native dish of Valencia, a city on Spain's Mediterranean coast. Authentic paella is made with foods that were commonly found or grown in the area, including beans, snails, rabbit or chicken, shellfish, fresh vegetables, and saffron, traditionally cooked outside over a fire using a wide, shallow pan specially shaped to cook rice in a thin layer. These days, many recipes for paella call for seafood of all kinds.

Regardless of the specific ingredients used, it is the rice that is the real key to exceptional paella. You can't use just any rice; it must be medium-grain rice that, like rice for risotto, has the *perla*—the amylose-rich pearl in the middle of the kernel. This allows for both proper al dente texture and maximum ability to absorb liquid and soak up the essence of this flavorful dish. Paella differs from risotto in that the rice should ultimately be dry and separate rather than creamy. There are some basic similarities in how the two are prepared, including not rinsing the rice before cooking and cooking the rice uncovered for 18 to 20 minutes. However, there is a major distinction: paella is not stirred after the rice is distributed evenly in the pan. Crusty, caramelized rice that sticks to the bottom, called the *socarrat*, is considered the delicious prize of the paella. Paella is covered for just the last 5 to 10 minutes of cooking, allowing all the flavors to meld fully.

Spanish medium-grain rice for paella is designated primarily by where it is grown, and then is usually further defined by the variety of rice. Choosing among them is a matter of carefully reading the label to make sure you're getting the real thing—and then determining how much you're willing to spend. There are three primary paella rice–producing regions in Spain: Ebro, Valencia, and Calasparra.

The Ebro delta in northeastern Spain is distinctive in that the rice is grown within a protected bird sanctuary, with the rice fields providing a good habitat for aquatic birds such as herons, egrets, ducks, gulls, and flamingos during much of the year. Rice from the other two regions, Valencia and Calasparra, is identified by Denominación de origen (DO) labeling. This designation guarantees that the rice is truly grown in that area, that it is from a pure strain unique to the region, and that it was grown according to certain standards.

The three varieties of DO-labeled medium-grain paella-type rice grown in Valencia are Bahía, Senia, and Bomba. Valencia, the birthplace of paella, is Spain's major rice-producing region. Located within the marshy wetlands of the protected Albufera nature preserve, the rice fields here, like those in the Ebro delta, provide habitat and forage for many species of birds, including cranes, herons, and terns.

The two varieties of DO-labeled rice grown in the Calasparra region are Balilla Sollana and Bomba. Located in the mountains of Murcia in southeastern

Spain, the Calasparra region is known for the exceptional quality of its rice. This is largely due to the cooler weather at high altitude and the practice of irrigating with cold mountain water, both of which extend the time required for the rice to mature, making for a harder grain with less moisture—and a greater ability to absorb liquid. Both varieties of Calasparra rice will be more expensive than their counterparts from other regions, but they're well worth it for special occasions.

Any of the varieties of rice from these three regions will work well in paella. However, Bomba is the preferred choice, as it can absorb as much as six parts liquid to one part rice—two to three times more than the other varieties. Because Bomba is harder to grow and has lower yields, it is more expensive. So top honors for quality and flavor—and top price—goes to Calasparra Bomba.

Spanish rice varieties need not be used only for paella. They are also good in rice salads, soups, and stews. To cook Spanish varieties of rice using the absorption method, use 1¾ cups of water per cup of rice. Combine the water and rice, bring to a boil, then lower the heat, cover, and simmer for 15 to 18 minutes. Remove from the heat and let stand, covered, for 10 to 15 minutes before fluffing.

Short-Grain Rice

Short-grain rice is almost round; it's only slightly longer than it is wide. Because it has more amylopectin and less amylose than do long-grain or medium-grain rice, it has a moist, soft, sticky texture when cooked. It's perfect for Asian cuisine, rice puddings, croquettes, and casseroles, as well as for rice dishes prepared during colder weather, when its inherent warming nature feels especially welcome. Short-grain rice is often cooked using the absorption method, but there are several techniques and special types of cooking apparatus that can give better results for certain types of short-grain rice. Short-grain brown rice and sweet brown rice can also be pressure-cooked. Short-grain brown rice can be presoaked for several hours, cutting cooking time to about 35 minutes. To retain nutrients, cook them in their soaking water. If the ambient temperature is warm (above 75°F), place the soaking rice in the refrigerator until ready to cook.

Short-grain brown rice is a hearty, somewhat sticky rice that's particularly appealing during the colder months. Pressure-cooking enhances its sweet flavor and compact texture. It's also a great whole grain alternative for making sushi or nori maki.

- For the absorption method, use 2¼ cups of water per cup of short-grain brown rice. Combine the water and rice, bring to a boil, then lower the heat, cover, and simmer for 50 minutes.
- To pressure-cook, use 2 cups of water per cup of rice and cook at pressure for 40 to 50 minutes. Experiment with the amount of time to find the texture you most prefer.

Short-grain white rice is milled to remove its bran layer and germ. It has a soft, sticky texture and mild, plain flavor. To cook short-grain white rice, use 1¼ cups of water per cup of rice. Combine the water and rice, bring to a boil, then lower the heat, cover, and simmer for 15 minutes.

Sticky rice, also known as sweet rice or glutinous rice, is very high in amylopectin, making it very sticky when cooked and therefore easy to form into bite-size pieces for dipping into sauce. This increased starchiness also makes the uncooked kernels look chalky white when raw but translucent after cooking. Sticky rice is used to make traditional Asian desserts, amasake (a beverage), rice wine, and mochi (a delicious food that puffs up like a biscuit when cooked). For more nutrients and flavor, choose the brown version, known as sweet brown rice, over the more refined white version. Sticky rice can be cooked using the standard absorption method, but it will turn out mushier than if steamed.

The best way to prepare sticky rice is to first soak it in water for 6 to 12 hours, then drain it and steam it in a woven bamboo steamer or Thai sticky rice steaming basket over a pot of boiling water. Steam white sticky rice for about 30 minutes and sweet brown rice for 40 to 45 minutes.

- For the absorption method, use 1½ cups of water per cup of sticky rice. Combine the water and rice, bring to a boil, then lower the heat, cover, and simmer for 30 minutes for white sticky rice or 50 minutes for sweet brown rice.
- To pressure-cook sweet brown rice, use 1 cup of water per cup of rice and cook at pressure for 45 minutes. A combination of ¼ cup of sweet brown rice and ¾ cup of short-grain brown rice pressure-cooked with 1½ cups of water for 50 minutes makes a delicious cool-weather rice blend.

Sushi rice is a semipolished, white, very sticky short-grain rice traditionally used to make nori-wrapped sushi rolls. Before cooking it, rinse and drain the rice several times until the rinse water

Clockwise, from top: (1) Mountain Violet sticky rice, (2) Ifagao Diket sticky rice, (3) Kalinga Jerkot sticky rice, (4) short-grain brown rice, (5) sticky rice

is almost clear, then allow it to drain for 30 to 60 minutes. Combine equal amounts of water and sushi rice, bring to a boil over medium heat, cover, and cook for 1 minute. Then turn down the heat to low and cook for 8 to 10 minutes. Turn down the heat once again, to very low, and cook 10 minutes longer, being sure to keep the cover on at all times during cooking. Remove from the heat and let stand, covered, for 10 minutes before fluffing the rice.

Rice Flavor Enhancers Onions, sautéed mushrooms, garlic, curry powder, bay leaf, raisins, dill, roasted red bell peppers, parsley, basil, thyme, lemon thyme, ginger, and grated lemon zest. Cooking rice with a cinnamon stick and a few whole cloves and cardamom seeds is a nice touch.

RYE

Contains gluten

Rye berries are bluish brown kernels that are longer and thinner than wheat. Although primarily ground into flour and eaten in the form of breads and crispbreads, rye's delicious, hearty flavor is equally as good when it's cooked as a whole, cracked, or flaked grain. Rye is grown predominantly in Eastern Europe, where it's long been a staple—in part because it grows well in poor soil and cool, moist conditions—and is still most often used in cuisines of that region, though its popularity continues to increase throughout the world due to its exceptional nutritional profile. Rye is particularly recognized for a unique type of soluble fiber it contains: long chains of polysaccharides called pentosans, and specifically arabinoxylans. Present throughout the entire kernel of rye, pentosans act much like the beta-glucan fiber in oats and barley, helping to decrease absorption of cholesterol and also making rye digest more slowly, so it keeps blood sugar levels stable and provides a steady source of energy. Lignans, compounds thought to help reduce the risk of cancer, are present in rye's bran layer.

Varieties and Cooking Guidelines

Whole rye berries have only their outer hull removed. They can be cooked alone or with other grains, such as brown rice or barley. They make a nice addition to soups, salads, and breads. It's best to presoak rye berries before cooking. To retain nutrients, cook them in their soaking water, using 3 cups of water per cup of rye berries. If the ambient temperature is warm (above 75°F), soak in the refrigerator.

- For the absorption method, use 3 cups of water per cup of rye berries. Bring the rye berries and their soaking water to a boil, then lower the heat, cover, and simmer until tender, about 60 minutes if presoaked or 1½ to 2 hours if not. With further cooking, the rye berries will split open, making for an even softer, more cereal-like texture.

- To pressure-cook, use 3 cups of water per cup of rye berries and cook for 40 minutes if presoaked, or 50 minutes if not.

- For slow-cooking, presoaking is optional. Use 4 cups of water per cup of rye berries and cook on the high setting for 3½ to 4 hours or on low for 8 hours.

Rye flakes are made from whole rye that is steamed, pressed, and rolled into thick flakes. Add them to breads for flavor and texture, or use them to make a hot breakfast cereal. Even better, combine them with other flaked grains, such as oats, Kamut, or spelt, to make a breakfast cereal medley. To cook rye flakes, use 3 cups of water per cup of flakes. Bring the water to a boil, stir in the flakes, then lower the heat, cover, and simmer for 25 to 30 minutes.

Rye grits, or steel-cut rye, is whole rye cracked into small pieces. It is ideal as a hot cereal or for adding to casseroles. To cook rye grits, use 3½ cups of water per cup of grits. Bring the water to a boil, then gradually pour in the grits, whisking all the while. Lower the heat, cover the pot, and simmer for 35 to 40 minutes.

Rye Flavor Enhancers Caraway seeds, fennel, anise, orange zest, raisins, maple syrup, roasted pecans, roasted walnuts, roasted sunflower seeds, onions, potatoes, parsley, peas, red bell peppers, and cabbage.

SORGHUM
Gluten free

Whole grain sorghum (also known as milo) has a round shape similar to that of millet but is significantly larger. Native to the tropical areas of Africa, the plant itself looks somewhat like corn, and the grain is nutritionally similar to white corn. Not too surprisingly, in western Africa it is known as great millet, kaffir corn, or Guinea corn. Due to sorghum's ability to adapt to and grow in a variety of environments, including arid as well as tropical and subtropical conditions, it is widely cultivated for both food and fodder. There are many varieties of sorghum with just as many colors. Although both sweet sorghum and grain sorghum are grown for human consumption, sweet sorghum is only used to make a sweet syrup (see page 275). Traditionally, grain sorghum is fermented and used to make beer, porridge, and flat bread—including Ethiopia's *injera* bread (where it serves as an alternative to the grain teff). Not only do the lactic acid bacteria in the fermented sorghum create a slightly sour taste that's appreciated in the areas of Africa where it is a staple, but it also helps to naturally preserve the food and protect against harmful bacteria. Sorghum is high in dietary fiber, and its protein and starch components digest more slowly than those of other grains, which helps stabilize blood sugar levels and provides steady energy for several hours.

Varieties and Cooking Guidelines

To provide a more versatile grain and appeal to prospective cooks, a white sorghum hybrid that is low in tannins has been developed. Its lighter color and neutral flavor make it a natural for cooking with more assertive seasonings or serving with a flavorful sauce. When cooked, whole sorghum has a taste and texture similar to that of untoasted buckwheat groats. It is an excellent grain to use for a main dish

pilaf or breakfast cereal. It's also a good alternative to pearled barley, bulgur, or couscous in salads. Or for variety and more well-rounded nutrition, cook it along with other grains with a similar cooking time, such as brown rice and barley.

- For the absorption method, use 3 cups of water per cup of sorghum. Combine the sorghum and water, bring to a boil, then lower the heat, cover, and simmer until the water is absorbed and the grains are tender, about 60 minutes.
- To pressure-cook, use 3 cups of water per cup of sorghum and cook at pressure for 45 minutes.
- To slow-cook, use 4 cups of water per cup of sorghum and cook on the high setting for 3½ to 4 hours or on low for 8 hours.

Sorghum Flavor Enhancers Curry powder, orange, rosemary, onions, chives, parsley, black pepper, bay leaf, thyme, garlic, ginger, sun-dried tomatoes marinated in olive oil, and miso-tahini sauce.

SPELT
Contains gluten

Spelt is an ancient grain originating in the Middle East at least six thousand years ago, and a very distant cousin of modern varieties of wheat with the same hexaploid genetic structure of forty-two chromosomes. Over the millennia, it became popular in parts of Germany, Switzerland, Austria, France, and Spain as a major variety of bread wheat. In Italy, it is referred to as *farro grande*. Known as *dinkel* in Germany, spelt was so significant that they named several towns in its honor, including Dinkelhausen and Dinkelsbühl. Hildegard of Bingen, a twelfth-century herbalist, mystic, and abbess of a convent in Germany, further popularized spelt through her teachings on using natural remedies to create a healthy balance in body, mind, and spirit. Hildegard considered spelt to be the best, most digestible grain one could eat for overall good health, and it remains a fundamental food in German health clinics that follow her teachings.

European immigrants established spelt in the United States, and it was a commonly grown grain until 1900, when it was largely replaced by newer, hullless hybrids of wheat that produced higher yields and were easier to harvest and process. Recently, however, it has become valued once again for its unique nutritional properties and superior flavor, which is sweeter and nuttier than wheat. And, although its sturdy hull makes spelt harder to process, it also makes it naturally resistant to insects, so it typically is grown without any pesticides.

Although spelt is different than modern wheat, it still contains gluten. While some people who are sensitive to modern varieties of wheat may find they better tolerate spelt, anyone with gluten intolerance and severe allergies or sensitivity to wheat should always consult with a medical professional and be evaluated carefully before trying any new grain.

Varieties and Cooking Guidelines

Whole spelt isn't nearly as familiar as spelt flour, but it's easy to cook and very versatile. It's terrific for cooked cereal, makes a great foundation for a pilaf or salad, and is a delicious, chewy addition to casseroles, soups, and breads. It takes a long time to cook, but you can reduce the amount of time by presoaking it. If you use the cooking times recommended below, the kernels will remain whole and somewhat chewy. Further cooking will cause the kernels to split open, making the spelt softer and more like a cereal. To add texture to other cooked whole grains in a pilaf, soup, or cereal, combine cooked whole spelt with cooked quinoa, bulgur, millet, barley, or any variety of rice.

It's best to presoak whole spelt for 6 to 12 hours. To retain nutrients, cook it in its soaking water, using 3 cups of water per cup of spelt. If the ambient temperature is warm (above 75°F), soak it in the refrigerator.

- For the absorption method, use 3 cups of water per cup of spelt. Bring the spelt and its soaking water to a boil, then lower the heat, cover, and simmer until tender, about 50 minutes to 1 hour if presoaked and 1½ to 2 hours if not.
- To pressure-cook, use 3 cups of water per cup of spelt and cook at pressure for 40 minutes if presoaked, or 50 minutes if not.
- For slow-cooking, presoaking is optional. Use 4 cups of water per cup of spelt and cook on the high setting for 3½ to 4 hours or on low for 8 hours.

Spelt bulgur is whole spelt that has been steamed, dried, and cracked, making it a delicious and quick-cooking foundation for pilafs, salads, and stuffings. Use 2 cups of water or broth per cup of spelt bulgur. Bring the water to a boil, then stir in the bulgur, season with salt and any herbs or spices you like, then lower the heat, cover, and simmer for 25 minutes. Remove from the heat and let stand undisturbed for 10 minutes before serving or using in a recipe.

Spelt flakes are made from whole spelt that has been steamed, dried, and flattened. It can be used like any other flaked grain for hot cereals, granolas, cookies, and casseroles. For a hot cereal, use 2 cups of water per cup of spelt flakes. Combine the water and spelt in a pot, bring to a boil, then lower the heat, cover, and simmer for 15 to 18 minutes. Spelt flakes can also be combined in any proportion with other flaked grains for variety in flavor.

Spelt Flavor Enhancers Onions, chives, dill, mushrooms, black pepper, garlic, curry powder, parsley, and cilantro. Sweet flavor enhancers include cinnamon, ginger, and allspice.

TEFF

Gluten free

Teff's name means "lost," an appropriate moniker considering its seeds are so tiny that if they were dropped on the ground, you'd be hard-pressed to find them. Introduced to the United States during the 1980s, teff is the most commonly cultivated grain in Ethiopia. It is traditionally used to make soup, porridge, beer, and especially *injera*, the crepelike Ethiopian bread that is used as plate, fork, and food during the meal.

Teff is only available in whole grain forms because it would be impossible to refine away the bran or germ on each tiny seed. While its protein content is similar to other grains, teff is particularly high in fiber, calcium, and iron. The grain itself is often accompanied by a symbiotic yeast that easily ferments when moisture is added, resulting in a sweet, slightly molasses-like, malty taste.

Varieties and Cooking Guidelines

White teff has the most delicate and mild flavor, while **red** and **brown teff** have a nuttier flavor. To add flavor and texture to familiar grains, include 2 tablespoons of teff when cooking 1 cup of rice, millet, or barley. Uncooked whole teff can also be added to soups and stews, casseroles, and puddings as a thickener and for variety in texture and flavor. As it needs only about 20 minutes of cooking time, whole teff is a good choice for making hot cereal, side dishes, or polenta. Its cooked texture is similar to that of wheat farina, although slightly crunchy.

For the absorption method, use 2 cups of water per ½ cup of teff. Bring the water to a boil, stir in the teff, then cover, lower the heat, and simmer until all of the liquid is absorbed, about 15 to 20 minutes. For extra flavor, toast the teff in a pan before adding boiling water. Pressure-cooking and slow-cooking are neither recommended nor necessary.

Teff Flavor Enhancers Chives, onions, thyme, and parsley. Sweet flavor enhancers include cinnamon, allspice, raisins, dates, pecans, walnuts, and maple syrup.

TRICTICALE

Contains gluten

Triticale has grayish brown, oval-shaped kernels that are larger than wheat and plumper than rye. Its name is a combination of the genus names of wheat (*Triticum*) and rye (*Secale*), and indeed, it's a hybrid of the two. It was first developed in the late 1800s but didn't become commercially viable until the 1950s. This nutritious grain combines the nutty flavor and higher yields of wheat with the better balance of amino acids and hardiness of rye. Still a newcomer in the history of grains, it remains a relatively obscure grain with high hopes for increased recognition and use. Look for it in natural foods and specialty stores.

Varieties and Cooking Guidelines

Whole triticale can be used as wheat berries: for breakfast cereal, as a foundation for pilafs or salads, or in bread dough, for texture. It takes a long time to cook, but presoaking will shorten that time. If you use the cooking times recommended below, the kernels will still be whole and somewhat chewy. Further cooking will cause the kernels to split open, making the triticale softer and more like a cereal. For variety, cook whole triticale along with long-cooking grains such as brown rice and barley. If adding triticale to quinoa, millet, or shorter-cooking grains, cook it separately and then add it to the other grain during the last few minutes of cooking.

It's best to presoak whole triticale for 6 to 8 hours or overnight. To retain nutrients, cook it in its soaking water, using 3 cups of water per cup of triticale. If the ambient temperature is warm (above 75°F), soak it in the refrigerator.

- For the absorption method, use 3 cups of water per cup of triticale. Bring the triticale and its soaking water to a boil, then lower the heat, cover, and simmer until tender, about 50 to 60 minutes if presoaked, and 1½ to 2 hours if not.
- To pressure-cook, use 3 cups of water per cup of triticale and cook at pressure for 40 minutes if presoaked, or 50 minutes if not.
- For slow-cooking, presoaking is optional. Use 4 cups of water per cup of triticale and cook on the high setting for 3½ to 4 hours or on low for 8 hours.

Triticale flakes can be used like other flakes: in granolas, cookies, and meat loaf or a vegetarian version of it. To make a hot cereal, use 2 cups of water per cup of triticale flakes. Bring the water to a boil, stir in the triticale flakes, then lower the heat, cover, and simmer for 15 to 20 minutes. For variety and more well-rounded nutrition, combine triticale flakes with barley flakes, oatmeal, or rice flakes for a hot cereal medley.

Onions, sage, black pepper, garlic, dill, basil, oregano, and thyme. Sweet flavor enhancers include cinnamon, ginger, raisins, and dates.

WHEAT

Contains gluten

Wheat is the most commonly used grain throughout the world. What we know as wheat today has been hybridized throughout the years for higher yields, easier harvesting, and specific baking and cooking properties. Heirloom forms of wheat that are still produced include einkorn, farro (emmer), Kamut, and spelt. While wheat may be most familiar and most often used in the form of flour for pasta, bread, and other baked goods, it also has tremendous versatility as a whole grain. Ironically, both wheat bran and wheat germ, the very components of wheat that are removed during refining, are often added to foods to boost levels of fiber and other nutrients.

Varieties and Cooking Guidelines

Whether in the form of whole wheat berries or cracked, wheat serves as the basis for chewy breakfast cereals, pilafs, salads, stuffing, and casseroles; both forms are also often added to breads for texture. Wheat berries also make excellent sprouts. Though couscous is technically pasta, it's used much like cracked wheat and bulgur are, especially in salads and side dishes. Wheat flakes are as versatile as any other grain flake, and when wheat is coarsely ground into farina and cooked, it makes for soft and creamy comfort food. Wheat bran and wheat germ also see wide use in a variety of applications, particularly cereals and baked goods.

Wheat berries are short, round kernels of varying shades of brown. While they take a couple of hours to cook, you can shorten that time if you presoak them. Cooked whole wheat berries are delicious when combined with cooked rice or barley. If you use the cooking times recommended below, the kernels will still be whole and somewhat chewy. Further cooking will cause the kernels to split open, making the wheat berries softer and more like a cereal.

It's best to soak wheat berries for 6 to 8 hours or overnight. To retain nutrients, soak them in their cooking water, using 3 cups of water per cup of wheat berries. If the ambient temperature is warm (above 75°F), soak them in the refrigerator.

- For the absorption method, bring the wheat berries and their soaking water to a boil. Lower the heat, cover, and simmer until tender, about 1 hour if presoaked, and 1½ to 2 hours if not.
- To pressure-cook, use 3 cups of water per cup of wheat berries and cook at pressure for 40 minutes if presoaked, or 50 minutes if not.
- For slow-cooking, presoaking is optional. Use 4 cups of water per cup of wheat berries and cook on the high setting for 3½ to 4 hours or on low for 8 hours.

Wheat flakes are made from whole wheat berries that have been steamed, dried, and flattened. Use them as an alternative to oat flakes for hot cereal, in baking, or in meat loaf or a vegetarian version of meat loaf. If you make granola, try substituting ½ cup of wheat flakes for oatmeal next time you make it. To cook wheat flakes, use 3 cups of water per cup of dry flakes. Bring the water to a boil, stir in the wheat flakes, then lower the heat, cover, and simmer for 15 to 20 minutes.

Cracked wheat is made by coarsely cracking wheat berries between rollers. It cooks much more quickly than do wheat berries and is more versatile. It has many uses beyond tabbouleh: use it as a cereal, a substitute for rice, or in casseroles and stuffings. To cook cracked wheat, use 2 cups of water per cup of cracked wheat. Bring the water to a boil, then stir in the cracked wheat, lower the heat, cover, and simmer for 20 minutes. For best texture, remove from the heat and let stand, covered, for 5 minutes before serving or using in a recipe.

Bulgur is similar to cracked wheat, but the wheat

berries are parboiled and dried before being cracked into one of three granulations, each with its own cooking properties and preferred uses:

- Fine granulation bulgur is best for making tabbouleh, hot cereal, Lebanese kibbe, and desserts.
- Medium granulation bulgur, the type most widely available, is considered all-purpose, appropriate for a wide range of dishes, including tabbouleh, pilafs, and stuffings.
- Coarse granulation bulgur is used like medium bulgur, but it will be chewier.

A mainstay of traditional cuisines for thousands of years, bulgur remains a popular ingredient because it's so quick and easy to prepare. As a bonus, the process of creating bulgur from wheat berries also yields a product that's more tender than cracked wheat and also has a longer shelf life. Since bulgur is partially cooked, it has a nuttier and richer flavor than that of cracked wheat. Further differences in flavor and aroma depend on the type of wheat used to make the bulgur and the skill of the processor. Bulgur made from red wheat is more commonly available. It has a mild flavor, nutlike aroma, and soft texture. Golden or tan bulgur made from white wheat has a sweeter flavor and coarser texture. Whichever variety you choose, look for uniform-size particles to ensure more even cooking results.

Bulgur can be prepared using the absorption method or by soaking it in hot water. The soaking method results in a coarser, chewier texture.

- For the absorption method, use 2 cups of water per cup of bulgur. Bring the water to a boil, stir in the bulgur, lower the heat, cover, and simmer for 20 minutes. Then, remove from the heat and let stand, covered, for 10 minutes before serving or using in a recipe.
- For the soaking method, use 2½ cups of boiling water per cup of bulgur. Pour the boiling water over the bulgur, cover, and let stand for 1 hour. Drain the bulgur in a colander lined with cheesecloth, then squeeze out the excess moisture.

Bulgur is handy for adding texture to soups and stews. For example, to give chili a texture reminiscent of ground beef, add ½ cup of bulgur per 4 to 5 cups of chili during the last half hour of cooking. Because bulgur absorbs a lot of liquid, you may need to add extra water or tomato sauce to get the final consistency you desire. For variety, experiment with cooking bulgur with vegetable broth or chicken broth instead of water. Or for breakfast fare, use fruit juice for the liquid. To further broaden the possibilities, try a different herb or spice each time you make bulgur.

Although technically pasta, **couscous** is more commonly regarded as a grain due to its use in a wide variety of recipes spanning the range of breakfast, lunch, dinner, and dessert. There are four varieties of couscous—Moroccan couscous, fregola, Israeli couscous, and Lebanese couscous—each unique in size and cooking method. With the exception of Moroccan couscous, which is also available in a whole wheat version, couscous is typically made with refined wheat.

Moroccan couscous is the smallest and most familiar variety. A staple food in northern African nations, especially Morocco, Algeria, and Tunisia, couscous is traditionally made using a labor-intensive process in which refined durum wheat flour is sprinkled with water, rolled into small pellets by hand (between the palms), steamed and cooled twice, and then dried.

In these countries, couscous is typically steamed over a hearty meat and vegetable stew in a special two-tiered steaming pot called a *couscousière*. The couscous is first moistened, then after steaming a bit, it's removed to break up any clumps, and then replaced over the stew to steam again. The result is couscous that is very light and fluffy, with each grain soft and separate—and saturated with flavors and aroma absorbed from the stew. Even though the process takes about an hour from start to finish, it is very easy and needs only minimal hands-on cooking during that time. If you don't have a *couscousière*, you can improvise with a heatproof colander that fits snugly into a stockpot. The steaming method also yields delicious couscous even if it's just cooked over plain water. It's well worth the extra effort if you have the time.

On the other hand, Moroccan couscous can easily be prepared and enjoyed in just a matter of minutes, including whole wheat varieties, which cook in the same amount of time but have more flavor and nutrients. It's one of the fastest-cooking grains around, not to mention a real lifesaver when extra guests show up unexpectedly for a meal. Just add it to boiling water and let it stand for 5 to 10 minutes. Although couscous made this way tends to be drier and clump together more, it is still very good. Try different brands of couscous until you discover your favorite, as they can vary quite a bit in flavor and texture.

Couscous is especially good when cooked with fruit juice, cinnamon or other sweet spices, raisins or dates, and chopped nuts. The mixture can then be pressed into a baking dish that has been quickly rinsed with water but not dried. Once cooled, the couscous can be cut into squares for a sweet snack or dessert. If cooked with vegetable broth, pressed and cooled couscous is transformed into a wheat-based polenta.

Fregola or *fregula* (the Sardinian spelling) is a traditional version of couscous from Sardinia. It is coarser and rougher than Moroccan couscous, and since it is toasted, it has a nuttier flavor. Traditional uses include adding fregola to soups and stews for thickening and texture, serving it with clams and tomatoes, or baking it topped with tomato sauce, herbs, and Pecorino Romano.

Israeli couscous (also known as pearl couscous), which is the size of tapioca pearls, is a delicious and versatile food that bears little resemblance to Moroccan couscous. It is truly more akin to pasta. Created in Israel in the 1950s, it is traditionally made from semolina that's extruded into shape and then dried by toasting. It's much larger than Moroccan couscous and has a nutty flavor and different texture. It's also prepared differently. Whole wheat Israeli couscous is also available, which has a nuttier flavor and, because it is made from whole grain flour, is more nutritious than its white counterpart.

Like pasta, Israeli couscous can be used as the basis of a pasta salad or in any recipe that calls for pasta. It's cooked like pasta, too: add it to boiling salted water and cook for 7 to 8 minutes, then rinse it briefly under cold water to stop the cooking and remove some of the sticky starch. It can also be added to soups during the last 10 minutes of cooking. Or use it to make a creamy risotto-like dish, substituting Israeli couscous for the rice and stirring until the broth is absorbed, about 12 minutes altogether. Use 2 cups of broth for each cup of Israeli couscous.

For a texture suitable for pilafs, with separate rather than sticky grains, first sauté 1 cup of Israeli couscous in oil or butter for a few minutes, then

Clockwise, from top: (1) Israeli couscous, (2) fregola (3) Lebanese couscous, (4) Moroccan couscous

add 1¾ cups of water and a bit of salt. Bring to a boil, then lower the heat, cover, and simmer until the water is absorbed, about 15 minutes. When cooking whole wheat pearl couscous, reduce the water per cup of couscous to 1¼ cups. After adding the couscous to boiling water, reduce the heat and simmer, covered, for about 20 minutes or until the water is absorbed. The cooked couscous can be served immediately as a side dish or cooled for use as the basis for a salad.

Lebanese couscous, also known as *moghrabieh*, is even larger, the size of small peas. It, too, can be cooked like risotto or as an addition to soups or stews to provide a chewy texture, but the more traditional method is to cook it on its own and serve it topped with stew. First soak 2 cups of Lebanese couscous by pouring boiling water over it. Cover and let stand for 45 minutes. Drain the couscous, then cook it in 4 cups of broth for about 30 minutes, until the liquid is absorbed and the couscous is tender.

For cooking it directly within soups or stews as a textural addition, use ¼ cup of Lebanese couscous for about 12 cups of soup, adding it about 30 minutes before the soup is done. Then cover the pot and cook until the Lebanese couscous is tender.

Farina is a hot cereal made from wheat that has been ground to a medium-fine consistency. Although when cooked it's often generically referred to as Cream of Wheat, that's just one specific brand name. The more accurate term is *farina*, a word originating from the Latin (and modern Italian) word for "flour." True to its roots, farina can be substituted for some of the flour in some recipes. It can also be cooked like polenta.

For optimal nutrition and the best flavor, look for products labeled "whole wheat farina" (you may have to check the ingredient listing). Products labeled as simply "wheat farina" are made from refined wheat, processed to remove the fiber-rich bran layer and nutrient-rich wheat germ. Disodium phosphate is added to some brands of refined farina to help speed cooking by causing the grains to swell and gelatinize faster. Proteolytic enzymes may also be added to decrease cooking time by weakening the grain to facilitate the penetration of water. While these timesavers are not harmful, neither are they essential, especially when you consider it only takes 10 minutes to cook farina without these additives.

To cook whole wheat farina, use 3 cups of water or milk per cup of farina. Bring the liquid to a boil, then slowly pour in the farina, stirring all the while to prevent clumping. Continue stirring until it returns to a boil, then lower the heat, cover, and simmer for about 10 minutes, stirring occasionally. Serve with fresh or dried fruit, nuts, milk, or soymilk.

Looking like a coarsely cracked greenish bulgur when cooked, **roasted green wheat**, also known as *farike* (or *frikeh* or *freekeh*), is a traditional food in Middle Eastern and North African cuisines, served in Syria, Lebanon, Jordan, Palestine, and Egypt for over two thousand years. It is made from durum wheat that is picked at a critical time: while still in its green stage (before it is fully ripe), when the endosperm of the grain is still soft. It is then sun-dried, set on fire to char the wheat's outer hull to make it easier to remove, and then spread out for further roasting. The moisture in the soft seed prevents the grain from thoroughly burning, which explains the smoky, nutty flavor that is characteristic of *farike*. The grain is then threshed to remove the straw and chaff, and finally dried in the shade to prevent the sun's bleaching the grain's green color. The word *farike* comes from the Arabic word for "rubbed," referring to rubbing off the chaff, which traditionally had been done by hand before threshing machines were made available. Although some brands offer whole *farike*, it is more commonly ground coarsely for regular cooking as a pilaf or finely for making a special *farike* soup.

When cooked, *farike* has a coarse, chewy texture, with some grains cracked and some whole, and an outstanding nutty, earthy, slightly smoky, albeit indescribably fresh, flavor. Very high in fiber, the grain has a low glycemic index like other whole grains, metabolizing slowly for lasting energy.

While the best quality roasted green wheat will

be free of stones and debris that may otherwise be a result of traditional *farike* processing, it is always a good idea to clean the grain before cooking. First pick through the grain and then rinse by placing it in a bowl or pot and covering it with water. Let sit for a few minutes, then pour off any debris that floats to the top.

Use *farike* as you would cracked wheat or bulgur: as a cooked breakfast cereal; in pilafs, stuffings, cold grain salads like tabbouleh; or as a great medium for combining beans, fresh herbs, chopped colorful sweet bell peppers, and arugula for a quick lunch. It can be added to soups, too, either as uncooked *farike* at the start of the cooking process or adding cooked grain closer toward the end.

For the absorption method, use 2½ cups of water per cup of cracked *farike*. Bring the water to a boil, stir in the grain, lower the heat, cover, and simmer for 20 minutes, until the water is absorbed. For best results, remove from the heat and let stand, covered, for 10 minutes before serving or using in a recipe. When cooking whole, uncracked *farike* increase the water to 3 cups and cook for 40 to 45 minutes.

Wheat bran is the outer protective covering of the wheat berry, sometimes called miller's bran or unprocessed bran. If you're already eating whole wheat cereals and other whole grain products, you're automatically getting bran in your diet and really don't need to supplement it. But if you choose to do so—perhaps sprinkling it on cereals, soups, or salads or adding it to muffins and other baked goods—limit the amount of bran to no more than 2 tablespoons per serving. Too much bran can have the negative effect of binding up minerals such as copper, iron, and zinc, preventing their absorption. And because it readily absorbs water, it is important to always drink plenty of liquids for digestive ease when consuming bran.

Wheat germ is the embryo of the grain, and as such it is particularly rich in nutrients, including fiber, protein, vitamin E, thiamin, folic acid, iron, zinc, magnesium, and healthful fats. As with bran, if your diet already includes whole wheat products,

you're automatically getting the benefits of wheat germ. Still, its nutty flavor and crumblike texture make it a popular addition to recipes for pancakes and other baked goods. It also makes a nice topping for smoothies, cereals, entrees, and desserts and can be used as a substitute for bread crumbs when coating a variety of foods.

Because it is so high in natural oils and thus very prone to rancidity, wheat germ should never be purchased in bulk. Instead, look for it in shelf-stable nitrogen-flushed packages or vacuum-packed jars or packages. Once opened, wheat germ should always be refrigerated or stored in the freezer. It is time to throw it away when it has that telltale unpleasant aroma and bitter flavor—as with all rancid foods, any health benefits are more than outweighed by the rancidity. Really fresh raw wheat germ that is only a few days old would undoubtedly be the most nutritious choice, but for most of us, this is impossible to procure; raw wheat germ should be used within a week of opening. Toasted wheat germ is a better option. Because heat inactivates enzymes that can accelerate rancidity, toasted wheat germ retains its freshness longer than raw wheat germ does. It will keep up to three months if stored in an airtight container in the freezer or refrigerator. It also imparts a delicious flavor that's even nuttier than regular wheat germ. Stabilized wheat germ is also available, on which a specialized heat treatment is used to kill bacteria and mold, extending storage time for up to six months if refrigerated and even longer if stored in the freezer. And finally, the most stable (although least nutritious) type of wheat germ is defatted. Since all the oils are removed (along with their nutrient value), it is not as essential to store defatted wheat germ in the refrigerator or freezer.

Wheat Flavor Enhancers Onions, chives, dill, mushrooms, black pepper, garlic, curry powder, parsley, cilantro, and mint. Sweet flavor enhancers include dried fruits, cinnamon, pumpkin pie spices, apple pie spices, ginger, and allspice; another option is to replace the water with fruit juice when cooking.

WILD RICE

Gluten free

Wild rice is not a variety of rice. Rather, its long, dark brown kernel is the seed of an aquatic grass that grows primarily in marshy areas of northern Minnesota, Wisconsin, and southern Canada; it is the only grain native to North America. Early North American inhabitants called it *manoomin*, meaning "good berry"; early English explorers came up with the name *wild rice*. Nutritionally, wild rice is a good source of protein, containing more than common rice, and it's rich in lysine, the amino acid that's usually limited in grains. Its texture is chewy and its flavor is often described as nutty, earthy, subtly smoky, and somewhat reminiscent of green tea.

Laws in Minnesota, Wisconsin, and Canada regulate wild rice harvesting, both to protect the rights of the Native American communities considered to be the official hand-harvesters of wild rice, and to preserve the native wild rice beds. A limited number of wild rice harvesting permits are issued, and they require strict adherence to the season, harvesting methods, and hours of harvesting allowed per day. Traditional harvesting is done manually, using only a canoe and two ricing sticks called knockers. While one person guides the canoe, another person uses one stick to pull the head of rice into the boat, then knocks the ripe seeds loose with the other stick.

However, most of what is marketed as wild rice is actually one of several hybrid versions cultivated and mechanically harvested in rice paddies in California and Minnesota—a practice that started years ago when the demand for wild rice exceeded the wild supply. While nontraditional growing and harvesting methods make "wild rice" less expensive, the flavor of these varieties is not as robust or nutty as that of authentic wild rice. Also, cultivated wild rice is more likely to be grown with fertilizers, herbicides, and insecticides.

Whether harvested in the wild or cultivated, wild rice is cured for a couple of weeks to further develop its flavor and to make it easier to husk. The rice is then parched—traditionally over a fire, or commercially within a large rotating drum—to reduce its moisture content and enhance its characteristic flavor. As a final process, the chaff is removed in a thresher and fanning mill. Since the specific techniques used vary from producer to producer, each brand of wild rice is unique in flavor.

Varieties and Cooking Guidelines

Only cultivated hybrid "wild rice" is graded according to its size. Wild rice designated as **giant** wild rice has grains that are one inch in length. **Extra fancy** wild rice is medium in length. The least expensive type, **select** wild rice, generally includes uneven lengths and sizes of kernels and broken kernels; it can be used in muffins, pancakes, soups, stuffings, and anywhere uniform appearance doesn't matter.

Wild rice is excellent for pilafs or as an ingredient in pancakes, breads, salads, soups, and stuffings. When cooked, it expands to three or four times its dry volume. To cook it, use 3 cups of water per cup of wild rice. Bring the water to a boil, stir in the wild rice, then lower the heat, cover, and cook for 50 to 60 minutes, or until the grains begin to split open and become tender but not mushy. However, some wild rice is mechanically scarified, meaning its hard black bran layer is scratched to reduce cooking time, so be sure to consult the instructions for the variety you purchase. It can be cooked together with brown rice without sacrificing its hearty flavor. Or it can be cooked separately and mixed with other cooked grains, providing a striking color contrast and chewy texture.

Wild Rice Flavor Enhancers Onions, chives, leeks, dill, mushrooms, parsley, sage, thyme, celery, and red bell peppers.

Whole Grain and Specialty Flours

All whole grains can be ground into flour, as can some other foods, but using them in cooking and baking is seldom just a matter of substituting them for wheat flour. Each contributes its own unique flavor and texture. Some are mildly flavored, while others are downright assertive. Textures range from silken to sandy. Some have gluten and others don't, which can significantly affect the texture and volume of baked goods, particularly breads that are kneaded. And even within the category of wheat flours, protein content can vary widely, making them perform quite differently in baking. Some types of wheat flour are more appropriate for certain types of baking than others. Recognizing the characteristics of each type of flour can not only make experimentation fun and interesting but also yield delicious baked goods as a reward for all your efforts.

GRINDING METHODS

Flour can be ground in several ways: stone ground, hammer milled, or roller milled. Whole grain flours are typically stone ground or hammer milled. Refined flours, from grains stripped of their bran and germ, must be roller milled.

Stone-ground flour is ground between two flat millstones that rub against each other, the most traditional way of grinding flour. The stones slowly crush the entire grain, distributing its bran and nutrient-rich germ throughout the flour, an essential component for making excellent whole grain breads. Since this slower method of grinding generates less heat than hammer milling or roller milling does, the flavors and nutrients within the grain are better retained. Also, since stone grinding creates larger particles of flour, products made with stone-ground flour may be digested and absorbed more slowly by the body. This keeps blood sugar levels more stable and, consequently, helps maintain a steady energy level. Since stone grinding can be just one part of the process, look for products labeled "100 percent stone-ground."

Hammer-milled flour is ground in a mill in which bars swinging on an axle rotate inside a steel cylinder, crushing the grain against the inner surface. A faster way to grind grains, hammer milling also yields a more consistent grade of finely ground

flour. However, the speed of the process generates higher temperatures, which can destroy some nutrients within the flour.

Roller-milled flour is ground in a machine that features several rollers with different surfaces, ranging from smooth to coarse, set various widths apart. Unlike stone grinding and hammer milling, grinding flour in a roller mill makes it possible to quickly separate the bran and germ from the endosperm and completely control the particle size of the flour through various stages of grinding and sifting. The miller can then analyze each grinding, or stream, to assess many characteristics, including the quality of the starch, the type of gluten, and the amount of protein. This also allows millers to create customized flour blends geared for various purposes, such as commercial bread baking or home use, and specific products, such as specialty breads, cakes, crackers, pastries, and pasta. Because roller milling, like hammer milling, generates more heat, some oxidation and damage to the nutrients within the flour can occur.

There are significant and surprising differences in quality and overall performance among the many brands of flour. Some of the key factors involved in this variation include the type of grain, growing conditions, quality control measures during processing, conditions in which the flour is stored (including in any warehouse along the way as well as the grocery store), and how old the flour is by the time you buy it—and actually use it. But it doesn't stop there: humidity and other factors in your home at the time of baking can also affect how flours perform, and different brands work better in different situations. It's definitely worth the time and investment to experiment with various brands of flour to discover which provides the best results.

You can also grind whole grain flour at home, which guarantees it's as fresh as possible, delivering appreciable differences in flavor and overall results in bread and other baked goods. Several home manual and electric flour mill models are available, some with millstones and others that rely on metal burrs. The best are millstone grain mills that have strong, quiet, efficient motors, good quality durable millstones that require little or no maintenance and that grind at very low temperature, the capacity to grind all types of whole grains as well as lentils and dried beans, and the ability to adjust from extremely fine flour to cracked grain without having to stop the milling process

Flour-grinding attachments are also available for some juicers, food processors, high speed blenders, and electric mixers, with varying results. The high heat typically generated by their grinding can destroy heat-sensitive nutrients within the flour. Recognizing this as a real problem, some manufacturers suggest grinding grain that has been stored in the freezer. Certain grains, such as rice, millet, oats, and quinoa, can be ground in a blender, but too much grinding could burn out the motor unless your blender is particularly heavy-duty. Also, a blender tends to grind flour unevenly. A small electric coffee grinder does a good job if only small amounts of flour are needed.

PROCESSING METHODS

The process of making refined wheat flour by removing the bran and wheat germ may also include further processing, including the addition of bleaching and maturing agents, dough conditioners, and enzymes, as well as vitamins for enrichment. Artificial bleaching agents began to see use in the United States in the early 1900s as a quicker, cheaper way to mature refined flour and condition the gluten. Traditionally, refined flour was stored for two to three months to allow oxygen to naturally bleach the flour's yellow tint to a creamy white color. It also oxidized the protein, making the gluten stronger and more elastic for better baking results.

Since storage involves some expense and the flour has to be rotated to make sure all of it is exposed to oxygen, artificial measures to get the job done in less than a couple of days—a process discovered in the early 1900s—was enthusiastically accepted by many millers. Either benzoyl peroxide or chlorine dioxide can be used to

chemically mature and condition flour depending on what type of flour is being produced. Benzoyl peroxide is used in some all-purpose flours and some bread flours. Chlorine dioxide yields a whiter color, as well as a more acidic flour, which makes for finer texture, so it's used in cake flour and also sometimes in all-purpose flours.

However, artisan and high-quality scratch bakers insist on using only unbleached wheat flour, finding that it far surpasses bleached wheat flour in every respect. Not only do the yellow carotenoids make for a pleasing creamy white tint in baked goods, but they also contribute to the overall taste and fragrant aroma of products baked with wheat. And since natural aging also oxidizes the flour's protein for stronger gluten and better baking results, there is simply no good reason why anyone should use bleached flour.

In addition to bleaching agents, refined flour is often subjected to oxidizing agents, such as potassium bromate and azodicarbonamide, to more quickly mature the flour and strengthen its gluten. Even whole wheat flour sometimes contains these additives to create a higher-rising bread. Although potassium bromate is allowed in the United States, it is banned in several countries, including the United Kingdom, Canada, Mexico, and Japan, as a potential carcinogen. Since remarkable bread is made in countries that have banned potassium bromate, it is clear that it is an unnecessary additive, and the alternatives, including azodicarbonamide, are equally unnecessary. While these additives significantly reduce the time and labor required for mass-production bakeries to develop dough, they don't make any contribution to crafting bread that is as tasty as it is nourishing.

The only additive that can truly enhance flour is alpha-amylase, an enzyme that helps break down some of the complex starches in flour into sugar. This helps provide readily available fuel for yeast, which in turn helps dough rise properly when making bread. Grains naturally contain some alpha-amylase, but the amount increases dramatically during sprouting. The source for supplemental alpha-amylase is often sprouted barley that's been ground into flour, which is generally known as barley malt powder or diastatic malt powder. Flour is typically tested at the mill using the falling number test to measure how much alpha-amylase is naturally present, as the level can vary depending on the variety of wheat, the weather during growing and harvest, and the storage conditions. If the level is too low, a small amount of diastatic malt powder may be added, and the precise amount is very important: too much will produce breads with a sticky texture, but too little will yield bread with a dry, crumbly texture.

Alpha-amylase can also be derived from *Aspergillus oryzae*, which synthesizes the enzyme during its growth. This is the same type of mold that is cultured to inoculate soybeans in the production of miso. Because fungal alpha-amylase is inactivated earlier in the baking process than diastatic barley malt is, the amount added need not be so precisely calibrated, as there isn't the same potential for sticky bread if too much is added. However, since fungal enzymes may be from a genetically engineered source, it's best to stick with flour supplemented only with diastatic barley malt unless you're sure that the specific brand of fungal alpha-amylase used is derived from a natural source.

ENRICHMENT

Enrichment of refined wheat flour and other grain products, including breads, pastas, cornmeal, and white rice emerged as a result of health surveys in the late 1930s that revealed alarming wide-spread nutritional deficiencies in B vitamins, iron, and iodine. The American Medical Association, National Research Council, National Academy of Sciences, and several public health authorities decided a good strategy to remedy the situation would be to fortify commonly consumed refined foods.

In 1941, the US Food and Drug Administration set standards for the use of the term *enriched* on grain products. To use this term products must

be supplemented with iron and three B vitamins: thiamin (B_1), riboflavin (B_2), and niacin (B_3). In response to research showing that adequate intake of folic acid (B_9) prior to conception dramatically reduces the incidence of neural tube defects (spina bifida and anencephaly), folic acid was added to the enrichment list in 1993. Although enrichment isn't federally mandated, most states have accepted the enrichment standards, in part because of interstate commerce—manufacturers want to ensure their products receive wide distribution.

Considering that only five out of the nutrients depleted during refinement are replaced, enrichment is just a drop in the bucket. As many as thirty nutrients are significantly depleted, including magnesium, potassium, calcium, zinc, selenium, vitamin B_6, and vitamin E.

GLUTEN AND ITS ROLE IN BAKING

Gluten is a protein complex comprised of two types of protein, gliadin and glutenin, which are responsible for giving dough flexibility, strength, and elasticity. When liquids are added to flour and the dough is manipulated, gliadin and glutenin combine to form gluten. The gentle stretching and folding of the dough during kneading helps develop quite a bit of gluten in breads. In cookie dough and cake and quick bread batters, where a lesser amount of gluten is desirable, stirring suffices. However it's developed, the gluten then captures the carbon dioxide produced by the yeast, sourdough starter, baking powder, or baking soda, leavening the dough and creating baked goods with a lighter texture and more volume.

The gliadin component of gluten gives dough its ability to be stretched and shaped, referred to as "extensibility," as well as the ability to expand to accommodate the gas bubbles produced by the leavening agent. Glutenin, on the other hand, is responsible for the dough's elasticity, letting it hold its original shape and spring back when stretched, which helps improve the dough's ability to capture and contain the gas bubbles.

Flours at a Glance

Flour	Gluten Free?	Flavor	Baked Texture	Best Used In
Amaranth	yes	spicy, nutty, woody	moist, fine crumb	protein and flavor booster in tortillas, breads, muffins, pancakes, and cookies
Arrowroot	yes	neutral	lightens heavy textures	sauces and gluten-free baking
Barley	no	sweet, malty	moist, cakelike crumb	breads, muffins, pancakes, cakes, quick breads, and gravies
Bean-based	yes	rich, sweet (light type), hearty (dark type)	moist, fine crumb	protein and flavor booster in breads, cakes, and cookies
Buckwheat	yes	hearty, earthy	moist, fine crumb	pancakes, crepes, and noodles
Carob	yes	chocolaty	dry, light crumb	brownies, cakes, desserts, candy, and beverages
Chestnut	yes	sweet, nutty	silky, dense crumb	pastries, breads, muffins, gnocchi, and pancakes
Cocoa	yes	chocolate	dry, light crumb	brownies, cakes, desserts, candy, and beverages
Cornmeal, blue or red	yes	sweet, nutlike	grainy, denser crumb	tortillas, cornbread, muffins, and pancakes
Cornmeal, white	yes	delicate corn flavor	grainy, slightly dry crumb	cornbread, tortillas, and porridge
Cornmeal, yellow	yes	deep, rich corn flavor	grainy, slightly dry crumb	cornbread, tortillas, polenta, tamales, muffins, and pancakes
Cornstarch	yes	neutral	lightens heavy-textured crumb	sauces, gluten-free baking aid, and thickener in fruit pies
Einkorn	no	toasted, nutty	dense, slightly sticky crumb	sourdough breads, cookies, brownies, muffins, quick breads
Emmer	no	sweet, malty, nutty	dense crumb	sourdough breads, cookies, brownies, muffins, quick breads,
Garbanzo-fava	yes	nutty, somewhat sweet	moist, tender crumb	flatbreads, fritters, breads, muffins, quick breads, cookies, cakes sauces, and gravies
Garbanzo	yes	sweet, rich	dry, delicate crumb	flatbreads, fritters, breads, sauces, soups, gravies, veggie burgers, and for added protein
Gluten flour	no	tangy	fine, chewy crumb	breads (as a rising aid and for added protein)
Kamut	no	sweet, rich, buttery	dense, heavy crumb	pasta, breads, and flatbreads
Kudzu	yes	neutral	not used in baking	sauces, soups, and dairy-free puddings and pies
Mesquite	yes	sweet, with molasses and mocha tones	dry crumb	seasoning savory or sweet foods, boosting nutrition and flavor in breads, muffins, and cookies
Millet	yes	mildly sweet to bitter, depending on age	dry, delicate crumb	breads, muffins, quick breads, and cookies
Nut-based (almond, hazelnut)	yes	rich, nutty	soft, delicate crumb	pie crusts, quick breads, pancakes, muffins, cakes

Oat	yes*	sweet	moist, cakelike crumb	breads, cakes, cookies, pancakes, crackers, sauces, and gravies
Potato flour	yes	sweet, strong potato flavor	moist, chewy crumb	soup thickener and gluten-free baking blends
Potato starch	yes	neutral, mild potato flavor	lightens heavy-textured crumb	sauces and gluten-free baking aid
Quinoa	yes	nutty, earthy	delicate, cakelike crumb	quick breads and cookies
Rice, brown	yes	nutty	dry, fine crumb	breads, muffins, and pancakes
Rice, sweet	yes	sweet	springy crumb	sauces and piecrusts
Rice, white	yes	neutral	dry, fine crumb	gravies, sauces, breads, quick breads, and muffins
Rye	no	tangy	moist crumb	breads, pancakes, waffles, and crackers
Seed-based (sesame seed, sunflower seed)	yes	nutty, earthy	soft, delicate crumb	nutrition-and flavor-booster in breads, muffins, quick breads, and cookies
Sorghum	yes	sweet	fine crumb	injera, breads, cookies, cakes, muffins, and quick breads
Soy	yes	pungent, slightly bitter, nutty	moist, fine crumb	protein booster in breads, muffins, and quick breads
Spelt	no	sweet, nutty	moderate-texture crumb	breads, muffins, quick breads, crackers, and piecrusts
Sprouted grain flour	no**	sweet	lighter, springy crumb	breads, muffins, and quick breads
Tapioca	yes	slightly sweet	chewy, springy crumb	sauces and gluten-free baking aid
Teff	yes	sweet, with malty molasses tones	light, dry crumb	injera, pancakes, waffles, muffins, and cookies
Triticale	no	nutty, tangy	dense crumb	breads, quick breads, and muffins
Wheat, durum	no	sweet, somewhat buttery	fine, delicate, dense crumb	pasta
Wheat, semolina	no	sweet, somewhat buttery	fine, delicate, firm crumb	breads and pasta
Wheat, refined white and all-purpose	no	sweet to neutral	fine, tender crumb	breads, cookies, muffins, quick breads, piecrusts, crackers, gravies, and sauces
Wheat, white whole	no	sweet, nutty	coarse, large crumb	breads, cookies, cakes, muffins, quick breads, piecrusts, crackers, gravies, and sauces
Wheat, whole	no	slightly bitter, nutty	coarse, large crumb	breads, muffins, quick breads, piecrusts, crackers, and sauces
Wild rice	yes	earthy, nutty	dry, fine crumb	pancakes, quick breads, gravies, and coating fish and poultry

*Although oats do not contain gluten, in North America they are often listed as being inappropriate for a gluten-free diet, but this is only out of concern that they may be contaminated by wheat during harvest and processing.
**Sprouted grain flour typically contains wheat.

International Flour Labeling

British equivalents for US flour classifications:

Soft flour—cake and pastry flour
Plain flour—all-purpose flour
Strong flour or hard flour—bread flour
Self-raising flour—self-rising flour
Wholemeal flour—whole wheat flour

Italian flour specifications

The classifications "1," "0," and "00" refer to how fine the flour is ground and how much of the bran and germ have been removed. "00" is the most highly refined and is talcum-powder soft.

AMARANTH FLOUR

Gluten free

Amaranth flour adds an unusual nutty, spicy flavor and a moist texture to cookies, muffins, pancakes, waffles, and breads, along with a smooth, crisp crust. Widely used in early Mexican and Central American cultures in traditional breads, it is valued these days for its high-quality protein, which can boost the nutritional content of any recipe. Although rich in protein, it's gluten free, so it can't be used on its own in baked goods intended to rise. Rather than using it as the sole or primary flour in recipes, combine amaranth flour in small amounts with other flours to create the right balance in flavor and texture. While too much may result in dense baked goods with a strong flavor, a small amount can add an extra spark that accentuates without overwhelming. A good rule of thumb is to substitute amaranth flour for up to 25 percent of the flour called for in a recipe. Substituting amaranth flour in a recipe may require a slightly extended baking time.

ARROWROOT

Gluten free

Obtained from a narrow, six-inch-long root that hails from the West Indies, arrowroot is true to its name, having been used by Indians to draw poison from arrow wounds. These days it's used for more peaceful purposes, serving as an easily digested thickener and flour substitute. Arrowroot is sometimes used in teething biscuits and cookies for toddlers, for its velvety consistency and because its starch is in a form that makes these foods easier to chew, swallow, and digest. It is typically sold ground as a light, white powder, although sometimes it may be found in small chunks that can be crushed quite easily with a mortar and pestle or the back of a spoon.

Arrowroot has several things going for it as a thickener. Unlike grain-based flour, which makes sauces that are cloudy and opaque, arrowroot yields clear sauces with a beautiful glazed appearance. As it is virtually neutral in taste, arrowroot also allows the true flavors of the sauce to come through, and it doesn't require precooking, as flour does, to eliminate unpleasant, raw, floury flavors. Because it starts to thicken more quickly and at lower temperatures than flour does, arrowroot is perfect for delicate sauces and also good to use for last-minute corrections to consistency. While it is the best choice for thickening foods that will be frozen after cooking and when thickening acidic liquids like fruit juices, it doesn't work well in dairy-based sauces, where it develops a slimy texture. Substitute an equal amount of arrowroot powder for either cornstarch or potato starch; if using it as a thickener in place of flour, use half the amount.

Use approximately 1 tablespoon of arrowroot to thicken 1 cup of liquid. To prevent clumping, first dissolve the arrowroot in a bit of cold water, then slowly pour it into hot, not boiling, liquid, stirring or whisking all the while, and continue to stir just until thickened. Lower the heat immediately and serve the sauce within 15 minutes. With prolonged cooking, sauces thickened with arrowroot will start to break down. Like other root-based starches, it isn't particularly heat stable. For the same reason, sauces made with arrowroot don't reheat well.

Arrowroot is also used as a baking starch in some gluten-free recipes, helping to complement other, more sandy-textured flours that lack the binding properties gluten would provide. It makes for a smoother texture and contributes to a crisper crust. It's particularly useful for lightening the texture of wheat-free baked goods made with amaranth, brown rice, or millet flour. You can use up to 50 percent arrowroot flour in a flour blend. If stored in an airtight, moisture-proof container, arrowroot will keep almost indefinitely. For those who are allergic to corn, arrowroot can be substituted for cornstarch on a one-to-one basis in any recipe.

BARLEY FLOUR
Contains gluten

Ground from whole barley, barley flour contributes a sweet, malty flavor, a moist, cakelike crumb, and a firm, chewy crust to baked goods. It is a delicious addition to breads, cakes, cookies, muffins, pancakes, and quick breads. For optimal flavor, lightly toast barley flour in a dry skillet before adding it to recipes. Although barley contains some gluten, bread made solely with barley flour won't have enough gluten to rise properly. Limit the amount of barley flour to 25 percent in these breads.

While it can be substituted equally for wheat flour in most baked goods leavened with baking powder or baking soda, some recipes may benefit from decreasing the amount of barley flour and adding in other types of flour to achieve a drier, less moist crumb. For cakes, cookies, muffins, pancakes, and quick breads, a good place to start is to substitute barley flour for up to 25 percent of the flour called for in the recipe. If that goes well, experiment with a higher proportion of barley flour the next time to explore the possible variations in both flavor and texture. On its own, barley flour performs well in unleavened flat breads and even piecrusts, though crusts made with barley flour will be heartier and less flaky. It also makes for an interesting flavor twist in flour-thickened gravies and other cooked sauces.

BEAN-BASED FLOURS
Gluten free

Flour ground from dried beans can be combined with other flours to boost levels of protein, soluble fiber, B vitamins, and minerals in baked goods. Because beans are high in methionine, an amino acid that is lacking in most grains, adding some bean flour will also improve the quality of the protein. Soy flour and garbanzo flour are the most familiar forms of bean flour, and each of these is described below, in its own listing. However, a wide variety of bean flours is available, typically categorized by the color of the bean. For any recipe calling for light bean flour, possibilities include fava bean flour, garbanzo flour, garbanzo-fava flour, white bean flour, and navy bean flour. Dark bean flour options include pinto bean flour, black bean flour, and Romano bean flour (made with cranberry beans). Light bean flours are generally milder in flavor than dark bean flours. For best digestibility, look for sprouted bean flour or, alternatively, products described as "micronized," "processed," "precooked," or "toasted."

Bean flour contributes body, flavor, and a moist, fine crumb to baked goods. Because it is gluten free, bean flour must be combined with flours that contain gluten when making baked goods that are intended to rise, using up to 25 percent bean flour. Alternatively, it can be included as a component within gluten-free baking blends with added xanthan or guar gum and emulsifiers to enhance the structure of breads and enable the leavening agents to do their job. Bean flour can similarly be used when making cakes and cookies.

BUCKWHEAT FLOUR
Gluten free

Buckwheat flour, with its robust, somewhat musty flavor, is the basis for Japanese soba noodles, and it also lends its distinctive flavor and functional qualities, including a soft crust, to hearty pancakes and traditional Russian blini, paper-thin crepes classically served with sour cream. Light buckwheat flour is made from hulled buckwheat, while stronger-flavored dark buckwheat flour includes some of the hull. As usual, the darker, more whole grain form is more nutritious. For a drier texture and mellower flavor, you can grind white, untoasted buckwheat groats into flour in a blender, electric coffee grinder, or grain mill. Due to its gummy texture when cooked, buckwheat flour is not a good choice when thickening sauces and gravies.

Because buckwheat is gluten free, it must be combined with a high-gluten flour, such as whole wheat, to make breads leavened with yeast. Even then it should be used in only limited amounts because its flavor is strong and it can create a gummy texture. Don't use more than $1/3$ cup of buckwheat flour per loaf of bread. Pancakes, muffins, and crepes can handle a higher proportion of buckwheat flour—up to 50 percent. It all depends on just how robust you'd like the flavor to be. However, the higher the proportion of buckwheat flour, the more leavening and/or binding assistance the recipe will need from ingredients such as eggs or yogurt.

CAROB FLOUR
Gluten free

Carob is the dried, roasted, and pulverized pod of a tree that grows primarily in countries surrounding the Mediterranean. Easily digested and rich in pectin, carob is a traditional remedy for soothing an upset stomach. With a flavor similar to that of chocolate but milder, carob is generally used as a substitute for cocoa. But unlike chocolate, carob is naturally sweet, high in fiber and calcium, very low in fat, and free of theobromine, a naturally occurring caffeinelike substance found in chocolate that some people prefer to avoid.

Substitute carob equally for cocoa in cookies, cakes, candies, and beverages. Because of its high fiber content—which, in baking, lends a dry, light crumb—use a blender when making carob drinks, otherwise it will settle at the bottom of the glass. To replace 1 square of baking chocolate in a recipe, use 3 tablespoons of carob flour plus 1 tablespoon of milk. Since carob is sweeter than cocoa and contains less fat, it's usually a good idea to decrease the amount of sweetener and increase the amount of fat when substituting it for cocoa. It is also sometimes added to bread dough to make loaves with a deep, rich color. For this purpose, add 1 to 2 tablespoons of carob powder per loaf of bread.

CHESTNUT FLOUR
Gluten free

Even though chestnuts are classified as a nut, a glance at their nutritional profile, especially when dried and ground into flour—high in carbohydrates (78 percent) and low in fat (less than 4 percent)—makes it seem they could just as easily be classified as a grain. Flour made from dried chestnuts can be used like any other gluten-free grain flour.

For many centuries, chestnuts have been an important seasonal staple food in Italian mountain communities, where chestnut trees flourish. In fact, chestnut flour, not cornmeal, was the original basis of polenta. Now considered a specialty item for both gourmet and gluten-free cooking, chestnut flour has a silky texture and sweet flavor that make it perfect for use in breads, muffins, pancakes, and pastries, as well as savory dishes, including chestnut gnocchi.

Chestnut flour can be substituted for up to 25 percent of the flour in yeasted bread recipes and up to 50 percent of the flour in recipes leavened with baking powder or baking soda. It can be substituted for cornmeal or oat flour on a one-to-one basis. Since it is very low in fat, chestnut flour will keep for twelve to eighteen months without going rancid.

COCOA POWDER
Gluten free

Unsweetened cocoa powder has more to offer than just its rich, delicious flavor. It performs similarly to a grain flour or root-based starch, providing structure, absorbing moisture, and serving as a thickening agent in desserts, baked goods, frostings, and fillings.

Cocoa powder is derived from cocoa beans, which grow in large pods on the cacao tree, a tall understory species that grows in humid tropical forests. The beans are fermented to help develop the flavor we associate with chocolate, and then dried and roasted for further expansion of flavor. They are cracked into small pieces known as nibs, which are then crushed to produce a thick, dark paste. Called chocolate liquor, this paste is hydraulically pressed to separate most of the cocoa butter from the cocoa particles. The extracted cocoa butter is utilized as a key ingredient in a wide variety of chocolate products.

The remaining cocoa particles are pulverized to make cocoa powder, which has a strong, complex, bitter chocolate flavor. Depending on how much cocoa butter is separated from the solids, as much as 24 percent cocoa butter can remain in the cocoa powder. This is one of the primary factors distinguishing the many brands of cocoa powder: the higher the fat, the richer the flavor.

Another key distinguishing factor is whether the cocoa is treated with an alkali. Cocoa powder is naturally acidic, which contributes to its bitter flavor and affects its performance in baking. In 1828, a Dutch chocolatier developed a method for treating cocoa powder with a solution of potassium carbonate, a harmless alkaline chemical substance, to neutralize its acidity and produce cocoa with a milder, less bitter flavor and a darker brown color. As a salute to its developer, cocoa that has been alkalized is referred to as Dutch process cocoa or Dutch cocoa. The process also makes cocoa powder more absorbent, so it's easier to mix with liquids. It is important to note, however, that the beneficial flavonoids within cocoa, which are credited as the primary basis for the health benefits of chocolate, are destroyed as a result of the Dutch process.

Whether to use natural, nonalkalized cocoa powder or Dutch process cocoa is sometimes just a matter of personal flavor preference, but in some recipes the distinction is important, as the degree of acidity can affect the final outcome. Many recipes will specify which form of cocoa to use, but to help you decide in other situations, it often comes down to whether the recipe is leavened with baking powder or baking soda. Baking soda must react with an acidic ingredient to produce its leavening effect, so natural, nonalkalized cocoa powder is generally used with baking soda. In recipes that use baking powder or contain other acidic ingredients, Dutched process cocoa is the better choice. In situations where neither baking powder nor baking soda is used, either type of cocoa should work well.

CORN FLOUR
Gluten free

Corn flour is ground to a finer consistency than cornmeal. Use it in breads, pancakes, or waffles if you'd like a smoother, less grainy texture than that of cornmeal. It can also be used in cakes and cookies. If you have trouble finding corn flour, make your own by grinding regular cornmeal (not whole corn!) in a blender or coffee grinder until it's more flour-like. (Be aware that in the United Kingdom, Australia, and New Zealand, the term *cornflour* means "cornstarch"—it's not the same thing.) Sprouted corn flour is great for making tortillas.

CORNMEAL
Gluten free

Because it is mildly sweet and nutty and has a granular and slightly dry texture, even a small amount of cornmeal makes a wonderful contribution to muffins, pancakes, and breads. Often used to prevent breads and pizza crusts from sticking to pans, it also adds a delicious flavor and texture to the crust. Stone-ground cornmeal from whole corn is the best option in terms of flavor, texture, and nutrition, but because the oil-rich germ is present in whole cornmeal, it should be refrigerated and used within three months. Degerminated cornmeal, made by grinding the corn between massive steel rollers that separate out the fiber and germ, is more shelf stable because most of the natural oils are removed in the process. But as usual, this comes at a cost in terms of valuable nutrients and flavor.

Cornmeal is available in a variety of grinds, from very fine to very coarse. In some cases, a specific grind is important to the outcome of the recipe, but in other cases it's just a matter of personal preference. It's also available in an assortment of colors, each with its own unique flavor. Whether yellow, white, blue, or red, these can be used interchangeably in recipes as long as you are open to the possibilities.

Blue cornmeal, ground from corn with deep purplish blue kernels, is pale gray but develops a lavender hue when mixed with water. Sweet and nutlike in flavor, blue cornmeal generally has a coarser, grittier texture than yellow or white cornmeal, since it is ground from flint corn, a type of corn with tough, starchy outer layers that are harder to grind. Tortillas made with blue cornmeal will be denser than those made with white or yellow corn. Blue corn contains more protein than yellow or white corn, and more of the amino acid lysine, giving it a more complete amino acid profile. It is also higher in minerals, including iron, potassium, and zinc.

High-lysine cornmeal is made from a hybrid strain of yellow corn that contains up to 70 percent more lysine than ordinary corn, along with higher levels of tryptophan, isoleucine, threonine, and other amino acids, resulting in a more complete protein profile. It was developed as a way to prevent protein deficiency among populations that depend on corn in their diets. Although not as easy to locate as cornmeal from regular yellow corn, it's worth seeking out, as it has an exceptionally delicious nutty, sweet flavor.

Red cornmeal, which can be difficult to come by, is ground from a type of flint corn that has a beautiful red color. It is similar to blue cornmeal in its sweet, intense flavor and in its nutritional profile. It can be used like any other cornmeal in baking or as a coating for fish. **White cornmeal** has a less pronounced, more delicate corn flavor. It's

considered to be essential for true Southern-style cornbread, as well as for genuine johnnycakes, a Northern specialty. **Yellow cornmeal**, rich in beta-carotene, has a deep, rich corn flavor. Use medium or coarsely ground yellow cornmeal for cornbread. Use coarsely ground for polenta or better yet, look for cornmeal expressly ground for polenta. Made from flint corn, which is harder, it yields polenta that's soft but not mushy.

Masa harina is made from corn masa, also known as *nixtamal*, a dough made by treating whole corn with alkali to improve its nutritional properties (see page 55). To make masa harina, the wet dough is dried and finely ground into a flour. Typically used for tortillas, corn chips, and tamales, masa harina provides a characteristic subtly sour flavor. Although fresh masa is ready to use and has a better flavor, masa harina is easier to store and keep on hand.

Great-tasting cornbreads can be made solely from cornmeal, or blend it with whole wheat or white flour for a lighter, softer texture. Suggested proportions vary, but three parts cornmeal to one part wheat flour is a good place to start. Fold in cooked fresh corn kernels for added sweetness and texture.

- To cook cornmeal as a breakfast cereal, use four parts water to one part cornmeal. Bring the water to a boil, then slowly pour in the cornmeal, whisking all the while to prevent clumping. Turn down the heat as low as possible, cover, and simmer for 25 to 30 minutes.

- For polenta, use 3 cups of water and about ¾ teaspoon of salt for each cup of cornmeal, which should be coarsely ground. Bring the water to a boil, add the salt, and then slowly pour in the cornmeal, whisking all the while to prevent clumping. Lower the heat to medium and continue to cook, stirring constantly, until the polenta thickens and stiffens, about 20 to 30 minutes. Spoon onto plates or onto an oiled platter and serve topped with your favorite sauce. Or transfer it to an oiled baking dish, smooth it to an even layer, and allow it to cool. To serve, cut it into slices or other shapes and bake, broil, or pan-fry.

CORNSTARCH
Gluten free

Next to wheat flour, cornstarch (known as cornflour in the United Kingdom, Australia, and New Zealand) is the second most commonly used thickener. To be transformed into cornstarch, corn kernels go through a rather extensive refining process. After the hull and germ are removed, the corn is further processed to separate out any remaining protein, resulting in pure starch that is then washed, dried, and ground into a fine powder. On account of the high level of processing cornstarch undergoes, and because it has little nutritional value, many people prefer to use arrowroot powder instead. Another good reason to choose an alternative thickener is that much of today's conventionally raised corn is genetically modified, and organic cornstarch can be difficult to come by.

Although it has a fairly neutral flavor, the taste of cornstarch is somewhat more apparent than that of arrowroot. Unlike sauces thickened with flour, those thickened with cornstarch have a smooth texture and are clear, though not as glossy as sauces made with arrowroot or tapioca. Cornstarch is an excellent thickener for dairy-based recipes, but it doesn't work in acidic liquids, nor should it be used in sauces or gravies that will be frozen and used later. Like root-based starches such as arrowroot, cornstarch thickens at lower temperatures than flour does, but if it's overcooked, it will break down, causing the sauce to become thin. For thickening, substitute cornstarch equally for arrowroot powder or potato starch; use only half the amount if substituting for flour. As with other thickeners, dissolve the cornstarch in a bit of cold water before adding it to the liquid to be thickened. Stir the mixture constantly until thickened, then lower the heat and serve as soon as possible.

From top: (1) Einkorn flour, (2) emmer farro flour, (3) Kamut khorasan wheat flour, (4) spelt flour, (5) mesquite flour

In baking, adding some cornstarch will help smooth the crust of gluten-free baked goods, and it will lighten the crumb without adding a flavor of its own.

EINKORN FLOUR
Contains gluten

Very high in protein and light amber in color, einkorn flour is ground from an ancient form of wheat, distinct from Kamut, spelt, and modern varieties of wheat. Because it has a higher proportion of gliadin to glutenin, it is unable to retain the gas bubbles created through rising, creating a slack bread dough that needs to be proofed and baked in a sided bread pan to hold its shape. It also has a low water retention capacity and while kneading, the dough will be sticky. While einkorn flour can be substituted in equal amounts for whole wheat flour in recipes, it is best used to make rustic breads where a bread with low volume is acceptable or in cookies, brownies, muffins, quick breads, and biscuits in which strong gluten is not desired. When making bread from einkorn flour, best results come from using sourdough culture as a leavening agent, as the acidity of the sourdough and longer leavening time strengthens the flour's gluten to help the bread hold its shape. The loaf will rise modestly and be somewhat compact with a dense, slightly sticky crumb and a delicious toasted nutty flavor.

Although the gluten in einkorn is distinct from modern varieties of wheat, anyone with gluten intolerance and severe allergies or sensitivity to wheat should always consult with a medical professional and be evaluated carefully before trying any new grain.

EMMER FLOUR
Contains gluten
Also known as farro, emmer is an unhybridized, ancient variety of wheat with a tetraploid genetic structure (in contrast to einkorn's diploid makeup and the hexaploid of modern wheat). It was common throughout Europe, northern Africa, and the Near East well before the early days of the Roman Empire and continues to be grown in Ethiopia and some areas of northern and central Italy, especially in Tuscany, Umbria, and areas around Rome. High in protein and with a delicious flavor reminiscent of a cross between wheat and barley, emmer is more commonly cooked in its whole, semipearled or cracked form for salads, soups, and farrotto—risotto made with farro. However, like any grain, it can also be ground into flour.

Performance-wise, emmer flour's gluten is weak, higher in proportion in gliadin than glutenin within the grain's gluten ratio, making its use and results in baking fairly similar to those of einkorn flour. Sourdough remains the best leavening agent to use with emmer flour, as the acidity of the starter and longer leavening time will help strengthen the flour's gluten. The dough will need to be held in shape within a bread pan while proofing and baking. While it will have a dense crumb, the flavor will be very good, reminiscent of a combination of roasted nuts, wheat,

and barley. Emmer flour can also be used when making cookies, brownies, muffins, quick breads, and biscuits. Adding a small amount, about 25 percent of the wheat flour called for in a recipe, can provide variety to familiar recipes.

Although its genetic structure and gluten makeup is different than that of modern wheat, anyone with gluten intolerance and severe allergies or sensitivity to wheat should always consult with a medical professional and be evaluated carefully before trying any new grain.

GARBANZO-FAVA FLOUR
Gluten free
This flour blend, made from a combination of garbanzo beans and fava beans, is a good substitute for rice flour in recipes for gluten-free baked goods, providing more volume, tenderness, and moisture. It is tan in color and its flavor is somewhat sweeter than that of rice flour. Garbanzo-fava flour has long been used in international cooking and baking, and small amounts of fava flour (2 percent or less) are often added to wheat flour in France to provide a subtle, sweet, buttery flavor and promote better rising.

Garbanzo-fava flour adds extra protein and fiber, which are often low in the flours typically used in gluten-free baking. It's usually best to use no more than 25 percent garbanzo-fava flour in a flour blend. As it provides a better flavor and lighter texture in baked goods than garbanzo flour alone, try it in muffins, pancakes, cakes, cookies, and quick breads, as well as in bread recipes. Like garbanzo flour, it can also be used as a binding agent or to thicken gravies and sauces. For best digestion of foods made with bean flour, look for products described as "micronized," "processed," "precooked," or "toasted."

GARBANZO FLOUR
Gluten free
Like the garbanzo beans, or chickpeas, from which it is ground, garbanzo flour is rich in protein and has a sweet, rich flavor. Unroasted garbanzo flour, also called besan or chana flour, is used to make

batter for the deep-fried Indian fritters called *pakoras*, a French flat bread known as *socca*, and an old Italian form of polenta called *panissa*. Roasted garbanzo flour makes it a snap to prepare falafel or hummus; just mix 1 cup of roasted garbanzo flour with ⅔ cup of cold water to equal 1½ cups of cooked, mashed garbanzo beans. This also works for other dips, spreads, and patties, and even casseroles. Either unroasted or roasted garbanzo flour can be used to thicken soups, stews, and sauces, and to bind ingredients together to make bean or grain burgers. Because it's high in protein, garbanzo flour is especially suitable as a substitute for soy flour in many recipes. In baked goods, it contributes a dry, delicate crumb. Another consideration is that bean-derived flours have a more pronounced flavor than flour ground from grain, so it's often best to use them in moderation, or in recipes that contain ingredients with stronger flavors and aromas, such as chocolate, cocoa, carob, applesauce, maple syrup, honey, and cinnamon. Since garbanzo flour contains no gluten, when making breads leavened with yeast or sourdough, it should be combined with wheat or spelt flour and should comprise no more than 25 percent of the total flour in the recipe. It can also be combined up to 25 percent with other gluten-free flours and starches, such as sorghum flour, cornstarch, and tapioca flour to make gluten-free breads. For best digestion of foods made with bean flour, look for products described as "micronized," "processed," "precooked," or "toasted."

GLUTEN FLOUR AND VITAL WHEAT GLUTEN
Contains gluten

Gluten is extracted from wheat flour in a process similar to how seitan, or "wheat meat," is made. The flour is formed into dough that's kneaded to help develop the gluten, then allowed to rest to further develop the gluten, and finally rinsed under water to separate the starch and bran from the gluten.

There are distinct differences between gluten flour and vital wheat gluten. Gluten flour is white flour with concentrated wheat gluten added to it;

it contains up to 14.5 percent protein. In contrast, vital wheat gluten is pure gluten that's been dried and ground; it contains about 75 percent protein. Adding either of these to dough will increase the amount of protein in the bread. However, since gluten is very deficient in lysine, one of the essential amino acids, it isn't a high-quality protein.

The addition of small amounts of gluten—about 5 to 10 percent of the total amount of flour for gluten flour, or 2 to 3 percent for vital wheat gluten—will help dough rise higher and more quickly, creating a lightly textured bread with a fine, chewy crumb that doesn't crumble when sliced. It is especially useful when baking with flours that contain little or no gluten, with the caveat that anyone who has gluten intolerance issues will not be able to use gluten flour or vital wheat gluten. Quick breads leavened with baking powder can also benefit from the addition of a bit of gluten flour or vital wheat gluten. It will improve the shape and texture of quick breads, but they won't necessarily rise higher.

While it may otherwise sound like a dream come true, adding gluten flour or vital wheat gluten to dough has its drawbacks. Because the dough has more gluten than normal, it requires more kneading to allow the gluten to fully develop. Gluten also imparts a distinctive flavor and chewy texture to breads that isn't universally appreciated. On top of that, breads made with extra gluten stale more quickly. But the biggest problem with using gluten flour or vital wheat gluten is that, because it is so concentrated, some people who don't usually have an adverse reaction to wheat may find breads made with gluten difficult to digest. Clearly, anyone who is allergic to wheat or gluten will also experience a problem if gluten flour is added. Accordingly, those on wheat-free or gluten-free diets shouldn't eat breads made with these products, even if the bread is otherwise free of both wheat and gluten.

Use up to 2 tablespoons of gluten flour per cup of flour in whole grain breads. Since white flour lacks the bran and germ, cup for cup it contains more gluten than whole wheat flour. Therefore, less gluten flour is needed when making breads with white flour; use up to 4 teaspoons per cup. When adding vital wheat gluten to bread dough, use up to 1½ teaspoons per cup of flour in whole grain breads and up to 1 teaspoon per cup of flour in white breads. Breads that contain bran, nuts, raisins, or seeds may need slightly more gluten flour or vital wheat gluten to compensate for the increased bulk.

KAMUT KHORASAN WHEAT FLOUR
Contains gluten

Ground from the large kernels of an ancient variety of khorasan wheat, Kamut flour lends a terrific sweet, nutty, buttery flavor and beautiful amber color to baked goods. The name Kamut is a registered trademark for this variety of wheat, which is always grown organically by virtue of its trademark requirements. Nutritionally, Kamut flour is higher in protein, minerals, and essential fatty acids than typical wheat flour. Since Kamut has a genetic makeup like durum wheat, it, too, is an excellent flour for making pasta. However, compared to modern varieties of wheat, its gluten ratio has more gliadin and less glutenin. Therefore, breads made with Kamut flour will have a denser texture than those made with conventional wheat flour. Also, as the glutenin type of gluten is weak, the dough will require a bread pan during the final proofing and baking to help maintain its structure.

Still, just a few tricks can help produce bread with a lighter (albeit still hearty), satisfying crumb, and the exceptional flavor of bread made with Kamut is definitely worth the effort. Keeping the dough moist, kneading it a few minutes longer, and allowing it to rest longer will all help create lighter baked products with Kamut flour. Accordingly, the longer leavening times involved in sourdough baking make it a perfect method for baking with Kamut flour.

Because the gluten isn't as springy as is in modern varieties of wheat, it is best to use Kamut flour for loaves that are intended to be denser or lower in overall volume. This helps minimize the volume of dough to be leavened, ensuring that loaves are as voluminous as possible. Baked goods that are intentionally lower in height, such as flat breads, crackers, cookies, pizza crusts, and pancakes, are also good candidates for using Kamut flour. The use of sprouted Kamut flour—Kamut that has been slightly sprouted, dried, and ground—provides an extra boost, with a noticeable increase in volume for breads and baked goods, along with a slightly darker, flavorful crust.

Kamut has a different genetic makeup and gluten profile than modern wheat, but it still contains gluten. While some people who are sensitive to wheat but not gluten may find they able to tolerate products made from Kamut, still, anyone with gluten intolerance and severe allergies or sensitivity to wheat should always consult with a medical professional and be evaluated carefully before trying any new grain.

KUDZU
Gluten free

Kudzu powder is made from the huge, white root of the kudzu plant. It is indigenous to Japan and China, where it grows vigorously in the mountains and is valued both as a cooking starch and as a traditional remedy for digestive disorders. Scientific research on kudzu's phytonutrients has confirmed that it has a number of positive effects on the body. However, in some parts of the southeastern United States, where it was originally planted to control soil erosion, kudzu is a noxious weed. Its vines are capable of overtaking anything—including roads, bridges, and power lines. Ironically, despite this overabundance, it is imported from Japan for use as a cooking starch and medicinal herb.

Kudzu is a remarkable thickening agent. Because the dried, pulverized powder sticks together when exposed to the slightest moisture, it's sold in small chalky-looking chunks, and is best stored in a tightly sealed jar. Like arrowroot, it has a neutral flavor, thickens quickly, and yields sauces and desserts that are smooth and transparent. As an added bonus, foods thickened with kudzu remain set after cooling, making creamy textured dairy-free pies and puddings a delicious possibility.

Before measuring kudzu, crush any chunks with the back of a spoon or in a mortar and pestle. Dissolve the kudzu powder in cold water and add it at the end of the recipe's cooking time, stirring constantly for 2 or 3 minutes until the desired thickness is achieved. Use about 1 to 1½ tablespoons per cup of liquid in sauces or soups. To create a thicker, puddinglike consistency, use 2 to 2½ tablespoons per cup of liquid.

MESQUITE FLOUR

Gluten free

Until the sixteenth century, mesquite flour was a principal food for Native Americans in what is now Mexico and the southwestern United States; they also valued the tree for many other purposes, including fuel, tools, and medicine. Today, the tree is considered infamous or renowned, depending on whom you ask. For ranchers in the southwestern United States who would prefer to see grass growing on their land to feed their cattle, the mesquite tree is a hardy, pesky, prolific plant with a very deep root system, making it hard to eradicate. However, the tree is highly respected in many parts of the world, and many cooks prefer mesquite when grilling because of the smoky sweet flavor it imparts.

Although mesquite flour slipped into oblivion for several centuries, it has recently regained its reputation as a valuable food, most notably as a gluten-free flour that can boost nutrition and flavor in flour blends. Ground from the ripened, roasted pods of the mesquite tree, this high protein flour has a sweet flavor reminiscent of molasses and mocha. Even just a bit makes a delicious statement.

To further accentuate its high protein content (11 to 17 percent), mesquite flour is a good source of lysine, an essential amino acid typically lacking in grain flour. It is also rich in minerals, namely calcium, magnesium, potassium, iron, and zinc. It derives its sweetness primarily from the simple sugar fructose, a form of sugar that's metabolized more slowly and without insulin, so it doesn't have much effect on blood sugar levels. Additionally, its high fiber content is largely from galactomannan, a soluble fiber that slows digestion. This also helps stabilize blood sugar levels.

You can use up to 25 percent mesquite flour in flour blends for baking muffins, cakes, breads, and cookies, whether with wheat flour or with other gluten-free flours. It contributes to a dry crumb. Since the flavor is strong, you may want to start with just 2 tablespoons of mesquite flour in each cup of flour in a recipe. While mesquite flour doesn't contribute any specific structural characteristics beyond fiber, its natural sweetness can boost the flavors of baked goods and dessert sauces while also providing the opportunity to cut down on sugar in the recipe or at the table. Use a couple of tablespoons in a recipe or just a sprinkle, depending on your mood. As a seasoning, it works well on protein-based foods, imparting a wonderful, sweet, smoky mesquite flavor. Sprinkle it on fish, meat, poultry, tofu, or tempeh before cooking; if using it to season beans, add it after cooking.

MILLET FLOUR

Gluten free

Baked goods made with millet flour have a mildly sweet and nutty taste, a dry, delicate, crumb, and a smooth, thin crust, as well as a slight yellow color. It is particularly important for millet flour to be freshly ground. At its prime, it has an appealing sweet flavor, but when even slightly old, it makes anything baked with it taste bitter. For optimal freshness, grind your own millet flour at home in a blender, electric coffee grinder, or flour mill. Store any unused flour in the freezer and use it as soon as possible.

You can use up to 50 percent millet flour in cookies and muffins. Combine it with whole wheat flour, brown rice flour, or a combination of brown rice flour and tapioca flour to enhance millet's sweet flavor and to balance its texture. Because it contains no gluten, it must be combined with a high proportion of wheat or spelt flour when making yeasted or sourdough breads. For best flavor and texture, limit the millet flour to ½ to ¾ cup per loaf.

NUT-BASED FLOURS
Gluten free

When ground fine as flour, nuts can be used as a thickener or a breading agent, or to replace some or all of the grain-based flour in recipes for piecrust, quick breads, pancakes, muffins, cookies, and cakes.

Raw or roasted almonds and hazelnuts are most commonly used when making nut-based flour, with both providing best results when used as a primary ingredient in a recipe for baked goods. Pecans, walnuts, and dried coconut also perform well as nut flour, although any other nut can be considered a candidate, especially when added in only small amounts. Still, each will be unique, contributing its own distinctive flavor, texture, and fat and fiber content. In general, nut-based flours contribute both protein and fiber to a recipe, enhance flavor and texture, and help soften the crust of baked goods (this is due to their fat content).

As nuts are gluten-free, when used as flour, they perform best when used in combination with other gluten-containing flour or within gluten-free baking mix formulas. Like many gluten-free baked goods, those made solely or primarily with nut-based flour depend heavily on the use of eggs to contribute volume, structure, and binding properties

Finely ground **almond flour** and **hazelnut flour** are available in specialty stores and from online merchants; these are typically produced from blanched nuts, which makes them somewhat ivory in color. For ultimate freshness, nut flour can be made at home by grinding cool, raw, or roasted nuts in a high-speed blender or, if only a small amount is needed, in an electric seed grinder or coffee grinder. The trick is to grind them enough to get a finely ground flour but not so much that you end up with a meal or nut butter. If lighter colored almond or

hazelnut flour is preferred, first blanch the nuts, allowing them to cool before grinding into flour.

For starters, experiment with replacing one-quarter to one-third of the flour called for in a recipe with nut flour to see how it turns out; then increase or decrease the amount in subsequent trials until you're happy with the results. The greater the proportion of nut flour used, the more potentially fragile the final results. Because nut flour can be heavier than wheat flour, slightly increase the quantity of leavening agents including eggs, within a recipe. Lining the baking pan with oil and parchment paper will assist with easier removal of baked goods.

As nut-based flours are high in natural fats, be sure to always store them in the refrigerator or freezer to extend freshness, ideally using them within 3 to 4 months.

OAT FLOUR
Gluten free

Baked goods with a high proportion of oat flour are especially moist and flavorful, with a cakelike, somewhat crumbly texture and firm crust. Oat flour's characteristics are primarily due to its bran, which is much higher in soluble fiber than is wheat bran. An added benefit with oat flour is that baked goods made with it remain fresher longer, thanks to its natural antioxidants. Before chemical preservatives were available, bakers often added a small amount of oats to their products to prevent them from going stale too quickly.

Although oats do not contain gluten, North American gluten-free diet associations often list it as a grain to avoid because of concern that oats may not always be adequately segregated from wheat during growing and processing. Oat flour is readily available in natural foods stores, but it can also be ground fresh at home in a home grain mill or high speed blender; 1¼ cups of rolled oats will make 1 cup of oat flour. Because oats are gluten free, don't use more than 25 percent oat flour in breads leavened with yeast or sourdough. Muffins, cakes, cookies, and pancakes can be made with up to

50 percent oat flour. Oat flour is also a good thickener in sauces, soups, and stews.

POTATO FLOUR
Gluten free

Potato flour is made from cooked potatoes that have been dried and ground. Used primarily as a thickener and binder, it yields sauces that are translucent and glossy. To thicken sauces, substitute potato flour equally for arrowroot and cornstarch, but when substituting it for flour, use only about half as much. It can also be added to cakes and cookies to provide a moist, chewy texture. In gluten-free baked goods, it will help harden the crust. Only use a very small amount of potato flour, about 1 teaspoon per cup, in flour mixes, as it has a much stronger flavor than potato starch.

POTATO STARCH
Gluten free

Rather than being made from the whole potato, as is the case with potato flour, potato starch is a fine-textured flour made from only the starch of the potato. Because it has a very bland flavor and is free of gluten, potato starch is often used in gluten-free flours and baking blends. It contributes a moist, light, and airy texture to baked goods. Use up to one-third potato starch in flour blends. Potato starch can also be used as a thickener in soup, sauces, and stews. It is unstable at high heat and shouldn't be boiled or cooked for prolonged periods of time. When using potato starch as a thickener, mix it with cold water before adding it to a hot liquid. To thicken sauces, substitute potato starch equally for arrowroot and cornstarch, but when substituting it for flour, use only about half as much.

QUINOA FLOUR
Gluten free

Baked goods made with quinoa flour have a delicate crumb, making it a nice addition to muffins and breads. It provides the same delicious, earthy, nutty flavor of cooked whole quinoa. Depending on how much is used in a recipe and what other flours it is paired with, it may lend baked goods a light yellow color, almost the color of cornbread. Quinoa flour is an effective nutrient booster, contributing high-quality, complete protein because it contains the amino acid lysine, which is usually deficient in grains. It's also high in minerals, particularly calcium, magnesium, potassium, iron, and zinc.

While the quinoa flour you purchase has a more consistent grind, you can easily grind your own in a blender, an electric coffee grinder, or better yet, a home flour mill, which makes for fresher and tastier flour; ¾ cup of whole quinoa will yield 1 cup of flour with a texture similar to that of finely ground cornmeal. Dry-roasting the flour will enhance its flavor. Because quinoa flour is gluten free, don't use more than 25 percent quinoa flour when making yeasted or sourdough breads. For best flavor and texture, use up to 30 percent quinoa flour in quick breads, cookies, and pancakes. Quinoa flour can be used to thicken sauces and gravies, too.

RICE FLOUR
Gluten free

For a long time, rice flour was the primary flour used in gluten-free baking. It has a fine, somewhat sandy texture that, in turn, creates finely textured but crumbly baked goods. Now, thanks to the increasing variety of alternative grains available, rice flour can be balanced with other gluten-free flours, such as arrowroot flour, potato starch, tapioca flour, and quinoa flour, which complement what rice flour has to offer. As a result, it's now possible to create baked goods with rice flour that have a more pleasing texture and flavor.

To compensate for rice flour's lack of gluten, xanthan gum or guar gum is typically added to help bind the dough together and provide some structure to capture the gas bubbles created by leavening agents. Because guar gum has laxative properties, xanthan gum is typically preferred. The general rule of thumb is to use about 1½ teaspoons of xanthan gum or guar gum per 2 cups of flour, but if guar

Use no more than 25 percent soy flour in quick breads, cookies, and cakes. It should be used even more sparingly in yeasted breads—no more than 10 percent of the total flour—since too much can overcondition the dough and make the bread rise too soon. When substituting soy flour for other flours, lower the oven temperature by 25°F to compensate for its tendency to brown prematurely. Save your taste buds and don't even bother trying to use it as a thickener for sauces and gravies.

SPELT FLOUR
Contains gluten

A distant cousin of modern varieties of wheat, spelt has good baking characteristics but also possesses traits that make it distinct from typical wheat flour. It has a sweeter and nuttier flavor, more protein, and a different type of gluten, and it contributes a moderate crumb. Spelt was commonly grown in the United States until 1900, when other varieties of wheat emerged that were easier to grow and harvest. However, it made a comeback in the 1980s due to emerging interest in heirloom crops and its overall terrific flavor, rustic color, and nutritional attributes.

From breads to piecrusts, spelt flour can be substituted equally for wheat flour in any recipe, providing richer flavored results. As spelt flour has higher water absorption than typical modern wheat flour, reduce the amount of liquids when substituting spelt flour for wheat flour. Start by reducing the recipe's liquids by 25 percent and add more liquid only if it seems necessary to obtain the optimal consistency of batter or dough for a particular recipe. Too much water will make the dough weak and sticky, undermining its ability to rise or, in the case of piecrusts, to roll out properly. Spelt also is lower in the gliadin fraction of the gluten protein complex, which means spelt doughs don't hold their structure as would dough made from wheat. The sponge method, preferably using a sourdough-type culture, will give the best results when making bread, particularly in regard to helping increase volume and establish a stronger structure. Kneading for less time

than one would with whole wheat flour and being careful not to overmix will also help compensate for its fragile gluten.

While whole grain spelt flour is the most flavorful and nutritious, white spelt flour, which has the bran and germ removed, is also available and can be used for lighter breads or in pastries. Sprouted spelt flour made from slightly sprouted spelt that has been dried and ground into flour provides for an extra boost in volume for breads and baked goods, along with a slightly darker crust and toasty flavor.

Although spelt is different than modern wheat, it still contains gluten. While some people who are sensitive to modern varieties of wheat may find they better tolerate spelt, anyone with gluten intolerance and severe allergies or sensitivity to wheat should always consult with a medical professional and be evaluated carefully before trying any new grain.

SPROUTED GRAIN FLOUR
Often contains gluten

The emergence of sprouted grain flour is revolutionizing whole grain flour baking, creating some of the lightest textured naturally sweet bread and baked goods. Breads that are more typically dense in nature, such as Kamut, spelt, and rye, have an astoundingly increased volume and lighter crumb when made with sprouted flour. It is especially notable when using a sourdough culture to make bread with these weaker gluten flours, as the additional acidity from the sourdough helps to further strengthen the gluten. And, even though it already contains plenty of gluten, sprouted whole wheat flour yields equally remarkable improvements in volume and crumb texture, along with enhanced flavor.

Sprouted flour from nearly any kind of grain is available. To make sprouted flour, the grains are first soaked, and allowed to sprout just until a nub begins to appear—before alpha-amylase, an enzyme naturally found in many grains that helps break down the grain's starch into more easily usable sugars, is allowed to fully develop.

Even so, enough of the alpha-amylase enzyme is present at this early stage of sprouting to add an extra boost to help bread dough rise better. The conversion of some of the grain's starch into maltose during the sprouting process also makes for a sweeter, fuller flavor and a darker color in the crust.

While technically one could make sprouted grain flour at home, companies dedicated to its production generally have the food safety measures down pat, and they have the experience to ensure the right amount of alpha-amylase to produce a good quality product. For the best of all worlds, buy the dried sprouted grain and grind it yourself at home in a flour mill for the freshest flour possible.

Sprouted flour can typically be substituted cup for cup for its regular unsprouted counterpart in recipes. Sprouted flour is also good in combination with other flours within recipes to help create lighter baked goods. Since it is much drier than flour ground directly from the grain, modify recipes by either adding more liquid ingredients or using less flour, depending on the recipe. Compensating for the inherent dryness of the sprouted flour is very important, as inadequate moisture within a recipe can lead to dry, dense baked goods; dry dough will lead to the gas bubbles created by leavenening agents becoming trapped, inhibiting their expansion that would otherwise help breads and other baked goods to properly rise. Experienced bread bakers will easily know by how the dough feels whether they'll need to add more water. When it comes to muffins and quick breads, some of it may be trial and error.

For optimal flavor, store sprouted flour in a cool but dry environment, such as a tightly sealed container in the refrigerator or freezer.

TAPIOCA FLOUR
Gluten free
Tapioca flour is a gluten-free, grain-free, slightly sweet powdered starch made from the root of the cassava plant, which is cultivated in South America and Florida. Don't confuse it with quick-cooking or pearl tapioca, which would be inappropriate for a sauce. Tapioca flour's thickening and baking properties are very similar to those of arrowroot. Sauces, glazes, and pie fillings thickened with tapioca flour will be translucent and shiny and have a thick, soft consistency when cool that's not unlike puddings made with pearl tapioca. Like arrowroot, tapioca flour is a good thickener for foods that will likely be frozen after cooking. Like other root-based thickeners, it can be added to sauces at low heat, whereas flour requires higher temperatures to thicken. To use it as a thickener, first mix it with a bit of cold water before adding it to hot liquids. Cook just until thickened; like most root-based thickeners, it isn't heat stable and doesn't stand up well to prolonged cooking. Tapioca flour adds a chewy texture, smooth, crisp crust, and elasticity or springiness to baked goods, making them lighter in texture. It can be substituted equally for arrowroot flour. Use up to 33 percent tapioca flour in flour blends.

TEFF FLOUR
Gluten free
Teff flour is ground from the seeds of a grass that is indigenous to Ethiopia and has been cultivated in the United States since the 1980s. It is a seed so small that its very name means "lost." As there would be no way to refine such small kernels, teff flour is only available in whole grain form. Most famous as the preferred grain for making injera, the spongy-textured traditional Ethiopian flat bread, teff comes with its own naturally occurring wild yeast living on the grain itself, which helps ferment the batter. In addition to being gluten free, it is also high in potassium, calcium, iron, protein, and fiber.

Brown and white teff flour are ground from two different varieties of teff, each with a distinctive flavor. Brown teff flour, the type most commonly available, gives baked goods a rich, molasseslike flavor, while white teff flour has a subtler taste. The sweet, malty flavor of teff and the light, delicate crumb it contributes to baked goods make it an interesting flour to experiment with in muffins and other quick breads, unyeasted flat breads, piecrusts, cookies, pancakes, and waffles. Substitute up to 20 percent teff flour in your favorite recipe, and if substituting for wheat flour, feel free to experiment with more. However, because of its naturally occurring wild yeast, teff should never be added to yeasted breads, as it would be too much of a good thing, overwhelming the dough with yeast.

Teff flour can also be used to make a delicious, creamy breakfast cereal. Toast ½ cup of flour in a dry pan over low heat, stirring constantly for just about 3 minutes, teasing out its malty aroma. Slowly pour in 1½ cups of water, whisking all the while, and season with salt. While continuing to stir constantly, bring to a boil, then lower the heat, cover, and simmer for 5 minutes. For an unusual twist on polenta, spread the cooked teff in an 8 by 8-inch baking dish that's been rinsed in cold water but not dried. Set aside for about an hour to cool and solidify.

TRITICALE FLOUR
Contains gluten

Triticale, a cross between wheat and rye, is slightly higher in protein than wheat and has a better amino acid balance than many other grains. Baked goods made with triticale flour have a delicious nutty, rye-like flavor. Its gluten is delicate, specifically lower in gliadin than wheat is, and it is about as tricky a flour to work with as rye, so its popularity has been limited. Although triticale flour is not commonly found in retail markets, it is available through specialty and mail order suppliers.

When making yeasted breads, use up to 50 percent triticale flour in combination with wheat flour. Since its gluten is weak, knead the dough with a gentle hand. Only allow the dough to rise once, otherwise the loaves will be overly dense. Triticale flour can generally be substituted for some or most of the wheat flour in recipes for quick breads, drop biscuits, cookies, and pancakes.

WHEAT FLOUR
Contains gluten

It's no wonder that flour made from wheat reigns in baking. With its high quality and quantity of both gliadin and glutenin, the components of the gluten protein complex, wheat can respond to all types of leavening to yield a wide variety of textures, from flaky pastries to dense, hearty breads. The different varieties of wheat flour are categorized according to the color, the season in which it's grown, the relative hardness of its kernels, and whether it is refined or a whole grain.

Wheat can be red, white, or amber, depending on the color of the bran on the outside of the kernel. Flavor varies, too, depending on the color of bran. Red wheat's outer bran layer contains somewhat bitter-tasting tannins and phenolic acid, whereas white wheat's bran contributes a sweeter flavor. Red wheat is the type most often grown in the United States. However, there is increased interest in white wheat, primarily because of its color, as breads baked with it look like they're made with white flour.

Spring wheat is planted in the spring and harvested in late summer. It is better suited for machine production of bread, where its higher gluten levels (12 to 14 percent) are up to the demands the mixers put on the dough. Bread flour, purposely formulated to be higher in gluten, is often made from spring wheat. Winter wheat is planted in fall and harvested in early summer and is preferred by artisan and home bakers for its moderate gluten content (10 to 12 percent), which allows the dough to be more easily stretched and worked by hand. Flour sold to consumers may be made from spring wheat, winter wheat, or a combination. Some brands indicate this on the package to help people choose the best flour for the intended use.

Wheat flour is also classified by the ratio of protein to starch in the endosperm—an indication of how much gluten is present and the best application for the flour. Wheat ranges from very hard to soft, and the harder the kernel, the higher the protein content and the stronger the gluten. This factor is

From top: (1) Semolina flour, (2) whole wheat flour, (3) white whole wheat flour, (4) white unbleached flour, (5) whole wheat pastry flour, (6) unbleached pastry flour

wheat, there are times and applications where only wheat will do. In those cases, it helps to understand the qualities of the different types of wheat flour and how that affects their performance so you can choose the right one for the job.

Heirloom wheat varieties are now being revived, and treasured for their distinctive flavors, color of their bran, and baking properties. One of the oldest wheat varieties in North America is **White Sonora wheat**, a soft, light-colored winter wheat with a round kernel that was introduced from Mexico into Arizona and California by Spanish missionaries. It was widely planted by the early 1800s and was a primary wheat crop in the area through the Civil War. White Sonora wheat was especially prized for its ability to make large white whole grain flour tortillas. Rich and nutty in flavor, White Sonora wheat has been used for making a dense, moist, and chewy bread in its comeback—even though its softness makes it a good choice for pastry, quick breads, and piecrust.

Hard wheat heirlooms include Turkey Red and Red Fife. **Turkey Red** wheat was a dominant hard red winter wheat in much of the Great Plains during the 1920s through to the mid 1940s and is considered a foundation for almost all American hard red winter wheat varieties. As its name implies, Turkey is most likely where Turkey Red wheat had its early origins. It was brought to the United States in 1873 by immigrants from southern Russian who had had good success with Turkey Red wheat in Ukraine after discovering it in the Crimea, just across the Black Sea from Turkey. Now in the midst of a revival as a prized heirloom, Turkey Red wheat is known for its unique, rich, complex flavor and excellent baking qualities.

Red Fife wheat, whose name gives credit not only to the color of the grain but also to the Scottish man who introduced it to Canada in the 1840s, David Alexander Fife, set the standard for wheat in Canada between 1860 and 1900 for its superior quality, and fine milling and baking properties. It is also the variety to which most of the bread wheat

most responsible for differences in baking performance among the various types of wheat flour.

Whole wheat flour is labeled as such only when the entire grain has been ground into flour. Refined white flour is usually bleached to remove its natural beta-carotene pigments. Unbleached white flour is the only type of refined flour worth buying. Not only is it less processed and free of unnecessary additives, but it also provides baked goods that taste better and are more aromatic than those made with bleached white flour.

All of these variables combine to create a wide array of wheat flours, only some of which are described below. Professional bakers have access to even more specialized types of flour, including custom blends they may request directly from flour mills and specialty baking suppliers. While it's always a good idea to explore alternatives to varieties grown in Canada at least partially owe their heritage. Red Fife's revival has been boosted by artisan bread bakers in Canada who highly value the grain's outstanding performance, flavor, and color, and the aroma of bread made from it.

Durum Flour

Durum wheat, a very hard wheat, contains the most protein and the least starch of any variety of wheat. It is available as flour in three forms: whole durum flour, durum flour, and semolina flour.

Whole durum flour is the flour of choice for making pasta, as gliadin is the more predominant component in its gluten complex, making for strong dough that can stretch into various shapes when extruded and expanded without disintegrating during cooking. (Think of the word *durable*.) Whole wheat pastas and whole wheat couscous are made from unrefined durum wheat.

Durum flour, also called fancy durum flour, is refined durum wheat that is finely ground. Unlike most refined wheat flours, durum flour is never bleached, since its buttery yellow color is generally valued in pasta and breads. The refined version of couscous is also made from refined durum wheat.

Semolina is coarsely ground refined durum wheat. Famous for its yellow hue, it is commonly added to bread to provide extra flavor and texture. It can also be used instead of cornmeal to prevent dough from sticking to surfaces during rising. Bread labeled as "semolina bread" may be made with a high percentage of finely milled durum wheat or, more frequently, it may have some coarse semolina added along with other types of wheat flour. It contributes a fine, delicate crumb and crunchy crust. High-quality dry pasta is made from finely ground semolina flour, which is higher in protein than other refined wheat flours, making it less starchy when cooked.

Hard Wheat Flours

Whole wheat flour, ground from the entire kernel— bran, endosperm, and germ—is hearty, flavorful, and significantly higher in fiber and nutrients than refined flour is. Products sold simply as whole wheat flour will be ground from hard red wheat. Although it is high in protein, its bran cuts into the gluten strands, resulting in bread that doesn't rise as much as those made with refined flour. It also contributes a coarse, large crumb. Nonetheless, whole wheat breads have a full-bodied flavor and coarser texture that make them satisfying and delicious. Whole wheat flour can also be used in quick breads, cookies, and cakes, although their texture will be denser. While their textural qualities are enjoyed by many, if you're looking for a lighter texture, use whole wheat pastry flour instead, or combine whole wheat flour with white flour.

Use less whole wheat flour when substituting for white flour. Initially, try replacing each cup of white flour with about ¾ cup of whole wheat flour to compensate for the fact that the bran in whole wheat flour absorbs liquid more readily than the bran in white flour. Alternatively, you can increase the liquid in the recipe.

Sprouted whole wheat flour is made from slightly sprouted wheat that has been dried and ground into flour. The process provides a noticeable extra boost in volume and lighter texture for breads and baked goods, a naturally sweet flavor, along with slightly darker crust.

Store whole wheat flour and sprouted whole wheat flour in the refrigerator or freezer and use it within three months, since it contains the natural oils from the wheat germ.

White whole wheat flour is a pale golden, mild-flavored flour ground from whole grain, hard white wheat. In contrast to whole wheat flour ground from hard red wheat, it produces baked goods that look as though they were made with white flour. Accordingly, when baking for people who object to the more pronounced nutty flavor and brownish color of products made with regular whole wheat flour, white wheat flour may appease without sacrificing nutrition.

Use white whole wheat flour for bread or as an all-purpose type of flour. Even though it contains the bran and germ, which are often assumed to contribute to less voluminous baking results, white whole wheat actually creates breads that rise better due to its high levels of gluten-forming proteins. And because of its subdued flavor and subtle color, white whole wheat flour works very well for cookies, quick breads, muffins, and cakes, despite being less light in texture than pastry flour. Store white whole wheat flour in the refrigerator or freezer and use it within three months, since it contains the natural oils from the wheat germ.

Bread flour, which is generally ground from hard spring wheat, is high in protein and has strong gluten that is ideal for baking light, airy loaves. Bread flour is sold in both whole wheat and refined white versions. Check the label to avoid additives such as potassium bromate, used to artificially age the flour.

Graham flour is another name for coarsely ground hard whole wheat flour. It is named after Sylvester Graham, who promoted the use of whole grain flour as a healthful practice in the 1830s to counter the growing popularity of refined white flour. It's most famous as the flour in graham crackers, but it can be used for other baked goods, too, where it lends a coarse and chewy texture.

Soft Wheat Flours

Compared to durum and hard wheat, soft wheat is higher in starch and lower in gluten (containing only 10 to 11 percent), making it most appropriate for cakes, cookies, piecrusts, quick breads, and any application where a lighter, less dense texture is desired. It's also the best type of wheat flour to use when making gravies, thickening quicker than those with more gluten. Soft wheat flours, ground primarily from winter wheat, are available in both refined and whole form.

Whole wheat pastry flour, ground from the whole kernel of soft wheat, contains the bran, germ, and endosperm. Like regular whole wheat flour, it provides more nutrients and fiber than refined pastry flour. Because it contains less gluten than regular whole wheat flour, it's less appropriate for breads

and better for lighter textured cookies, piecrusts, and quick breads and muffins leavened with baking powder or baking soda. It may take a little practice to make piecrusts with it, but once you've mastered the technique, the results are delicious, although not flaky. You might want to start by using a combination of whole wheat pastry flour and unbleached all-purpose flour.

Unbleached pastry flour, made from soft wheat with the bran and germ removed, is designed to provide light-textured pastries. However, this functionality comes at a high price in terms of nutrition. Still, it is neither bleached nor treated with chlorine gas, giving it an edge over cake flour.

Cake flour is made from soft wheat with the bran and germ removed. It is ground finer than whole wheat pastry flour and chemically bleached with chlorine gas, not just to whiten the flour, but also to make it slightly acidic so the cake will set more quickly and have a finer texture. In the interest of nutrition, whole wheat pastry flour remains a better bet. If you prefer light-colored, feathery-light baked goods, use unbleached pastry flour or a combination of whole wheat pastry flour and unbleached pastry flour. In most cases, 100 percent unbleached all-purpose flour can work satisfactorily, too.

Wheat Flour Blends

All-purpose flour is a blend of hard wheat and soft wheat. Its protein content depends on the specific brand's product specifications. True to its name, all-purpose flour works satisfactorily for breads and rolls leavened with yeast and sourdough and also performs well in cookies, cakes, muffins, and pies. If a recipe doesn't specify a particular type of flour, all-purpose flour is a safe bet. However, all-purpose flour often contains bleaching and maturing agents and dough conditioners, so read labels carefully before purchasing.

Self-rising flour is all-purpose flour with salt and baking powder added for convenience. If a recipe calls for self-rising flour, for each cup use 1 cup all-purpose flour and add 1 to 1¼ teaspoons of baking powder and ½ teaspoon of salt. Should you choose to buy self-rising flour, try to find a brand that uses aluminum-free baking powder.

WILD RICE FLOUR
Gluten free

Wild rice flour, which is ground from whole wild rice, provides a rich, hearty, nutty flavor and dry, fine crumb to pancakes, quick breads, muffins, and cookies. It can be difficult to come by, but you can easily grind your own in a blender or an electric coffee grinder. Since wild rice flour is gluten free, it needs to be blended with other flours for best baking results. Use up to 25 percent wild rice flour in flour blends. Try using it as a flavorful substitute for wheat flour when coating fish, poultry, or wild game before cooking. It can also be used to thicken gravies, stews, and sauces.

Artisanal Breads

Throughout the history of civilization, bread has provided sustenance and comfort and has symbolized community and sharing; it has even been used as currency. Discovering bread that goes far beyond the soft, smooth textured, refined white sandwich breads is life changing; it's often the entry point to realizing that food can be more than just fuel, but can hold nuances of flavor and texture that leave one feeling satisfied in every sense of the word. Not surprisingly, the recent renaissance of remarkable bread can be traced back to the natural foods movement starting in the 1960s (with its appreciation for good, wholesome ingredients that) and to today's renewed respect for traditional foods and the craftsmanship of artisanal bakers. Each country and culture has its own traditional forms and varieties of bread that have been developed over the centuries to complement its unique climate, local grain, and mode of cooking and baking. So visiting bakeries is one of the first things I do upon arrival in a new place.

The skill of the baker and the type of leavening agent used can distinguish one bread from another in terms of flavor, texture, nutrition, and overall digestibility. While saving time is a virtue in other venues, when it comes to making a loaf with exceptional flavor, structure, and texture, slowing down the process to develop the dough is essential to making artisan quality breads. Key to the process is the use of a pre-ferment—a dough that is mixed ahead of time and allowed to ferment for many hours before being used to leaven breads. Bakers will often indicate which type of leavening method they use when describing their breads; each has its own process of development into the final loaf. These include:

- The uniquely American sourdough cultures that create richly flavored, slightly tangy, pleasantly chewy breads
- The European-style wild yeast–powered levains that are still technically sourdoughs but are less tart in flavor
- The batterlike poolish pre-ferment, a slow-rising yeast starter that uses a small amount of baking yeast in its development as a boost
- The firmer-dough biga-style pre-ferment, which uses regular baking yeast rather than wild yeast in its development for use in bread dough that has a higher water content
- The unique Flemish desem starters that depend on natural enzymes in flour rather than wild yeasts for their development

NATURAL LEAVENING AGENTS

Sourdough breads, also known as naturally leavened breads, depend on the interaction of microorganisms ever present in our natural environment. Considered the oldest form of leavening agent, a **sourdough culture** or **starter** is a mixture of flour and water that has been cultured from a variety of wild yeasts and bacteria found naturally in the air as well as on the grain and the flour itself. These various strains of wild yeasts in sourdough culture are predominantly of the species *Saccharomyces exiguus*.

In the process of making sourdough bread, a pre-prepared starter culture is added to flour, water, and salt to make dough that is allowed to ferment and rise for several hours before baking. Because the wild yeasts and lactobacillus bacteria vary according to the environment in which the bread is made, sourdough bread made within each bakery and household will truly be unique. In a well-known example, the bacteria found exclusively in San Francisco, conveniently called *Lactobacillus sanfrancisco*, is responsible for the distinctive sour flavor and the crust that's even thicker than can be found in sourdough breads made from other cultures around the country.

The enhanced depth and complexity of flavors of sourdough breads occur when lactobacilli ("friendly" bacteria originating in the environment that grow in the dough along with the wild yeast) are given enough time to do their magic. The longer the dough ferments during its rising time, the more opportunity for the natural lactobacillus bacteria within the environment to come into play, creating both lactic acid and acetic acid as byproducts as they feed off sugars in the dough. As the acids slowly accumulate, their flavor permeates the dough. While lactic acid produces rich, sweet, mellow flavors, acetic acid is responsible for a tart tang that increases with time. The increased acidity of the dough also improves overall digestibility of the final loaf, including slower and more sustained absorption of nutrients.

The extended rising time also allows for better availability of minerals, such as magnesium, iron, copper, and zinc. Otherwise bound by phytic acid, a substance found in the bran layers of whole grains, these minerals are released when phytic acid is broken down as the dough ferments. Although the fermentation process for yeasted bread can also help break down some of the phytic acid, the longer fermentation time required by naturally leavened breads more fully liberates the minerals and makes them available to the body.

Baking yeast is also often included as an ingredient in sourdough breads purchased from a bakery. Even though baking yeast is not necessary to make sourdough, some bakers add a small amount to reduce rising time, lighten the texture of the bread, and create more consistent flavor results. However, since baking yeast grows best in neutral or alkaline dough, the natural bacteria, which require a more acidic environment, are not given the full opportunity to do their work within the bread dough, reducing some complexity of flavor. Shelf life will also be affected. Since the acidic conditions in the dough help hinder mold growth and staling, yeast-assisted sourdough bread won't last as long.

A starter needs to be refreshed every seven days to keep it active. Additionally, the starter should be always be refreshed the night before you plan to use the sourdough culture in baking. At least 1 cup of starter should always be kept on hand to ensure starter's viability is maintained. If, between feedings of the culture, a dark liquid with an alcohol-like aroma appears at the top, looking like it has separated from the thicker culture below it, just stir the water back into the culture.

It is a good likelihood that in the process of keeping your starter refreshed you will accumulate more starter than you use. Just give some of it to a friend to let them try sourdough baking or discard what you don't need.

The basic sourdough starter replenishing formula is to add 1 to 1½ parts water to 2 parts starter and 2 parts flour. For example:

- 1 cup sourdough starter
- ½ to ¾ cup water
- 1 cup organic whole wheat bread flour

Transfer the sourdough starter to a mixing bowl and add in the water, mixing well. Add in the flour, mixing well again to create a somewhat thick batter consistency. Wash and dry the starter jar. Then put the starter back into the jar. Cover the mouth of the jar with a damp cloth and let the starter sit on the kitchen counter at room temperature for 5 to 7 hours, or overnight if you are baking the next morning. Remove the amount of starter you need for baking and return the starter to the refrigerator until it is time to replenish it again.

Desem is a fermented culture with traditional Flemish origins. It is created from the interaction of organisms and enzymes that naturally exist in the whole wheat flour itself; this is in contrast to relying on wild airborne yeasts and bacteria as in classic sourdough and similar wild yeast–created cultures. The culture development begins with a ball of dough made from whole wheat flour and water that is buried in more flour under cool temperature conditions for five days, being refreshed and kneaded daily with additional flour and water. It is then transferred to a covered crock, and the daily "feeding" and kneading are continued through a further week, at which time the desem starter is ready to use. Three-fourths of the desem is removed the day before baking to be used as a pre-ferment for making bread. The remaining desem is stored in the crock under cool conditions and kept active with twice weekly refreshing. Although the process and temperature conditions necessary for creating and keeping the desem are a bigger commitment than many people have the opportunity or time to invest, fortunately several artisan bakeries specialize in producing desem-based breads; they generally indicate this is the case on their labeling and product information. Desem bread has a delicious, complex, subtly sweet rather than tangy flavor and light texture.

Modern baking of yeast-leavened breads has its roots in antiquity. Around 300 BCE, Egyptian bakers made bread by combining the yeasty froth from beer with flour and water and allowing the dough to ferment. Even through the nineteenth century, breweries were the source for packaged cakes of yeast made from starch, water, and the yeast skimmed off the top of the beer-brewing vats. Modern-day **baking yeast** is derived from a pure culture of a specific strain of yeast (*Saccharomyces cerevisiae*, meaning "brewer's sugar fungus") that is grown in large fermentation vessels and fed with molasses supplemented with nitrogen, phosphate, vitamins, and minerals. The yeast broth is then concentrated in a centrifuge to create a creamy yeast,

and from there it is made into three types of baking yeast: cake yeast, active dry yeast, and instant yeast. These differ primarily in duration of shelf life and ease of use, and choosing between them is mostly a matter of personal preference. They can easily be substituted for one another as follows: 0.6 ounce cake yeast = 0.25 ounce (2¼ teaspoons) active dry yeast = 2 teaspoons instant yeast.

In bread machines, both cake yeast and active dry yeast can be used in regular cycles, but not in cycles of less than an hour. Instant yeast can be used in cycles of any length. Yeast specially labeled for use in bread machines is essentially instant yeast with some ascorbic acid added to help the dough stretch easily and enhance volume and structure in the final loaf. Nutritional yeast and brewer's yeast cannot be substituted for baker's yeast. Used for their nutritional value rather than for leavening, both of these are inactivated forms of yeast.

Cake yeast, also known as compressed yeast, is made by filtering cream yeast to remove water and further concentrate the yeast. Used by many commercial bakers, cake yeast is sold for home use in the form of small squares wrapped in foil. Since it is fresh and not dried, cake yeast is ready to use without having to do anything to activate the yeast cells beyond dissolving it in warm liquid (90°F to 95°F) before baking. On the other hand, it is more perishable, requiring constant refrigeration. It must be used within ten to fourteen days, or by the date indicated on the package. It can also be frozen for up to three months.

Active dry yeast was developed during World War II to provide a low-moisture product with a longer shelf life. Going a step beyond cake yeast, active dry yeast is dried at controlled temperatures to further reduce its moisture content, making it less perishable than cake yeast. Although it need not be refrigerated, it will keep longer if stored at cool temperatures in an airtight container: three months in the refrigerator or up to six months in the freezer. To give the yeast a good jump-start, it must be dissolved in lukewarm water (105°F to 115°F) before use, a process known as proofing.

Instant yeast, sometimes referred to as rapid-rising yeast, is a special strain of yeast developed in the late 1960s, and it's also processed with an improved drying method. Not only does it have more viable yeast cells than active dry yeast, but it can also be added directly to flour without first being proofed in water. However, do avoid combining it with cold liquids and even cold dry ingredients. Another advantage of instant yeast is its long shelf life—one to two years—thanks in part to its protective vacuum packaging. Still, once the package is opened, any unused instant yeast should be refrigerated and used within one week or frozen for up to three months.

CHEMICAL LEAVENING AGENTS

Baking soda, ammonium carbonate, ammonium bicarbonate, and baking powder are all chemical leavening agents. Although the word *chemical* may sound disconcerting, it merely describes the process that takes place when a leavening agent is mixed with wet ingredients and reacts to create gas, typically carbon dioxide. The bubbles of gas are trapped in the dough or batter, and during baking they expand, causing the dough to rise. The optimal reaction and rise depends on a proper proportion of acidic to alkaline ingredients.

Baking soda (sodium bicarbonate) is the most common chemical leavening agent. Being an alkaline substance, it is the only chemical leavening agent needed when the batter includes acidic ingredients such as sour milk, buttermilk, sour cream, yogurt, vinegar, honey, barley malt, molasses, rice syrup, lemon juice, or fruit juice.

Baking powder is a combination of an alkali (baking soda) and one or two acids (such as cream of tartar, calcium phosphate, or sodium aluminum sulfate), along with an inert filler (such as cornstarch or calcium carbonate), which serves as a buffer to prevent the alkaline and acid substances from reacting with one another during storage. Since baking powder is a properly proportioned blend of alkaline and acidic ingredients, baking powder can be used in recipes that don't contain acidic ingredients.

Originally, baking powder was single-acting, meaning it reacted as soon as it was moistened—more often than not before the pan even made it into the oven. These days, most baking powder is double-acting, reacting twice to give off carbon dioxide—first when moistened during mixing, and then a second time when heated. Beyond that, the primary distinction between types of baking powder is whether they contain aluminum compounds.

Products that contain sodium aluminum sulfate as an acid release most of the carbon dioxide gas when the product is heated, not just moistened, making it less critical to get baked goods into the oven as quickly as possible. However, if too much is used it can create a bitter aftertaste. On the other hand, baking powders that contain monocalcium phosphate or cream of tartar react very quickly, with most of the reaction happening when the baking powder is moistened.

Although there are some differences in how the products may work, the bigger issue has been whether using products with aluminum compounds is linked in some way to Alzheimer's disease. Whether this disease or others can be caused by accumulation of aluminum remains controversial. Until the verdict is in, nonaluminum baking powder remains a good option, requiring only that you get baked goods into the oven quickly.

Low-sodium baking powders are made with potassium bicarbonate instead of sodium bicarbonate (baking soda) to reduce the amount of sodium in baked goods. For best results, use one and a half to two times more low-sodium baking powder than the amount of regular baking powder called for. Another way to reduce sodium, unless your doctor recommends against it, is to use regular baking powder but cut back on the amount of salt in the recipe.

Pasta and Noodles

With its rainbow of colors and variety of shapes and textures, pasta provides an option to fit any whim and enhance any meal, whether it's topped with a sauce, tossed into soup, or served on the side. Though there are a few exceptions, most varieties fit into two main categories—Italian-inspired pastas and Asian noodles—and many are available both fresh and dried. Within these broad groupings, pastas can be further distinguished by type of flour used, shape, and whether they have added ingredients for color and flavor. No matter which kind you choose, all pasta is quick and easy to cook, providing the perfect base for a meal in minutes.

A Healthy Choice

Cooked just to al dente, pasta is metabolized slowly, thanks to its unique combination of starches and proteins, and as a result, it helps maintain steady blood sugar levels. Among the foods rich in complex carbohydrates, it's one of the most easily digested, explaining why it's often a favorite food of athletes; it's one of the most nutritious ways to help restore depleted muscle glycogen.

Although most people assume pasta is only made from wheat, that's far from the case. Until recently, the predominant grain grown in a region often dictated what the local pasta was made from and how it was made. Over the millennia, pasta has been made from everything from rice to buckwheat, including many now uncommon varieties of wheat. This was strikingly illustrated in 2005, when archaeologists found the oldest recognizable evidence of pasta to date, a four-thousand-year-old container of Chinese noodles made from millet. These days, the selection of pasta has expanded to include versions made from corn, quinoa, and even bean flours. Not only do these serve to accommodate wheat-free and gluten-free diets, they also provide even more variety in flavor, texture, and nutrition for anyone who loves pasta. And for visual interest, various coloring agents may be added, from pureed vegetables, herbs, and spices to squid ink, creating striking green, golden, red, and even black pastas.

For optimal flavor, texture, and nutrition, choose pasta made from whole grain flour, containing all the nutrients and fiber in the whole grain. When it comes to taste and texture, whole grain pasta contributes a delicious nutty flavor enhanced with the unique character of the grain from which it was made; a pleasantly chewy, satisfying texture; and shades ranging from tan to medium brown, all helping to enhance the overall experience of a meal.

The next best choice in terms of nutrition is pasta made from a blend of whole grain flour and refined flour (usually wheat). Although it has less fiber and fewer vitamins and minerals than 100 percent whole grain varieties, it offers a good compromise, having a lighter texture while still containing more of the flavor and nutrients of the whole grain. A blended flour base also allows pastas to be made using grains (such as quinoa) and beans (such as pinto beans and soybeans) that couldn't be made into pasta on their own.

Fresh or dried pasta made from refined flour is a distant third choice, getting most of its nutrients from those added back into the flour during enrichment. Remember, enrichment only replaces five of the nutrients depleted during refinement of the flour, even though levels of up to thirty nutrients are significantly diminished.

Fresh Pasta and Noodles

Like dried pasta, fresh pasta comes in many shapes, but the most common are ribbon shapes rolled out by hand or in a pasta machine. Unique shapes formed by hand are also available, often as specialties of a given region or pasta producer. Stuffed pasta varieties are made by encasing a vegetable, cheese, or meat filling seasoned with a variety of herbs and spices within squares or other shapes cut from sheets of pasta. With its wide range of imaginative and inspired flavors, colors, and fillings, fresh artisanal pasta can be savored with all the senses.

At its best, fresh pasta is tender, delicate, and flavorful, needing only a light sauce or broth as accompaniment. Most familiar are Italian-inspired fresh

pastas made from wheat. Since fresh pasta made with 100 percent semolina as used in good-quality, store-bought fresh pasta would be too difficult to roll out by hand or in many home pasta machines, homemade versions usually use unbleached all-purpose flour and eggs, sometimes with semolina flour added to provide more strength to the dough. The use of eggs makes for dough that is softer, more elastic, and easier to handle. Some of fresh pasta's amber color and subtle flavor can be attributed to the eggs, which also provide extra nutrients.

A wide variety of freshly made Asian noodles are also available, including Chinese wheat noodles made with or without egg, Southeast Asian rice noodles, and Japanese buckwheat soba and wheat-based udon. Fresh Asian noodles made with wheat use soft wheat flour, so they cook up softer than fresh pasta made with any amount of sturdy semolina. Most soba is also made with some wheat flour to increase strength and elasticity, making it more resilient during cooking.

When handmade with attention to detail and cooked the day it is prepared, fresh pasta is well worth seeking out. Think of gnocchi that melts in your mouth, chilled soba served with the simplest of dipping sauces to further spotlight its exceptional flavor, and heavenly fettuccine so soft and flavorful it takes your breath away. Outside of making it fresh at home, to find such high-caliber fresh pasta you'll likely need to go to a specialty market that makes its own pasta daily or to a small restaurant devoted to the craft of producing fresh handmade pasta.

Because of its high moisture content, fresh pasta is very perishable. To sell it beyond its usual two-day shelf life, many manufacturers steam-pasteurize the pasta and pack it on trays enveloped with plastic barrier films to minimize spoilage. Many manufacturers further treat their fresh pasta using a packaging process in which oxygen present within the package is displaced by a high concentration of carbon dioxide, which helps control growth of microorganisms. The use of specialized oxygen-scavenging packaging materials can further extend shelf life. Depending

The Shape of Things

Ever wonder why the shapes of pasta are so varied? Aesthetics has something to do with it, but the primary reason is that the different shapes have different properties in terms of retaining heat, absorbing liquids, and holding sauces.

Shape	Example	How to Use
Strands: long cylinders with or without a hollow center	angel hair (capelli d'angelo), bucatini, capellini, cellophane noodles, soba, somen, spaghetti, vermicelli	Italian varieties: Best with finely grated cheese and smooth, not-too-chunky tomato-based sauces that are intended to coat or cling to the pasta. Also good for tossing with olive oil or butter and seasonings. Asian varieties: Use in soups, salads, and side dishes, or in stir-fries with a sauce, dressing, or light broth.
Ribbons: flat strips	fettuccine, kluski, lasagna, lasagnette, linguine, mafalda, pappardelle, rice sticks, tagliatelle, trenette, udon	Italian varieties: Best with pesto, creamy or béchamel sauces, or rich ragout-type sauces. Dried ribbon pasta can stand up to thicker, heavier sauces while fresh versions call for lighter toppings. Asian varieties: Use like Asian strands (see above).
Tubular: hollow shapes	cannelloni, elbow macaroni, maccheroni, manicotti, mostaccioli, penne, penne rigate, rigatoni, trenette, trenne, ziti	Best with chunky vegetable and meat sauces, or thick cheese sauces that will cling to the pasta and be trapped in the bends and crevices. Match smaller shapes with sauces with more finely chopped ingredients. Also a good choice for casseroles and pasta salads. Larger versions can be stuffed and baked.
Novelty shapes	conchiglie (shells), farfalle (bowties), fusilli, gnocchi, orechiette, radiatore, rotelle, rotini, ruote	Use like tubular pasta.
Tiny soup shapes	alfabeto, ditali, fregola, orzo, stelline (stars), wonton noodles	Use sparingly in soups and stews to thicken and contribute texture, using larger shapes in thick soups and smaller shapes in broth-based soups.
Stuffed fresh pasta	cannelloni, cappelletti, mezzaluna, ravioli, ravioloni, tortellini, tortelloni	Traditionally, the shape of a given stuffed pasta was based on the filling, but these days anything goes!

on the product and the specific technology used to treat and pack the pasta after manufacture, the shelf life of fresh pasta can be extended to as much as 120 days. Although pasta treated as such can be labeled as "all natural" and may contain no preservatives or additives, it stretches the definition of the term "fresh." Unfortunately, flavor and texture can be adversely affected in the process, too, making the final result thick, heavy, and rubbery—and an unpleasant eating experience—in which case dried pasta is a better option.

Alternatively, all types of fresh pasta can be purchased frozen, which turns out to be the best way to extend the shelf life of fresh pasta. Unlike pasteurization, flash-freezing can preserve the flavor and texture of fresh pasta. Another advantage is that frozen pastas generally don't have added preservatives, such as sorbic acid and potassium sorbate, or stabilizers, which may be added to the fillings of refrigerated stuffed pastas.

HOW TO COOK FRESH PASTA AND NOODLES

Plan on cooking about 4 ounces of fresh pasta for a 1-cup cooked serving. Add the pasta to a generous amount of salted boiling water, and cook for the amount of time recommended on the package. In general, fresh unstuffed pasta cooks within 3 minutes, whereas it can take up to 5 minutes until the edges of stuffed pastas are al dente. Uncooked fresh pasta should be refrigerated and used within three days or by the date indicated on the package. Stored in an airtight container, leftover cooked fresh pasta can be stored in the refrigerator for up to three days or in the freezer for up to a month.

Fresh pasta that has been frozen should be cooked without thawing in order to retain its integrity and texture. This adds a couple of minutes to the cooking time required for fresh pasta.

When it comes to cooking fresh Asian noodles, cooking time varies, depending on the specific noodle and the type of flour used in its manufacture. Cooking time can run from 1 to 3 minutes for fresh

Chinese egg noodles and 2 to 4 minutes for Chinese wheat noodles, depending on size and thickness. Alternatively, these fresh noodle varieties can also be added directly to soups without precooking. Fresh soba and udon cooking time can take between 1 and 4 minutes, again depending on size and thickness. An additional step of rinsing Chinese wheat noodles, soba, and udon in cold water after cooking to stop cooking and remove excess starch is recommended. On the other hand, fresh rice noodles simply need a brief soak in hot or boiling water to soften them up enough that they are ready to eat.

Italian-Style Dried Pasta

The best wheat-based dried pastas are made from flour ground from durum wheat, which includes whole durum flour, refined durum flour, and semolina. Particularly high in protein, durum flour makes sturdy dough that enables pasta to both stretch and expand without disintegrating during

From top left: (1) Kamut khorasan wheat spirals, (2) einkorn linguine, (3) farro penne, (4) spelt ribbons

127

cooking. Pasta made with durum wheat is a light amber color, and its cooking water should look fairly clear, not starchy.

Using good-quality flour is not enough to make great pasta. It also takes a great deal of skill and the right type of equipment. Because durum flour is high in gliadin, the type of gluten that makes for a stretchable though strong dough, it is difficult to knead into a smooth, elastic dough and most of the manufacturing processes are done by machine rather than by hand. The dough is generally rolled into sheets, which are then cut into strands or shaped mechanically (extruded) by being forced through dies, metal molds designed to produce various shapes, sizes, and patterns.

The speed at which the dough is squeezed through the die is very important. If processed too fast, as is often the case in factories geared toward efficiency rather than quality, the excess heat generated affects the wheat and has negative impacts on flavor, quality, and nutrient levels. Even the composition of the die makes a difference. The best shaped pastas are extruded through bronze dies that produce pasta with a rough, porous surface, which will better capture sauces. In contrast, pastas with a smooth, polished look are extruded through Teflon dies. Although Teflon is a longer lasting material and also allows dough to flow more easily through the die, Teflon's effect on pasta is similar to what it does to pans: sauces don't tend to stick to the pasta.

Dried ribbon pastas, such as fettuccine, linguine, lasagne, and egg noodles, are more tender and flavorful if made from dough that is rolled and cut (laminated) rather than extruded. In the lamination process, once the dough is mixed and kneaded it goes through a series of rollers until it reaches the appropriate thickness. The long, continuous sheets are then cut as they pass through a series of knives. Although it is a more time-consuming and intricate process, the extra effort makes for firmer pasta with better texture and taste.

Drying time and temperature also affect flavor. Pasta dries from the inside out. If dried too fast,

it will become brittle; if dried too slowly, it could sour. At home, drying is accomplished by hanging fresh pasta on special drying racks (or sometimes on the backs of kitchen chairs!) for several hours, until it's very dry. The goal is to lower the moisture content, which is initially about 60 percent, down to 12.5 percent, so that it can be stored for a long time under normal conditions. The best commercial dried pasta is dried at low temperatures with circulating air. Drying time may be as long as fifty hours, depending on the type of pasta.

These days, Italian-style pastas are made from a wide range of ingredients beyond durum wheat. There are gluten-free options based on rice, corn, quinoa, or bean flour, as well as pastas made from heritage forms of wheat, including Kamut, spelt, einkorn, and farro, and selections made from a combination of sprouted grains and beans. And sometimes the flavor and nutrition of durum wheat pastas are enhanced by the addition of unconventional flours, such as Jerusalem artichoke flour.

Pasta made from durum wheat is often considered to be superior because of its texture and ability to cook al dente, whereas many alternative types of pasta have tended to be stickier or more fragile. However, pastas made from other types of flour have improved significantly over the years. Better manufacturing techniques and refinement of cooking methods allow some of these pastas to rival durum-based varieties. Without gluten to bind them, many gluten-free pastas are made by cooking the starch before it is extruded; this allows the starch structure to hold the pasta together.

Even if you aren't on a gluten-free or wheat-restricted diet, it's worthwhile to explore the new generation of alternative pastas. They provide interesting variety in terms of appearance, taste, and texture. Plus, eating a wider variety of grains and grain products provides more well-rounded nutrition.

BEAN PASTAS

Bean pastas (made from black beans, white beans, lentils, or garbanzos) may at first seem hard to comprehend, but they've actually been made for centuries in Asia in the form of cellophane noodles made from mung beans. Nutritionally, the Italian-style bean pastas have a lot going for them. The beneficial fiber, protein, iron, magnesium, zinc, and folate in beans make for a better nutritional profile than that of other pastas. While some brands are made entirely from bean flour, most use a blend of bean flour with corn, wheat, or other types of flour.

CORN PASTA

Corn pasta is available in several forms and shapes, including spaghetti, rotini, and elbows. Made from a blend of refined corn flours, it has a rich natural corn flavor that is nicely complemented by cheese and black, pinto, or kidney beans. In addition to plain corn pasta, look for corn combined with quinoa flour and for colorful corn pasta made with dried vegetable powders. Corn pasta contains about half the amount of protein and less vitamins and minerals than pasta made from durum wheat. Since corn pasta doesn't have the benefit of gluten to help it keep its shape, it is particularly important to avoid overcooking.

EINKORN PASTA

Einkorn pasta is made from what is considered the first cultivated form of wheat, with a history of about ten thousand years. Einkorn's slightly sweet, complex and nutty flavor and great texture makes for a uniquely delicious whole grain pasta. It is also high in protein and antioxidants, most notably lutein and zeaxanthin, which accounts for its somewhat brownish orange color.

Einkorn contains gluten, but as its genetic structure is very different than that of modern varieties of wheat, some people who are sensitive to common wheat may find they can better tolerate einkorn pasta. Still, anyone with gluten intolerance and severe allergies or sensitivity to wheat should always consult with a medical professional and be evaluated carefully before trying any new grain

FARRO PASTA

Farro (emmer) pasta is made from an ancient type of wheat that is in the same class of hexaploid wheat as Kamut and durum wheat; all these are noted for their high protein and overall dough strength. Most commonly produced in Italy, where farro is still cultivated, this brown whole grain pasta has an excellent wheat/barley flavor and light texture. It is recommended to refrain from stirring the pasta during the first minute of cooking, as farro pasta is more fragile than its durum flour counterparts.

Because it is distinct from modern hybridized wheat and is lower in gluten, some individuals who are sensitive to common wheat find that they can better tolerate farro. Nevertheless, anyone with gluten intolerance and severe allergies or sensitivity to wheat should always consult with a medical professional and be evaluated carefully before trying any new grain.

JERUSALEM ARTICHOKE PASTA

Jerusalem artichoke pasta is made from a blend of durum wheat flour and flour made from dried Jerusalem artichokes. This root vegetable in the sunflower family looks like a knobby potato and is more typically cooked as a vegetable. In pasta, it contributes a somewhat nutty and sweet flavor, a lighter texture, and a lower level of carbohydrates. Up to 80 percent of the carbohydrate in Jerusalem artichokes is in the form of inulin, which isn't broken down in the digestive system by the enzymes that normally help digest starch. To the extent that it is digested, bacteria in the colon do the job. As a result, it functions more like fiber and has a stabilizing effect on blood sugar.

KAMUT KHORASAN WHEAT PASTA

Kamut pasta is an exceptionally good whole grain pasta with a golden color, rich, buttery flavor and great texture. Kamut, a registered trademark for an ancient variety of khorasan wheat, is in the same tetraploid class of hard wheat varieties as farro and durum wheat. In addition to its high protein content, the gliadin component of gluten, which produces a stronger dough, is predominant, making it a perfect grain for pasta. There's a shape of Kamut pasta available suitable for any recipe, from salads to soups to entrées. Kamut pasta also freezes well, retaining its cooked texture. Nutritionally, it is higher in protein, minerals, and essential fatty acids than are typical wheat-based pastas. Kamut contains gluten, but as it is distinct from modern-day varieties of wheat, some people who are sensitive to common wheat may find they can better tolerate Kamut pasta. Still, anyone with gluten intolerance and severe allergies or sensitivity to wheat should always consult with a medical professional and be evaluated carefully before trying any new grain.

QUINOA PASTA

Quinoa pasta is always made by combining quinoa flour with another type of grain flour, such as corn, rice, or wheat. Along with contributing a delicious, unique nutty flavor and lighter texture, quinoa flour also makes the pasta higher in protein and minerals.

RICE PASTA

Rice pasta, once heavy-textured and starchy, has improved a lot over the years and now looks and cooks up like traditional wheat-based pastas. Not to be confused with Asian rice noodles, these pastas are gluten-free versions of fettuccine, penne, elbow macaroni, and other Italian-style pastas. One reason they're better these days is because they incorporate parboiled white rice flour, which lends the pasta a drier, less sticky texture. To make this type of rice flour, manufacturers start with brown rice that is soaked in warm water, steamed, and dried before it is milled into white rice and then ground into flour, a process that retains more nutrients. Excellent brown rice pasta is also available, made in the same fashion. It is light brown and has a subtle nutty flavor.

RYE PASTA

Rye pasta made entirely from rye flour is dark brown and has a deep, rich flavor reminiscent of pumpernickel bread. It is particularly good with mild-flavored ingredients or as a side dish alongside salmon or cooked beans, especially white beans or garbanzo beans. It's a nutritional dynamo, especially because it's an excellent source of soluble fiber, which provides a sensation of fullness sooner, stabilizes blood sugar levels, and helps decrease absorption of cholesterol. If made from whole grain rye flour, it also contains lignans, which can help reduce the risk of cancer.

SPELT PASTA

Spelt pasta, made from a distant relative of modern-day wheat, has a somewhat sweeter, nuttier flavor that is equally wonderful whether it's served with a sauce, in a dish, or on its own. It's available in both whole grain and refined forms, and either can be used in any recipe that calls for wheat pasta. It is higher in protein than traditional pasta and considered very easy to digest. While some people who are sensitive to modern varieties of wheat may find they better tolerate spelt, anyone with gluten intolerance and severe allergies or sensitivity to wheat should always consult with a medical professional and be evaluated carefully before trying any new grain.

SPROUTED GRAIN PASTAS

Sprouted grain pasta is usually made from a combination of grains and beans that are sprouted then dried and ground into flour. It is higher in protein than most pastas, and the sprouting process makes the minerals more readily absorbed. These pastas are also high in fiber, making them very filling. The conversion of some of the grains' starch into maltose during the sprouting process also gives the pasta a sweeter taste and a darker color. To avoid stickiness, sprouted grain pasta must be rinsed before serving. Because their flavors are stronger than those of most pastas, sprouted grain pastas are best used in conjunction with mild-flavored ingredients and dishes.

Asian Noodles

Although rice has long been synonymous with Asian cuisine, noodles have been an equally key component. Used in soups, salads, stir-fries, and braised dishes, noodles have been highly esteemed over the centuries, and these days they're also prized as a convenient and healthy fast food and snack. Asian noodles look somewhat like Italian strand and ribbon pastas, and in most cases the two could be used interchangeably. However, there are some important distinctions between the two, mostly due to the types of flour used to make Asian noodles.

In contrast to the firm Italian pastas made from durum wheat flour, most wheat-based Asian noodles are softer and more porous because they're made with soft wheat, or with hard wheat that contains less gluten. Other Asian noodles are made with rice flour, buckwheat flour, or a variety of vegetable starches, lending them remarkable flavors and textures. As none of these contains gluten, making noodles from them requires different techniques, and many of them are cooked differently, too. For example, many varieties of Asian noodles require presoaking before cooking. Others, including soba, somen, and udon, must be rinsed with cold water after cooking to remove excess starch.

Like Italian-style pastas, Asian noodles come in a wide variety of colors, from translucent to white, green, or brown. Because they're made from a wider variety of grains, they vary in flavor, too. Many have rich, distinctive flavors, while others are neutral, allowing them to absorb the flavor of the foods they're cooked with. All of this variety makes exploring the world of Asian noodles an especially fun experience.

CELLOPHANE NOODLES

Also known as bean thread noodles and glass noodles, cellophane noodles are very thin, translucent noodles made from mung bean starch and water. Before packaging, they are boiled, then dried; then they're soaked in water, shaped into bundles, and

From top: (1) Harusame, (2) cellophane noodles, (3) ramen, (4) hiyamugi, (5) kuzukiri, (6) rice sticks, (7) buckwheat soba, (8) yomogi soba, (9) somen, (10) whole wheat udon

dried again. They have a slippery, springy, chewy texture and are virtually tasteless until they absorb flavors from other foods. Nutritionally, they are a good source of iron, and because they are primarily starch, they're easy to digest. Cellophane noodles are popular in many Southeast Asian countries and are especially prized as a key ingredient for refreshing summer salads. They shouldn't actually be cooked; rather, soak them in hot but not boiling water just until softened, about 5 to 15 minutes. Loosen and separate the noodles, then rinse and drain them before adding them to a dish. They may benefit from cooking a few minutes in a dish, but they'll become gelatinous if cooked too long. They are quite long and have a tendency to clump together, so you may wish to cut them into more manageable lengths with clean kitchen scissors. Since cellophane noodles can expand up to three times in volume, start with a small amount the first time you use them.

CHINESE EGG NOODLES

Made from refined hard wheat flour, eggs, and water, the golden yellow strands of Chinese egg noodles come in various round thicknesses or flat widths. Soft, silky fresh Chinese egg noodles are shaped into nests and sold refrigerated; dried, they're packaged in tight, rectangular bundles. While some of their yellow color can be attributed to the egg yolks, most of it is from the action of kansui, an alkaline solution made from potassium carbonate or sodium carbonate, on the natural pigments in wheat. Kansui also helps improve the elasticity of the noodles and contributes to their characteristic flavor. If the noodles are a very bright yellow, it's likely that artificial color was used.

Use Chinese egg noodles in soups or serve them with a sauce; cold cooked egg noodles are especially good with a soy-sesame dressing. Depending on size, cooking time is 1 to 3 minutes for fresh noodles and 3 to 6 minutes for dried. Fresh Chinese egg noodles can be added directly to soups, whereas dried noodles should be precooked (actually slightly undercooked).

CHINESE WHEAT NOODLES

These are round or flat, cream to yellowish beige strands of various thicknesses and widths. Fresh Chinese wheat noodles are shaped into nests and sold refrigerated; dried, they're packed in tight, rectangular bundles. Made from hard wheat, water, kansui (an alkaline solution made from potassium carbonate or sodium carbonate), and salt, they can be used in soups and stir-fries or served with a sauce. Depending on size, cooking time is 2 to 4 minutes for fresh noodles and 4 to 7 minutes for dried. After cooking, rinse the noodles in cold water and drain before using in a recipe. Fresh noodles can be added directly to soups, whereas dried noodles should be precooked (slightly undercooked).

HARUSAME

These translucent five- to seven-inch-long Japanese noodles look like cellophane noodles, but they may be made from rice starch, potato starch, mung bean starch, or soybean starch. Like cellophane noodles, they are not boiled but rather are soaked in hot water just until softened, about 5 to 15 minutes. Loosen and separate the noodles, then drain and rinse them before adding to stir-fries, soups, and other dishes.

HIYAMUGI

These Japanese noodles made from wheat flour, salt, and water are somewhat wider than somen but thinner than udon. Like somen, they are traditionally served only in the warmer months in chilled noodle dishes with a dipping sauce. A whole wheat version is also available, sometimes referred to as whole wheat somen. Cook in boiling water for 4 to 6 minutes, just until tender, then rinse in cold water to stop the cooking and remove excess starch.

KUZUKIRI

These light-colored, nearly transparent Japanese noodles are made from kudzu starch, and sometimes with added potato starch. Extracted from the fibrous root of a vinelike plant native to Asia, kudzu starch has long been valued for its thickening properties and, in Japanese folk medicine, as an easily digested, restorative carbohydrate. To make kuzukiri, the starch is dried, then ground and mixed with water to make a batter, which is cooked briefly until it solidifies. After cooling, it is cut into strips and dried. It is cooked like regular pasta and used in salads, sukiyaki, or sweet-and-sour soup, or simply in a light broth.

RAMEN

These familiar long, thin, extruded noodles are made from wheat flour, water, salt, sometimes eggs, and kansui, an alkaline solution made from potassium carbonate or sodium carbonate. Kansui is essential in making ramen noodles, giving them their springy texture and characteristic flavor, and also lending them their yellow color, which results from its action on pigments in the wheat flour.

In the United States and many other countries, ramen is synonymous with instant ramen, a cheap and easy noodle soup flavored with a seasoning packet. But in Japan, where some restaurants specialize in this traditional dish, ramen can be elevated to an art form. The noodles are served in a meticulously prepared broth and topped with everything from green onions, bean sprouts, and bamboo shoots to sea vegetables, wood ear mushrooms, and meat. Instant ramen, created in 1958 by the Japanese company Nissin Foods as a way to make ramen available anytime and anywhere, is also extremely popular in Japan but is seen as distinct from its namesake dish.

Japanese standards for instant ramen noodles stipulate they are to be made with wheat flour, water, salt, and kansui to give the noodles their characteristic flavor, texture, and color. After the raw noodles are steamed and pressed into a mold, they are either dried in a hot air drying machine or deep-fried in palm oil, lard, or sesame oil for a couple of minutes to reduce their moisture content. Not surprisingly, there are noticeable differences in flavor and texture between deep-fried and air-dried ramen, with the air-dried noodles having a more delicate texture, fresher taste, and better retention of nutrients.

The flavor packet in packages of instant ramen provides a quick gauge of quality. If it contains monosodium glutamate (MSG), artificial flavors, sugars, artificial colors, preservatives, or flavor enhancers such as disodium inosinate and disodium guanylate, look for another brand. Although high-quality ramen costs more, you'll get a seasoning packet that contains natural ingredients such as shoyu powder from naturally aged soy sauce, freeze-dried miso, and preservative-free dried seaweeds, vegetables, and spices. You may even get ramen noodles made with some whole wheat flour—although perhaps not traditional, they are more nutritious.

RICE NOODLES

These fresh white noodles are made from a mixture of rice flour and water that is formed into a sheet and precooked by steaming, then cut into various widths (or sold as folded sheets), and coated with oil to prevent sticking. Since they are already cooked, all the cooking they require is a brief soak in hot or boiling water to soften them up and to rinse off the oil. Fresh rice noodles have a very limited shelf life and harden quickly, so ideally they should be used the day of purchase.

RICE PAPER WRAPPERS

These circular or triangular sheets used to make spring rolls are made with the same ingredients as fresh rice noodles and dried rice sticks, but they are much thinner and they're dried on bamboo mats. To use them as wrappers for spring rolls, either soften them in water for 30 to 60 seconds or brush them with water. Don't use hot water and don't soak them too long, or they'll start to fall apart. Like rice sticks, they are steamed before being dried, so they're ready to eat as soon as they're soaked and softened.

RICE STICKS

These brittle, opaque, white dried noodles made from rice are available in thin, medium, and wide widths. Popular throughout Southeast Asia, they are known by a plethora of names, including mai-fun, bifun, sen yai, and banh pho. To make them, rice is soaked in water, ground into a paste, made into dough, and then extruded in various widths. The noodles are precooked with steam, then cooled and maintained in this state for many hours to help stabilize their structure before they are dried with hot air.

Prepare rice sticks by soaking them in hot water for 3 to 15 minutes, depending on the width of the noodles and how they will be further cooked or served. Drain the noodles after soaking, and rinse them in cold water to remove excess starch.

If you plan to use the noodles in soup, soak them in hot water for just 3 to 5 minutes, then add them to the soup for the last 2 to 3 of minutes of cooking. Presoaking time for stir-fries is, likewise, about 3 to 5 minutes before adding to the stir-fry for the last

3 to 5 minutes of cooking. For salads or serving the noodles with sauce, soak the noodles in hot water for 8 to 15 minutes, until tender.

Alternatively, the noodles can be soaked in cold water for an hour or until tender. This takes longer, but it helps prevent the noodles from sticking together during cooking and also gives more wiggle room in finishing the dish, as the noodles don't have to be used immediately.

SOBA

In Japanese, *soba* means "buckwheat," and these thin, square-cut brownish gray noodles are indeed made from buckwheat flour. Although all are based on buckwheat, the many types of soba vary in taste, texture, and color depending on the percentage of buckwheat flour used and whether any vegetables or other ingredients are included. The best soba is rolled (laminated) into sheets that are cut into long strands, slowly air-dried, and then hand cut, similar to the traditional Japanese method of making soba by hand.

Soba is traditionally served hot during colder months, in a broth or stir-fry, and served cold in summer, in salads, in cold broths, or with a dipping sauce. It also makes excellent noodle sushi. And, it is great as a side dish with other meals beyond Asian cuisine, especially when served with smoked salmon, tofu, or tempeh, and vegetables such as peas, steamed potatoes, and sautéed onions and red bell peppers. For best results, avoid stir-frying 100 percent buckwheat soba, ito soba, mugwort soba, and green tea soba.

Soba made from 100 percent buckwheat flour has a delicious flavor that's hearty and rich. As it contains no gluten, it is more delicate, so it's important not to overcook it, and to rinse it in cold water to stop the cooking process once it reaches the al dente stage. For this reason, most soba is made with at least 20 percent wheat flour to provide more strength and resilience. The more wheat used, the lighter the color of the soba and the milder its flavor. Soba made with added wheat also typically contains salt. Most varieties of soba are fairly thin, about like linguine. All vegetable soba noodles are based on soba made from a blend of buckwheat and wheat flours. Contemporary versions of soba sometimes use Kamut or spelt flour in place of the wheat flour, providing new options in flavor and nutrition.

Ito soba is very thin, about the width of angel hair pasta, whereas most soba is about as thick as linguine. Ito soba is made from a blend of buckwheat and wheat and has a very light texture.

Yomogi soba (mugwort soba) is deep green, a color it derives from dried mugwort leaves. This mineral-rich plant lends the soba added nutritional value and a delicious, slightly bitter flavor slightly reminiscent of spinach. **Cha soba** (green tea soba) is made with green tea powder, which contributes a lovely green color and a delicate, aromatic flavor. It is typically served cold with a simple dipping sauce on the side rather than in broth.

Jinenjo soba (wild yam soba) is light brown from the addition of dried Japanese wild mountain yam, a root vegetable that naturally contains diastase and amylase, two enzymes that help facilitate the digestion of starches. Wild yam soba has a particularly delicious nutty flavor and smooth, slightly slick texture. The wild yam also provides good binding qualities, making it sturdier than other sobas. **Lotus root soba**, a light-colored soba similar to wild yam soba, contains dried, ground lotus root. It has a delicious nutty flavor and aroma similar to that of freshly cooked lotus root and a smooth texture.

Korean-style buckwheat noodles, known as naengmyon, contain some potato starch in addition to buckwheat flour, which makes them slightly chewier than Japanese-style soba. Naengmyon is typically served cold but can also be used in soups.

Cooking time is 1 to 4 minutes for fresh soba or 5 to 7 minutes for dried. Cook just until al dente, drain, and then immediately rinse with cold water to stop the cooking process. Alternatively, use the cold water shock method, in which the soba is added to boiling water, then 1 cup of cold water is added after it returns to a boil. Another cup of cold water is added two or three more times, until the soba is at the al dente stage. After cooking, drain and rinse with cold water.

SOMEN

These very thin, delicate, white, round noodles made from wheat flour, water, and salt are often found packaged in small bundles secured by a band. Light and refreshing, they are traditionally served cold during the warmer months, often in salads, and sometimes directly on ice with a light dipping sauce on the side. Somen was originally made by hand stretching, folding, and restretching the dough into one long strip, a process that took considerable time and skill, making somen an expensive food eaten primarily by the wealthy. Hand-stretched somen is still made by artisans, including two- and three-year-old varieties that are valued for their smooth texture and enhanced flavor. Needless to say, these varieties are significantly more expensive. Cook somen in boiling water for about 2 minutes, just until tender. Drain, rinse in cold water, and drain again before serving.

TANGMYON

Also known as dangmyun, tangmyon is a Korean version of cellophane noodles made with sweet potato starch. They are prepared as cellophane noodles are: soaked in hot water for 10 to 15 minutes. They're typically added to stir-fries and soups.

UDON

These thick and delicious noodles made from wheat flour and whole wheat flour, salt, and water are nearly as wide as linguine. Soft and slippery, udon is typically served in a hot or chilled broth or with dipping sauce, but it is equally good in salads or topped with a simple sauce. Fresh udon is generally thick and flat, with the fresh version somewhat thinner and either round or flat. The best tasting, best textured udon is made using the roll and cut method, in which the kneaded dough is repeatedly rolled to yield thin, large sheets that are cut into shape, slowly dried, and then cut into the final length. Udon made from a blend of unbleached white and whole wheat flour or from other types of flour is also available. Genmai udon contains some brown rice flour, which contributes a nutty flavor. It's also available made from spelt and Kamut.

Cooking time is 2 to 4 minutes for fresh udon and 5 to 7 minutes for dried. After cooking, drain the udon and rinse with cold water to stop the cooking and remove excess starch. An alternative method for cooking dried udon is the cold water shock method, in which the udon is added to boiling water, then 1 cup of cold water is added after it returns to a boil. Another cup of cold water is added two or three more times, until the udon is al dente. After cooking, drain, rinse with cold water, and drain again.

Beans, Peas, Lentils, and Soy Products

ᴐᴠ

It wasn't until I was twenty-one years old that I first learned how to cook beans from scratch—both from sheer curiosity and, truth be told, to impress my husband in our early dating days (he was a good innovative cook who appreciated the great flavors and versatility of beans within a meal). Admittedly, my first attempt left much to be desired; I learned the hard way that beans are best presoaked and that they need plenty of water when cooking. Nonetheless, it quickly became apparent that they were easy to cook and that their chameleon nature suited them for any part of a meal, whether in salads, soups, spreads, snacks, casseroles, dips, wraps, or treasured accompaniment to any grain or pasta. Tofu and tempeh, made from soybeans, expand the bean lover's horizons even more; each can be enjoyed on its own merit as a substitute in a wide variety of egg and meat-based recipes.

Virtually every culture and cuisine incorporates dried beans, peas, and lentils in one way or another, often combined with grains, pastas, and vegetables in unique combinations. Falafel and hummus, both based on garbanzo beans, hail from the Middle East, while tempeh with peanut sauce is native to Indonesia. Soy-based miso soup is traditional in Japan, just as tofu pad thai is long established in Thailand. Italian pasta e fagioli and cannellini-based minestrone are both time-honored recipes, as is red kidney bean curry from India. This is just a minor sampling of the many ways beans have long been incorporated into menus worldwide.

No matter which you use, the range of colors, flavors, and textures of beans is remarkable; you owe it to yourself to try as many of them as possible. And just as knowing one's ancestry provides more color and insights to one's life, knowing the particular genus and species of a bean will enhance the enjoyment of cooking and the dining experience—such knowledge helps provide some clues to a bean's taste and texture, and also helps a cook decide what kind of recipes it may best be used in.

The Fabaceae Family Tree

All beans, no matter where they originated, started as wild plant species that were later domesticated. Although it's true that beans, peas, and lentils are different, for the sake of simplicity, the term *bean* is used here generically to refer to all legumes. Within Fabaceae, the vast family of legumes, those used principally for food include the eight major genera listed below. (Note that while peanuts are classified as a legume—species *Arachis hypolgaea*—they will be explored in the Nuts and Seeds chapter, in keeping with common usage.)

- *Cicer arietinum*: garbanzos, also known as chickpeas,
- *Glycine max*: soybeans
- *Lens culinaris*: lentils
- *Lupinus* genus (*L. albus, L. angustifolius, L. luteus, L. mutablis*): lupini beans
- *Phaseolus* genus (*P. acutifolius, P. coccineus, P. lunatus, P. vulgaris*): this genus includes, to name a just a few, tepary beans, scarlet runner beans, lima beans, black beans, and pinto beans
- *Pisum sativum*: peas
- *Vicia faba*: fava beans
- *Vigna* genus (*V. angularis, V. mungo, V. radiata, V. umbellata, V. unguiculata*): this genus includes adzuki beans, urad dal (black gram and its peeled white/ivory lentil), mung beans, rice beans, black-eyed peas, cow peas, and pigeon peas

Interestingly enough, the number of areas around the world from which beans have their roots is actually quite concentrated with nearly half of the genera—the four related to garbanzos, peas, lentils, and fava beans—originating in the ancient Fertile Crescent region, which included Babylonia, Assyria, Egypt, and Phoenicia. In modern-day geography, the Fertile Crescent corresponds to Israel, Lebanon, Jordan, Syria, and Iraq. Both soybeans' *Glycine* genus and the *Vigna* genus came from Asia, though Vigna also has one of its species originating in Africa. The *Phaseolus* genus, sometimes referred to as the New World beans, hailed from both the Andes Mountains in South America and from Mesoamerica, which includes Mexico and Central America. *Lupinus* is thought to have two origins, both in the Mediterranean and in South America, depending on the species.

Taking it a bit further, there are links in flavor among the various species within the basic genera. Many of the individual genus categories include a single primary species, as occurs with chickpeas, soybeans, peas, and fava beans. Each of these beans is individually well known for its very distinct flavor and texture, with a bevy of classic recipes from which adaptations are easy to create.

Others, like the *Vigna* genus, include many species. The *Phaseolus* genus of beans has the most extensive and seemingly diverse number of species of all. Still, even with multiple species within a genus it is easy to generalize what flavors will be in store when trying a bean, as multiple species within a genus have similarities to one another. Take the *Vigna* genus, for example. There are five species included in the list given here, and yet their unadorned flavor can generally be described as distinctively "vegetable-like." All these beans are definitely made more delicious when cooked along with other ingredients in soups, stews, or as with Indian dals, not to mention the quintessential Hoppin' John black-eyed pea preparation. Meanwhile, beans within the *Phaseolus* genus range from mild to richly flavored with many varieties within the various species able to perform simply seasoned as center stage within a meal or as a supporting player.

HEIRLOOM BEANS

As with fruits, vegetables, and grains, heirloom bean varieties have experienced a resurgence of interest, greatly expanding the repertoire beyond the more familiar pinto beans, black beans, and navy beans. Thanks to their propensity to open pollination, natural selection has had a field day with beans, generating a variety of beans that withstand various climates, have a pleasing flavor and/or

Cranberry beans

are placed in a pot, again with enough water to cover them by a couple of inches, and brought to a boil for 3 minutes. They are then removed from the heat and soaked for 1 to 4 hours. Soaking the beans in hotter water speeds their absorption of water and also more effectively leaches out the water-soluble oligosaccharides. The drawback is that it also leaches out many of the water-soluble nutrients and some of the flavor and color components. However, if the cold-soak method doesn't remove enough of the oligosaccharides for you, using the hot-soak method and sacrificing some nutrients and flavor may be a good compromise. The hot-soak method is also handy when you need to prepare beans more quickly.

2. Cook the beans until tender.

It's essential to ensure the beans are thoroughly cooked. The combination of presoaking and thorough cooking will ensure maximum breakdown of the oligosaccharides and other resistant starches. The simple way to test for doneness is with a fork. If the beans can be easily mashed, they're ready to eat.

If there is some resistance, or when you bite into a single bean, it is apparent that the bean isn't cooked evenly all the way through, they need further cooking. Undercooking them is neither the answer nor necessary when cooking beans for use in salads. Rest assured, properly cooked beans will still be able to retain their texture and shape.

3. Choose beans that are easier to digest.

Navy beans, lima beans, and whole dried soybeans are notorious for containing higher levels of hard-to-digest oligosaccharides. In contrast, Anasazi beans, adzuki beans, black-eyed peas, lentils, and mung beans have the least amounts of these complex sugars. Even so, centuries ago, traditional cultures found ways to prepare soybeans to make them easier to digest and more nutritious. In the process of making tofu and soymilk, the oligosaccharides are removed, and the fermentation of tempeh, miso, tamari, and shoyu also eliminates or breaks down most of the oligosaccharides.

4. Eat smaller quantities of beans until your body adjusts.

The good news is that many people who eat beans regularly find their digestive system fairly quickly adapts, making for easier eating. Start off by eating only ¼ cup to ½ cup at a time a couple of times per week, gradually increasing the amount and frequency.

5. Avoid eating beans cooked with sweeteners.

Some people who would otherwise have little difficulty digesting most beans have trouble with beans cooked with sweeteners, presumably because it adds more carbohydrate fuel for bacteria in the large intestine. Experiment to see whether this is the case for you. If the after-effects of baked beans made with a sweetener make life a bit uncomfortable, opt for plain beans. Or, if you prefer your beans sweetened, cook them with naturally sweet root vegetables such as carrots.

6. Cook beans with carminative herbs and spices.

Certain herbs and spices have carminative (gas-reducing) properties in addition to their delicious flavor. A sprig or two of fresh epazote, a pungent plant native to Mexico and South America, or a couple of teaspoons of dried epazote, can be very helpful. Add it to the pot of beans during the last 15 minutes of cooking to avoid a bitter flavor. Both cilantro, the fresh leaves of the coriander plant, and coriander seeds are also effective, with the seeds not surprisingly a key ingredient in many curry blends (underscoring the fact that coriander seeds are best enjoyed when combined with other spices). Turmeric, another common spice in curry powder, likewise has a carminative effect, although the amount of turmeric curry powders contain can vary. However, turmeric is also good as a spice on its own when cooking or sautéing. Still others find bay leaf or cumin cooked with beans useful, not to mention the good flavor they impart in the process.

7. Consider cooking sprouted beans.

Sprouting beans before cooking them also makes them more digestible. There are two general forms of sprouted beans: the fresh vegetable form, usually referred to as bean sprouts; and presprouted, in which beans are sprouted slightly, dried, and then used as one would use a dried bean. In the germination process, the young shoots use the complex oligosaccharides as fuel, thereby reducing the amount that can potentially be a bother. The degree to which the oligosaccharides remain is a factor of how long the sprouts have been allowed to grow. As an extra benefit, the sprouting process can increase nutrient availability and enhance digestibility of the bean from which the sprouts are made, including tofu made with sprouted soybeans. On the other hand, the sprouting process changes the character of the bean, giving any recipes made with presprouted dried beans a lighter quality and more of a slight vegetable flavor. In any case, all bean sprouts or sprouted beans must be cooked to reduce any food safety risks that could potentially arise from contaminated seed or improper production practices or storage. It is especially important to never eat sprouted kidney beans and sprouted lima beans raw, as they contain toxic enzymes that must be inactivated by cooking at high heat for at least 10 minutes.

8. Use a commercial enzyme product containing alpha-galactosidase.

If all else fails, you can take supplemental alpha-galactosidase in liquid or tablet form. This enzyme, developed from a food-grade mold, breaks down the oligosaccharides into smaller, more digestible sugars before they reach the colon. It helps improve digestion of beans by supplying an enzyme not normally found in the human body. Take the tablets (swallow or chew them, or crumble them on the food) or sprinkle the liquid form directly on the food with the first bite, using the amount indicated on the product label. While cooking beans with the alpha-galactosidase may sound like a good idea, it isn't. High heat will render the enzyme ineffective.

BUYING AND STORING BEANS

Not only are beans nutritious, they are also inexpensive and readily available. **Fresh shell beans**, such as black-eyed peas, cranberry beans, fava beans, garbanzos, and tongues of fire beans, can often be found in produce departments or at farmers' markets. Prepare and serve them as a tender vegetable. Unlike their dried bean counterparts, they cook quickly in boiling water, taking between 15 and 30 minutes, depending on the bean and its size, and don't require presoaking. Approximately 2½ pounds of fresh beans in their pods will yield about 3 cups of shelled beans. Although they're best used within a few days of harvest, they can be stored in a plastic bag in the refrigerator for up to a week.

Dried beans are available throughout the year. Virtually every grocery store sells a variety of packaged dried beans, and many sell them in bulk. You'll likely find packages of mixed beans specially formulated for soups and stews, too. Each year the catalog of beans continues to expand with both heirloom and new hybrid varieties.

Select dried beans with smooth surfaces and bright colors. While dried beans can, in theory, be stored for years, when it comes to cooking, it is important to know that after about a year from harvest they lose moisture and then require longer cooking. Likewise, beans that are stored too long at warm temperatures and high humidity will never get tender.

The same variety of bean can taste so great or just so-so, depending on where it is purchased. To make sure you are buying "fresh" dried beans, look for an expiration date on the package and use them within the suggested time frame. If the package has no expiration date or if you're buying in bulk, you may need to stick to buying only common varieties of beans, as they have faster turnover, and select those that aren't wrinkled or dull in color. Or, better yet, experiment with buying beans from a variety of sources, including sources that sell through mail order or online, from companies specializing in growing dried beans. After some trial and error, the best options will become apparent. And, while some companies specialize in a certain variety of beans, spending the time to cultivate a couple of good sources will provide a wider expanse of beans from which to try. After purchase, store beans in an airtight container in a cool, dry place away from sunlight. Rather than topping off a small amount of beans left in a container, use up the old beans first, implementing a "first in, first out" inventory control.

Canned precooked beans are also an excellent choice to have on hand. While it's hard to beat the flavor of freshly cooked beans, canned beans are a lifesaver when you need to prepare a meal quickly. A bit of seasoning is all you need to perk them up. Before you buy, look at both the nutrition information panel and the ingredient label to ensure the brand you choose contains only beans, water, and low amounts of sodium or, preferably, no added salt. Avoid brands that contain high-fructose corn syrup or other forms of sugar. Ingredients such as disodium

EDTA (for color retention) or calcium chloride (a firming agent) are also unnecessary. Drain and rinse canned beans before adding them to a recipe. This will lower the sodium level by one-third, help to reduce any amount of oligosaccharides in the beans, and also freshen the flavor. For best flavor, canned beans should be used by the freshness date on the container or within a year of purchase. As a rule of thumb, a 15-ounce can is equivalent to approximately 1¾ cups of cooked beans.

Cooked beans, including canned beans, will keep for five days in the refrigerator and up to six months in the freezer. Planning ahead, cooking a quantity of beans at a time, and keeping a few varieties of canned beans around for quick meals can all make it easier to incorporate these delicious and nutritious foods into your menu planning.

Preparing Beans

Regardless of whether you use the cold-soak or the hot-soak method, first sort through the beans to remove any defective beans, small pebbles, and other debris. Wash the beans several times under cold water, discarding any that float to the surface. For best flavor and nutrition, cook the beans with just enough fresh water, always making sure the beans are covered with water throughout the cooking process. Avoid using too much water. Not only will this dilute the flavor of the beans, but also any liquid you drain away after cooking will represent a loss of valuable nutrients.

SEASONING

Chopped onion, garlic, herbs, and spices may be cooked along with dried beans for added flavor. Adding the sea vegetable kombu can help tenderize the beans and enhance their flavor by virtue of its naturally occurring glutamic acid. It also can help replace minerals that are lost down the drain when the bean soaking water is discarded. Use about a 2-inch strip of kombu per pot of beans, rinsing it under water before adding to the pot to remove excess sodium.

On the other hand, don't add salt, sugars, tomatoes, wine, lemon juice, or vinegar until the end of cooking. Salting the beans before they are done will slow the rate at which they absorb water, prolonging the time until they become tender. Sugar added before cooking reinforces the cell walls and slows down the process of softening the starch within the cells. Acidic ingredients added early make the cell walls more stable but won't allow the starches to swell and soften. So while sugar or acidic ingredients like tomatoes, lemon juice, and vinegar added at the end of cooking can help retain the texture of beans, they'll prevent the beans from becoming tender if added during cooking.

Some cooks and books have suggested adding baking soda to beans while they're cooking. Unless your water is exceedingly hard and baking soda's alkalinity would allow the beans to cook more quickly, it's best to forgo it. Excess alkalinity can break down the cell walls of the beans. Not only will you be left with a mushy texture, but valuable protein and vitamins will also leach into the cooking water. Baking soda can also deplete thiamin. If you decide you still need or want to use baking soda in your beans, keep it to $1/8$ teaspoon per cup of dried beans.

BOIL AND SIMMER

In a large covered pot, combine the beans with fresh water, using 4 cups of water for each cup of beans. Bring the beans to a boil, then lower the heat to a simmer to help prevent the skins of the beans from bursting during cooking. Toward the end of the cooking time, it's okay if there isn't much water above the beans, but be sure to check periodically to make sure there's enough water to keep the bottom from scorching. The beans will be done when they are tender, requiring approximately $1\frac{1}{2}$ to 2 hours for most varieties, with some outliers requiring less and others more, depending on the particular bean and its overall quality. Remember that beans older than one year from harvest will need additional cooking time.

PRESSURE-COOKING

With a pressure cooker, you can prepare beans in less than one-third the time it would take with the boil and simmer method. Since the temperature inside a pressure cooker is around 250°F, beans cook much faster, saving a lot of preparation time and eliminating the need to be at home and babysit the beans for a couple of hours while they cook. If you cook a lot of beans, the investment in a pressure cooker is definitely worth it! Because less water escapes as steam, you'll only need to add water to a depth of about 1 inch above the surface of the beans before securing the lid. Vegetables such as onions, carrots, and celery may be combined with the beans before cooking, if desired. Since some beans tend to foam and clog the pressure release vent, keep the total amount of beans and water to no more than two-thirds of the pressure cooker's capacity. To prevent the beans from splitting and losing their shape, after bringing the cooker to pressure, reduce the heat just enough to keep the pressure at a low, steady level. After the cooking is complete, let the pressure come down naturally (this is called the "natural pressure release" method) to help them retain their shape and to allow for continued cooking and proper flavor formation. Usually taking about 15 to 20 minutes, natural pressure release should be factored into your cooking plans and valued as essential extra time when cooking the beans. In fact, all pressure cooker manufacturers advise it over using a quick release option, comprehending all the benefits of natural pressure release. Actual high pressure cooking times will vary, depending on the variety, quality, and age of the bean, as well as with the actual pressure per square inch (psi) at which your pressure cooker operates. Cooking at elevations higher than 2,000 feet will also increase cooking time by about an additional 5 percent per every 1,000 feet above 2,000 feet.

Another critical component of effective pressure cooking is to make sure to routinely replace the pressure cooker's rubber or silicone gasket, the essential sealing ring that allows a tight seal, trapping steam so internal pressure can build up. Replacing worn out gaskets is a common trouble-shooting solution when pressure-cooking the same bean seems to take longer or when steam or water drips down the sides of the cooker during the cooking process. Plan on replacing the gasket at least annually or, if you're using the pressure cooker several times per week, more frequently; consider every six months as a good rule of thumb.

Pressure-cooking lentils and some other beans is not recommended because of the tendency of their skins to loosen or for foam to develop during the cooking process, each of which can clog the pressure vent. The cooking guidelines for each variety listed below will clearly indicate when the use of a pressure cooker is not advised.

BAKING

Before baking beans, first boil them for 15 to 20 minutes in 4½ cups of water for each cup of beans. Then transfer the beans and their cooking water to a covered baking dish and bake at 350°F for about 3½ hours.

SLOW-COOKING

Slow cookers are good for making soups or stews with beans, but manufacturers recommend using only precooked or canned beans in slow cooker recipes rather than starting with dried beans. The suggestion is based both on recipe testing conducted by the manufacturers and on concerns about whether the cooking temperature of slow cookers is high enough to safely cook beans from scratch. This is of special importance when cooking kidney beans, which need to be boiled or cooked at boiling temperatures for at least 10 minutes to inactivate toxins they inherently contain that could otherwise cause symptoms similar to food poisoning.

If you still want to use a slow cooker to cook dried beans, manufacturers recommend that you first boil the beans for at least 10 minutes before placing them in the slow cooker. Add water to cover the surface of the beans by about 1 inch, and then cook on the high setting, which is approximately 212°F, until tender, 5 to 8 hours.

FINDING TIME TO COOK BEANS

No matter how little preparation time you have to spare before mealtime, there's bound to be a bean or bean-based product you can use. In general, smaller beans and lentils cook faster, and no presoaking is required for lentils. Soy-based tofu and tempeh are also quickly cooked, taking no more than 30 minutes. And, of course, you can always reach for canned beans when cooking isn't an option.

The total amount of time it takes to cook beans is determined by several factors: the variety of bean, pea, or lentil, the simmering temperature, the soaking time, the quality and age of the legumes, and the altitude. Consequently, consider the "boil and simmer" cooking times I have listed for each of the beans below simply as approximations; actual cooking time will vary depending on the beans and the situation. Also adjust the time depending on the intended use. Beans destined to be used whole in salads are usually cooked less than those destined for soups. Even so, they should also be cooked until tender and easily mashed with a fork. And it makes sense to make extra to take advantage of the time saving benefits of the creative use of leftovers.

For beans other than lentils, my family relies on a pressure cooker as our primary way to cook beans, as it significantly decreases cooking time, making them relatively quick and easy to prepare even on busy days. For approximate cooking times for the beans listed below, refer to the bean cooking timetable provided by the manufacturer for your specific brand of pressure cooker. Experiment with their suggestions, testing for doneness after the "natural pressure release" part of the process, which brings the cooker's pressure down enough to enable you to open the pressure cooker. If the beans need more time to get soft and finish cooking, put the pressure cooker lid on again, place the pressure cooker on the stove, and bring it back to pressure for 5 minutes. Take the pressure cooker off the heat and allow the pressure to go down until it is safe to open the lid. Test for doneness again, repeating the process if necessary. Note the total pressure-cooking time and use it to gauge future batches.

Exploring Beans and Peas

Given the immeasurable number of bean varieties available, including those that have a limited regional availability, no book could possibly ever catalog every bean known to humankind. Still, there are many that deserve special attention, from familiar friends that warrant permanent status on our tables to amazing heirlooms whose appearance, flavor, or story are so rich that they impart a bit of history with every bite.

ADZUKI BEANS
Vigna angularis
Boil and simmer for 1 to 1½ hours.
Also known as aduki or azuki beans, these are small, round, reddish brown beans marked with a distinctive thin white line down the side. Traditionally used in both Japanese and Chinese cuisines for festive meals, they are slightly sweet and nutty in flavor. Although adzuki beans have often been used as an ingredient in desserts and confections, they are equally, if not more, delicious when prepared in a savory manner. Serve them with rice or barley or, for an exceptional dish, add cubes of winter squash during the last half hour of cooking and season with tamari. Stretch tradition and try adzuki beans in Southwestern cuisine, too. Their color contrasts beautifully with yellow corn tortillas. Adzuki beans are also easy to sprout.

ANASAZI BEANS
Phaseolus vulgaris
Boil and simmer for 1 to 1½ hours.
This heirloom variety has been cultivated in the American Southwest since about 130 CE. After the cliff-dwelling Anasazi abandoned their homes in the Four Corners region around 1200 CE, the beans were left to survive in the wild. Though the bean was officially rediscovered in the Anasazi ruins by archeologists in the 1950s, cultivation had actually continued throughout the centuries in family gardens. Commercial production was rekindled by agronomist Bruce Riddell and entrepreneur Ernie Waller, who shared a common interest in this native bean. In 1983, they named the bean "Anasazi" from the then-current name for the people now known as the Ancestral Puebloans.

Anasazi beans are as striking in appearance as they are delicious. While similar in both size and shape to pinto beans, they are dappled burgundy and white, markings that fade with cooking to a light pink. They are also sweeter and more flavorful than pinto beans and hold their shape better once cooked. Much of the Anasazi bean's popularity can be attributed to its ease of digestion. Many people report it is less problematic in terms of intestinal gas, and this is well grounded in reality. The level of hard-to-digest oligosaccharides is 25 percent less than in many other beans. Anasazi beans can be used in any recipe that calls for pinto beans.

APPALOOSA BEANS
Phaseolus vulgaris
Boil and simmer for 1½ hours.
This heirloom bean is long and slender, with its color a mottled dark purple and ivory white on the diagonal. Hailing from the Palouse region of Washington and Idaho, the bean was named for the Appaloosa horse, whose markings are similar. During cooking the color fades to a pinkish burgundy. The flavor of appaloosa beans is mild, earthy, and herbaceous. Holding their shape when cooked, they are a good choice in any soup, chili, dip, or refried bean recipe that calls for black beans, pintos, or kidney beans.

ARIKARA YELLOW BEANS
Phaseolus vulgaris
Boil and simmer for 1½ to 2 hours.
True to its name, the Arikara yellow bean is yellow-tan in color. However, once cooked, it turns a

variety is the Eston lentil. Fortunately, when cooking, you won't have to struggle with which is which as these basic brown and green varieties have similar cooking times and water-to-lentil proportions. Still, learning more about each lentil's characteristics enhances the enjoyment both in cooking and in dining.

BLACK BELUGA LENTILS

Use 2¼ cups water to 1 cup lentils. Boil and simmer for 25 to 30 minutes.

These are tiny black lentils that look remarkably like shiny, glistening caviar when cooked. Their rich, earthy flavor and soft texture is perfect in salads and soups or featured with pasta, rice, or sautéed vegetables. Not only does their deep black color present a dramatic, striking contrast when cooked with a variety of colorful green and red vegetables, but it also indicates they are high in the antioxidant anthocyanin.

CASTELLUCCIO LENTILS

Use 2 cups water to 1 cup lentils. Boil and simmer for 30 minutes.

Although Castelluccio lentils (Umbrian lentils, *lenticchie di Castelluccio*) are tiny, about 2 millimeters across, they have a big presence in the culinary world, where they are highly prized for their complex, delicately nutty, slightly earthy flavor and tender texture. The small, round, flat seeds vary in color from light brown to a dull yellow, sometimes speckled and sometimes striped. They are grown by a cooperative of farmers in the high plains areas surrounding Castelluccio di Norcia, in Umbria's Monti Sibillini national park. The farmers' commitment to the lentil involves strict agricultural production and harvesting requirements, including their centuries-old tradition of a three-year crop rotation alternating lentils, wheat, and pasture to continually allow the land to be restored. In 1998, Castelluccio lentils achieved Europe's Protected Geographical recognition, a testament to the area's special microclimate, which, along with its calcium-rich soil, account for the distinctiveness of the Castelluccio lentil. A label with the words "Lenticchia di Castelluccio di Norcia—Indicazione Geografica Protetta" ensures you are purchasing authentic Castelluccio lentils that are grown in the official area by and in accordance with the cooperative's guiding principles.

Castelluccio lentils retain their shape when cooked. They are excellent simply prepared, simmered in water or vegetable stock and lightly seasoned with aromatic herbs and spices, allowing the lentil's natural flavor to shine through.

CRIMSON LENTILS

Use 1¾ to 2 cups water to 1 cup lentils. Boil and simmer for 10 to 15 minutes.

The reddish orange color of these tiny lentils turns golden once they're cooked. While still whole and not split as are red chief lentils, they are peeled, with their rusty brown outer seed coat removed to expose the beautiful inner color. They cook quickly and generally lose their shape in cooking. As such crimson lentils are good for soups, stews, and puréed side dishes, and as a flavorful way to thicken soups and sauces. They may be used in any recipe that calls for split red lentils. Their mild, celery-like flavor works well with a variety of seasonings and cuisines.

ESTON LENTILS

Use 2½ cups water to 1 cup lentils. Boil and simmer for 30 to 35 minutes.

The small Eston lentil is 4.5 to 5.5 millimeters in size. It is khaki green in color with a yellow interior that has a relatively neutral earthy flavor. As it holds its shape somewhat less readily than the larger green lentils, it works well in soups, stews, and recipes that call for mashed lentils.

FRENCH GREEN LENTILS

Use 2½ cups water to 1 cup lentils. Boil and simmer for 40 to 45 minutes.

Known for their distinctive rich, peppery flavor, French green lentils are further distinguished by their slate green color with bluish black undertones, and their small size, about one-third the size of green lentils. They are also rich in antioxidant phytochemicals similar to those in blueberries and black grapes and in minerals, particularly iron and magnesium.

While French green lentils are grown using the same variety of lentil as the famous Puy lentils, since they are grown in North America or Italy rather than the Puy region in central France, they are never referred to as *lentilles du Puy*. Nonetheless, they can be substituted in any recipe that calls for Puy lentils, not to mention being less expensive, as well. As French green lentils hold their shape well, use them as a side dish in accompaniment with vegetables and pasta, in salads, in a light soup, or as a focal point in a meal.

IVORY LENTILS

Use 2 cups water to 1 cup lentils. Boil and simmer for 30 to 35 minutes.

Just when you think everyone's on the same program, there's always one that dares to be different. While with a name like ivory lentil, it would seem logical that this bean would be a variety of the *Lens culinaris* species. But ivory lentils are actually from a completely different species, the Asian-based *Vigna mungo*. As it turns out, ivory lentils, also known in India as urad dal, are actually peeled and split black lentils (black gram). Tiny and ivory colored in appearance, when cooked, ivory lentils have a mild, earthy flavor and a creamy texture. They cook fairly quickly, taking about 30 minutes or so until soft. Traditionally in India, ivory lentils and rice are ground together into a flour to make idlis (steamed rice cakes) and dosas (savory pancakes). Ivory lentils can, likewise, be used to make soup, dips, and purees.

LAIRD LENTILS

Use 2½ cups water to 1 cup lentils. Boil and simmer for 40 to 45 minutes.

The Laird variety is a large lentil, ranging from 6 to 7 millimeters in size. In addition to its size, the Laird

Clockwise from top left: (1) French green, (2) petite estoria, (3) Spanish pardina, (4) marrow, (5) petite castillo, (6) lenticche verdi, (7) black beluga, (8) Puy

lentil is celebrated for its robust, earthy flavor. Depending on where it is grown, its texture and specific flavor may vary, although it remains a favorite type of green lentil due to its overall richer taste. As they hold their shape well, Laird lentils can be used in side dishes seasoned with herbs served along with pasta, rice, or a favorite whole grain, and in soups and stews.

LENTICCHIE VERDI

Use 2½ cups water to 1 cup lentils. Boil and simmer for 40 to 45 minutes.

Literally translated from Italian as "green lentils," lentils labeled *lenticchie verdi* were grown in Italy, a country that appreciates lentils and includes them often in its cuisine. These green lentils are typically large-sized, flat, disk-shaped, and khaki-colored. Along with their robust earthy flavor, they have a hearty texture that, although they keep their shape are cooked by steaming or boiling them in their pods for 3 to 5 minutes. After they are drained and allowed to cool, split open the pods, remove the beans, and eat them as an appetizer with or without added salt, or add them to soups.

Whole soybeans are as easy to prepare as any other dried bean—they just take longer. Soybeans must always be soaked and then cooked thoroughly to deactivate protease inhibitors that would otherwise block the body's enzymes from doing their job of digesting protein. Pressure-cooking and boiling and simmering are the preferred methods for cooking whole soybeans. If a slow cooker is used, the soybeans must first be boiled on the stove for 10 minutes to ensure that the protease inhibitor is deactivated. Because they contain less starch, soybeans will remain firmer in texture and retain their shape rather than becoming creamy like other beans, even though they must be cooked longer— for up to 3 hours.

There are two types of dried soybeans: yellow and black. They may be used interchangeably in salads, soups, and stews or can be served with pasta or grains, especially rice.

Yellow soybeans are the basic variety of soybeans used for cooking and processing. As they have a bland, beany flavor and are less digestible than other cooked whole beans, yellow soybeans are most commonly eaten in the form of tofu and tempeh. Still, they can be jazzed up with a variety of seasonings or served in a flavorful sauce or stew.

Black soybeans, when cooked in their whole form, are much more flavorful than yellow soybeans, with a flavor somewhat reminiscent of regular black beans. They are also used as an ingredient within some brands of tofu and the basis of salty, spicy Chinese fermented black beans, which are added to dishes before steaming or stir-frying. Black soybeans are also featured in Chinese black bean sauce, a strong, salty sauce used in many Chinese dishes. For a delicious twist on hummus, substitute black soybeans for garbanzo beans.

Two of the tastiest and most digestible ways to enjoy soybeans are **tempeh** and **tofu**. Quick to cook, both readily absorb seasonings, making them very versatile. Their textures also make them good substitutes for meat in sauces, sandwiches, stir-fries, and casseroles.

TEMPEH

Tempeh is a traditional Indonesian soy food with a tender, chewy texture and a mild flavor reminiscent of mushrooms. It is made by culturing cooked, cracked soybeans with the fungus *Rhizopus oligosporus*, in a process similar to making blue cheese. After an incubation period of eighteen to twenty-four hours, the soybeans are bound into a cakelike form created by the mycelia of the fungus, a network of white, cottony filaments. Grains such as rice, millet, and quinoa, as well as sesame seeds are often combined with the soybeans before inoculation for increased flavor.

Tempeh contains all the nutrients and phytonutrients of whole soybeans, including the beneficial fiber. Its protein is particularly high in quality and quantity, providing nearly fifteen grams of protein per three-ounce serving. The fermentation process involved in its production makes it very digestible, a benefit common to all fermented foods, whose proteins, fats, and carbohydrates are broken down into simpler compounds during the fermentation process. Fermentation also neutralizes phytic acid, a compound found in many plant foods that binds with minerals and impedes their absorption. Therefore, the fermentation of tempeh makes it easier for the body to absorb the many minerals present in soybeans, including zinc, iron, and calcium.

Although there are many claims to the contrary, tempeh processed in the United States and Europe is not a vegetarian source of B_{12}, as tempeh produced traditionally in Indonesia is. However, the source of B_{12} in Indonesian tempeh is neither the soybeans nor the *Rhizopus oligosporus*, but one of two bacteria, either *Citrobacter freundii* or *Klebsiella pneumoniae*, which develop as a result of "accidental" inoculation that can occur when sanitary conditions are less than optimal. As most Western tempeh producers use a pure *Rhizopus oligosporus* culture in tightly regulated environments, the presence of these bacteria, and the B$_{12}$ they produce, would be unlikely.

Buying and Cooking Tempeh

Tempeh can be found either in the refrigerated or frozen food department. Its texture, flavor, and overall quality vary widely depending on the specific methods and equipment used, the quality of the ingredients, and the manufacturer's skill, so it's a good idea to experiment with different brands. While the flavor of tempeh is milder when its surface color appears completely white, tempeh with small black spots, which can occur during the process of fermentation, is still safe to eat. Keep tempeh refrigerated, cooking it prior to the use-by date indicated on the product's label. Once cooked, it should be consumed within five days. Alternatively, uncooked tempeh can be frozen in its original packaging in the freezer for up to six months. Throw it away if it begins to smell like ammonia or grows patches of rainbow colors.

Preparation of tempeh is very simple. It's best to season it prior to cooking and cook it for at least 30 minutes. An easy and delicious way to prepare tempeh is to season it lightly with tamari and herbs or spices, add it with about ½ inch depth of water to a baking dish, then bake it at 350°F for 30 to 35 minutes. Alternatively, it can be marinated for an hour prior to baking for deeper flavor. Use the baked tempeh as a filling for sandwiches or wraps, or serve it with pasta, rice, or a whole grain. Tempeh can be cooked in many other ways, as well, both on its own and with other ingredients: stir-fried, grilled, pan-fried, broiled, braised in a small amount of water or broth, or added to stews and soups. When crumbled, it has a meatlike texture that goes well in spaghetti sauces and on pizza instead of sausage.

TOFU

First produced in China about two thousand years ago and introduced to Japan a thousand years later, tofu remains an integral component of Asian cuisine while becoming a major source of protein worldwide. In 1770, Benjamin Franklin sent a friend soybean seeds from England, along with a note about the fascinating idea that soybeans were being used to produce "cheese" in China. But it wasn't until two hundred years later, in an era of increasing exploration of the diversity of global ideas and cultures, that tofu went from relative obscurity in Western nations to become a food emblematic of the times.

William Shurtleff and Akiko Aoyagi's comprehensive *Book of Tofu*, first published in 1975, introduced its readers not only to the countless ways to prepare tofu but also to the idea of right livelihood through the production of tofu. Consequently, scores of local tofu shops sprang up, both large and small, many of which continue to thrive to this day.

Nutritionally, tofu is an excellent source of high-quality protein, providing seven grams protein for a three-ounce serving of firm tofu. And, with the exception of fiber, which is removed as part of the tofu-making process, it contains all the nutrients, including the phytoestrogenic isoflavones, that are found in whole soybeans. It is also very easy to digest, thanks to the fact that the oligosaccharides, the complex carbohydrates that make soybeans (and all beans) difficult to digest, are removed during the manufacturing process. Protease inhibitors found in raw soybeans that can impede the digestion of its protein are also mostly destroyed during the cooking process that occurs when making tofu.

Although the flavor of plain, unseasoned tofu is extremely mild, it is this very quality that makes tofu so versatile. Depending upon how it is seasoned, what it is cooked with, and how it is cooked, every tofu dish you prepare can be unique.

Types of Tofu

There are four main types of tofu, differentiated by their density and texture: soft, firm, extra-firm, and silken. Some tofu is specially made with soybeans that were sprouted before they were used to make tofu; the sprouting process itself may enhance both the availability of nutrients and the digestibility of the tofu. **Soft, firm**, and **extra-firm tofu** are made in somewhat the same way as soft cheese. The process starts by soaking soybeans overnight, then grinding them with water and cooking them to make a soy-milk slurry. After straining it to remove the soybean pulp (which is known as *okara* and can be used to flavor or thicken soups or vegetable and grain dishes), a coagulant is added to curdle the soy milk. The type or blend of coagulant used determines the final density, texture, and flavor of the tofu. Magnesium chloride, which can be obtained from seawater or created synthetically, creates a firmer, denser tofu with a subtle natural sweetness. Calcium sulfate yields a soft, smooth consistency and a mild flavor, as well as additional calcium content. The curds are then separated from the liquid and placed into containers or forms where they are pressed to expel more moisture, the extent depending on the density desired. The finished tofu is then either vacuum-packed or packaged in water-filled plastic tubs. As tofu is a very perishable product, most packaged tofu is pasteurized during the manufacturing process to prevent spoilage from potentially harmful microorganisms while it remains in the unopened package. Avoid any packages that appear bloated and never use tofu that has a sour odor or a slimy texture upon opening. All of these indicate spoiled tofu caused by some glitch in the packaging process.

Silken tofu, popular in traditional Japanese cuisine, is much lighter, more delicate, and sweeter tasting than regular tofu, resembling a custard or thick cream. Modern manufacturing of silken tofu depends on a thicker, richer soy milk that is neither strained nor pressed. After mixing the pasteurized soy milk with coagulating agents, glucono-delta-lactone and calcium chloride, it is poured directly into individual cartons that are then sealed in an aseptic, sterile atmosphere. Immersion in hot water activates the coagulant to form the tofu inside the carton. Since the curds and whey are not separated in the process as with regular tofu, silken tofu has a higher water content, which accounts for its softer, smoother consistency. Firm and extra-firm versions of silken tofu are made through the addition of soy protein isolates during manufacture. An advantage of aseptic-packed silken tofu is that it is shelf stable under cool, dry conditions and need not be refrigerated until after it's opened. It must, however, be used by the date stated on the package.

Choosing Tofu

Deciding which of the four types of tofu to choose depends on its intended use. Silken tofu has a creamy, custardlike texture and therefore works well in dips, sauces, soups, smoothies, and salad dressings. Soft tofu can be used in similar ways, and because of its similarity to ricotta cheese, it can also be used as a nondairy substitute for ricotta and cottage cheese in recipes. Because firm tofu holds its shape better, it's a good variety to use in tofu salads and scrambled tofu and as the basis for nondairy cheesecakes. Extra-firm is best when using tofu in cubed or sliced form, whether baked, sautéed, stir-fried, or fried.

Still, there are ways to make soft tofu harder and, conversely, hard tofu softer. Soft tofu can be made firmer by pressing some of the liquid out of it. Place the tofu in a cloth or between paper towels on a hard surface, then put a plate or cutting board on top and place something heavy on top, such as a thick book or a skillet. Allow it to set for 30 minutes to expel the liquid. Conversely, if a recipe calls for soft tofu and you have hard tofu on hand, simply soak the tofu in water or, if the tofu is used in mashed form, mash it with a bit of extra liquid.

Cooking Tofu

As with tempeh, one of the easiest ways to cook tofu is to bake it. Slice or cube it, sprinkle it with tamari and any combination of herbs and spices, place it in a baking dish—no need to oil the bottom of it—and bake at 350°F for 25 to 30 minutes. If you wish, marinate it for up to 30 minutes prior to baking to infuse additional flavor into the tofu. You can also simmer an entire block of fresh or home-frozen tofu (see below for more on frozen tofu) in a pan on the stovetop. First season it with tamari and your choice of herbs and/or spices and place in a pot of boiling water, at a depth about half the height of the tofu. Reduce the heat, cover, and simmer for 30 minutes. When added to stews, soups, chili, and vegetable medleys, tofu will contribute its soft texture to the dish while absorbing the flavors in which it is immersed. It is delicious stir-fried with a lot of vegetables, and its soft texture makes it excellent for blending with other ingredients to make dips and sandwich spreads.

Tofu can also be substituted for dairy and eggs in recipes. It can be transformed to emulate the flavor and texture of dairy products such as cream cheese, sour cream, cottage cheese, and whipped cream, and it does a good job of replacing ricotta in pasta dishes. When crumbled and sautéed with onions, scrambled tofu makes a worthy stand-in for scrambled eggs, especially when a pinch of turmeric is added to give the dish its characteristic yellow hue.

When using unpasteurized tofu in dips and other recipes that won't undergo any cooking, boil it in water for at least 5 to 10 minutes, then allow it to cool before proceeding with the recipe. For extra assurance, even pasteurized tofu should be briefly boiled before it's used in uncooked recipes. Any unused raw tofu can be kept in the refrigerator for up to six days as long as it's stored in water that is drained and replenished daily. Cooked tofu should be stored in the refrigerator and used within five days.

Frozen and Freeze-Dried Tofu

Another way to change the texture of tofu and increase its ability to absorb flavors is to freeze it. When thawed and cooked, it has a chewy, meaty quality. Once it's crumbled, it's a perfect substitute for ground beef in casseroles, pizza, stews, or spaghetti sauce. Sliced or cubed frozen tofu is delicious baked, sautéed, or stir-fried and finished with a sauce or seasoned with a splash of tamari and any variety of herbs and spices. To freeze tofu, simply place it in the freezer for a minimum of thirty-six hours but no longer than four months. Vacuum-packed tofu can be frozen as is. Water-packed tofu should be drained and then frozen in a container or plastic bag. Silken tofu should be removed from its aseptic packaging and sliced before freezing. The tofu will turn yellow while in a frozen state but return to its original color once thawed. Thaw frozen tofu in the refrigerator. Placing it (still in its container or packaging) in a pan of water while in the refrigerator will accelerate defrosting. Once it's thawed, squeeze out the excess liquid before cooking.

When available, freeze-dried tofu can be found in the Asian food section of natural foods stores or specialty grocers. In its packaged form, it looks unusual, perhaps even inedible, resembling a pack of small, pale beige sponges. But, when reconstituted, it has a finer, firmer-grained texture and is more absorbent than regular tofu. The production of freeze-dried tofu actually began well over a thousand years ago, and the traditional manufacture is still practiced. In the mountains of Japan, the tofu is suspended on wooden racks, where it is allowed to freeze at night and thaw during the day, allowing for evaporation of its moisture. After about twenty days, the tofu is extremely dry, light in weight, and finely textured. Some freeze-dried tofu is now made in factories, in a process that takes over a year, using tofu coagulated with calcium chloride and ammonia gas to set the color.

Freeze-dried tofu needs no refrigeration, but to ensure best flavor, use it by the freshness date on the package. (Freeze-dried tofu past its prime will turn a yellowish brown color.) Once the package is open, the tofu should be stored in an airtight plastic bag or container and used within four months. To reconstitute, soak the cakes in hot water on each side for 5 minutes. Press between towels or the palms of your hands to squeeze out excess liquid. Then cover the tofu with hot water again, soaking for an additional 5 minutes, and squeeze out the liquid. Repeat this process a few times, until the soaking water remains clear rather than becoming milky white. Cook reconstituted freeze-dried tofu for at least 20 minutes in soups or stews, with vegetables, or alone with your choice of seasonings. When shredded, it can be used as a meat substitute in spaghetti sauce, chili, and casseroles. It can also be marinated for 30 minutes before cooking. Since freeze-dried tofu is such a concentrated food, one cake is usually enough per person.

Yuba

One of the by-products of making tofu is yuba, also known as tofu skin and bean curd skin. Mildly sweet in flavor and creamy yellow in color, yuba is a film of concentrated protein and fat that forms on the surface of soy milk as it cooks; it is removed before a coagulant is added to curdle the soy milk into curds that will be pressed to make tofu. However, production of yuba is usually a dedicated process unto itself; rich soy milk is heated in open shallow pans, allowing for the formation of the film or skin—the effect is not unlike what often occurs when one is slowly heating dairy milk. As the skin forms, it is gently removed and hung to drain and dry; multiple sheets of yuba form and are removed until all the soy milk in the pan or pot has evaporated. Sold fresh in Asian markets, tofu shops, and some farmer's markets, yuba will last up to five days if refrigerated. Yuba is also sold dried, as beige-colored, crisp sheets; it's available from Asian groceries and online merchants. Dried yuba is likewise sold as beige-colored tofu sticks, also known as bean curd sticks and bamboo yuba; these are made by rolling fresh sheets of yuba together and hanging them over a line.

Fresh yuba can be simply prepared: served warm with a dipping sauce; used as a wrapper for making sushi or spring rolls; or cut into ½-inch strips, warmed briefly in hot water and used as a grain-free and gluten-free pasta substitute. As yuba is already cooked, it doesn't need a lot of cooking—just about 30 seconds to warm it up. And that's not all. It can also be cut into small pieces or strips and added directly to soups or even to stir-fries toward the end of cooking. Yuba has been the source for some meat analogs as well, taking advantage of its slightly chewy but tender texture and chameleon nature. Traditionally, seasoned yuba was stuffed into animal-shaped hollow molds, steamed for almost an hour, removed from the molds, and finished off with deep frying. An easier alternative is to fold a sheet of yuba in thirds and roll it into a tube, or fold it several times to make a square, lightly fry it in oil, and then cut into small pieces and braise it in a flavorful stock or light sauce until the liquid is absorbed by the yuba.

Dried yuba sheets can be used as above after first reconstituting individual sheets. Fill a large container that will accommodate the yuba sheet half way with warm water, soak the sheet for 20 to 30 seconds, and then transfer it to a clean dish towel. Pat it dry and place it on a plate or cutting board, at which point it is ready to use like fresh yuba.

Rehydrating dried tofu sticks by covering them with water in a large container will take about 6 to 8 hours. After soaking, cut the reconstituted tofu sticks in half, transfer them to a pot, add broth or seasoned stock to cover, and braise for 30 to 40 minutes, allowing the tofu sticks to absorb most of the liquid. Serve them with vegetables and your favorite rice or pasta.

Nuts and Seeds

ↄ

At my house, nuts or seeds are a fundamental food. Breads, appetizers, snacks, soups, salads, veggies, pasta, entrees, and desserts—you name it—all are enhanced with nuts and seeds in one way or another. Breakfast might be almond butter on muffins or oatmeal and raisins sprinkled with roasted pecans. At lunch, we might combine tahini with pureed beans of any type for a quick and easy sandwich spread, or the crunchy texture of roasted sunflower seeds might make a welcome appearance in whole wheat tortilla encased wraps. Savory lentils and Kamut pasta topped with roasted walnuts is a standard dinner at least once a week, and anything served with rice and roasted almonds is an instant success.

Each type of nut or seed provides a unique taste, texture, and aroma that is both satisfying on its own and a wonderful complement to other elements in a dish or meal, adding depth, interest, and visual appeal. When you add in the variety of flavors, textures, and functional properties provided by basic preparation techniques, such as toasting and roasting, grinding into nut and seed butters, and making creamy nut and seed milks, the possibilities these nutritious foods offer are endless. Cooking with their oils provides yet another way to experience and benefit from nuts and seeds, but we'll explore that in the Culinary Oils chapter (see page 217).

A Compact Source of Nutrients

Botanically speaking, only a few of the foods we think of as nuts fit the technical definition of nuts: a dry indehiscent one-seeded fruit with a woody pericarp—think of chestnuts, hazelnuts, and acorns. Other culinary nuts fall into the less-than familiar category of drupes—a type of fruit with fleshy tissues surrounding a pit that holds a seed inside. While we usually eat drupes in the form of fruit (apricots, cherries, peaches, plums, and other stone fruits, as well as mangos and avocados), almonds and pistachios are a couple of drupes we think of as nuts. Other culinary nuts fall into other obscure botanical categories, like capsules and kernels, and as most of us know, the ubiquitous peanut is actually a legume and grows

Grams of Protein per Ounce

Almonds	6 grams
Brazil nuts	4.1 grams
Cashews	5.2 grams
Chestnuts	0.9 grams
Chia	4.7 grams
Coconut (dried)	2 grams
Flaxseeds	5 grams
Hazelnuts	4.2 grams
Macadamia nuts	2.2 grams
Peanuts	7 grams
Pecans	2.6 grams
Pine nuts	4 grams
Pistachios	5.8 grams
Pumpkin seeds	7 grams
Sesame seeds (with hulls)	5 grams
Sesame seeds (without hulls)	5.8 grams
Sunflower seeds	6.5 grams
Walnuts, black	6.8 grams
Walnuts, English	4.3 grams

A GOOD SOURCE OF PROTEIN

It's not just by chance that nuts are sometimes referred to as nutmeats. While a few varieties provide only low to moderate amounts of protein, others contain significant amounts, most notably almonds, black walnuts, pistachios, and peanuts, supplying as much protein in a single ounce as an egg, half a cup of cooked dried beans, or one ounce of meat, poultry, or fish. Most varieties of seeds provide a similar amount of protein, with pumpkin seeds, hulled sesame seeds, and sunflower seeds being exceptionally good sources. Whether as a primary source of protein or just an adjunct, nuts and seeds are a good source of protein that is low in saturated fat and free of cholesterol.

HEALTHY FATS, PHYTOSTEROLS, AND ANTIOXIDANTS

The predominance of beneficial fats in nuts and seeds is another nutritional bonus. With few exceptions, their fats are monounsaturated and polyunsaturated, both of which are much more healthful than the saturated fat that predominates in most animal foods. Monounsaturated fat, often dubbed the heart-healthy fat, can reduce levels of LDL cholesterol (bad cholesterol) while sparing HDL cholesterol (good cholesterol). The polyunsaturated fats found in nuts and seeds provide essential fatty acids (EFAs): linoleic acid (an omega-6 fatty acid) and alpha-linolenic acid (an omega-3 fatty acid). Collectively, EFAs help maintain the structure of healthy cell membranes, particularly in nerve tissue and the retina, and promote healthy skin. EFAs also help regulate many vital systems within the body, including the inflammation response, immune function, blood pressure, and blood clotting. Because nuts and seeds are a good source of these healthful fats, consuming them regularly may also help reduce the risk of cancer, diabetes and other chronic diseases, and even macular degeneration, an age-related eye disease that limits vision. It can also help reduce blood cholesterol levels and decrease incidence of cardiovascular disease.

underground. Some of the "nuts" we eat are botanically defined as seeds, such as cashews and pine nuts. Of course, most of the foods we think of as seeds are indeed seeds, including sunflower seeds, sesame seeds, pumpkin seeds, and flaxseeds.

Regardless of how they are categorized botanically, all nuts are indeed seeds in the sense that they are reproductive structures and can sprout and grow into a new plant. As such, they are packed with nutrients to support the new plant until it begins producing nutrients on its own. The same is true of grains and beans, also foods with an excellent nutritional profile. So what is it that makes nuts and seeds so special? Their high protein content is one thing that sets them apart from most plant foods, but even more important is the healthful oils they contain.

Nuts and seeds provide an extra heart-healthy boost due to their high phytosterol content. These naturally occurring components of plant cell membranes have a chemical structure similar to that of cholesterol but act differently in the body. They block the absorption of dietary cholesterol that's circulating in the blood and reduce the liver's reabsorption of the cholesterol that your body naturally produces.

Nuts and seeds are also a good source of certain vitamins and minerals (including calcium, vitamin E, iron, and zinc) and of antioxidants. In particular, antioxidants work within the body to help prevent and moderate damage from oxidative stress—whether from external sources, such as pollutants, toxins, and rancid fats, or from internal sources, such as the normal oxidation processes involved in metabolism and the production of energy. Although fruits and vegetables are the foods most commonly associated with high levels of antioxidants, nuts and seeds, particularly pecans, walnuts, hazelnuts, and pistachios, are also an exceptional source, often in the form of the same compounds that provide their color and astringent flavors.

What about weight gain from eating nuts and seeds? Because they're high in fat, they are indeed more calorie dense. However, as long as they're eaten in moderation and included as a substitute for (rather than an addition to) other snacks or foods high in saturated fat, weight gain shouldn't be an issue. In fact, including more healthy fats in the diet can actually help with weight loss, providing not only the nutrients the body needs to function properly but increased satisfaction as well.

Buying, Storing, and Using Nuts and Seeds

As you can see, nuts and seeds are extremely healthful—if they're fresh and properly stored. However, once they become rancid, they pose significant health hazards, including weakening the immune system and promoting aging. Even worse, they become carcinogenic. Although because many nuts are somewhat expensive, it can sometimes seem difficult to discard them, let this be your motivation to purchase only nuts in good, fresh condition. Buy them in smaller quantities, and store them properly. Consuming nuts that are even only slightly rancid is simply not worth the health risk.

The best way to purchase whole nuts and seeds is in the shell. If fresh and in good condition when purchased, they can be kept at room temperature for up to three months. They will last for up to six months if refrigerated or one year if frozen. Look for unshelled nuts that are heavy for their size and free of cracks or holes.

Shelled nuts are, however, more convenient, and some nuts, like cashews, macadamia nuts, and black walnuts, are only available shelled. For optimal freshness, flavor, texture, and nutrition, the best way to buy nuts and seeds is in bags or containers that have been vacuum-packed or nitrogen-flushed, or packed in oxygen-barrier plastic or foil packaging. This especially pertains to varieties that contain a high proportion of polyunsaturated fats, which are more susceptible to rancidity. Otherwise, look for whole and shelled nuts and seeds that are fresh and stored in cool and clean conditions away from direct light. In general, nuts and seeds should look firm and have uniform color inside and out. Avoid any nuts and seeds that are shriveled, moldy, or discolored.

Shelf life for shelled nuts can range from one month to one year, depending on the particular nut or seed and how well it has been stored from harvest to sale. After you purchase nuts and seeds, store them in glass jars or tightly sealed containers at temperatures below 50°F and away from light and moisture. It's best to refrigerate them if you have the space available to do this. Freezing will extend freshness, stretching shelf life from six months to one year. Chopped, sliced, or ground nuts are extremely susceptible to rancidity, so it's best to buy whole nuts and process them at home just prior to use.

Both raw and roasted nuts are available. Raw nuts have a milder, sweeter taste, while roasted nuts have a deeper color, intensified flavor, and crisper, crunchier texture. Roasted nuts are also less likely to sink to the bottom when baked in muffins, quick breads, and cakes. However, because the fat within the nuts is exposed to oxygen during the roasting process, roasted nuts have a shorter shelf life than raw nuts do and require special attention for storage.

When buying roasted nuts, dry-roasted varieties are your best bet, since the oil used to roast them adds an extra element of risk if it is less than fresh or of poor quality. Not only can this make the nuts more susceptible to rancidity and subsequent oxidation, but it can also affect their flavor. In fact, unless you're confident the nuts are freshly roasted, just buy raw nuts and roast them at home, storing any extra in the refrigerator in a glass jar or tightly sealed container for up to four weeks; frozen, they'll keep for nine to twelve months. The process is very easy, and as a side benefit, the alluring aroma of roasting nuts will waft and linger throughout the house.

ROASTING AND BLANCHING NUTS AND SEEDS

Nuts and seeds can be toasted in a skillet on top of the stove or roasted in the oven. To pan-toast nuts and seeds, preheat a skillet over low heat and then add a thin layer of nuts or seeds. Stir constantly, checking for doneness after 5 minutes and every few minutes thereafter to prevent burning. Don't even think of walking away, even if "just for a minute," as they can burn very quickly. Even though pan-toasting may seem quicker, it's difficult to toast the nuts and seeds as evenly in a skillet as in the oven, where the heat is evenly distributed.

To oven-roast, preheat the oven to 275°F to 280°F, spread the nuts or seeds on a baking sheet, and bake for anywhere from 5 to 11 minutes, depending on the nut or seed, stirring occasionally. Using these lower temperatures will ensure more even roasting throughout the nut and actually increase shelf life. As with pan-toasting, check the nuts frequently; it's all too easy to burn them. Since they will continue to roast while cooling, remove them from the heat

just before you think they're done. The nuts will become crisper as they cool.

For a special treat, toward the end of roasting, sprinkle nuts with tamari shoyu, stir to coat, and then place them back in the oven to dry for about 2 minutes. Alternatively, immerse nuts in tamari shoyu prior to roasting, using about 2 tablespoons per cup of nuts, and then roast the nuts at 300°F for 10 to 15 minutes. Tamari-roasted nuts are terrific as a snack, especially when combined with raisins or sprinkled on foods as a condiment.

Blanched almonds or hazelnuts are also best prepared at home. Like roasting, blanching accelerates the oxidative process, even more so since the process removes the skin, which is a natural barrier to oxygen. You might also consider whether blanched nuts are truly necessary in a given application. Since the skin contains tannins and other phenolic compounds that are excellent antioxidants, removing the skin not only reduces fiber but also significantly lowers the phytonutrient value of the nut.

If you still choose to blanch nuts, the method for almonds is different than that for peanuts, hazelnuts, and pistachios. To blanch almonds, simply pour boiling water over the nuts, allow them to set for 3 minutes, and drain. Then put the almonds in cold water for 1 minute. Gently rub the almonds between your thumb and fingers to slip off their skins. If desired, the blanched almonds can be dried by lightly roasting them in 300°F oven for just a few minutes.

To blanch peanuts, hazelnuts, or pistachios, first roast them, then immediately wrap them in a clean terry-cloth or coarsely textured towel to steam for about 5 minutes. Briskly rub them in the towel for 1 to 3 minutes, or until the skins are removed.

NUT AND SEED BUTTERS

Nut butter (referred to as nut paste in Europe if made without sugar) is another way to enjoy the flavors and nutrition of nuts. In general, two tablespoons of nut butter is the equivalent of one ounce of nuts. Typically used as spreads for bread and crackers, nut butters can also be used as the basis for sauces, gravies, dips, and cookies. Nearly any raw or roasted nut can be processed into nut butter, but the most commonly sold varieties are almond butter, cashew butter, hazelnut butter, sesame butter or tahini, and, of course, peanut butter. Nut butters are also sold freshly ground by a machine in the store. If made from very fresh nuts or seeds and ground at low temperatures, these usually provide the best flavor. All prepacked freshly ground nut butters should be stored and sold refrigerated and labeled with a "best sold by" date.

Thanks to the force of gravity, the oils and solids of natural nut and seed butters tend to separate. However, once the oils are stirred in, they will remain suspended in the solids if the nut butter is refrigerated. Another trick is to store unopened jars of nut butter upside down at room temperature to help distribute the oils. You'll still have some stirring to do, but it will be much easier. Avoid nut butters that have hydrogenated fat added to prevent separation. And although palm oil can be used as a natural, nonhydrogenated stabilizer, not only is it unnecessary, but it also adds additional fat.

Making Nut and Seed Butters

You can also make your own nut and seed butters at home, ensuring the freshest and likely the best tasting you'll ever have. The basic rule of thumb for making nut butter is that the higher the natural fat content of the nut or seed, the easier it will be to process. While it is easy to make raw pecan, macadamia, and walnut butters, first roasting nuts and seeds with moderate fat content will make blending much easier and faster: the roasting process brings the oils to the surface, which means you won't need to add extra oil to facilitate grinding and create a better consistency. Even using the right variety of a specific nut or seed can make the difference between success and something merely ho-hum. For example, when making almond butter, be sure to use only the higher fat "Mission" variety of almonds rather than the more commonly available "nonpareil."

Unfortunately, making nut butters in a basic no-frills home blender is often a sure-fire way to eventually burn out its motor, so if a basic home blender is what you have to work with, it may end up being cheaper simply to purchase the nut butter and not have to buy another blender! Electric nut and seed grinders, if equipped with heavy-duty motors, may be able to make small amounts of nut butters in the process of continual grinding, but this is not recommended for the inexpensive grinders that are made for grinding coffee beans, nuts, and seeds into coarse to somewhat fine textures. Food processors can make nut butters using the multipurpose blade, processing the nuts continuously until smooth. Still, when it comes down to it, a high-speed blender with a powerful motor or a juicer that has an attachment specifically for making nut butters at home will provide the best results. What's more, these machines' ability to grind more finely, which helps disperse the natural oils within the nut or seed, provides yet another way to avoid having to add extra oil during the process.

NUT AND SEED MILKS

Nut and seed milks can be used like dairy milk: as a hot or cold beverage, poured over hot and cold cereals, as the basis for making yogurt or ice cream, as an ingredient when baking, and for all cooking applications, including sauces, gravies, puddings, and custards. However, they should never be used for infant formula, as their nutritional profile doesn't fulfill babies' dietary needs, even if enriched with calcium and other vitamins.

Nut and seed milks are hardly a recent phenomenon. Almond milk and walnut milk were common ingredients in European medieval cooking among both peasants and the aristocracy. Not only were they safer alternatives to dairy milk, which spoiled quickly in the days before refrigeration and pasteurization, but they also made the official list of foods approved by the Roman Catholic Church for use during Lent and on other days when animal foods were not allowed. Even now, *latte di mandorle*, made from a sweetened almond paste (*crema di mandorle*), remains a traditional thirst-quenching summer drink in Italy and Sicily and an important ingredient in delicious desserts and sweets.

On the other side of the ocean, Native Americans made pecan milk and sweet hickory milk for use as beverages and as ingredients in corn cakes and hominy. Not only that, tribes in the western part of what is now the United States put milk they made from piñon nuts outside to freeze, creating an early version of ice cream.

Making Nut and Seed Milks

Freshly made nut and seed milk is incredibly easy to make and the flavor and overall nutrition far surpasses commercially prepared milks sold refrigerated in cartons or in shelf-stable aseptic packages; these are often sweetened and high in sodium. The fundamental process for making nut and seed milks hasn't changed much over the centuries: grind any nut or seed and blend it with water—that's basically it. One part nuts or seeds to four parts water is the proportion most commonly used when making nut milk; blend it on high for a couple of minutes until it's creamy. Less water makes it richer and creamier, which is handy for thickening soups or as a substitute for half-and half. More water makes it thinner, with a consistency similar to that of skim milk. While a basic home blender can be used to make nut and seed milk, a high-powered blender will create significantly better results. With the exception of cashew milk (which has a naturally creamy consistency because of the nut's higher starch content), most nut and seed milks should be strained through a fine-mesh strainer or cheesecloth, or, better yet, a nylon nut milk–filtering bag; these easy to find and inexpensive, and the results are silky in texture. Nut and seed milks taste even better if you allow them to set for a couple of hours before filtering and drinking, allowing the flavors to meld.

The creamy texture of almonds and cashews makes them the best candidates for nut milks, but any nut or seed or combination of them can be used. Blanching almonds and hazelnuts first to remove their skins isn't necessary nor is it advised; doing so will eliminate valuable phytonutrients found in the dark skins, though it does make for a whiter color and smoother consistency. Nut and seed milks can be customized with other ingredients as desired. For a sweeter tasting milk, blend in pitted dates, a banana, or any liquid sweetener, such as honey, maple syrup, or agave nectar. Fruit juice can be used for a portion of the liquid, too, and will also boost sweetness.

Homemade nut milk generally won't keep for more than four days in the refrigerator. Commercially prepared versions sold in aseptic packaging may last for seven to ten days after opening, since they are sterilized to destroy microorganisms that could affect safety and shelf life of the product. Stabilizers such as guar gum, xanthan gum, carrageenan, carob bean gum, and soy lecithin are also typically added to help keep the fat and liquid components within the milk in suspension. Ground flaxseeds or lecithin granules can be added to homemade nut and seed milks as stabilizers; however, if the fiber is filtered immediately after the milk is made, there is no need to add stabilizers to create that suspension. If the milk hasn't been filtered, giving it a vigorous shake before using will usually do the trick.

COCONUT WATER AND COCONUT MILK

Coconut milk is made in a different manner than other nut milks, and coconut water is very different than coconut milk. The fresh coconut water found in the center of a young coconut has a slight almond flavor and is very nutritious, being especially high in potassium and other minerals; unlike coconut milk, it contains no fat. However, it is important to note that unlike plain water, coconut water does contain calories and carbohydrates. Often enjoyed where it is grown (sipped through straws stuck straight into young, green coconuts), it is also extracted and pasteurized and packed into cans, bottles, and shelf-stable aseptic containers, making it widely available many miles away from the tropics.

It is the white pulp, or meat, of a mature coconut that is used to make coconut milk—and it's not difficult to do at home. Starting with a fresh coconut, remove the pulp from the shell, cut it into small pieces, then add boiling water to cover and let steep for about 10 minutes. Allow the mixture to cool briefly before transferring to a blender. Because hot liquids have a tendency to spew when blended, leave the lid slightly ajar and cover with a towel before blending. Process until the coconut is finely grated, about a minute or so. Then, using a nut milk–filtering bag or a strainer lined with a double layer of cheesecloth, strain the coconut milk into a bowl and squeeze the pulp to extract as much liquid as possible. You can add more hot water to the remaining pulp and strain and squeeze it again for a lighter coconut milk. For an extra-light coconut milk, do a third extraction.

Although the results aren't quite as tasty, dried unsweetened coconut can also be used if fresh coconut is unavailable. Combine 2 cups of coconut with 2¾ cups of water in a pan and bring to a boil, then lower the heat, cover, and simmer for 10 minutes. Transfer to a blender (observing the same cautions noted above) and process for about 1 minute. Strain the mixture as described above.

If allowed to set, coconut milk (including canned coconut milk) will separate, just as raw whole milk does, with the higher fat "cream" rising to the top and the thinner, more watery "skim" layer staying on the bottom. Just shake the milk vigorously and the layers will combine once again. Use coconut milk as a beverage, on cereals, and in curries, desserts, soups, and sauces. Unless a recipe specifies otherwise, cook coconut milk and coconut cream over low heat, stirring constantly to avoid curdling and separation of the natural oils from the milk. Coconut milk is very perishable, lasting only about two days when refrigerated, so use it quickly.

Exploring Nuts and Seeds

Each and every nut and seed has its own story, including its origins and where it is currently grown, unique nutritional attributes, special varieties available, how to store, and, in particular, its own special culinary opportunities, sparking the imagination to bring nuts and seeds out of the snack bowl and onto your plate.

ALMONDS

Predominantly monounsaturated fat
1 ounce = slightly less than ¼ cup
Almonds are related to peaches, nectarines, and other members of the rose family. Originally native to the Mediterranean region, almonds are now grown throughout the world, with the United States (California), Spain, Syria, Iran, and Italy being the five countries with the greatest production. **Sweet almonds** are the edible variety, whereas **bitter almonds** are used in cosmetics and to make almond extract.

Both the standard nutrients and phytochemicals in almonds contribute to their cholesterol-reducing effects when eaten on a regular basis. They are high in heart-healthy monounsaturated fat, and their skins are a good source of fiber (3.3 grams per ounce) and of antioxidants. The skin contains most of the almond's flavonoids, including proanthocyanidins, which are responsible for the slightly astringent flavor and brown color of the skin. Almonds also contain more calcium than any other nut, supplying 70 milligrams per ounce, and are one of the best nut sources of protein (6 grams per ounce) and vitamin E (7.3 milligrams of alpha-tocopherol per ounce). Beta-sitosterol is the primary phytosterol found in almonds, providing additional help with lowering cholesterol.

Almond Varieties

There are hundreds of varieties of almond, each with its own unique combination of flavor intensity, shape, color, and texture, making some more appropriate than others for specific purposes. However, only a few are widely available. Here are some of the most common varieties.

"**California almonds**" is a classification that covers a number of varieties that generally have a medium-thick shell and slightly wrinkled, medium-brown kernels. They're a good all-purpose nut and considered good for blanching. **Marcona almonds**, from Spain, are a heart-shaped variety generally sold blanched, fried in oil, and salted. They have light brown, flat, smooth kernels and a very rich and somewhat sweet flavor. Fried Marcona almonds are good as a snack; raw, they're best for baking. **Mission almonds** have a thick, hearty shell encasing a small, wide kernel that is dark brownish red, plump, rounded, and deeply wrinkled, with a strong almond flavor. They're exceptionally good for roasting and are the almond of choice to use for making almond butter.

Nonpareil almonds, likely the most commonly available, are a medium-size almond with a thin outer shell and smooth, flat, light brown kernels.

From top: (1) Smoked almonds, (2) slivered almonds, (3) tamari roasted almonds, (4) "California almonds," (5) Marcona almonds, (6) sesame honey almonds, (7) raw almonds in the shell

They are an all-purpose type of almond, and the variety that is most used for blanching as the skin is easily removed. By contrast, **Pizzuta almonds**, from Sicily, are an heirloom flat, pointed, oval, broad-shaped almond variety that is orangey brown in color. Limited in production, it is worth the hunt to experience its flavor that is milky and sweet, yet bitter, like almond extract. Grown in southern Sicily near the Mediterranean Sea, the Pizzuta almond owes its essence to the area's sunny but humid weather and its calcium-rich soil. Best for savoring as a snack or dessert, they can also be used in baking for a special occasion.

Storage and Use

About 1 pound of almonds in the shell will yield 1¼ cups of shelled almonds. Store shelled almonds in the refrigerator for up to nine months and in the freezer for up to one year. Due to their edible but tough brown skins, which are retained after shelling, almonds resist rancidity better than any other nut.

Thanks to its combination of fiber and moderate fat content, which makes for a dry texture, **almond flour** can be used as a gluten-free substitute for some of the flour in baked goods or as a thickener or breading agent. Although commercially ground almond flour may prove to be finer textured, almond flour can be made at home in a high-powered blender, or, when only small amounts are needed, in a small electric seed grinder or coffee grinder. Be sure to use California almonds or nonpareil almonds for best results.

Delicious **almond butter** can be used instead of butter or cream cheese as a spread on muffins, toast, and bagels, or like peanut butter in sandwiches, cookies, sauces, and spreads. Whether made from raw or roasted almonds, its flavor is exceptional, with raw almond butter being mellower overall. Like peanut butter, almond butter comes in smooth and crunchy versions. It has about the same amount of protein as peanut butter, but it's lower in saturated fat and higher in monounsaturated fat, giving it a preferable fatty acid profile.

Almond paste, a dense mixture of finely ground blanched almonds, sugar, corn syrup, water, and sometimes almond extract, is used as an ingredient in cookies, cakes, candies, and pastries, sometimes as a filling and sometimes standing in for flour. It's sold in tubes or cans that, once opened, should be stored in the refrigerator. Made with essentially the same ingredients, **marzipan** contains a higher percentage of sugar to create a more pliable consistency, making it easier to sculpt into decorative shapes and to roll out for use as a smooth cake covering.

BRAZIL NUTS

About equal monounsaturated and
  polyunsaturated fat
1 ounce = slightly less than ¼ cup (but limit to
  no more than 2 Brazil nuts per day)

Brazil nuts are the seeds of trees that grow in the Amazon—in Brazil, Peru, Bolivia, Colombia, Venezuela, and Guiana—and reach heights of over 130 feet. The tree's fruit looks like a coconut with a woody shell; inside are the long, wedge-shaped Brazil nuts with their own hard shells, found in clusters of twelve to twenty-four.

Remarkably, Brazil nuts contain 543 micrograms of selenium per ounce. This trace mineral is known for its excellent antioxidant properties and ability to support the immune system, but a little goes a long way. Too much selenium over long periods of time can manifest in symptoms of selenium toxicity, most notably hair and nail brittleness and loss, as well as skin rashes, gastrointestinal disturbances, and fatigue. Since 400 micrograms of selenium is the upper daily intake limit recommended for adults, consumption of Brazil nuts should be limited to no more than two per day.

Storage and Use

Brazil nuts are primarily sold shelled, as cracking the shell is a more challenging venture than with many other nuts. Store shelled Brazil nuts in the refrigerator for up to six months or in the freezer for up to nine months.

Brazil nuts make a delicious snack, especially when eaten with fresh or dried fruit, such as apples, pears, raisins, dates, and figs. Their flavor and texture have a tropical flair, somewhat reminiscent of coconut and macadamia nuts, and they contribute a creamy texture to smoothies. Try a few chopped Brazil nuts in cookies, cakes, salads, and even poultry stuffing for extra texture and flavor.

Brazil nuts can be ground into a smooth, very creamy butter, although it's seldom sold commercially. It can be used like any other nut butter but, since it's exceptionally rich, it is best to use it sparingly. In comparison to peanut butter, it is lower in protein and higher in fat, including saturated fat.

CASHEWS

Predominantly monounsaturated fat
1 ounce = slightly less than ¼ cup

Cashews, which are in the same plant family as mangos and pistachios, grow near the equator on bushy, medium-size trees. India, Mozambique, and Brazil are the principal producers. The grayish brown, kidney-shaped shell surrounding the cashew nut (the plant's true fruit) hangs from the lower end of the cashew apple, a pear-shaped, yellow or red fruit (technically a pseudofruit). After the cashew apple drops to the ground, the cashew nut is separated from the fruit. Cashew apples, which spoil very quickly, are eaten fresh locally or processed into juices, syrups, preserves, and alcoholic beverages.

Within the shell, the cashew is at one end and at the other end is a honeycomb of cells that contain a toxic fluid that can blister the mouth. Surrounding the nut itself is another thin brown shell. Because of the danger from the toxic oil that lies between the outer shell and the inner shell, cashews are sold only in their shelled form and are extracted using methods that ensure their safety.

Cashews contain more iron (1.9 milligrams) than other tree nuts. They are also a good source of betasitosterol, which helps reduce serum cholesterol. Since they contain more carbohydrates than most nuts, mostly in the form of starch, they're also lower in fat.

Storage and Use

Store cashews in the refrigerator for up to six months or in the freezer for up to nine months. Their high starch content makes cashews a very effective thickener when ground and added to soups, smoothies, curries, and stews. They also yield creamy cashew milk and sauces. Their higher level of carbohydrates also means that raw cashews have a sweet flavor, one that develops more depth and complexity when they're roasted. If left whole, cashews are a wonderful addition to stir-fries and East Indian dishes. Since they become unpleasantly soggy when cooked too long, they should be added at the end of cooking to maintain crispness.

Cashew butter contains a small amount of oil to compensate for the nut's higher starch content and drier consistency, creating a smoother texture. When buying cashew butter, check the label to ensure that only high oleic oil is used; this will ensure optimal quality and greater resistance to rancidity. Cashew butter is a treat as a spread, in soups as a nondairy substitute for cream, and in dips, salad dressings, and sauces. Although it has a similar amount of saturated fat as peanut butter and less protein, it is higher in monounsaturated fat.

CHESTNUTS

About equal monounsaturated and
*   polyunsaturated fat*
1 ounce = 3 roasted and peeled chestnuts

Chestnuts have been used as food around the world for a very long time—in Asia for nearly six thousand years, in Europe for about three thousand years, in the United States certainly long before the pioneers settled the country, and in Australia since the 1850s. Though chestnut trees once grew prolifically from Maine to Georgia, a devastating blight introduced in 1904 from imported Chinese chestnut trees nearly wiped out native North American chestnut trees by 1950. Although a few surviving natives have been found and different hybrids have been developed in attempts to reinvigorate chestnut cultivation in the United States, most chestnuts purchased in the

Chestnuts

United States are imported. Worldwide, China reigns as the largest producer, with Korea as the second-largest producer. In Europe, Italy grows and exports the most chestnuts, followed by France and Spain.

Chestnuts are unique among nuts. They have a high water content, are very low in fat, and contain almost 50 percent carbohydrates, making them seem more like a starchy vegetable than a nut—which is exactly how they have been used and valued for thousands of years. They are also good sources of potassium and even a small amount of vitamin C. Although chestnuts are also low in protein, it is of high quality.

Varieties

The size and flavor of chestnuts vary widely among species. Though there are many wild varieties used locally, these are the primary types found commercially: **American chestnuts** (*Castanea dentata*) are small, with excellent, concentrated flavor. They have softer shells than other chestnuts and no astringent pellicle (a brown membrane that clings to other varieties of chestnuts). **Chinese chestnuts** (*Castanea mollissima*) are medium-size and have good flavor. **European chestnuts** (*Castanea sativa*) range in size from small to large and also taste good. Smaller varieties are also fairly flat sided. The more commonly available variety is larger and more rounded, making it the better choice for roasting. **Japanese chestnuts** (*Castanea crenata*), confusingly, are sometimes called Chinese chestnuts, even though they are a different species. They have fair flavor and come in various sizes.

Fresh chestnuts are fun and festive, but they're only available a few months per year. As an alternative, roasted and peeled chestnuts are available in vacuum-packed cans and bags. Once opened, they should be stored like freshly cooked chestnuts. Dried chestnuts are also available, and because they're shelf stable, they're very convenient. Store them as you would dried beans, in airtight containers for up to a year. As the natural drying process converts some of the starch within fresh chestnuts into sugar, dried chestnuts are sweeter in flavor when reconstituted. They also double in size after they are reconstituted, so use half the volume of dried chestnuts as the total amount you want when cooked. To use them in recipes in place of shelled fresh chestnuts, first soak them in cold water for 6 to 8 hours. Or, use the quicker hot-soak method by covering them with boiling water and allowing them to soak for an hour. The chestnuts can then be added directly to a recipe that will be simmered for at least an hour. Alternatively, precook the soaked chestnuts if they will be added to recipes that require less cooking time, adding extra water, if needed, to cover the surface of the chestnuts by about 1 inch. Bring them to a boil, reduce the heat, and simmer them for an hour, or until tender. For a richly flavored rice dish, cook dried chestnuts with rice in a pressure cooker.

Storage and Use

Boiled and mashed like potatoes, made into flour for bread or noodles, roasted for a snack, or even eaten raw, chestnuts have been for thousands of years a staple in the diet wherever chestnut trees have grown. They remain a highly valued snack and ingredient in contemporary times, adding flavor and texture to soups, stuffings, pastas, stir-fries, and desserts. Chestnut flour, ground from dried chestnuts, can be added to other flours when making pasta, bread, and other baked goods.

About 1 pound of chestnuts in the shell will yield 2½ cups of shelled chestnuts. Fresh chestnuts in the shell contain up to 50 percent water, making them prone to mold and thus highly perishable, so only purchase fresh chestnuts if they're sold refrigerated. Chestnuts should have smooth, shiny brown shells free of pinholes, mold, and splits. The best ones will feel heavy for their size. Store fresh chestnuts in a plastic bag in the refrigerator for up to three weeks or freeze them for up to nine months. Cooked chestnuts will keep for a similar period of time; store them in an airtight container.

CHIA SEEDS
Predominantly polyunsaturated fat, primarily omega-3 fatty acids
1 ounce = 2¾ tablespoons

If a chia-sprouting novelty planter is what most comes to mind when chia seeds are mentioned, you're not alone. But, like other seeds, chia has a lot to offer.

Originating in Mexico—where the ancient Mayans and Aztecs recognized the seeds as an exceptional source of nutrients—chia is also grown in Central and South America. Depending on the amount of water available where it is grown, the chia plant can grow from just a couple inches tall up to 24 inches high. Tiny tubular flowers can be found on the several stems that emerge from the base of the plant, which, after they naturally dry later in the season, are shaken to harvest their seeds. These very tiny seeds, only about 1 millimeter in diameter, prove multicolored on close inspection—brown, gray, black, and white. They have a very mild, nut-like flavor, making them quite inconspicuous in dishes despite their long list of healthy attributes.

Like flaxseeds, chia seeds are rich in the valuable omega-3 fatty acid alpha-linolenic acid (ALA), which is often deficient—and out of balance in relation to omega-6 fatty acids—in many people's diets. Chia seeds are higher in dietary fiber than flaxseed, with their soluble fiber forming a gel when mixed with liquids. In addition to its thickening properties being handy when making desserts and smoothies, chia seed helps support normal functioning of the digestive tract, and can have a positive effect on cholesterol. Its fiber is also helpful in preventing constipation. Along with providing a good variety of minerals, chia seeds are also a good source of antioxidants, which also aid the seeds' ability to be stored longer without becoming rancid.

Chia seeds can be used whole or ground. There is no need to grind them, though—even when consumed whole, their nutrients are available to the body.

Storage and Use

Chia seeds can be sprinkled on cereals, salads, vegetables, or yogurt, tossed into smoothies, stirred into juices, or used in baking either whole or ground and mixed with flour. Refrigerate the chia seeds after opening the package, storing in a tightly sealed container and being mindful of the suggested use-by date.

COCONUT

Predominantly saturated fat
1 ounce = ¹/₃ cup dried shredded coconut

The coconut palm has been highly valued since ancient times as a source of water, nutrients, fiber, and fuel. Although fresh coconut meat is often classified as a fruit, in its dried form it is treated more like a nut. Chewy and subtly sweet, coconut meat is actually the endosperm of the plant—the nutrients designed to support the palm tree embryo as

it sprouts through one of the eyes in the hard, hairy husk. Coconut palms grow in hot, rainy tropical regions, with the Philippines, Indonesia, India, Brazil, and Sri Lanka being the top five coconut producers. Dried shredded or flaked coconut is made from coconuts that have been split open to remove the internal liquid. The meat is dried in the sun or in kilns until it has a 2.5 percent moisture content, at which point it's known as copra.

Dried coconut is high in fiber (4.6 grams per ounce). Unlike other nuts and seeds, its fats are primarily saturated. However, unlike the saturated fats in meat and dairy products, which are comprised primarily of long-chain fatty acids, the saturated fat in coconut is made up of short- and medium-chain fatty acids (primarily lauric acid followed by myristic, caprylic, and palmitic acid), which have been found to not increase cholesterol levels. These medium-chain triglycerides, also known as MCTs, are not stored as fat but rather are metabolized quickly.

Storage and Use

One medium fresh coconut will yield 3 to 4 cups of freshly grated coconut. (You can also use a vegetable peeler to make coconut flakes.) Store fresh coconut in a tightly sealed container for up to four days in the refrigerator or up to four months in the freezer. Dried coconut also keeps best when refrigerated, tightly sealed, and used within six months. Purchase only unsweetened coconut rather than the presweetened varieties. Not only is it more nutritious, but it also has better flavor. And because the amount of sweetener added varies, you can most effectively control the sweetness of foods cooked with coconut if you use the unsweetened form. Like other nuts, coconut's flavor is enhanced when it is roasted. Preheat the oven to 275°F, spread fresh or dried unsweetened coconut on a baking sheet, and bake for about 5 to 10 minutes, until the coconut becomes golden in color.

While coconut milk made from fresh or dried coconut is a familiar ingredient in sweet and savory

Asian, Indian, Hawaiian, Latin, and Caribbean cuisines (see Making Nut and Seed Milks, page 174), flaked and grated coconut can also be used like nuts, added to cookies, muffins, granola, puddings, cobblers, and cakes. Or enjoy it simply sprinkled on fresh fruit, such as strawberries and mangos, as an accent on cereal, or as a flavorful garnish on vegetables, main dishes, and desserts.

FLAXSEEDS

Predominantly polyunsaturated fat, primarily
   omega-3 fatty acids
1 ounce = 2¾ tablespoons whole flaxseeds
1 tablespoon whole flaxseeds = about 1½ tablespoons
   ground flaxseeds

Flaxseeds are tiny, oval, reddish brown or golden seeds from the blue-flowered flax plant, now grown primarily in Canada, China, the United States, and India. Flax fiber has been used for food, clothing, and even building materials throughout the world for more than seven thousand years. When it comes to food, flaxseeds have long been prized for their flavor, fiber, and nutrient value. Flaxseeds were a valued remedy in ancient Egyptian and Greek medicine, and around 750 CE, Charlemagne thought flaxseeds so essential for health that he enacted laws requiring their regular consumption.

Half of the total fat in flaxseed (and 80 percent of its polyunsaturated fat) is from alpha-linolenic acid, making it one of the richest plant sources of omega-3 fatty acids. Each tablespoon of ground flaxseeds supplies 1.8 grams of omega-3 fatty acids, which are deficient in most modern diets (and they're also underconsumed in relation to omega-6 fatty acids). Because flaxseed contains three times more omega-3 fatty acids than omega-6, adding flaxseeds to your diet may help correct the typical imbalance and provide significant health benefits, including helping reduce inflammation and possibly helping to lower the risk of heart disease and cancer. And although polyunsaturated fats are normally very sensitive to heat (this is discussed in the next chapter), when flaxseeds are included in baked goods or otherwise cooked, their omega-3 fatty acids have shown to be very heat stable.

Flaxseed is also very high in fiber, providing 2.2 grams of fiber per tablespoon of ground flaxseeds. Mucilage gum is the main type of soluble fiber found in the seed coat; when moistened, it expands and becomes thick and sticky, making it effective in helping promote bowel regularity. Soluble fiber may also help stabilize blood glucose levels and lower cholesterol levels.

Flaxseed is also an excellent source of lignans, a type of fiber (found within its cell walls) that is acclaimed as a phytoestrogen, and also for its antioxidant capabilities. Flaxseed's primary lignan, secoisolariciresinol diglycoside, thankfully referred to simply as SDG, is broken down by bacteria in the digestive tract and converted into the hormone-like substances enterodiol and enterolactone (these are referred to as mammalian lignans because they are produced in the mammalian colon and not by plants). Depending on the amount of stronger estrogens, like estradiol, available in the body, these can either act as weak estrogens and help balance hormone levels or function as estrogen antagonists, possibly helping protect against hormone-sensitive cancers, such as some forms of breast cancer. Flax contains many antioxidants beyond its lignans: flavonoids, carotenoids, lutein, zeaxanthin, and gamma-tocopherol (a form of vitamin E). All of them, as well as the metabolites enterodiol and enterolactone, help protect the body from oxidative damage and thus help guard against chronic diseases.

Although flax oil is a more concentrated source of omega-3 fatty acids than whole and ground flaxseeds, it lacks the fiber and, consequently, the potential benefits of the lignans. Some flax oil manufacturers add purified lignans back into their oils, but a better solution may be to use both flax oil and flaxseeds to get the best of both worlds.

Varieties

There are two types of flaxseed available: brown and golden. Both provide similar nutritional benefits. The main differences between the two are color, flavor, and price. Brown flaxseeds are reddish brown and have a nutty flavor. They are best for use in hearty-flavored foods or those that would be complemented by a stronger flavor. In contrast, golden flaxseeds are light yellow and have a milder flavor. They are best for use in lighter-flavored foods. As they aren't as widely available as brown flaxseed, they're typically more expensive.

Storage and Use

Whole flaxseeds can be stored in a glass jar or other airtight packaging in a cool, dry place for up to a year after harvest. However, since few labels indicate a use-by date or you may have purchased flaxseeds from a bulk bin, using whole flaxseed within six months after purchase is probably a good idea. When indoor temperatures are warm, store whole flaxseeds in a tightly sealed container in the refrigerator.

Flaxseeds have many uses in the kitchen. They are often used in their whole form to provide extra crunch, color, a lot of fiber, and a pleasant nutty flavor, perhaps as a topping applied before baking, or as an ingredient in cereals, crackers, breads, muffins, and other baked goods. But because their tough, protective seed coat is so hard, it isn't broken down by either chewing or digestion, so they must be ground if their omega-3 fatty acids and other nutrients are to be assimilated. Simply sprinkle ground flaxseeds over cereals, soups, salads, or vegetables, or mix it into juices or smoothies.

Because flaxseeds are high in fiber and they swell and increase in bulk when moistened, start out with just a couple of teaspoons, and be sure to consume them with plenty of liquid. These same mucilaginous properties of flaxseeds allow them to be used in place of eggs to help increase the volume of baked goods. For the equivalent of 1 egg, combine 1 tablespoon of ground flaxseeds, also known as flaxseed meal, with 3 tablespoons of water. Set the mixture aside for a few minutes to allow it to gel, and then add it to your recipe as you would an egg.

Ground flaxseed can be substituted for one-fourth to one-third of the flour in muffins or quick breads; however, too much flaxseed will weigh down the batter, limiting the amount it can rise. Just as extra liquid is needed when sprinkling ground flaxseed over food, add 1 tablespoon of extra liquid for every 3 tablespoons of ground flaxseed used in a recipe. Baked goods made with ground flaxseed tend to brown quickly, so you may need to reduce the baking time slightly or lower the oven temperature by 25°F. Unlike most other seeds, flaxseeds don't make a good seed butter, as they are too gritty when ground.

HAZELNUTS

Predominantly monounsaturated fat
1 ounce = slightly less than ¼ cup

For nearly five thousand years, hazelnuts have been prized for their mild, rich, slightly sweet flavor and crisp texture, which is enhanced when they're roasted. They range in color from reddish brown to dark brown on the exterior and cream to tan-colored in the interior. Today, the principal countries producing hazelnuts are Turkey, Spain, Italy, and the United States (Oregon).

The names *hazelnut* and *filbert* are often used interchangeably, and different authorities make different distinctions between the two (wild versus cultivated varieties, or American versus European varieties, for example). Given that both are delicious, don't worry too much about the nomenclature, which is apt to be misapplied anyway. Several explanations have been given for the origin of the name *filbert*. Some say it arose because the day that harvesting of the nuts usually began was on the feast day of St. Philbert, a French monk who lived in the seventh century. Others believe it to be derived from the German word *vollbart*, which means "full beard," referring to the appearance of the shell that covers the entire nut. Practically speaking, large, round hazelnuts are the kind usually sold for snacking, roasting, and general cooking. The European variety, more often called filberts, are smaller in size and easier to blanch and are consequently preferred by many European bakers and confectioners, who often grind them to use as flour.

In addition to their heart-healthy monounsaturated fat, hazelnuts are an excellent source of phytochemicals. Proanthocyanidins, a type of flavonoid found in hazelnuts, are present in particularly high amounts. These compounds, which are responsible for the astringent flavor of hazelnuts' skins, can neutralize both water-soluble and fat-soluble toxins in the body. Hazelnuts are also a good source of phytosterols, which help reduce cholesterol and boost the immune system, as well as vitamin E in the form of alpha-tocopherol.

Storage and Use

About 1 pound of hazelnuts in the shell will yield 1½ cups of whole nuts. Hazelnuts in the shell can be kept at room temperature in dry conditions for two to three months or in the refrigerator or freezer for up to one year. On the other hand, shelled hazelnuts always need cool conditions. Store them in the refrigerator for up to six months or in the freezer for up to one year.

Simply appreciated when eaten out of hand, especially when roasted, whole hazelnuts are also exceptional in salads, providing a nice contrast in shape, texture, and flavor. As with almonds, many cooks like to blanch hazelnuts to get rid of the fibrous, somewhat astringent brown skin that surrounds the meat. However, removing the skins also strips away the protective action of the phytochemicals. Use whole hazelnuts, including the skin, for optimal nutrition and complexity of flavor, and blanch them only when truly necessary. Chopped or sliced, they make a nice addition to baked goods.

Both blanched and whole hazelnuts can be ground into flour and substituted for one-fourth to one-third of the flour called for in a recipe. **Hazelnut flour** is particularly good in muffins, breads, and biscuits. Its mealier texture, in comparison

to almond flour, may provide grainier and denser (albeit delicious) results, depending on the recipe.

Hazelnut butter or **paste** is another way to enjoy hazelnuts while taking advantage of their many nutritional benefits. It is usually ground from roasted hazelnuts and has a very rich flavor and a smooth, silky texture. Use it like peanut butter, add it to cookie recipes, or spread it on bread and baked goods in place of butter. Thinned with fruit juice, it makes a terrific sauce for sliced bananas, apples, and pears. In comparison to peanut butter, hazelnut butter is lower in protein and higher in overall fat; however, it has a higher percentage of monounsaturated fat and is lower in saturated and polyunsaturated fats. Since it contains more natural oil than peanut butter, it will also have a thinner consistency.

MACADAMIA NUTS
Predominantly monounsaturated fat
1 ounce = ¼ cup

Macadamia nuts are produced from evergreen trees indigenous to Australia. Named after John Macadam, the Scottish scientist who first cultivated the tree in the mid-1800s, the macadamia tree was originally grown only for ornamental purposes. Fortunately, somewhere along the line someone realized that beyond the tree's natural beauty, its nuts are delicious. They are mildly sweet and buttery with a smooth, creamy texture. About the size and shape of a marble, they are light beige in color. Introduced to Hawaii in 1882, the macadamia tree is now the most important tree crop grown there, making Hawaii one of the top producers, along with Australia and New Zealand.

Since the shells of macadamia nuts are very hard to crack, requiring special equipment to do the job, they are sold shelled. Once the husk and shell are removed, the actual kernel ends up being only 15 percent of the whole nut, explaining why macadamia nuts are among the more expensive nuts.

Macadamia nuts are a good source of phytosterols, especially beta-sitosterol, which can help lower cholesterol. They also have the highest percentage of calories from fat of all nuts, although most of it is monounsaturated. Their percentage of polyunsaturated fat is low, and they don't contain an inordinate amount of saturated fat.

Storage and Use

Store macadamia nuts in the refrigerator for up to six months or in the freezer for up to nine months. Because macadamia nuts can stand up to higher heat, they are a good, flavorful addition to stir-fries and sautés. Like hazelnuts, they are a complementary addition to salads because of their unique shape and taste. And, of course, they are often added to baked goods and are delicious eaten as a snack.

Macadamia butter is very rich. Because it is very high in fat in comparison to other nut butters, it should be used in moderation, but you can use it as you would any other nut butter. It's a wonderful nondairy alternative to cream in soups.

PEANUTS

Predominantly monounsaturated fat
1 ounce = slightly less than ¼ cup

First cultivated thousands of years ago in South America, peanuts have since become an important component of traditional cuisines worldwide. The three top producers worldwide are China, India, and the United States. Although peanuts are actually members of the legume family, they are higher in fat and lower in carbohydrates than other legumes, so they're commonly used like nuts and are included in many of the same reference charts as nuts. They mature underground (explaining their other common moniker, groundnuts), yielding two or three peanuts within each brown shell.

In addition to their high levels of protein (7 grams per ounce), niacin, and heart-healthy monounsaturated fat, peanuts are an excellent source of phytochemicals. The phytosterols in peanuts may help reduce cholesterol levels in the blood. They are also very high in antioxidants, including proanthocyanidins, resveratrol, and p-coumaric acid. Although resveratrol is most often associated

with grapes and wine, one ounce of peanuts contains the same amount as two pounds of grapes or about half an ounce of wine. Resveratrol has been associated with reduced risk of atherosclerosis and with increased blood flow to the brain, which may help reduce the risk of stroke. And because it's been shown to help stop the growth of damaged cells within the body, resveratrol may also help reduce the risk of cancer. P-coumaric acid is known for its strong antioxidant properties; roasting peanuts actually increases their p-coumaric acid content by as much as 22 percent.

Peanuts are often added to many kinds of foods to boost nutrient values. Nonetheless, nutritious as they are, peanuts are one of the most common allergenic foods, causing severe reactions in highly sensitive individuals.

Varieties

There are four primary varieties of peanuts, each with a different size, shape, flavor, and set of uses. **Runner**, a higher yield variety with uniform intermediate kernel size and good flavor when roasted, is used for peanut butter and salted peanut products. **Virginia**, a variety with large oval kernels and good peanutty flavor, is used for candies, salted peanut products, and nut mixes, and is sold both raw and roasted in the shell. **Spanish**, a small, mild-tasting variety with round kernels with reddish brown skin, is used for peanut candies, nut mixes, snacks, and peanut butter. **Valencia**, a medium to small, sweet, richly flavored variety with oval kernels with bright red skin, is a good roasting peanut, in or out of the shell. Valencias are used for boiled peanuts and peanut butter, and are sold both raw and roasted in the shell.

Storage and Use

About 1½ pounds of peanuts in the shell will yield 1 pound or 3½ cups of shelled peanuts. Although peanuts are susceptible to contamination by aflatoxins (carcinogenic substances produced by certain strains of a mold), better storage and handling methods, along with testing, have lowered rates of contamination in recent years. Since the fungus grows in humid, hot conditions, especially between 86°F and 96°F, and because peanuts tend to go rancid quickly, it's especially important to keep peanuts in cool, dry conditions. Store peanuts in the shell in a cool, dry place for up to two months or in the refrigerator for up to nine months. Shelled peanuts should be refrigerated and used within three months or frozen for up to six months. For best flavor, freshness, and nutrition, avoid buying and storing chopped peanuts. Instead, chop them by hand or in a food processor immediately before use.

As a garnish for soups, salads, noodles and rice dishes, chopped and whole peanuts provide a complementary flavor and a crunchy textural contrast. Add them to stir-fries, too. Blend ground peanuts into sauces and spreads to provide extra nutrition, flavor, and bulk. They are also often used as the basis for Asian sauces and dressings. And freely substitute peanuts for other nuts when making cookies and muffins. In addition to being convenient and having great flavor, peanut butter is a good source of protein and monounsaturated fats, although somewhat higher in polyunsaturated fats than many other nut butters. The antioxidant capacity of peanut butter is, likewise, increased by 22 percent, which occurs when whole peanuts are roasted, as they are when making any commercial peanut butter.

Peanut butter is made by grinding roasted peanuts until they are smooth and creamy. Chunky versions are generally created through the addition of peanut granules. The differences among the various brands of peanut butter begin after this basic common platform.

The standards for peanut butter in the United States require that it be made from at least 90 percent peanuts from either blanched peanuts, with or without the highly nutritious germ, or unblanched peanuts, including the skins and germ. Up to 10 percent seasonings and stabilizing agents may be added, such as salt and sweeteners, along with emulsifiers and stabilizers to help keep the peanut oil from separating and rising to the top. Since 1996, adding vitamins has also been permitted. Artificial sweeteners, artificial flavors, chemical preservatives, lard and other animal fats, and coloring additives are not allowed.

Commonly used sweeteners include sugar, evaporated cane juice, honey, dextrose, corn syrup, and high-fructose corn syrup, often in combination with one another. Molasses is sometimes added, but more to complement flavor than as a sweetener. Emulsifiers, typically monoglycerides and diglycerides derived from vegetable oil, interact with the proteins in peanut butter to help keep them suspended within the oil base. Stabilizing ingredients help prevent oil separation and make the peanut butter less prone to oxidation so it doesn't need refrigeration. Stabilizers include a blend of vegetable oils, both fully and partially hydrogenated vegetable oils, with rapeseed, cottonseed, and soybean oil most often used.

Be aware that the trans fat listing on the nutrition panel may not tell the full story. Even though the ingredient label may list hydrogenated fats, labeling regulations allow a zero claim to be used if the amount of trans fat per serving is less than 0.5 gram. Unlike the process of partially hydrogenating fats, full hydrogenation (which transforms an oil into a hard fat) doesn't create trans fats. When fully hydrogenated fats are combined with partially hydrogenated fats, they're easier to work with, and also keep the overall amount of trans fat low enough to be under the radar of labeling requirements. A better type of stabilizer is palm oil. A natural alternative to hydrogenated vegetable shortening that's free of trans-fatty acids, it functions similarly, including helping protect against oxidation.

Brands made with fresh, high-quality peanuts need no additives, including flavor enhancement from sweeteners. Although oil separation occurs soon after production, an initial stirring followed by refrigeration will keep the oil from separating again without additional emulsifiers or stabilizers.

them to couscous and rice pilafs for subtle crunch and extra seasoning.

PISTACHIOS

Predominantly monounsaturated fat

1 ounce = slightly less than ¼ cup of shelled pistachios

The delicious pistachio nut is unique in many ways. Not only does it come with a precracked shell, but the kernel is green, thanks to the presence of chlorophyll. Pistachios, which originated in the Middle East and have been used for food for more than ten thousand years, are now primarily cultivated in Iran, the United States (California), Turkey, Syria, China, and Greece. The pistachio is a small tree that thrives in hot, dry, desertlike conditions. Its fruits, which grow in clusters, consist of a thin hull that tightly surrounds an inner shell and the kernel. When the fruit ripens and the internal kernel matures, the hull begins to loosen its grip on the inner shell and changes to a rosy pale yellow color. In the meantime, the internal kernel (the pistachio nut) expands, ultimately cracking the inner shell as it fills it to capacity.

Traditionally, the ripe fruits were knocked to the ground and dried with the rosy-colored hulls still attached, which meant that some of the inner shells, which are naturally grayish beige, became stained from the pigments in the hull. Early importers decided to stain all the shells red to disguise the staining, as well as to make pistachios more noticeable amid the other nuts in the marketplace. These days, pistachios are typically hulled before they are dried, which eliminates any staining issues, and most consumers view dyed shells as unnatural.

Pistachios have the distinction of being slightly lower in fat than most of the other nuts and seeds, and a majority of their fat is monounsaturated. They also have an outstanding range of phytochemicals, including phytosterols, which may help in the reduction of blood cholesterol levels, as well as the antioxidant proanthocyanidins, which not only lend pistachios their slightly astringent flavor but may help reduce the risk of cardiovascular disease and cancer. Likewise, they contain a significant amount of carotenes, especially lutein, an antioxidant associated with eye health. They also contain high levels of the antioxidant gamma-tocopherol, a form of vitamin E that helps prevent oxidation of fats both in foods and in the body. To top it off, pistachios are high in protein, earning them a high rating as a snack.

Although pistachios are available shelled, most are sold in their shell, either raw or roasted. Discard any shells that are not split open, as they usually contain immature kernels. Slightly split shells are usually fine; they just require a bit of extra effort to wedge them open. Cooking raw pistachios at low temperatures or roasting them can help retain the green color of the pistachio kernel. Pistachios are also available salted in the shell. These are made by first dipping them into a salt solution before they are dried or roasted.

Storage and Use

About 1 pound of pistachios in the shell will yield 2 cups of shelled pistachios, or in terms of cup measurements, 1 cup of pistachios in the shell yields ½ cup shelled. Store pistachios in an airtight container in the refrigerator for up to six months or in the freezer for up to one year.

Although typically eaten as snacks out of hand, pistachios also make a great addition to salads, vegetables, pasta dishes, muffins, quick breads, and desserts—including, of course, ice cream.

Pistachio butter is another option; it is green like the nut and mildly sweet. It is best served as a rich dip for fruit or vegetable slices, making for a nice snack or a simple, satisfying dessert. Try a dab stuffed into a halved, pitted medjool date. In comparison to peanut butter, pistachio butter is somewhat lower in protein but similar in terms of its fat profile.

PUMPKIN SEEDS

Predominantly polyunsaturated fat

1 ounce = about 3½ tablespoons of pumpkin seeds

Pumpkins are native to North America, where they

have been used for food for thousands of years, primarily in areas that correspond to current-day central and northern Mexico and the southwestern United States. All parts of this squash were used for food, including the seeds. Today, the pumpkin seeds sold commercially come from special varieties of pumpkin that yield long, flat, dark green seeds that are typically hullless, rather than from jack-o'-lantern pumpkins or sugar (pie) pumpkins, which have small pale seeds encased in pale fibrous hulls. Pumpkin seeds, also known as pepitas, have a subtle sweet flavor and a chewy texture.

Pumpkin seeds are especially celebrated for their impressive nutritional portfolio. High in protein (7 grams per ounce), pumpkin seeds are also a very good source of zinc (2 milligrams per ounce) and iron (4 milligrams per ounce). Their green color comes from chlorophyll. Two primary carotenes, lutein and beta-carotene, provide important antioxidants. Pumpkin seeds are high in gamma-tocopherol (5.4 milligrams per ounce), a form of vitamin E that prevents oxidation of fats, as well as lignans, a type of fiber in its cell walls, adds extra antioxidant depth. Pumpkin seeds are also an excellent source of phytosterols, a phytonutrient that can help lower cholesterol levels. The virtues of pumpkin seeds have been known for quite some time, as they've traditionally been used medicinally for bladder conditions and as a remedy for parasitic worms.

Storage and Use

Because they are high in polyunsaturated fat, pumpkin seeds need special attention to keep them from going rancid. Their freshness window is a couple months at best when they aren't refrigerated, so it can be hard to find them in top condition unless they are sold in vacuum-packed containers. Look for seeds that have a deep green color and are full, not shriveled. Store them in an airtight container in the refrigerator for up to six months or in the freezer for up to one year.

Pumpkin seeds are commonly used as a snack and in Mexican and Southwestern cooking. However, they're very versatile and can be used in many other ways. Roasted, they're a nice addition to vegetables, any cooked grain, muffins, and cookies. Garnish soup or any kind of entrée, especially enchiladas, with pumpkin seeds just before serving. Ground roasted pumpkin seeds can imbue sauces with a deep, rich flavor while also serving as a thickener.

To roast seeds removed from a fresh pumpkin, first wash them to remove any lingering stringy membranes and blot them dry. Then roast the pumpkin seeds in a 280°F oven for about 15 minutes, testing for doneness and optimal flavor. Although much smaller and more fibrous than commercially available pumpkin seeds, they are tasty and nutritious. Shelling them is a lot of work; fortunately you can eat them whole—shells and all.

Pumpkin seed butter is decidedly green and richly flavored. It can be used as a spread, in salad dressings and sauces, and in baking. Although it has about the same overall fat content as peanut butter, pumpkin seed butter has a higher percentage of polyunsaturated fat and is lower in monounsaturated fat, so it should be kept under constant refrigeration and be used quickly.

SESAME SEEDS
*About equal monounsaturated and
    polyunsaturated fat*
*1 ounce = about 3 tablespoons of sesame seeds
    with hulls or 3½ tablespoons hulled*
Sesame seeds are yet another ancient crop, with cultivation most likely originating in Africa. They have been used for both food and medicinal purposes for several thousand years. Today, about two-thirds of the world's sesame seeds, grown primarily in India, China, Mexico, and Sudan, are processed into oil, with the rest being used predominantly as a topping, seasoning, or condiment. They can also be ground into flour and used in small amounts within baked goods to provide extra flavor and nutrition.

A sesame plant stands about two to four feet high and produces flowers that mature into seedpods; the hulls of the seeds within range in color from

Clockwise, from top left: (1) Sunflower seeds, (2) chia seeds, (3) hulled sesame seeds, (4) flaxseeds, (5) black sesame seeds, (6) pumpkin seeds

light tan to red, brown, or black. Inside each hull is a tiny, oval-shaped, creamy-colored seed. Traditionally, the seeds are gathered by hand, collecting the seeds that emerge from the pod after it bursts; however, hybrid varieties have been developed whose seeds don't scatter, and this allows harvesting by machine.

Despite their small size, sesame seeds pack in an impressive amount of nutrients and flavor. Grinding the seeds will ensure that more of their nutrients will be absorbed. Sesame seeds are a good source of protein and iron, but calcium is another issue. Although nutritional charts for whole sesame seeds show them to be very high in calcium, how much of it is really absorbed remains a question as their hulls contain oxalic acid, which can bind with the calcium and prevent its absorption.

Whole sesame seeds with the hull intact are an excellent source of fiber. Like flaxseeds, sesame seeds are an excellent source of the beneficial class of fiber called lignans; in fact, they contain their own unique lignan, which is called sesamin. In a metabolic process similar to the conversion of flax lignans, sesamin functions as a precursor of the hormonelike substances enterodiol and enterolactone. These compounds are thought to help protect against hormone-sensitive cancers, such as certain forms of breast cancer, or to exert weak estrogenic effects that can help balance hormone levels in the body. The lignans in sesame seeds also have potent antioxidant effects.

Sesame seeds are especially noteworthy for containing more phytosterols than any other nut or seed. These phytochemicals have been shown to enhance the immune response and may also help reduce cholesterol levels and decrease risk of cardiovascular disease and certain cancers. Unfortunately, removing the hull removes some of the seeds' other beneficial phytochemicals, including phytic acid, which is being studied as an agent that may prevent cancer. Hulled sesame seeds are also much lower in iron, calcium, and copper. But in the end, hulling is a mixed bag: although the nutrients in the hull are lost, the nutrients within become more accessible.

Varieties

Sesame seeds are sold both whole and hulled (decorticated). Whole sesame seeds, which are light brown in color, are used extensively in the baking industry, since they tend to stick well to crackers and bread while also providing a pleasant crunch. Black sesame seeds are a whole, unhulled variety that has a strong, earthy flavor. They are typically consumed raw as they can become bitter when toasted. They are often used in Asian cooking as an ingredient or a condiment, both for flavor and to create a striking color accent on vegetables, rice and noodle dishes, and fish.

Hulled ivory-colored sesame seeds have had their hulls removed to make them easier to digest or for a milder flavor. When buying hulled sesame seeds, look for the phrase "mechanically hulled" to ensure the hulls were not removed using caustic soda or other chemical solvents. Hulled sesame seeds are often used in Asian cooking as a seasoning, both sprinkled on and incorporated into the dish. Hull-less varieties are also used in candies and sprinkled on conventional hamburger buns.

Storage and Use

Store both whole and hulled sesame seeds in moisture-proof containers in the refrigerator for up to six months or in the freezer for up to one year. Because the fiber-rich hull provides a protective covering for the creamy white seed inside, whole sesame seeds last longer when not refrigerated, remaining relatively fresh for about two months, assuming they were purchased in top condition. Hulled sesame seeds are more prone to rancidity and therefore have a much shorter shelf life.

Toasting gives sesame seeds a more full-bodied nutty flavor and an attractive deep golden color. To toast them, place them in a dry skillet over medium-low heat for just a few minutes, until golden brown. Stir constantly to prevent burning, and don't even think of turning your back, even for just a moment—that's exactly when they'll burn.

Sesame seeds are also the main ingredient in gomasio, also known as sesame salt, a delicious, flavorful condiment made by roasting and grinding sesame seeds with salt. Proportions usually range from eight to fifteen parts sesame seeds to one part salt. Use it as a lower-sodium alternative to salt, and as an additional source of protein and other nutrients on grains, noodles, vegetables, beans, tofu, or fish.

Sesame butter and **tahini** are to sesame seeds as peanuts are to peanut butter. These delicious, creamy spreads, often used in Middle Eastern, African, and Asian cooking, are made by grinding raw or roasted sesame seeds. They provide an easy, convenient, and delicious way to get maximum nutrient value out of sesame seeds. In comparison to peanut butter, sesame butter and tahini are lower in protein but higher in iron, magnesium, and zinc. They have

similar amounts of total fat, but the sesame-based products are lower in monounsaturated fat and higher in polyunsaturated fat.

Sesame butter, made from ground whole sesame seeds, is darker in color, much stronger in flavor, and has a thicker consistency. It is used primarily as a spread for breads and such or as an ingredient in sauces, rather than as an ingredient in classic dip recipes like hummus. Because it's ground from whole sesame seeds, it is also more nutritious, containing all the phytochemicals, vitamins, and minerals found in the whole seed. Black sesame butter, sometimes incorrectly called tahini, is a variety of sesame butter made from ground whole black sesame seeds. It has a rich, complex, naturally smoky flavor.

In contrast, tahini is made from ground hulled sesame seeds, which gives it a thinner consistency than that of sesame butter. Both raw and roasted versions of tahini are available, and each has distinctive flavor qualities. Raw tahini is nutty and subtly sweet, while tahini made from roasted sesame seeds has a deeper, richer flavor. Which to choose is simply a personal decision.

All forms of sesame butter and tahini are versatile and can be used at any meal. The possibilities are endless. At breakfast, spread some on toast instead of butter, add a spoonful to a smoothie, or thin it with a bit of juice to make a sauce for fruit salads. At lunch or dinner, tahini can be both a binder and a flavor component in sandwich spreads, fillings, or dips. Or use it to make salad dressings or creamy nondairy soups. A simple nondairy milk substitute can be made by blending 1 tablespoon of tahini with 1 cup of water and a dab of sweetener. Refrigerate and consume within four days; use it as you would milk, whether as a beverage or in cooking and baking.

SUNFLOWER SEEDS

Predominantly polyunsaturated fat

1 ounce = about 3 tablespoons of shelled sunflower seeds

Sunflower seeds have their roots in what is now the southwestern region of the United States, where they were likely cultivated by Native Americans by 3000 BCE. In Mexico, they were domesticated about thirty-five hundred years ago and are now used extensively throughout the world. The popularity of sunflower seeds got a big boost in the eighteenth century when the Russian Orthodox Church declared them to be an acceptable food during Lent. By crossbreeding them for higher oil yield and larger seeds, Russia set the stage for commercial production, and Russia remains the world's largest producer, followed by the European Union, Eastern Europe, Argentina, China, India, the United States, and Turkey.

Sunflower seeds are particularly high in vitamin E (9.8 milligrams per ounce)—the highest of any nut or seed—making them an excellent source of antioxidants. They're also especially rich in phytochemicals, including phytosterols, which may help reduce cholesterol and the risk of certain types of cancer. They also provide a good amount of fiber (3 grams per ounce), including lignans, the type of fiber that can help lower cholesterol and protect against heart disease and some cancers. Phenolic acids, like chlorogenic acid, provide extra antioxidant protection. Sunflower seeds have a high protein content, too, providing 6.5 grams per ounce, near the amount found in pumpkin seeds and peanuts.

Varieties

There are two basic types of sunflower seeds: **oil-seeds** are small, oil-rich, black seeds used to make sunflower oil and meal; they're also the sunflower seed of choice for birdseed. **Non-oil seeds** are larger, black-and-white striped seeds used for snacking and general food use; they're available both in-shell and shelled. This type of seed has been developed so that its fibrous hull is only loosely attached to the kernel, making it easily shelled by hand or even by crunching the shell with one's teeth and spitting it out.

Storage and Use

About 1 pound of in-shell sunflower seeds will yield a bit over ½ pound of shelled sunflower seeds, or approximately 1¾ cups. For best nutrition, choose unsalted sunflower seeds, either raw or dry-roasted. In-shell sunflower seeds should be clean and unbroken and have a firm texture. Refrigerate or freeze in-shell sunflower seeds for up to one year, keeping out only the amount that will likely be consumed within a week. Shelled sunflower seeds should be uniform in color with no broken or discolored seeds, indications that the seeds may be rancid. If purchased in top condition, shelled sunflower seeds can last for up to six months in the refrigerator or nine months in the freezer, tightly wrapped.

Besides being a nutritious snack, sunflower seeds are a good addition to baked goods, whole, chopped, or ground, and a crunchy substitute for bacon bits and croutons on cooked vegetables and salads. Roast them for best flavor. Raw in-shell sunflower seeds can be sprouted.

Sunflower butter is sometimes available. It provides about the same amount of protein as peanut butter, as well as all the valuable phytochemicals and nutrients in sunflower seeds. However, it is very prone to rancidity due to its high percentage of polyunsaturated fat, so it's hard to find it in good shape. Once opened, its shelf life is very limited, even if it's refrigerated.

WALNUTS

Predominantly polyunsaturated fat, including omega-3 fatty acids

1 ounce = slightly more than ¼ cup of English walnut halves or about 3½ tablespoons of black walnut pieces

Walnuts have been used for food since at least 7000 BCE, and have also served medicinal purposes throughout the millennia. There are a variety of native species found throughout the world, including in southeastern Europe, ancient Persia (now Iran and Afghanistan), Asia Minor (Turkey), the Himalayas, and the Americas. Today, the top five producers are China, the United States (California), Iran, Turkey, and Ukraine.

Walnuts are most widely known for their alpha-linolenic acid content, making them one of the few plant foods and the only nut that contains appreciable amounts of this omega-3 fatty acid—2.6 grams per ounce (0.56 grams per ounce for black walnuts). When in proper balance with linoleic acid (an omega-6 fatty acid), omega-3 fatty acids serve to help increase immunity and reduce inflammation, risk of cardiovascular disease, and total and LDL (bad) cholesterol.

Walnuts are also known for their phytochemicals, which contribute to antioxidant activity associated with the nut. Walnuts contain high amounts of gamma-tocopherol, the form of vitamin E that reduces oxidation of fats (6 milligrams per ounce in English walnuts; 8 milligrams per ounce in black walnuts). Walnuts are also a source of melatonin. Although this hormone is more commonly known for its role in maintaining regular sleep patterns, it also serves as an antioxidant, helping to protect cells from oxidative damage and inhibiting certain types of cancer. The walnut's pellicle, the thin brown skin surrounding the meat of the nut, contains most of the phenolic substances found in walnuts. The function of the pellicle is to protect the kernel from oxidation and fungal attack, but it is also responsible for the nut's mild astringent flavor and is the source of much of its antioxidant activity. For example, the pellicle includes ellagic acid, flavonoids, and pro-anthocyanidins—all of which help protect against cardiovascular disease and cancer. Phytosterols, which help reduce cholesterol and enhance overall immunity, are also present in walnuts. Though the amount in English walnuts is low in comparison to most nuts and seeds, black walnuts are a richer source. Black walnuts are also higher in protein (6.8 grams per ounce) than English walnuts (4.3 grams per ounce).

Varieties

There are more than a dozen species of walnut trees with edible nuts, but **English walnuts** (*Juglans regia*) and **black walnuts** (*Juglans nigra*) stand out as the two varieties most widely known and used. English walnuts, also called Persian walnuts, are much more commercially significant than black walnuts. Though the species originated elsewhere, "English" became associated with this type of walnut because it was widely transported by English merchant sailors during medieval times. Black walnuts, native to North America, are more distinctively flavored and stronger in taste than English walnuts. Because their hull is very thick and hard to crack, requiring the nuts to be shelled between heavy rollers or wheels, black walnuts are usually sold in pieces rather than as halves.

Storage and Use

About 1 pound of English walnuts in the shell will yield 2 cups of shelled nuts. For best flavor and texture, avoid walnuts that rattle within their shells. Store walnuts in the shell at room temperature for two to three months, or for longer storage, keep them in the refrigerator or freezer for up to one year. Once shelled, walnuts tend to go rancid quickly. When possible, ask for a sample before purchasing. The more surface area exposed on a nut, the more opportunity for oxidation to occur, so when buying shelled walnuts, choose English walnut halves instead of walnut pieces; they can be easily chopped or crushed at home. (Black walnuts are only available in pieces since they are so hard to extract from the shell.) Store shelled walnuts in the refrigerator for up to three months or in the freezer for up to a year.

Use walnuts to top cereals, grains, vegetables, and salads, or as an ingredient in breads, stuffings, entrées, and cookies and other desserts. When ground into flour in a high-powered blender or small seed grinder or coffee grinder, they can be added as a flavor enhancer when making any type of baked goods and desserts.

Walnut butter is sometimes available; it's usually made from English walnuts. Lower in protein than peanut butter, it is also very rich and vulnerable to oxidation, and thus requires constant refrigeration.

Meat and Poultry

Buying meat used to be a rather straightforward process. But widening interest in how our food is produced has resulted in increased complexity, given the plethora of new labeling terms and claims that now confront shoppers. While initially it can be daunting, information that provides truthfulness and accuracy, including transparency of how an animal was raised throughout its life, is a good thing, as it sets up a win-win situation for animals and consumers alike. At the most basic level, the more an animal is raised with care and concern under good living conditions that allow it to express its natural behaviors—essentially providing as good a quality life as possible for the duration of its life—the higher the odds that consumers will, in turn, benefit from enhanced quality of meat, flavor, and nutrition.

Ideally, animals are allowed to graze year-round on open pastures, giving them the opportunity to eat perennial and annual grasses, broad-leaved plants, legumes, and a wide variety of seasonal plants, all of which are rich in nutrients and fiber. Outside the growing season, they may be given supplemental forage from dry hay or from crops that has undergone fermentation as a result of storage (known as silage, haylage, or baleage)—sweet-smelling, succulent, nutritious animal feed that is easy to digest. This varied diet—which is what animals ate in the wild and what they ate on the diversified small farms prevalent throughout history until World War II—means that animals' bodies developed primarily polyunsaturated and monounsaturated fats.

Grass-fed meat has a more favorable ratio of omega-3 to omega-6 fatty acids. Since too high a proportion of omega-6 fatty acids in the diet can increase the potential for heart attacks, strokes, thrombosis, arrhythmia, cancer, and arthritis and other inflammatory diseases, the more favorable ratio of omega-3 fatty acids in grass-fed meat may help reduce these risks. A better ratio of omega-3 fatty acids is also true of chickens and other poultry allowed to roam and peck outdoors looking for bugs, worms, and the like amid vegetation.

Meat from grass-fed ruminant animals (those that are cud-chewing, including cattle, sheep, bison, goats, deer, and elk), is also higher in conjugated fatty acids (CLAs), due to the high proportion of linoleic acid found in pasture grasses. CLA is the collective term for a variety of very specific forms of linoleic acid, and although they are trans fats, they occur naturally and appear to have certain health benefits, including helping to reduce or inhibit the effects of cancer-causing substances. The health benefits of CLAs are similar to those of omega-3 fatty acids.

But in the last century, many producers began to turn away from natural, grass-fed raising practices, for a number of reasons. One was that research that started during the latter part of the nineteenth century demonstrated that feeding grain to livestock in concentrated animal feeding operations (feedlots, also called CAFOs) produced more flavorful, tender meat marbled with fat, although simultaneously increasing the percentage of saturated fat. Other practices evolved and became common, all tending toward fitting animal husbandry into a larger-scale, more economically efficient, industrial mode. One of these was the addition of cheap animal by-products from ruminant animals to animal feed; this practice ultimately led to outbreaks of bovine spongiform encephalopathy (BSE), a fatal degenerative neurological disease of cattle also known as mad cow disease. Another has been the routine use of antibiotics in animal feed.

Poultry and pigs have been subjected to similar efforts to fit them into industrial scale production. In particular, they have been bred for particular traits to benefit the end consumer but that, for the animal, have had painful physical and/or abnormal behavioral outcomes. For example, pigs bred for less fat have exhibited aggressive behavior toward each other, including tail biting, an issue that many producers "solved" by cutting off their tails to minimize the problem. Poultry bred for more breast meat can have difficulty walking, a consequence of too much weight for their bones to handle. Crowded and dull living conditions, resulting from a focus on minimizing production costs, are devoid of the opportunity for both poultry and pigs to express their natural behaviors, and these take a physical and emotional toll on the animals.

The Good News and How to Choose

Fortunately, finding meat and poultry producers that feed their animals without animal by-products or antibiotics is becoming easier as the market responds to the growing consumer demand for meat from animals raised in a more compassionate and healthy manner. Knowing what your options are involves understanding general meat production techniques and the basics of animal welfare; it can help you make informed decisions and, possibly, discover previously unexplored resources. The following terminology can help guide you through the maze.

Air-chilled is a process of cooling chicken after slaughter by moving them through cold air chambers to keep bacteria to a minimum. The conventional method involves chilling them directly in a water chiller, which can add to water weight to the chicken, reducing flavor due to the chicken's natural juices being diluted in the process.

Animal welfare labeling is a way to know how the producer of the labeled meat or poultry raised their animals. Look for independent verification of the claims rather than declarations that are more akin to marketing. Information pertaining to the label should clearly state how the animal was raised, including living conditions, feed, and permissible and prohibited production and handling techniques. In addition to stating that the animal was never administered antibiotics, supplemental growth hormones, or animal by-products in its feed, the label can (and should) indicate whether the animal was raised on well-managed pasture or in a natural outdoor habitat for all, some, or none of the animal's life.

When animals are housed, background information should be available indicating the quality of indoor conditions, where conditions would ideally include dry, clean bedding and litter several inches in depth; good indoor air-quality control; and plenty of room for the animals to move, express natural behaviors, and rest. Look also for transportation and slaughter requirements related to an animal welfare labeling claim. The more detailed the labeling criteria the better, as this will help you identify producers who are trying to provide the best possible conditions to support the physical, emotional, and behavioral needs of the animals they raise.

Cured meats, including ham, bacon, sausage, hot dogs, and luncheon meat, are typically made with sodium nitrite, a synthetic quick-curing agent, and sometimes sodium nitrate (which converts to nitrite in the curing process) in order to maintain the pink or red colors, enhance flavor, and help protect against bacterial growth. Concerns about the safety of nitrites were raised in the 1970s, when it was discovered that they can combine with amines (substances derived from protein) to form nitrosamine, a very potent carcinogenic compound, especially when cured meat is heated at high temperatures; frying bacon is particularly problematic. However, in addition to mandating the use of significantly less sodium nitrite when curing meat, most governments also require the addition of a compound closely related to ascorbic acid (vitamin C), such as sodium ascorbate, which serves to effectively block the formation of nitrosamines. Some countries have special allowances for the amount of nitrites and nitrates allowed in the processing of certain traditional cured meats, for example, Wiltshire bacon and ham produced in the United Kingdom. Vegetable extract powders that contain naturally occurring nitrates, such as celery juice powder, parsley, cherry powder, beet powder, and spinach are allowed as alternatives to synthetic forms of nitrites as curing agents in many countries, including the United States and Canada.

Dry-aged beef has been stored for ten to twenty-eight days at temperatures between 34°F and 36°F and at 85 percent humidity, a process that allows the beef's natural enzymes to further tenderize the meat by breaking down the connective tissues in the muscle. The evaporation of moisture from the muscle concentrates the flavors of the meat, making dry-aged beef highly revered. It is usually found in specialty food markets and butcher shops. In contrast, most beef sold in grocery stores is wet-aged in vacuum-sealed bags for just a couple of days, so it is less tender than dry-aged beef.

"**Free-range**" is a labeling term used primarily for poultry that ideally should describe poultry raised with free access to outdoor areas with shade and areas in which to explore bugs and other morsels of interest. In the absence of an official global definition for free-range, look for information that describes what the producer, retailer, or certifier of a product means by the claim. When it comes to beef, sheep, bison, pigs, goat, deer, and elk raised primarily on pasture, they will usually be described as pastured or grass-fed.

"**Fresh**" is a term used on raw poultry products whose requirements were established by the Food Safety and Inspection Service of the United States Department of Agriculture in 1997 to designate whole poultry and cuts that have never been subjected to temperatures below 26°F—the temperature at which poultry freezes. While some ice may occasionally be evident on the skin, the poultry is never fully frozen.

Game is a general classification that can include deer, bison, elk, rabbit, pheasant, duck, geese, guinea fowl, quail, and squab. Although these and many other animals are hunted in the wild for personal consumption, game meats sold in supermarkets in the United States must be farm raised. Game animals can be raised any number of ways, from outdoor habitats where they forage on natural grasses and plants to confinement in small areas where they are may be fed grain-based feed. Added growth hormones are not allowed, but depending on the producer, antibiotics remain a possibility. Flavor, texture, and nutritional value will vary according to how the animal was raised. Game birds can be cooked like their poultry counterparts, while venison and bison meat are best cooked similar to grass-fed beef.

"**Grain-fed**" or "**grain-finished**" both refer to an animal that at some point in its life—usually the last several months of its life—is fed a grain ration instead of grass for quicker weight gain, as well as to increase marbling with fat and its signature flavor and tenderness. Although typically grain-fed animals are confined to feedlots, whether big or small, some producers turn the tables and bring the grain out to the animals in the pasture, allowing them access to both grass and grain.

Grass-fed is a labeling term that was codified by the United States Department of Agriculture in 2007 to designate ruminant animals whose diet throughout their lifespan consists solely of grass and any herbaceous plant that can be grazed or harvested for feeding (with the exception of milk or milk replacer consumed prior to weaning). Hay, haylage, baleage, silage, and crop residue without grain are also allowed. Mineral and vitamin supplementation is permitted as well. Requirements beyond a grass-fed diet, such as a prohibition of supplemental growth hormones or antibiotics or specific restrictions related to confinement of the animal (beyond the prerequisite for continuous access to pasture during the growing season), are not included within the USDA's grass-fed standard.

When it comes to cooking, grass-fed beef is delicious, typically with a somewhat stronger, more gamey flavor than grain-fed beef. It varies in tenderness depending on the climate conditions, variety of grasses and other forage found in the pasture, and the skills of the producer. As it is lower in fat than meat from grain-fed animals, a couple of key cooking hints can help enhance its full flavor and texture. In general, it is important to add or conserve moisture. To help lock in natural juices, sear the meat before roasting, then cover with a lid or foil while cooking; alternatively, it can be cooked in a slow cooker. Other cooking methods can also help retain moisture. The meat can be braised, stewed, cooked in a sauce, marinated before cooking, or basted during cooking. Add oil to the pan before browning the meat. The addition of sautéed onions and peppers, or cooking them along with the meat, will also help add moisture, along with extra flavor.

Because grass-fed beef is low in fat, keep cooking temperatures low; high heat can make for tough eating. It is at its best when cooked no more than medium rare, or medium at most. After cooking, allow it to rest for a few minutes before serving, to distribute the natural juices.

Halal meat and poultry have been slaughtered and processed according to Islamic dietary laws. Pork and its by-products are not considered halal, nor are carnivorous animals, birds of prey, and land animals without external ears. Likewise, halal meat products are prohibited from being made with blood and its by-products. Certification of meat and poultry as halal verifies that the ingredients, preparation, slaughter requirements, processing and all other compulsory procedures as specified by Islamic law have been maintained.

"**Heritage**" is a term used to describe classic breeds of livestock that had commercial viability in the past. Unlike modern breeding programs that focus on operational efficiency or enhancement of isolated traits, heritage breeds better support the health and well-being of the animal, including preserving characteristics more in tune with the animal's natural behaviors. Meat from heritage breeds usually has better flavor, too, in part due to genetics, and also because they usually have a more varied diet and more opportunities to graze and roam. Their size, shape, and texture may be unique, as well, preserving the genetic diversity that was common in the past.

Irradiation is a method for reducing pathogens such as *E. coli* and salmonella in fresh and frozen red meat and poultry by exposing it to a dose of gamma rays. However, its overall use is questionable as irradiation does not make the meat safe to eat raw, nor does it replace safe handling practices, including safe internal cooking temperatures. Irradiated meat can still become contaminated from bacteria after it goes through the irradiation treatment. US federal law requires irradiated foods to be labeled with the statement 'treated with irradiation" or "treated by irradiation," along with the international symbol

Seafood

ᴑ

There are few foods that exemplify "global" eating as well as seafood, which enables us to travel the world vicariously without leaving our dinner table. We can eat cod from Iceland, wild salmon and sablefish from Alaska, farmed salmon from Norway and Scotland, albacore tuna from the Pacific Ocean off the California coast, sardines from Mexico, halibut from British Columbia, Pacific cod from the Bering Sea and Aleutian Islands, hake from South Africa, scallops from eastern Canada, prawns from Australia . . . and the list goes on and on.

Ironically, though seafood is one of the easiest proteins to cook, often there is more apprehension cooking it than meat or poultry, with many folks more frequently eating fish at a restaurant than preparing it at home. Nevertheless, once you have a basic recipe down pat, it's all a matter of adapting cooking techniques to the type of fish or seafood at hand, with a focus on just keeping it simple. Accompanying sauces and side dishes should be complementary, subtly enhancing the flavor of the seafood rather than overpowering it.

While its great taste, ease of preparation, and versatility no doubt have played a large part in seafood's widespread popularity, its nutritional attributes are equally appealing, with fatty cold-water fish being a key source for obtaining the valuable omega-3 fatty acids within our diets.

How to Choose

Many terms and concepts are bandied about when it comes to seafood—gear type, sustainability, nutrition, safety, along with production and processing methods. Fortunately, there is no need to become or hire a marine biologist in order to understand them. The following exploration of fishing and aquaculture practices and terminology will help you navigate your way more confidently through your seafood shopping experience.

AQUACULTURE

Aquaculture, the raising of fish in tanks on land or in cages in open water, is hardly a recent phenomenon. The Chinese have been raising fish since before 1000 BCE, both as a source of fresh food and for ornamental purposes, to beautify the gardens of the wealthy. Over the years, they also developed polyculture practices, where raising fish was integrated with plant and animal husbandry, with each system supporting the others and all flourishing from their interaction. Ideas about aquaculture spread to other Asian countries and eventually to Europe, where, in the Middle Ages, fish ponds became common as a means of providing fresh protein.

In the latter part of the twentieth century, there was a resurgence of interest in these techniques, and aquaculture in general, as people began to realize that an alternative to wild-caught fish would help keep up with the increasing demand for fish from consumers. Innovative techniques and sophisticated equipment have brought aquaculture to a new level, helping us move toward the goal of long-term protection of the environment along with healthy, well-cared-for stocks. When purchasing farm-raised fish, shrimp, and mollusks, look for operations that use neither antibiotics or supplemental hormones nor toxic, persistent chemicals. Pens should be positioned in areas with active water exchange and away from vulnerable marine species or habitats. Feed should be based on the natural requirements of the species being raised, using fish meal and fish oil as needed, ideally from by-products of fish or shellfish processed for human consumption or from sustainably managed fisheries. Good water quality should be maintained within and outside the pens or tanks, for the benefit of both the fish and the environment. Systems should also be well designed to prevent any farmed fish from escaping.

When conducted in a conscientious manner, aquaculture can be one of the answers in the quest to protect our world fisheries, ocean habitats, and the earth itself, which depends on the health of the oceans.

"GEAR TYPE" OR CATCHING METHODS

The particular method used to catch a fish (also called "gear type") is increasingly being used to

Line-caught fish

help consumers learn more about what is factored into a seafood sustainability assessment. Different catch methods are used depending on the type of fish or seafood sought and where that species lives. The severity of bycatch (the incidental or accidental catch of species that are not the primary target of the fishery) and impact to the habitat depend on the particular type of fishing gear that's used to catch a fish, along with how and where it is used.

Dredges consist of a mouth frame with an attached bag made from metal mesh or rings that drags along the bottom of the sea to scrape up and collect oysters, scallops, mussels, and clams. Depending on the type of dredge used and the intensity of use, there can be an impact on the seafloor and on the species that live there.

Gill nets are comprised of vertical walls of netting that are set near the surface, mid-water, or deeper, to capture fish as they travel through an area. The name of the catch method comes from the fact that, as fish encounter the net, they their gills get caught or they become entangled. In certain areas, bycatch of marine animals including sea turtles, sharks and seabirds can be a problem, as are gillnets that get lost at sea and continue to entangle marine life.

Harpoons are the traditional way to catch large individual fish like swordfish as they come to the surface. A long harpoon is thrust directly into the animal, and then it is hauled on board. With this highly selective fishing method, there's virtually no bycatch and only mature adult swordfish are caught.

Longlines consist of a long main line that hangs horizontally in the water either near the surface (for example, when fishing swordfish), a bit deeper (for tuna), or on the sea floor (for bottom-dwelling species such as cod and halibut) and a series of baited hooks that hang vertically from the main line. Longlines can stretch for many miles and catch a high volume of fish at once. Depending on where and how the long lines are set, bycatch of non-targeted catch can be high.

"**Pole and line**" involves the use of a fishing pole and line with either a single hook attached or a few; after the fish takes the bait, it is swung onto the boat. Pole and line gear is operated by hand to catch tunas in some areas. Bycatch is low with this method.

A **purse seine** is a large net used to surround and capture schooling fish like yellowfin or skipjack tuna. It has rings at the bottom through which a rope or cable passes; when pulled, the rope draws the rings close together, forming a "purse" that prevents the fish from escaping. Depending on how the gear is used, bycatch of other species could be an issue.

Traps and **pots** are submerged wire, wooden, or steel-framed cages used to catch species like lobsters, crabs, and reef fish. They may be baited or not. Animals enter the traps but then cannot escape, although escape hatches included in many traps may allow unwanted species to escape.

Trawls are cone-shaped nets with a wide mouth and a closed off tail that are pulled behind or alongside fishing vessels. They can vary greatly in size and design depending where they're used (the sea floor versus in mid-water) and what they're intended to catch. Bycatch and habitat impacts could occur depending on how the gear is used.

Trolling is similar to hook and line except that the boat is typically moving and fishing lines are towed behind or alongside a boat and reeled in after the fish takes the bait. Fish like albacore tuna follow the moving bait. Bycatch is low with this method.

FRESH OR FROZEN

Fresh fish is a good, delicious choice when purchased from merchants that have their supply of fresh fish flown in several times per week. (The same is true of ordering fish in a restaurant.) Whether wild caught or farm raised, visual cues of freshness for whole fish include shiny skin and eyes that are bright, glassy, and convex, not sunken. Fillets should be translucent and light in color, not yellowed or uncharacteristically dark, with firm flesh that is springy when pressed. A strong, malodorous fishy smell is largely the product of decomposition and, as such, shouldn't be apparent in either the fish or in the market from which it is purchased.

Still, **frozen seafood** can often be better than fresh, given the fact that by the time fresh fish gets to a market hundreds or thousands of miles away, it could be several days old. Fortunately, frozen food technology has advanced dramatically over the years, so we can now buy fish frozen either immediately, on the boat, or very soon after coming to shore. Both the good flavor and the texture of such frozen fish can put to rest the idea that fish must be bought and cooked fresh to be at its best.

However, do avoid frozen fish treated with sodium tripolyphosphate (STP) and sulfites. STP is used to inhibit potential moisture loss in the freezing and thawing process, control enzymatic breakdown, and aid in the removal of shells from shrimp. While it's relatively harmless to health, STP retains water, so some of the cost per pound for a product may be for this elevated water content. STP can also adversely affect the overall flavor and texture of the fish.

Sulfites, which can cause severe allergic reactions in sensitive individuals, are a different issue. A collective term for sulfur dioxide, sodium sulfite, potassium or sodium bisulfite, and potassium or sodium metabisulfite, sulfites are often used to help prevent development of a black pigment on shrimp shells called melanosis or "black spot," or to bleach it out once it's occurred. This discoloration is the result of a natural chemical reaction that occurs in warm-water shrimp if they aren't properly rinsed and iced once their heads are removed. Melanosis itself is harmless, similar to the blackening of a banana peel as it ripens. However, its presence could indicate poor handling—that the shrimp were left out too long in warm temperatures after being caught. Ultimately, both sodium tripolyphosphate and sulfites are unnecessary additives, as evidenced by the many frozen seafood products processed without them, and they are usually indicative of a lower quality product.

MARINE STEWARDSHIP COUNCIL

The Marine Stewardship Council (MSC), an independent, global, nonprofit organization, was created to help consumers identify fish from wild fisheries proven to be well managed; such products are marked with a distinctive blue and white label. The market-focused program also allows those who engage in sustainable fishing practices to get recognition for doing so, thus creating extra incentive for others to do the same. The Principles and Criteria for Sustainable Fishing that underlie the program are based on the Code of Conduct for Responsible Fisheries of the UN's Food and Agriculture Organization. These include that the fishery should be conducted in a way to prevent overfishing; that the fishery must maintain the structure, function, and diversity of associated ecosystems; and that its management system must respect national and international regulations. Input from a multistakeholder group of scientists, fisheries experts, environmental organizations, and seafood-related businesses helps keep the organization and its programs current, relevant, and on target.

Assessments of fisheries are done by accredited certification agencies independent of the Marine Stewardship Council (MSC) to ensure evaluations are unbiased and reliable. Credibility of the label is further secured by a chain of custody system to trace MSC-labeled seafood from the label right back to the fishery to ensure only fish from certified fisheries is labeled as such.

The Marine Stewardship Council program has started putting sustainability of wild fisheries back on track, serving as a catalyst for real change, with fisheries having access to an international program that both creates incentives and gives credits to fisheries showing continued improvements in management methods. Concurrently, the MSC's eco-label helps provide a useful guide, accurately identifying healthy fish stocks to consumers.

METHYLMERCURY AND OTHER CONTAMINANTS

Through a process called bioaccumulation, toxic mercury can progressively accumulate in fatty tissues at each successive stage of the food chain, from small plant-eating fish to larger fish that eat them, and finally to humans who consume the various types of seafood. In general, smaller fish have less mercury than larger fish, as the older and larger the fish, the greater the potential for them to accumulate high levels of mercury. Though mercury often originates as an air pollutant from chlorine processing plants, coal-fired power plants, and the burning of medical waste, it can ultimately make its way into bodies of water. It's initially released in an inorganic form, but bacteria in the water convert it into a more readily absorbed and more toxic form: methylmercury. Longer-lived predatory fish, including shark, swordfish, tilefish (golden bass), king mackerel, and tuna tend to accumulate higher concentrations of mercury from their consumption of organisms lower in the food chain. Some varieties of fish obtained from recreational fishing in rivers, lakes, and streams may also be high in mercury, not to mention other pollutants, including dioxins

Fish with Highest Levels of Mercury

King mackerel
Shark
Swordfish
Tilefish

Fish with Lowest Levels of Mercury

Anchovies
Catfish
Clam
Crab
Flounder
Haddock
Hake
Herring
Mackerel (North Atlantic);
   chub (Pacific)
Ocean perch
Oysters
Pollack
Plaice
Rainbow trout
Salmon (farmed and wild)
Sardines
Scallops
Shrimp
Sole
Spiny lobster
Squid (calamari)
Tilapia
Trout

cal composition, they also bioaccumulate up the food chain, and some fish may contain all three contaminants. Each state's department of health or department of natural resources should be able to provide information about fish in certain areas that have a high risk of contamination, along with specific food consumption advisories. Neither cooking nor trimming can reduce mercury levels in fish, as it is most concentrated in the muscle tissue rather than in fat or oils. On the other hand, exposure to PCBs and dioxins can be minimized by removing the skin and surface fat from fish before cooking.

Human health risks depend not only on the methylmercury level in the fish but also on how much is eaten, the body weight of the consumer, and individual variation in the body's ability to handle mercury. Babies in the womb and young children are most vulnerable to mercury, as it can adversely affect the development of the cognitive, motor, and sensory centers within the brain. The more mercury that gets into a person's body, the longer the exposure time, and the younger the person, the more severe the effects are likely to be. In addition to children, all women of childbearing age are, therefore, advised by the United States Food and Drug Administration (FDA) to eat only up to twelve ounces per week of a variety of fish and shellfish known to be lower in mercury. When it comes to canned tuna, guidelines on albacore (white) tuna have been highlighted in particular, as, unlike canned tuna labeled "chunk light" or "chunk," which tends to come from smaller species, albacore tuna contains more mercury. Accordingly, the FDA recommends its consumption be limited to six ounces per week

and polychlorinated biphenyls (PCBs). Because these persist in the environment for long periods of time, they often make their way into bodies of water, where they are absorbed and transported into fatty tissues in fish and marine mammals. Although they are distinctly different than mercury in chemi-

"NO GENETICALLY ENGINEERED SEAFOOD"

A producer or merchant's buying policy statement may claim "no genetically engineered seafood," which declares nonsupport of the production or sale of genetically engineered fish. By deliberately altering the DNA of fish, inserting genes not normally found within fish itself, genetic engineering can achieve any number of enhanced attributes, such as quicker growth, increased size, and different nutritional profile or flavor. While scientifically feasible, many question the implications of genetically engineered seafood with regard to human safety, its environmental impact, and the ultimate welfare of the fish. Buying seafood raised and captured naturally and responsibly, which has been proven safe through the test of time, remains the best choice.

OMEGA-3 FATTY ACIDS

A commonly heard phrase used long ago to summarize the benefits of fish—that fish is brain food—is actually remarkably true. The two long-chain polyunsaturated omega-3 fatty acids: eicosapentaenoic acid and docosahexaenoic acid, fortunately commonly abbreviated and referred to as EPA and DHA, offer health benefits throughout life, starting even before we are born. In addition to being associated with reduced cardiac mortality from coronary heart disease or sudden death in persons with and without heart disease, EPA and DHA also help facilitate the growth of brain and nerve cells in the developing fetus and nursing infant. DHA, in particular, is a component in phospholipids, which are components of all cell membranes, including brain cell membranes, where they help facilitate release of neurotransmitters and general cell-to-cell communication within the brain. Emerging research shows these fatty acids in fish may also play further roles, such as supporting optimal health in the eyes and possibly helping to reduce depression in some individuals

In their report, the 2010 US Dietary Guidelines Advisory Committee suggested the consumption of two 4-ounce servings of seafood per week, particularly those varieties high in EPA and DHA and low in methylmercury, to provide an average of 250 milligrams per day of omega-3 fatty acids. The human body can synthesize both EPA and DHA, in limited amounts, from alpha-linolenic acid, the plant-based omega-3 fatty acid found in flaxseeds, walnuts, and canola oil. However, the preformed,

Seafood High in Omega-3 Fatty Acids

Although virtually all seafood contains some EPA and DHA, some, especially oily cold-water fish, are much better sources of EPA and DHA. Farm-raised fish can have comparable amounts of these omega-3 fatty acids as their wild cousins, but whether this is the case or not depends on the amount and quality of fish meal, fish oils, or algae included in their diet.

Anchovy
Herring
Mackerel
Mussels
Sablefish (black cod)
Salmon
Sardines
Rainbow trout
Pacific oysters

longer-chain EPA and DHA found in fish, which they derive from their diet of algae, plankton, and other fish, are a more reliable source and more easily used by our bodies.

SMOKED FISH

Curing with smoke and salt is a centuries-old method of preserving fish for months on end. Because refrigeration is now so readily available, most smoked fish is cured with new methods that concentrate on the absorption of flavors from aromatic smoke. The process begins with coating the fish in salt or placing it in a brine to bring out flavor and inhibit the growth of harmful bacteria. For extra flavor, sugar and other seasonings may also be used. Then the fish is rinsed and dried in cool, circulating air until the surface becomes glossy; this creates a natural seal on the exterior. Cold or hot smoking is the next step, using smoke from a variety of hardwoods, each contributing its own unique flavor. **Cold-smoked fish**, known for its delicious flavor and moist, tender texture, is processed at temperatures between 60°F and 110°F for twenty-four hours or more. In contrast, **hot-smoked fish** is cured at a minimum internal temperature of 145°F, perhaps up to 200°F, for a much shorter period of time than cold-smoked fish. Because hot smoking essentially cooks the fish, moisture content is reduced, yielding a firmer, drier texture and a slightly less rich flavor.

Since fish smoked by either method isn't processed enough to fully preserved it, both types must be refrigerated and consumed within fourteen days after processing, or by the date indicated on the package. For longer storage, smoked fish may be frozen for up to two months. Smoked fish sent through mail-order specialty houses needs no refrigeration until its special packaging is opened. Although it may be hard to imagine how the fish inside could be safe to eat, they are processed similar to canned fish except in this case the "can" is a thin metallic pouch.

SUSTAINABILITY

Sustainability is the term used to describe fishing practices that not only contribute to long-term viability of the species of fish, but are in balance with the marine environment and local ecology as well. Drastic reductions in fish populations typically result from overfishing (catching fish faster than they can reproduce) or taking too much bycatch, that is, catching and discarding fish and other aquatic creatures other than the specific species sought. But the problem goes beyond excessive fishing. Bycatch can also include seabirds who may inadvertently get killed while going after bait, and fishing in areas where mammals, such as sea lions, feed can also put their populations at risk. Dwindling seafood stocks can also be a consequence of building in and polluting coastal areas, estuaries, and reefs, which can destroy nursery habitats for young fish. This can

set off a chain reaction, adversely affecting the productivity and stability of entire ecosystems and also resulting in reduced water quality and increased human health risks.

The good news is that a return to abundance and biodiversity within the world's fisheries remains a very real possibility. The goal is to rebuild fisheries whose fish populations are low and overfished or in danger of being so while maintaining healthy stocks at or above sustainable levels. Restoration can readily occur through strict fishing quotas that are followed and respected, careful ecosystem management for healthy habitats, the use of different fishing gear, changes in management practices, and at least temporary closures of protected areas to allow species to recover before they're fished to extinction. Many such turnarounds have, indeed, taken place as a result of putting intent into action.

Using eco-labels showing seafood sustainability ratings as a guide when shopping is an easy way to support responsible fisheries. The Marine Stewardship Council's blue and white eco-label is the most internationally recognized and supported. Several seafood sustainability advocacy groups have also created consumer guides use a traffic light–style red/yellow/green visual for choosing fish that have not yet rated a Marine Stewardship Council certification. These are most reliable when reflecting the actual fishery in question (rather than the species in general), along with the location where the fish is caught and the type of fishing gear employed, all of which can be very helpful when trying to see how the fish you're wondering about rates.

Farmed fish, shrimp, and mollusks can also be raised sustainably, with mollusk aquaculture especially hailed, as such. When buying farmed seafood, ask for the market's buying standards so that you understand the environmental practices they require of producers who sell to them.

Dairy Products and Eggs

Distinctions in taste, consistency, and nutrition among the wide variety of dairy products come down to the source—the milk from which they were produced and, of course, the animals that supply it. While cow's milk may be the most familiar, whether in the form of milk, cultured dairy products, or cheese, products that use milk from other animals, including goats, sheep, and water buffalo, are also available.

And, that is just the beginning. An exploration of the wide array of dairy products and cheese provides both a journey through history and an opportunity to experience flavors and sensations unique to other countries and regions without leaving the comfort of your home. The passion and ingenuity demonstrated by individual artisanal cheese makers is likewise inspiring. When you factor in the different types of milk and the diversity of cultures, both in terms of civilizations and traditions as well as specific bacterial cultures and molds used to make cheese, the possibilities are endless, with offerings in every flavor, consistency, and style imaginable.

And where do eggs come into connection with dairy products? Although eggs are obviously different than dairy, both represent products that are supplied on an ongoing basis by the animal.

Starting from the Ground Up

As with animals raised for their meat, pasture is the basis of good flavor, superior nutrition, and animal welfare for dairy animals and egg layers. Milk from animals raised primarily on pasture has a preferable ratio of omega-3 to omega-6 fatty acids and is also higher in conjugated fatty acids (CLAs), forms of linoleic acid found primarily in foods from ruminant animals. It also makes sense to graze dairy animals on pasture that hasn't been treated with synthetic pesticides, herbicides, and fertilizers that can be persistent in the environment, in the bodies of the animals, and in our own bodies. Due to specific pasture and feed requirements in organic standards, choosing organic milk is one of the best ways to ensure the animals are raised on high-quality pasture that's monitored and well maintained. The benefits of pasture aren't just about advantages for humans. Well-managed pasture with a variety of grasses and plants provides superior nutrition for the animals, too, and gives them the freedom of movement and ability to exercise that are so important to their health and well-being. In every way imaginable, milk produced from animals raised on well-managed pasture, without antibiotics or growth hormones, is best for the health and well-being of the animals. It's best for us, too, in terms of health, nutrition, and flavor.

Plant variety and soil conditions in the pasture, along with the time of year the pasture is grazed, can also affect the flavor of the milk. Seasonal effects on the natural color of cow's milk is most apparent in cheese, due to the concentration of milk that occurs in production, though this doesn't apply to dairy products from goat, sheep, and water buffalo, whose milk is always pure white. In dairy products made from cow's milk, those created from summer milk will be darker, changing from an off-white to more yellow because of the smorgasbord of plants available, from which the cows naturally obtain more beta-carotene.

Other differences in milk and dairy products can be attributed to the specific breed of animal, the particular time within the animal's lactating cycle (the milk is more concentrated and rich toward the end of the cycle), and the time of day the animal is milked (evening milk is higher in fat than is morning milk). In fact, Morbier, a rich and delicious two-layered, semisoft French cheese, showcases this difference in milk quality. The bottom layer is made from morning milk and the top layer from evening milk, with the two separated by a thin layer of ash.

GOAT'S MILK

Goat's milk is a popular alternative for people sensitive to proteins in cow's milk. Unlike cow's milk, which has high levels of alpha-s1-casein, the protein involved in curd formation and firmness, goat's milk is fairly low in this protein. Not only does this help

explain why some people are less sensitive to goat's milk, but it also helps explain why goat cheese is more crumbly.

Goat's milk is only slightly higher in fat than cow's milk, and its fat profile is unique. It contains about twice the concentration of medium-chain fatty acids (medium-chain triglycerides, or MCTs) as cow's milk. Because MCT fatty acids are absorbed well and quickly, they are often used in the treatment of people with malabsorption issues. This unusual fat profile may be another reason why some people find goat's milk easier to digest than cow's milk.

SHEEP'S MILK

Milk from sheep contains twice as much butterfat as cow's milk. About 25 percent of the fat in sheep's milk is made up of medium-chain fatty acids, providing similar benefits as goat's milk in terms of enhanced absorption and utilization.

Sheep's milk is very concentrated, containing a higher percentage of solids than cow's milk. This means it contains higher amounts of many nutrients as well, including protein, calcium, magnesium, iron, and zinc, along with several of the B vitamins. However, because it is so thick and rich, sheep's milk is most commonly consumed as cheese or yogurt rather than in its liquid form. Its thickness also means that less milk is needed to make cheese and other dairy products.

WATER BUFFALO'S MILK

Long-lived animals with many important functions in southern and eastern Asia, water buffalo look very similar to cows, except for their long, curved horns. They are highly valued for their work power and for their milk; the river buffalo variety, in particular, is used for dairy production. Appreciation for water buffalo continues to grow, to the point that they are now being raised on five continents, including North America.

Like sheep's milk, the milk from water buffalo contains twice as much fat as cow's milk. Also like sheep's milk, milk from water buffalo has a higher percentage of total solids and less water, making it more concentrated than cow's milk, and richer in nutrients, including protein, calcium, and iron. This has benefits for dairy producers in that there's no need for additional thickeners in yogurt made with milk from water buffalo, and, as with sheep's milk, a lower volume of milk is needed to make cheese.

Artisanal Cheeses

As is so often the case in our modern world, mechanized processing methods, complete with computers to monitor every step along the way, have been developed for making cheese. This allows manufacturers to produce larger quantities of cheese and use less skilled labor, as well as to make cheeses that are consistent in flavor and texture from one batch to another. And many of these cheeses are very good and satisfying.

Fortunately, however, the fine art of creating hand-crafted cheese still exists, preserving traditional methods that have been used for centuries. In fact, demand for these cheeses is increasing as appreciation for their unique and full flavors, as well as the people behind them, continues to grow. Although fairly new on the scene, American hand-crafted cheeses have earned deep respect and appreciation, with many now included in lists of the world's great cheeses.

Artisanal cheeses are by definition produced on a small scale, providing more opportunity to produce distinctive, seasonal cheeses that reflect the breed of animal from which the milk is obtained, the plants it foraged upon, and the character, passion, and skill of the producer. Some of these artisans use milk from animals they raise on their own farms, creating cheeses referred to as farmstead or farmhouse cheese. Enhanced attention to detail also means more opportunity to age and ripen cheeses to their full potential, allowing for just the right humidity, temperature, and amount of time to develop the complexity of flavor and aroma to extraordinary levels.

Blue cheese

Artisanal cheeses are produced on a small scale locally and regionally throughout the world. Differences in cheeses from different countries and regions, or differences attributable to climate, types of livestock, local plants, and time-honored techniques, can be quite significant. Special designations have been created to protect the labeling of such cheeses (among other regional products), such as the French Appellation d'origine contrôlée (AOC), the Spanish Denominación de origen (DO), and the Italian Denominazione di origine controllata (DOC).

Any producer granted the right to use these name-controlled origin labels must follow very detailed production methods that help preserve cheese-making traditions and the physical characteristics and other attributes of different types of cheese. Species and breed of animal, amount of pasture, and time of year the cheese is produced can be among the many aspects specified for the production of a particular variety of cheese.

Exploring Cheese Varieties

Cheese Type	Sample Varieties	Length of Aging	How to Store
FRESH These high-moisture cheeses are unripened, don't have a rind, and are mild, with a milky flavor.	Chèvre, Cottage Cheese, Cream Cheese, Crème Fraîche, Feta, Fromage Blanc, Kefir Cheese, Mascarpone, Mozzarella, Neufchâtel, Ricotta, Skyr, Yogurt Cheese	A few days to a few months	Keep in the container in which it is purchased and use before the use-by date. Toss if mold develops.
SOFT-RIPENED OR BLOOMY RIND These high-moisture cheeses with a buttery, rich flavor are surface ripened after being exposed to specific strains of mold that are resident in the ripening room or sprayed on. They're developed under humid conditions, creating the characteristic soft, white, fuzzy or bloomy rind.	Brie, Brillat-Savarin, Camembert, Explorateur, Humboldt Fog, Mt. Tam, Pierre Robert, Saint-André	Up to 12 weeks	Loosely wrap in waxed paper or parchment paper, then light plastic wrap to retain moisture.
BLUE-VEINED These soft or semisoft cheeses are pierced and inoculated with a type of mold from the genus *Penicillium* during the ripening process, resulting in a bluish-green mold that grows throughout the cheese.	Bleu d'Auvergne, Blue Castello, Buttermilk Blue, Danish Blue, Fourme d'Ambert, Gorgonzola, Maytag Blue, Roquefort, Saga, Shropshire Blue, Stilton, Valdeón	4 weeks to 14 months	Loosely wrap in waxed paper or parchment paper, then light plastic wrap to retain moisture.
SOFT WASHED-RIND These high-moisture cheeses ripen from the outside in, during which time the exterior of the cheese is rubbed or washed regularly with a solution of brine, wine, beer, cider, or marc (grape brandy). This encourages the growth of certain bacteria, which creates a distinctive orange rind and strong, complex flavors.	Chaumes, Chimay, Espoisses, Limburger, Livarot, Mont St. Francis, Morbier, Munster (France), Reblochan, Red Hawk, Saint-Nectaire	Up to 12 weeks	Loosley wrap in waxed paper, then light plastic wrap to retain moisture.

Cheese Type	Sample Varieties	Length of Aging	How to Store
SEMISOFT These cheeses ripen from the inside out and are usually supple to the touch and mild in flavor.	Asiago, Bel Paese, Colby, Edam, Fontina, Gouda, Havarti, Kasseri, Monterey Jack, Muenster (US), Provolone (plain or smoked), Pyrenees, Swiss (baby)	3 to 12 months	Wrap in waxed or parchment paper, then put in a plastic bag, leaving it unsealed, or loosely wrap in plastic to help retain moisture. If mold develops, trim away at least 1 inch around the mold.
SEMIFIRM These cheeses are ripened from the inside out. Their nutty or fruity flavors develop more complexity with increased aging.	Cheddar, Cheshire, Comté, Double Gloucester, Emmental (French and Swiss), Gruyère, Jarlsberg, Manchego, Pleasant Ridge Reserve	3 to 24 months	Wrap in waxed or parchment paper, folding to seal the edges. If the cheese begins to dry out, loosely cover the paper-wrapped cheese with plastic. If mold develops, trim away at least 1 inch around the mold.
FIRM AND AGED These dry, low-moisture cheeses are ripened from the inside out and have complex flavors with sweet overtones.	Aged Asiago, Aged Gouda, Aged Manchego, Aged Provolone, Grana Padano, Parmesan, Parmigiano-Reggiano, Pecorino Romano, Vella Dry Jack	6 months and longer	Wrap in plastic or unwaxed parchment paper, leaving the rind exposed to allow it to breathe. If mold develops, trim away at least 1 inch around the mold.

Buying and Storing Milk and Cheese

Certain terms on labels can tell you a lot about how dairy products were produced, from how the animals were fed and treated to how the milk was processed to the additives and other substances found in the final product. Following are some of the key terms.

Bovine somatotropin is more commonly known as **rBGH** (recombinant bovine somatotropin) or rBST. This genetically engineered bovine growth hormone is injected into cows every fourteen days to increase milk production by about 10 percent. However, cows administered rBGH may have reduced pregnancy rates, increased risk for mastitis, enlarged hocks, and disorders of the foot region. To avoid buying milk with rBGH, look for organic milk or products that state that none has been administered to the cows. Unfortunately, because of threat of lawsuit by the developer of the drug and by regulation within the United States, all rBGH claims on labels must include the statement that no significant difference has been shown between milk derived from rBGH-treated and non-rBGH cows. The good news is that, in response to consumer demand, use of rBGH by dairies has diminished.

Chymosin, also called recombinant rennet, is made through a cloning process in which the calf chymosin gene is transferred into a microorganism, which then produces chymosin. As the process does not require continued sourcing from animals, some vegetarians find cheese made with chymosin as an acceptable choice. Rennet produced in this way functions nearly identically to rennet extracted directly from an animal and, unlike microbial enzymes, it can be used to make cheddar and other hard cheeses. (See below for more about microbial enzymes and rennet.)

Homogenization is a process that distributes fat particles evenly throughout cow's milk so the cream doesn't separate from the milk. Homogenization is accomplished by spraying milk at high pressure through a small nozzle onto a hard surface to break the fat down into very small particles. Some people prefer unhomogenized milk, enjoying the opportunity to use the cream that floats to the top, which can be carefully skimmed off and used as a topping for fruit, desserts, and cereals, or it may be whipped. Because the fat globules in milk from goats, sheep, and water buffalo are smaller and stay suspended, none need to go through the homogenization process.

Lactose intolerance is a condition caused by a deficiency in lactase, an enzyme produced in the small intestine that's responsible for digesting **lactose** (the natural sugar found in milk). Symptoms of lactose intolerance, which are usually experienced soon after consuming dairy products, include bloating, cramps, flatulence, and nausea.

"**Microbial enzymes**" is a term that may be found on cheese labels indicating that, instead of rennet, the enzyme used to make the cheese is derived from a variety of microorganisms via a controlled fermentation process. There are debates about whether cheese made with microbial enzymes can match the flavor and aroma of a rennet-based cheese, but their biggest drawback is that they cannot be used to make cheddar or other hard cheeses. Although microbial enzymes may be listed on a label as "vegetable rennet," in reality authentic plant-based rennet is rare. Some traditional Portuguese and Spanish cheeses are the exception; these are made with a coagulant extracted from the flowers of the cardoon thistle. This is considered a hallmark of Portuguese cheeses such as Queijo Azeitão, Queijo de Évora, and Queijo Serra da Estrela, and Spanish cheeses such as Queso de la Serena and Torta del Casar. Since the curdling properties of thistle work only on goat's milk and sheep's milk, no cow's milk cheese is available coagulated with true plant-based rennet.

Pasteurization is a heating process that destroys bacteria that contribute to spoilage or are pathogenic, ensuring the safety of milk within a certain time period. While cultured dairy products and cheese provided a solution in early civilizations for safely preserving milk, opportunities to consume fresh fluid milk increased with the advent of improved ways to keep milk cold, along with pasteurization, a method that emerged in the latter part of the 1800s.

Regulations for pasteurization require that milk be heated to a minimum of 161°F for at least fifteen seconds to kill yeasts, molds, pathogenic microorganisms, and most of the less harmful strains of bacteria. Also called the high-temperature, short-time method (HTST), basic pasteurization provides an extended shelf life of up to twenty days.

Raw milk cheese is cheese made from unpasteurized milk. The use of raw milk is considered to have a positive effect on the flavor, texture, and overall character of the cheese. Since some heat is needed in the process of making cheese, the main difference between raw and pasteurized cheese is the initial level and duration of heat the milk is subjected to. US regulations require that cheese made with raw milk, whether imported or domestically produced, must be aged for a minimum of sixty days prior to sale at temperatures not greater than 35°F to ensure food safety and quality.

Rennet is a preparation made from an enzyme extracted from the membrane lining the fourth stomach of a bovine calf. Rennet is used to separate the curds from the whey when making cheese. A hallmark of cheese made with rennet is its firm, dense texture.

Ultra-pasteurization is a method for pasteurizing milk that uses a higher temperature and a shorter time frame. The milk is heated to a minimum of 280°F for at least two seconds, although usually for about five seconds. Ultra-pasteurization (UP) eliminates more bacteria and microorganisms than regular pasteurization, extending shelf life to between 60 and 90 days. Some people buy ultra-pasteurized milk for its convenience factor, as it allows them to keep milk on hand for longer periods of time. Ultra-pasteurization is a boon for processors, enabling them to sell more of the milk they process, along with providing them a lot of extra time to distribute "fresh" milk across the country and still have plenty of shelf life remaining. On the

other hand, ultra-pasteurized cream can be a challenge to froth and whip to hold peaks, so some recipes advise against its use.

STORING CHEESE

Similar to other fresh foods, like fruits and vegetables, all cheese continues to ripen after purchase. Proper moisture and temperature are key to keeping cheese at its best.

Although cut-to-order cheese is optimum, plastic shrink-wrapped soft-ripened bloomy rind, washed rind, semisoft, and semihard cheese and cheese sold vacuum-packed in heavy plastic should ideally be rewrapped after purchase using waxed or parchment paper. If the cheese will likely not be consumed within a few days, these paper-wrapped cheeses can be loosely covered with plastic to help retain moisture. Hard grating cheeses are best in rewrapped in unwaxed parchment, leaving the rind exposed to air to let it breathe. As home refrigerators are set up for a drier, colder atmosphere than is best for storing most cheeses, put it in the area that has the highest humidity such as a vegetable drawer or, if available, special deli drawer set at the warmest temperature possible.

Avoid freezing cheese. While some semihard and hard cheeses can be frozen, their texture will be crumbly when thawed, making them only usable for cooking. The best idea is just to buy cheese frequently, and only enough to allow you to enjoy it while its flavor and texture are at their prime.

Cultured Dairy Products

"Cultured" refers to a fermentation process initiated by lactic acid–producing bacteria that break down the lactose in milk, resulting in a more flavorful, slightly tart, food. Friendly bacteria—bacteria that are essential to proper functioning of the immune and digestive systems—are introduced during the culturing process. To ensure optimal probiotic activity, look for labels on cultured dairy products that indicate they contain live cultures.

Egg Quality and Selection Guide

Egg Quality Grade	Characteristics	Best For
Grade AA (qualities found when less than 10 days old)	Firmly centered yolk; clear, firm, thick white; high overall height; clean, unbroken shell, and practically free from defects.	Poaching, frying, and making soufflés, meringues, and custards
Grade A (qualities found when up to 30 days old)	Moderately firm yolk; moderately firm white; lower overall height; spreads more readily; clean, unbroken shell; practically free from defects.	Frying, boiling, scrambling, and in general cooking and baking
Ungraded	May be equivalent to Grade AA or Grade A. Look for clean, unbroken shells and use-by dating.	Depends on quality of the egg

space. As the definition of "outdoor space" can vary, look for further details that describe the condition of the outdoor area and the hen's opportunity to find shade and to explore bugs and other morsels of interest.

Omega-3 eggs are from hens fed a diet supplemented with flaxseeds, marine algae, or other sources of omega-3 fatty acids to enhance the amount of alpha-linolenic fatty acid in the egg. Eggs from hens that are allowed to forage outdoors in areas teeming with insects will naturally contain more omega-3 fatty acids than those of hens confined to poultry houses or crowded wire cages.

Organic eggs are produced by uncaged hens raised on a certified organic farm that are fed an all-organic diet and have access to the outdoors.

Pasteurized eggs are rapidly heated and held at temperatures high enough to destroy dangerous salmonella bacteria, but low enough to not cook the eggs, coagulate their proteins, or affect color, flavor, nutritional value, or future use. Eggs in their shells, liquid eggs, and freeze-dried egg products may all be pasteurized. Powdered dried egg whites are also pasteurized during the process that makes them.

"**Pasture-raised**" is a term sometimes used to refer to eggs produced from hens that are raised outdoors with access to housing.

Quality grading is a voluntary measurement of the interior characteristics of the egg and the condition of the eggshell. Egg packers who want to use the USDA grade shield on their cartons must pay for monitoring services by a US Department of Agriculture grader. Cartons displaying a grade but without the USDA shield indicate monitoring by state agencies.

Ungraded eggs are packed and self-evaluated by the farmer. They may show characteristics similar to Grade AA or Grade A, depending on the skill and reputation of the producer.

Culinary Oils

Just as juice is extracted from whole fruits and vegetables, culinary oils are extracted from nuts, seeds, and oil-rich plants. Olive oil is considered to be one of the first cooking oils, coming into use soon after olive trees were initially cultivated, around 5000 BCE. Although almond, walnut, and flaxseed oils were also produced thousands of years ago, they were most often used for lighting, heating, and medicinal purposes. Still, throughout the years, these and many other oils have joined olive oil in the kitchen, both at home and in restaurants.

Oil is 100 percent fat. As such, it comprises varying proportions of all three types of fatty acid: saturated fat, monounsaturated fat, and polyunsaturated fat, the last of which also includes essential fatty acids. The predominant type of fat found within a type of oil is something you can easily discern with a glance. Saturated fats, like lard or butter, are solid when cold and fairly solid at room temperature. Monounsaturated fats, like olive oil, are thicker when cold but liquid at room temperature. Polyunsaturated fats, like safflower oil, are liquid whether cold or at room temperature.

While appreciation of the importance of fats in the diet has waxed and waned throughout the years, these days it's better understood that getting the right kind of fat in one's diet is important for optimal health and well-being. In addition to reducing saturated fats, it's important to achieve a better ratio between omega-3 and omega-6 fatty acids when choosing oils, increasing the use of sources higher in omega-3 fatty acids, which may help reduce inflammations, as well as the risk of heart disease and certain types of cancer. Monounsaturated fat, often dubbed heart-healthy, is associated with helping to reduce levels of LDL (bad) cholesterol, while sparing HDL (good) cholesterol.

While culinary oils can serve as a source of essential fatty acids, as a concentrated fat, they lack the fiber and phytonutrients found in the nuts, seeds, and other plant parts from which they're derived. And, when it comes to calories, oils pack it in stealthily, with 120 calories in just one tablespoon. So it makes a lot of sense to use nuts and seeds in their whole form as your main source of fats within your diet, including nut and seed butters, avocados, and the like, which provide great flavor, texture, and versatility, plus better nutrition.

APRICOT KERNEL OIL

Predominantly monounsaturated fat
Refined

Apricot kernel oil is pressed from the kernels found within apricot pits, which, botanically, are very similar to almonds. It has a mild, slightly sweet flavor. Apricot kernel oil is widely used in cosmetics, lotions, and massage oils. It has a smoke point of 495°F, making it a good all-purpose oil for all types of cooking. It's especially nice in salad dressings.

ARGAN OIL

Slightly higher in monounsaturated fat (44 percent)
  than polyunsaturated fat (37 percent)
Unrefined

Extracted from the nut of the argan tree, argan oil is a deep golden color and has a flavor similar to pumpkin seeds. The argan tree, which can live to be two hundred years old, grows only in a small area in southwestern Morocco. The hard-shelled nut, still typically cracked by hand, is found inside the tree's

From left: Avocado oil, toasted sesame oil, pumpkin seed oil, argan oil, hazelnut oil

small green fruit. Each nut can contain up to three kernels from which the oil is extracted. Argan oil has been used for many centuries as a flavoring ingredient in Moroccan cuisine. Due to its high omega-6 content, it is also used in traditional medicine—externally as a massage oil and internally as a good source of beneficial essential fatty acids.

Argan oil is light, similar in viscosity to sesame oil. Mix it with honey and serve with bread for a traditional Moroccan breakfast, or drizzle it over tagines—Moroccan stews made from meat or poultry simmered with vegetables, olives, and spices and served over couscous. It also makes a delicious salad dressing when mixed with lemon juice or vinegar. Or use it as a condiment to enhance the flavor of soups, vegetables, grains, pasta, grilled meat or fish, or beans, especially lentils.

AVOCADO OIL

Predominantly monounsaturated fat
Unrefined or refined

Avocado oil is pressed from the oil-rich pulp of the avocado fruit and may have some of the flavor and color of avocados depending on the degree of refinement the oil has undergone.

Unrefined avocado oil has a delicious, buttery, nutty flavor that's exceptional in salad dressings, sauces, and light sautés or simply drizzled over crusty bread, steamed vegetables, or pasta dishes. As processing essentially involves only pressing the oil from the pulp, unrefined avocado oil retains the beautiful green color of the original fruit. For best flavor and nutrition, use it only in no-heat or low-heat cooking applications.

In contrast, refined avocado oil has a very light color and is almost flavorless. It is distinguished from all other plant-derived culinary oils in having the highest smoke point—510°F. In addition to being the best oil to use for high-heat cooking, such as stir-frying, grilling, broiling, and frying, it also works well in salad dressings and low- to medium-heat applications when a mild flavor desired.

CANOLA OIL

Predominantly monounsaturated fat,
  including 11 percent omega-3 fatty acids
Refined

If you want to keep things simple and keep only one kind of oil in your refrigerator, this is the one to choose. Canola oil is an excellent all-purpose oil made from a fairly recently developed variety of mustard rape, a plant related to kale, cabbage, brussels sprouts, and other members of the *Brassica* genus. Although oil from conventional rapeseed plants has been a traditional cooking oil in China, Japan, and India for more than three thousand years, in the 1970s questions were raised about its safety because it contains fairly high levels of erucic acid, which had detrimental health effects on rats in a single animal study. As a result, several hybrids with lower levels of erucic acid were developed, even though subsequent studies have failed to show detrimental effects from erucic acid in humans. Nonetheless, this relatively new variety of oil, sometimes referred to as LEAR oil (low erucic acid rapeseed oil) turned out to be worth the effort.

Canola oil is always refined, making it heat stable at fairly high temperatures. Accordingly, it is suitable for all types of cooking, from salad dressings to sautéing and baking up to 425°F with regular canola oil and up to 460°F with super high-heat canola oil (which is from rapeseed bred to have a higher percentage of monounsaturated fats). Its neutral flavor and aroma are mild enough to allow the flavors of the foods it's cooked with to be the focus.

Although canola oil was developed before genetic engineering was used as a tool in plant breeding, genetically engineered versions of low erucic acid rapeseed have since been created. To ensure you aren't getting oil from genetically modified plants, use only certified organic canola oil or oil from producers who have verified their canola oil is from plants that were grown from non-GMO seed.

COCONUT OIL

Predominantly saturated fat
Unrefined or refined

Coconut oil is made from the fruits of coconut palm trees, which grow in hot, rainy tropical climates. It is thought to be one of the earliest plant oils used by humans, especially in tropical regions. Due to its saturated fat content, coconut oil is very stable, resisting oxidation and thus rancidity. This lends products made with coconut oil a longer shelf life and explains why it is widely used in food manufacturing, in nondairy creamers, and for frying products like potato chips and popcorn, for example. It is also appreciated for its subtle, slightly sweet and nutty flavor, making it a key ingredient used to make popcorn and many other products.

The coconut flavor is much more pronounced in unrefined coconut oil. Because all of the flavor components and the full spectrum of phytonutrients remain intact in unrefined coconut oil, it also has a lower smoke point (280°F), making it more appropriate for medium-heat cooking, including light sautéing in dishes where its coconut flavor will enhance the recipe. In comparison, refined coconut oil has fewer nutrients, but its smoke point of 365°F makes it the better option for cooking and baking at medium-high heat.

Different brands of coconut oil vary widely in quality. Coconut oil can be processed in many ways, some retaining nutrients and the natural coconut flavor better than others. Typical commercial production of coconut oil starts with copra, coconut meat that has been scraped out of ripe coconuts and dried for a couple of days in the sun or in a kiln, often by individual farmers in communities where coconut palms are grown. Because the copra is usually processed into coconut oil at facilities far from where it was dried, it can start to deteriorate along the way, especially because of the high humidity and unsanitary conditions that often prevail. To make it safe for human use, the coconut oil expressed from copra undergoes a thorough refining process, often at high temperatures and using solvents.

In contrast, expeller-pressed coconut oil is processed without solvents. It can be either lightly filtered and left unrefined or further refined, filtered, and distilled, giving it a higher heat tolerance but also removing some of the flavors and aroma of fresh coconut.

Virgin coconut oil is unrefined and may be processed in a couple of different ways. It can be expressed from quickly dried coconut meat within an hour of cracking open the coconut, using minimal heat and filtration, directly at the site where coconut palms are grown. Or it can be expressed from wet coconut meat by first making coconut milk and then separating the oil out of the coconut milk in any of a number of ways: by boiling, fermentation, or refrigeration, or by using enzymes or a centrifuge. For example, in the fermentation method, the coconut milk is fermented for twenty-four to thirty-six hours, during which time the oil separates out. Then, depending on the manufacturer, the oil may be heated at low temperatures for a short time to remove moisture that could eventually cause the oil to deteriorate. Finally, it is filtered. The best virgin coconut oils will have a wonderful taste and aroma of coconuts.

Free of trans fats and cholesterol, but still one to be used sparingly, coconut oil is often used as an alternative to hydrogenated fats and butter for frying, sautéing, or baking cookies, piecrusts, and cakes. When stored below 78°F, coconut oil has a thick consistency like shortening and is sometimes referred to as coconut butter. At warmer temperatures, it melts into a liquid oil. If your coconut oil is in a more solid form and a recipe calls for coconut oil in its liquid state, just put the container in hot water until it liquefies. Likewise, you may want to refrigerate liquid coconut oil until it solidifies if you're using it in a recipe that calls for fat in a solid form, such as shortening.

CORN OIL
Predominantly polyunsaturated fat
Unrefined or refined

An old American standby, corn oil was first produced in the late 1800s, several years after the development of processes for hydrolyzing cornstarch, in which the starch is separated from the oil-rich germ. Because it's inexpensive, corn oil is used extensively in making margarine and vegetable shortening, as well as for cooking and salad dressings.

Corn oil has a smoke point of 320°F if unrefined and 450°F if refined. Due to its tendency to foam and smoke at high heat, neither form of corn oil should be used for deep-frying. It's usually refined, in which case it has an almost nonexistent flavor and a light golden color. When unrefined, it has a buttery corn flavor and a deep yellow color that make it a good choice for baking, sautéing, and cooking pancakes. When using unrefined corn oil, don't exceed medium-hot temperature cooking and keep oven temperatures at or below 350°F. As the majority of corn is genetically engineered, use certified organic corn oil or oil that is verified as not coming from plants that were grown from genetically modified seed.

FLAXSEED OIL
Predominantly polyunsaturated fat,
*   including 57 percent omega-3 fatty acids*
Unrefined

Flaxseed oil, a golden colored oil with a nutty, buttery flavor, is pressed from the tiny oval seeds of the blue-flowered flax plant. As its polyunsaturated fat is comprised of an amazing 57 percent alpha-linolenic acid, flaxseed oil is prized as a plant-based, and therefore vegetarian, source of omega-3 fatty acids. A teaspoon of flaxseed oil provides 2.8 grams of ALA.

Lignans, a beneficial form of fiber found in the thin outer membrane of whole flaxseeds, are removed as a result of expressing the oil from the seeds. However, they are sometimes added back into flaxseed oil as an enrichment. The primary lignan found in flaxseed, secoisolariciresinol diglycoside

(SDG), is known for its antioxidant properties and balancing effect on hormones. Flaxseed oil enriched with lignans provides enhanced nutrition, richer texture, and nuttier flavor. As the lignans will sink to the bottom of the bottle, the oil must be shaken vigorously before use.

Flaxseed oil should only be used in no-heat recipes or added to foods at temperatures lower than 225°F, such as salad dressings, sandwich spreads, and dips. It makes a delicious and healthy replacement for butter or any oil on baked potatoes, steamed vegetables, rice, pasta, and cooked grains, and even drizzled on bread. Or you can add a spoonful to smoothies, shakes, or yogurt. Since flaxseed oil is so high in polyunsaturated fats, it is quite sensitive to light, heat, and oxygen, explaining why it's packaged in dark bottles. It should be refrigerated at all times, including in grocery stores.

GRAPESEED OIL

Predominantly polyunsaturated fat
Refined

Grapeseed oil, a traditional oil produced in many countries where wine grapes are grown, is pressed from the tiny seeds of grapes. Not surprisingly, it is a popular component in French and Italian cooking. Due to its nongreasy nature, it is also popular as a base for massage oils. Because the seeds are so small and hard and contain only 10 percent oil, most grapeseed oil is extracted with solvents and refined. However, varieties that use alcohol, rather than hexane, as a solvent are available and would be the better choice.

Unlike other oils high in polyunsaturated fats, grapeseed oil has a relatively high smoke point (425°F), due to its low levels of impurities, which are naturally present in most oils. Another benefit of its relative purity is that salad dressings and marinades made with grapeseed oil don't cloud when refrigerated. Chefs like it for its neutral flavor and light consistency, and also because it's suitable for a wider range of temperatures and cooking applications than olive oil is. Grapeseed oil is a good choice

when making sauces, sautéing, baking, and frying at medium-high heat. Mild in flavor, it's a good choice when making infused oils, and is also commonly used with other oils to tone down strong flavors.

HAZELNUT OIL

Predominantly monounsaturated fat
Unrefined

Hazelnut oil is a distinctively delicious oil made by hydraulically pressing hazelnuts that have been ground and then roasted. And like hazelnuts themselves, hazelnut oil is also a good source of phytosterols, which are phytonutrients that help reduce cholesterol while boosting the immune system.

To best appreciate its flavor, drizzle hazelnut oil on salads, bitter greens, steamed vegetables, cooked grains, or pasta as a flavoring accent, or use it in marinades, vinaigrettes, and sauces. Although hazelnut oil can also be used in baking, its flavor can dissipate when subjected to heat.

OLIVE OIL

Predominantly monounsaturated fat
Unrefined or refined

Olive oil has had a long culinary history (since 5000 BCE), and remains one of the most intriguing of the oils. Good-quality olive oil is pressed from coarsely crushed olives, most often in a hydraulic press, sometimes in a stone press, and occasionally by just letting gravity take its course, allowing the oil to drip out of the crushed olives and through a fine screen. The many types of olive oil vary in flavor, color, and aroma depending on the variety of olives used, the soil and climate in which they were grown, when and how they were harvested, and the skill of the processor.

The most flavorful and nutritious olive oils come from handpicked semiripe olives and have a fruitier, more robust taste accented by a spicy, peppery flavor. This zesty taste signifies the higher level of antioxidant phytochemicals present in olives before they ripen. Early-harvest olive oils contain at least thirty antioxidant phytochemicals, which provide

processing removes most of the protein, to the point that none would be detectable by standard laboratory methods. But with so many other choices available, it may not be worth the risk.

PUMPKIN SEED OIL

Predominantly polyunsaturated fat, including
  15 percent omega-3 fatty acids
Unrefined

Pumpkin seed oil has a dark, opaque green color and the rich flavor of roasted pumpkin seeds. Like pumpkin seeds, it is very high in antioxidants, including vitamin E, carotenoids, and chlorophyll, as well as phytosterols.

Though it is sometimes refined for use in cosmetics, for culinary purposes it's usually unrefined. And since it is very high in polyunsaturated fats, its smoke point is quite low. It is best used as a flavoring accent for salads, soups, hot crusty bread, and steamed vegetables or fish. For salad dressings or general cooking purposes, mix a small amount of pumpkin seed oil into a larger amount of another oil, preferably one high in monounsaturated fats. Not only will the combination moderate the robust flavor characteristic of pumpkin seed oil, but it will also increase its smoke point. Store pumpkin seed oil in the refrigerator, and use it quickly for optimal flavor and nutrition.

SAFFLOWER OIL

Predominantly polyunsaturated fat and unrefined
  or refined (regular safflower oil)
predominantly monounsaturated fat and refined
  (high oleic or very high oleic safflower oil)

Safflower oil is expressed from the seeds of a thistle-like plant whose flowers have long been used as a dye and as a coloring agent in food in place of the more rare and costly saffron. This is why the plant is sometimes referred to as saffron thistle or bastard saffron. Because regular safflower oil has the highest polyunsaturated fat content of any culinary oil, it was particularly popular in the 1970s, when then-current nutritional theory praised the virtues of polyunsaturated fats. Since then, however, newer information about fats indicates that polyunsaturated fats should be used in moderation because they are very vulnerable to oxidation.

Unrefined safflower oil, which has a unique nutty flavor and golden color, is best used unheated as a condiment on cold dishes and to make salad dressings. When cooking with it, don't exceed 225°F. It can also be blended with other oils that have a higher smoke point and used for cooking at medium heat. The smoke point of refined safflower oil, which has a very light color and flavor, is 320°F, making it appropriate for medium-heat cooking.

For cooking at medium-high to high heat, which includes sautéing, pan-frying, searing, stir-frying, grilling, broiling, and baking, choose high oleic or very high-oleic safflower oil. Both are made from new varieties of safflower developed through traditional plant breeding techniques, not genetic engineering, to significantly modify the fatty acid profile from predominantly polyunsaturated fats to monounsaturated fats. The term *high-oleic* simply refers to its high percentage of monounsaturated fats in the form of oleic acid. Not only do the high-oleic forms of safflower oil have a heart-healthy advantage over regular safflower oil, but they are also much more stable against oxidation and have a smoke point of 390°F. Very high-oleic safflower oil has an even higher percentage of monounsaturated fat, giving it a smoke point of 460°F.

SESAME OIL

About equal monounsaturated and
  polyunsaturated fat
Unrefined or refined

Sesame oil has been enjoyed for thousands of years for many reasons. Its rich, nutty flavor has long been used to enhance cooking, but sesame oil has also been used in Ayurvedic medicine, where it's revered for its beneficial essential fatty acids.

Sesame seeds contain more phytosterols (which help lower cholesterol) than any other nut or seed, and their oil has a very high amount of these compounds, especially when it undergoes minimal processing and isn't refined. Unlike other culinary oils, sesame oil's fatty acid profile consists of almost equal amounts of monounsaturated and polyunsaturated fats. Although such a high proportion of polyunsaturated fats would generally result in increased vulnerability to oxidation, sesame oil contains unique lignans, sesamin and sesamol, which act as potent antioxidants. They help protect the oil from rancidity and also allow it to be used at medium-high temperatures even in its unrefined form. The smoke point of unrefined sesame oil is 350°F, and that of refined sesame oil is 445°F.

As usual, the flavor and color of unrefined sesame oil is much richer. Its nutty flavor makes it a natural for sautés, sauces, salad dressings, and marinades, and it's also excellent simply drizzled over any cold or hot vegetable, pasta, or grain dish. Use refined sesame oil when stir-frying, for higher-heat sautés, or for general cooking purposes. It's a good choice for mixing with other oils to increase their smoke point.

Extracting the oil from toasted sesame seeds creates a very rich flavor and aroma, making toasted sesame especially good as a flavoring agent. It is often used in Asian cuisines, drizzled over soups, noodles, stir-fries, and vegetables. When using it as a cooking oil, rather than a condiment, don't exceed 350°F.

SOY OIL

Predominantly polyunsaturated fat, including
  8 percent omega-3 fatty acids
Unrefined and refined

For a long time, soy oil was considered to be inedible due to its tendency to have off flavors, so it was used primarily in the manufacture of industrial products. But by the early 1940s, new processing and refinement methods, including hydrogenation, were developed to remove or neutralize the various components responsible for its unpalatable flavor. Shortly thereafter, soy oil became the leading cooking oil in the United States and one of the oils most often used in vegetable shortening, margarine, and salad dressings. In fact, it became so common in the United States that it was often referred to generically as "vegetable oil." Even now, most vegetable oil is predominantly soy oil.

Because soy oil is so high in polyunsaturated fat, including an appreciable amount of the esteemed alpha-linolenic acid (an omega-3 fatty acid), it is more vulnerable to oxidation than many other oils. While hydrogenation (the process of artificially transforming polyunsaturated fats like soy oil into more solid fats, like margarine and vegetable shortening) has been used to help stabilize the oil, given all of the health risks of the resulting formation of artificial trans fatty acids, it is best to avoid any products in which soy oil is partially hydrogenated. Soy oil is also known for being high in vitamin E. About 30 percent of its vitamin content is lost during refining. (This is often collected and used in dietary supplements.)

Unrefined soy oil has a deep amber color and a very distinctive flavor, making it one that should be used sparingly, as it can easily overpower other ingredients within a dish or meal. It is best reserved for low- to medium-heat cooking; no higher than 320°F. With its light flavor and smoke point of 450°F, refined soy oil can be used for almost any application. Semirefined soy oil, which is mechanically expressed without chemical solvents, is also available; it has a smoke point of 360°F. Check product labeling to know whether you are buying unrefined, semirefined, or fully refined soy oil. Since the majority of soybeans grown in the United States are genetically engineered, use certified organic soy oil to ensure it isn't derived from genetically modified soybeans.

SUNFLOWER OIL

Predominantly polyunsaturated fat and unrefined or refined (regular sunflower oil)
Predominantly monounsaturated fat and refined (high oleic or very high oleic sunflower oil)

Although sunflowers have grown wild for millions of years and their seeds have been used for food for thousands of years, a method of extracting sunflower oil from the seeds wasn't developed until the early 1700s. Newer strains of sunflower, developed to contain up to twice the amount of oil in the seeds as traditional varieties, make the process easier.

Sunflower oil is a very good source of vitamin E, having the highest alpha-tocopherol level of any of the primary culinary oils. It also contains a moderate amount of phytosterols, which help cholesterol levels. While its specific fatty acid profile can vary depending on the strain of sunflower and the climate in which it was grown, sunflower oil is usually very high in polyunsaturated fats, making it more vulnerable to oxidation. Accordingly, unrefined sunflower oil, with its light yellow color and mild sunflower seed flavor, is best used for no-heat applications, such as salad dressings.

Refined sunflower oil can be made from traditional varieties of sunflower seeds, which are rich in linoleic acid (an omega-6 fatty acid), but most sunflower oil now available is made from new varieties of sunflowers developed to have high levels of oleic acid (a monounsaturated fat). First developed in Russia in the mid-1970s, these varieties were created using crossbreeding rather than biotechnology. In 1995, the culinary oil industry made a wholesale switch to high-oleic seeds because their oil is more stable. Because it has a smoke point of 460°F and is more resistant to oxidation, high oleic sunflower oil is a good choice for cooking at medium-high to high heat, including sautéing, pan-frying, searing, stir-frying, grilling, broiling, and baking.

WALNUT OIL

Predominantly polyunsaturated fat, including 10 percent omega-3 fatty acids
Unrefined or refined

Walnut oil is extracted from English walnuts that are first ground and then roasted before being pressed. It is one of the rare plant sources for omega-3 fatty acids, with 1 tablespoon of walnut oil providing 1.4 grams of alpha-linolenic acid, which is a precursor for eicosapentaenoic acid (EPA) and docosahexaenoic acid (DHA), the more biologically active omega-3 fatty acids. Like walnuts themselves, walnut oil is high in antioxidants. It has especially high amounts of gamma-tocopherol, a form of vitamin E that helps guard against the oxidation of fats, both in foods and in the body.

Unrefined walnut oil has a more vibrant color than does refined, and a rich, nutty flavor, but because it's more vulnerable to oxidation and has a fairly low smoke point (305°F), it isn't suitable for general cooking. Use it in salad dressings and sauces, or drizzle it over pasta, cooked grains, and steamed vegetables as a flavoring agent. Refined walnut oil has a higher smoke point (400°F), so it's suitable for baking, where it makes for especially delicious cakes and cookies, and is good for greasing baking pans. Or try brushing it on fish or chicken before baking or grilling.

Essential Seasonings

ᴀᴏ

There are many seasonings I just couldn't do without. Salt, miso, tamari, umeboshi plums, and umeboshi vinegar are some of the essential seasonings I use to enhance flavors. And, although edible seaweeds might seem more like a vegetable than a seasoning, I find they play a valuable role in heightening the flavor of other foods with which they are cooked or served.

Ask people to describe the primary flavors in food, and they're likely to list four: sweet, salty, sour, and bitter. That a fifth flavor exists may be surprising, but that elusive savory sensation experienced when all the flavor and aroma components come together in a food now has a name: umami. In fact, the term *umami* has been around for a long time. It was first identified in 1908, when research was conducted on kombu, the seaweed that provides the flavor-enhancing properties of dashi, a fundamental broth in Japanese cuisine. The study determined that when the amino acid glutamic acid exists in an unbound form (that is, not linked to other amino acids), it helps provide the subtle taste of umami, which has an ability to expand and round out flavors. Mushrooms, ripe tomatoes, Parmesan cheese, and cured ham all provide umami, as do sea vegetables, soy sauce, and miso. Use any of these ingredients when cooking and a kind of magic happens.

Long after discovery of the link between glutamic acid and umami, two other compounds, inosinate and guanylate, were also determined to provide the fifth taste. Most known for their work as building blocks for creating RNA and DNA within our cells, these compounds are found in bonito flakes and shiitake mushrooms, two ingredients that, like kombu, are also considered essential flavor enhancers within traditional Japanese cooking. In effect, science is merely corroborating what practice and tradition already determined centuries ago.

Synthetic monosodium glutamate (MSG), a salt form of glutamic acid, was developed once the amino acid was determined to be a source of umami, in an attempt to capture the taste and provide it cheaply—with a shake of the wrist rather than through the natural foods that contain it. However, as is often the case, trying to imitate nature turns out to be problematic, since MSG causes serious side effects in sensitive individuals. Synthetic forms of inosinate and guanylate are often used in combination with MSG to further enhance flavor. In addition to their questionable effects on health, these attempts to add the taste of umami artificially also deny us the opportunity to experience the extraordinary textures, colors, and other flavors—not to mention the nutrients—in real foods.

Umami can also be accentuated through fermentation and curing of foods. During the process of fermentation, proteins are broken down into their constituent amino acids, providing the opportunity for glutamate to exert its flavor-enhancing properties. Umami is further heightened by the synergistic effect of combining foods known to be high in glutamate, inosinate, and guanylate: adding mushrooms to tomato sauce, for example, or serving ham with cheese.

Many different sauces, seasonings, and condiments from across the globe provide umami, including, for example, ketchup, cocktail sauce, anchovy paste, and clam sauce. While each of these essential seasonings can be associated with a particular style of cooking, their use is truly universal and they can enhance flavor in any type of cuisine. Common to each is salt, the most essential seasoning of all.

Salt

As an indication of salt's significance to health and wealth throughout the ages, wars have been fought over it; towns were founded around salt deposits; and civilizations lived or died by its availability. Salt, which is a combination of sodium and chloride, was valuable in historic times because it allowed people to preserve food without freezing or refrigeration. As a result of its dehydrating action, salt helps to inhibit growth of both mold and bacteria. Pickled vegetables and cured meat and fish are classic examples of the superior preserving abilities of salt. It is also responsible for development of the rind and better consistency of texture in cheese, and strengthening gluten and controlling the rate of fermentation in bread.

Maldon flake salt

In the human body, the sodium in salt is a key player in maintaining the pressure and volume of blood and the correct balance of water in and around cells and tissues. Transmission of nerve impulses and proper digestion also depends on having enough salt in the diet. But we really don't need much salt to remain healthy, just about 500 milligrams per day. This number is remarkably close to the estimated daily sodium intake of our hunter-gatherer ancestors: about 690 milligrams, with 148 milligrams of it from plant foods and the remaining 542 milligrams from wild game. Today, however, some people may consume up to ten times that amount per day. Fast foods and processed foods are the biggest culprits, responsible for as much as 75 percent of the sodium intake of people who eat a lot of these foods.

In terms of dietary sodium from sources other than fast foods and processed foods, only 60 percent comes from the salt or salty seasonings we intentionally add, while 40 percent occurs naturally in foods. It should come as no surprise, then, that the most effective way to moderate sodium intake is to minimize consumption of processed foods, opting instead for simply prepared foods, seasoned only as needed to accentuate the natural flavors within.

NUTRITIONAL DIFFERENCES AMONG SALTS

Although all salt is mostly sodium chloride, with amounts ranging from 97 to 99.5 percent, there are distinctive nutritional differences between refined salt and unrefined salt, as the latter retains the spectrum of macrominerals and trace minerals found in the particular area from which it originates. However, despite unique local and regional variations in the mineral profile of seawater, its relative concentration of minerals has remained the same for millions of years.

The correlation between the profile of salts and trace minerals found in the sea and those within our bodies was recognized as far back as 1684, by the noted scientist Robert Boyle. Boyle's work was corroborated in 1776, when Hilaire-Marin Rouelle isolated cubic crystals that were similar to sea salt from inorganic materials in blood serum.

While the amount of minerals beyond sodium chloride that one actually receives in the small volume of salt consumed on a daily basis is fairly minimal, our growing understanding of the power of phytonutrients, found in trace amounts in plant foods, has repeatedly challenged the concept that nutrients in seemingly insignificant quantities have little value. The whole is typically greater than the sum of its parts, even if we don't always know exactly what we would be missing if the whole were fragmented. So when it comes to choosing between salt that retains the natural spectrum of minerals and refined salt, opting for more natural forms seems a prudent way to go, not only for finishing salts but for salt used in general cooking, too. Even on a purely practical basis, the extra minerals in sea salt have been found to be helpful in gluten development when making bread. And salt with a more diverse mineral profile tastes better, too.

One nutrient not to bank on in sea salt, however, is iodine. Even though most of the world's naturally occurring iodine comes from the oceans, it is present in seawater only in very small amounts that, even when concentrated, are not enough to ensure proper functioning of the thyroid gland and prevention of goiter. But rather than depending on commercial iodized salt, try to get enough iodine by eating fish or sea vegetables, or get it through a dietary supplement. Dairy products can also be a source of iodine, as iodine solutions are commonly used to clean milking equipment and cows' udders.

IODIZED SALT

Potassium iodide is often added to commercial salt to ensure that people get enough iodine. This critically important nutrient can prevent the development of goiter, an early warning sign of iodine deficiency. On a basic level, iodine helps ensure proper functioning of the thyroid gland, which regulates a wide variety of processes within the body, including growth, development, metabolism, and reproductive function. Iodine deficiency is also recognized as the number one cause of preventable brain damage worldwide.

Supplemental iodine was first added to salt in 1924, particularly for the benefit of people living in mountainous or landlocked regions where iodine is especially deficient in the soil. It also helps fill in the gaps for those whose diets do not include regular consumption of seafood or sea vegetables, both of which provide concentrated natural sources of iodine.

A very small amount of dextrose (0.04 percent) is added to iodized salt to stabilize the potassium iodide and prevent it from breaking down and evaporating. Pickling salt (specifically developed for pickling applications) isn't fortified with iodine or anticaking agents because they could discolor the pickles. In addition, the anticaking agents aren't water soluble, so they could settle on the bottom of the jar.

SALT CRYSTAL SIZE AND FLAVOR

Despite the many nuances in flavor that depend on where and how salt is obtained and whether it's enhanced with minerals or other substances, the primary differences among salts in terms of flavor and effect on food are largely determined by the processing techniques used to create the salt and the skill of the manufacturers. This is especially relevant when it comes to the size and structure of the salt crystal.

Small, dense, cubic crystals are produced in closed evaporation tanks in which crystallization occurs throughout the brine. In contrast, salt produced in open pools or containers with monitored, slow drying and hands-on processing creates broad, irregular plate-shaped or pyramid-shaped crystals. Not only do these provide the crunchy texture characteristic of fine finishing salts, but these very structures also enhance the tasting experience, producing a pleasant burst of flavor on the palate, very unlike the sharp taste that results from the small, solid crystals of common table salt. And here, too, the irregular crystals of fine finishing salts are superior. The size and shape of the crystals help the salt adhere to the surface of foods, allowing it to better perform as a condiment or topping.

Kosher salt, which can either be mined or made from seawater sources, provides yet another texture of salt. Its name derives from the fact that it is used to prepare meat according to Jewish dietary guidelines. Through the process of continually raking salt brine during evaporation, coarse, irregular crystals are created, which tend to cling to meat. This means the salt stays on the surface longer and does a better job of drawing blood and juices out of just-butchered meat, as kosher guidelines require. Beyond this traditional use, kosher salt works well in recipes that include enough water to allow it to dissolve and disperse. It can also be used as a crunchy, salty topping on meat, fish, pretzels, and breads.

Many chefs appreciate kosher salt for its flavor, which is less harsh than that of table salt. And due to its large crystal size, kosher salt is easier to pick up with the fingers when adding a pinch of salt to a recipe. Brands of kosher salt do, however, vary in the shape of crystal, depending on the manufacturer's processing methods. Some are cubic, with the large grains composed of many cubes stacked together. Other brands have crystals with a hollow, pyramidal shape, and as a result they dissolve twice as fast as table salt and granular kosher salt do. Because the pyramid-shaped crystals are less dense, it takes a larger amount to achieve the same saltiness. Most brands of kosher salt also are free of additives, including iodine. Still, some brands do include sodium ferrocyanide as an anticaking agent, which may leave a slight chemical aftertaste.

Gomasio, a traditional Japanese condiment used instead of plain table salt, is a blend of roasted sesame seeds ground with sea salt, generally using eight to fifteen parts sesame to one part sea salt. Especially good on whole grains, cooked vegetables, baked potatoes, cooked beans, and pasta, gomasio can be used to enhance the flavor of other foods while minimizing the amount of sodium consumed.

MEASURING AND STORING SALTS

The amount of salt called for in recipes is usually based on the assumption that the small crystals commonly found in table salt will be used. How much to use when substituting salt with larger crystals depends on the specific density of the salt in comparison to table salt. Finely ground salt can generally be substituted for common table salt on a one-to-one basis, whereas with flake salt you may need to use almost twice as much. You'll have to experiment to figure out how much to use of different varieties.

Finishing salts should be stored in a glass, ceramic, or wooden container with a loose-fitting lid, such as a cork stopper, which allows some air to flow to the salt but still keeps it dry. If a utensil is used to measure the salt or sprinkle it over food, it should be nonmetal. Cooking salts can be stored in similar containers. To keep excess moisture from causing clumping in salt shakers, add a couple of grains of uncooked rice.

Exploring Salt Varieties

One way or another, all salt originates from the sea or saltwater lakes, whether dehydrated from a current source of water or extracted from salt deposits formed as ancient bodies of water dried up. Even so, where the salt originates and how it is produced can make a big difference in how it affects the experience and flavor of food, and also in terms of what minerals it can provide beyond plain sodium chloride.

MINED SALT

Also known as rock salt, salt obtained from inland salt mines is used in a wide variety of ways: as an agent to deice roads in the winter, as a salt lick for livestock in the fields, as a freezing aid for making homemade ice cream, and, of course, as a seasoning agent. Through an extraction method called **room-and-pillar mining**, miners blast and drill to remove big chunks of salt, leaving large pillars of salt in place to hold up the roof of the mine. The extracted salt is brought up to the surface, crushed, and screened. Mined culinary salts may occur in a variety of colors, such as soft pink crystal salt from Pakistan or pinkish gray salt from Redmond, Utah, each manifesting and retaining the range of natural minerals of a long-gone ocean, as well as the sediment that settled between the different crystallization layers. Subtle flavor differences will also be apparent.

Mined culinary salts, with their cubic crystal structure, are best used in cooking, although they could also be used as finishing salts to provide a more flavorful and colorful alternative to common table salt. Typically, mined culinary salts are available both finely ground or in larger chunks to be used in home salt grinders.

Common table salt is often produced from deep underground salt deposits using the **solution mining** method. This involves pumping water down into the salt deposit to create a brine solution, then pumping it back to the surface and on to a purification plant, where impurities are removed, along with the more bitter chloride and sulfate salts of magnesium and many trace minerals, leaving about 99.5 percent sodium chloride. Evaporation in huge vessels yields very fine, dense, cubic crystals of salt that look like grains of sugar. Anticaking agents are often added, such as calcium silicate and magnesium carbonate, both white, odor-free and taste-free compounds that absorb moisture within the package.

SALT FROM EVAPORATED SALTWATER

Salt that is made by evaporating saltwater is often generically referred to as sea salt. Quality varies widely among these salts. Some brands of sea salt are hardly different from typical mined table salt, being harvested and dried on a large scale and refined to remove most minerals, ultimately yielding 99.5 percent pure sodium chloride. They may even be evaporated in such a way as to create the same small, dense, cubic crystals found in common table salt, and anticaking agents and iodine are often added. While refined sea salt, like common mined table salt, is fine for general cooking, its flavor is too sharp to function as a finishing salt, which needs to be able to complement and complete a dish.

At the other end of the quality spectrum, unrefined salt from unpolluted areas is still traditionally produced in much the same manner as it was centuries ago. In this seasonal process, which takes advantage of spring tides at their saltiest, seawater is first trapped in inlets, estuaries, large shallow ponds, or clay-lined pools (commonly referred to as salt pans). The water is then almost completely evaporated in the open air under the sun or, in humid or colder areas, with a controlled external heat source.

Next, during the crystallization stage, the salts in the seawater are encouraged to precipitate through the use of techniques that ultimately determine the size, shape, texture, and color of the finished salt.

This process may include carefully skimming off the delicate crystals that form on the surface and raking the crystals that form at the bottom of the salt pan. Special care is taken to minimize stirring up any clay or sediment in order to keep the salt crystals as pure and flavorful as possible. Traditional long wooden rakes are still used by many artisan producers, as metal implements are considered to have the potential to adversely affect the final flavor.

The surface crystals that are formed and collected each day are considered the crème de la crème of sea salt. These are known as **fleur de sel** in France and **flor de sal** in Portugal (and go by other names in other places); both these names translate to "flower of salt," which reflects how the crystals blossom on the surface of the water, and may also refer to the aroma of violets that is said to develop as the crystals dry in the sun, accentuating its special character. Like the cream that rises to the top of unhomogenized whole milk, this type of salt, with its light, flaky texture and sweet, delicate flavor, is considered the perfect condiment to complement simple dishes and foods. In fact, it is best used only as a finishing salt, as its nuances of flavor and its texture would be lost in the high temperatures and duration of most cooking processes. However, a light dusting of fleur de sel can accentuate the flavors of vegetables, meats, fish, beans, and baked potatoes once they're cooked. Even though various brands of French fleur de sel and Portuguese flor de sal are produced in essentially the same manner, they have subtle differences in flavor and aroma because they come from different harvesting areas.

French **sel gris** (gray salt) and the comparable, although naturally whiter, traditional Portuguese sea salt are made from the second layer of salt that doesn't rise to the surface. Skimmed off after the fleur de sel is collected, sel gris is coarser and somewhat bolder in flavor. Both French and Portuguese gray salts are excellent for all types of cooking, including roasting, baking, grilling, and brining, and also provide a more flavorful, mineral-rich alternative to common table salt.

From top: (1) Jurassic Ocean salt, (2) Peruvian Andes Warm Spring salt, (3) Lemon Flake salt, (4) Haleakala Ruby salt, (5) sel gris, (6) Hana Flake salt

Maldon sea salt is hand harvested off of England's Essex coast, a centuries-old salt-producing region that has low rainfall, strong winds, lots of sunshine, and low-lying salt marshes, qualities that come together to naturally trap seawater and begin the process of evaporation. The concentrated brine is collected and evaporated in large stainless steel pans over controlled natural gas heat. As the brine concentrates, small crystals shaped like hollow pyramids form, accumulate, and are hand harvested daily using traditional long-handled rakes. The result is very soft, light, flaky crystals of salt that are exceptional as a finishing salt.

Natural sea salt from the west coast of Sicily is also a special find. Look for salts like **Ittica d'Or**, a sea salt from the medieval saltworks along the salt road between Trapani and Marsala that is now designated as a natural preserve to protect it from industrial pollution.

Flower of Bali is another unusual finishing salt obtained by gathering crystals from the top of seawater evaporating in hollowed-out trunks of palm trees.

FLAVOR-ENRICHED SEA SALTS

Each sea salt has a unique flavor and color, reflecting the minerals found in the area where the salt originates and the skill of the salt worker, which can make a difference in how much of the clay bottom of the salt pan is scraped up in the raking process. Beyond these differences, some salts are endowed with natural minerals. Comprising up to 2 to 3 percent of the final product, the minerals (which may be retained in or added to sea salt) can make the final product taste slightly sweet, bitter, or briny.

Red Alaea sea salt from Hawaii derives its color from the natural iron oxides found in red volcanic clay. The red salt originally formed naturally, when, as a result of heavy rains, red clay river sediments seeped into tide pools. When evaporated naturally, the salt from these pools was dyed red. Hawaiian red sea salt, traditionally used in blessing and healing rituals, was valued as a sacred representation of the meshing of earth and sea. Today it is also used in Hawaiian dishes, not only for its flavor, but also in honor of tradition. Another example of enriched sea salt is **Cyprus black lava salt**. This flaky salt from tidal pools formed by lava flows has activated charcoal added for dramatic color and smoky flavor and aroma.

Sea salt can also be infused with a smoked flavor. A variety of shells or types of wood can be used to impart different aromas through a cold-smoking process. Examples include salt smoked over juniper, cherry, elm, beech, and oak; or from Chardonnay-imbued oak chips from seasoned French wine barrels; as well as salt smoked over red alder wood.

Miso

Sea salt is a significant ingredient in miso. Although this thick, versatile seasoning paste originated in China twenty-five hundred years ago, it is most commonly associated with Japan, where it is one of the hallmarks of traditional Japanese cuisine. It is made from cooked soybeans mixed with water and koji, which is cooked grain or soybeans inoculated with a mold that starts the fermentation process. Depending on the type of miso being produced, the aging process may range between two months and three years. Each variety of miso reflects the microorganisms native to the area in which it is made, giving it a unique flavor and sometimes a unique appearance.

The fermentation process enhances the fifth flavor, umami, explaining why miso is widely recognized for its ability to enhance flavor in soups, with classic miso soup being the most familiar. It also sets the stage for exceptional sauces, stews, gravies, salad dressings, dips, spreads, and marinades, and can even serve as a stand-in for Parmesan cheese for a new spin on pesto.

MISO AND HEALTH

An additional bonus of miso is its healthful, probiotic properties, arising from the "friendly" lactobacillus bacteria that proliferate during the process of making miso. Probiotics can help support the body's own native friendly bacteria, effectively providing a boost to the immune system, helping protect against disease, and aiding in digestion of food and absorption of nutrients. Since pasteurization is designed to kill microbes, unpasteurized miso has the best probiotic activity. This type of miso will always be sold refrigerated in glass jars or plastic containers. While pasteurized miso is fine in terms of flavor and easier to ship, the pasteurization process reduces the health benefits of miso, trading nutrition for convenience.

Studies have also shown that frequent consumption of miso soup is associated with decreased risk of stomach cancer and breast cancer. Other studies indicate that miso consumption can reduce the effects of radiation exposure and increase survival rates from cancer, particularly dark miso that has been fermented for a long time.

Miso at a Glance

Light Miso Types	Characteristics	How to Use
Sweet white miso (shiro miso)	Made from soybeans and rice Sweet, some caramel undertones; creamy texture, white or pale yellow to caramel color	Dips, spreads, salad dressings, glazes, topping for sweet corn or baked potatoes
Mellow white miso	Made from soybeans and rice Mildly sweet, subtly tart, smooth texture, medium yellow to light brown color	Dips, warm-weather soups, spreads, salad dressings, glazes, topping for sweet corn or baked potatoes
Chickpea miso	Made from chickpeas and rice Mild and sweet with chickpea flavor undertones, beige color	Dips, warm-weather soups, spreads, salad dressings, glazes
Dark Miso Types	**Characteristics**	**How to Use**
Red miso (aka miso)	Made from soybeans and white rice Salty, savory flavor, thick creamy texture, reddish brown color	All-purpose variety: use in miso soups, sauces, spreads, marinades, dips, salad dressings
Brown rice miso (genmai miso)	Made from soybeans and brown rice Salty, medium/strong savory flavor, thick creamy texture, golden brown color	Soups, sauces, spreads, marinades
Barley miso (mugi miso)	Made from soybeans and barley Salty, deep, rich winey flavor, subtle sweetness, thick texture, medium to dark brown color	Soups, sauces, spreads, marinades

HOW MISO IS MADE

The thick texture of miso and its inherent complexity of flavors result from a unique production process involving alternating cycles of fermentation and aging. The process begins by steaming grain, typically rice or barley, or cooked soybeans, and inoculating them with *Aspergillus oryzae*, the type of mold most widely used in Japan for initiating food-related fermentation processes.

After a two-day incubation period, the mixture, now called koji, is mixed in with cooked, mashed soybeans or garbanzo beans, sea salt, and water. During the subsequent aging process, the enzymes in the koji, along with natural microorganisms in the environment, break down the complex carbohydrates, fat, and protein in the beans and grains into more easily digested sugars, fatty acids, and amino acids, including glutamic acid, which is responsible for miso's umami flavor-enhancing properties.

Because fermentation requires warm temperatures, this phase occurs during the warmer months. Cold temperatures during the winter aging phase slow enzyme activity and kill undesirable bacteria that could otherwise taint the flavor and character of the miso. Both cycles are essential to the process of making miso. One-year miso has been fermented at least one summer, while "two-year" miso has gone through two summer fermentation seasons and at least one full summer-to-winter cycle. Similarly, "three-year" miso has gone through at least three summer fermentation seasons and at least two full summer-to-winter cycles, which accounts for its deeper flavors and thicker texture.

VARIETIES OF MISO

Differences among the various types of miso are based on the specific type of koji used, proportions of each of the ingredients, and the total fermentation time. There are two fundamental categories of miso based on color and taste: light miso and dark miso.

LIGHT MISO

Light miso includes all one-year misos, which are typically labeled generically as "mellow miso" or "sweet miso," or by the type of grain used in the koji, such as shiro (sweet rice miso). Misos in this category are less salty, lighter in color (white, yellow, or beige), and higher in carbohydrates than are dark misos. To achieve these characteristics, light miso is made with a high proportion of grain koji, along with a low percentage of salt (ranging from 4 to 6 percent) to speed up fermentation. Since the high protein content of soybeans naturally requires a longer fermentation time to break down the protein, fewer soybeans are used in light miso than dark.

Sweet miso varieties have even less salt and more koji than does mellow miso, producing a smooth, creamy texture and a flavor that's mild, slightly tart, somewhat sweet, and cooling. It's a good choice for use in soups, sauces, dips, spreads, and dressings in warmer seasons and climates. Using sweet miso can be as simple as mixing a small amount into mashed avocado and tofu for a fusion-style guacamole, or blending it with pureed cooked beans and fresh herbs for a quick spread. The creamy texture of light miso also makes it an effective substitute for dairy in soups, spreads, dressings, and even mashed potatoes, though you'd use only a moderate amount.

Try making a miso glaze by combining light miso with oil, honey, and vinegar, and brushing it on roasted vegetables or grilled fish, chicken, or tofu near the end of cooking. Miso marinades are yet another way to explore light miso; combine it into a pastelike mixture with ingredients such as mirin (sweet rice wine), lemon juice, or sake. It's an especially good way to prepare tofu or fish; not only does the marinade help accentuate flavors, but it also serves as a natural tenderizer. Marinate tofu for 2 to 24 hours in the refrigerator. Firm fish like salmon or sablefish (also known as black cod) can be marinated in the refrigerator for as little as 4 hours or up to a couple days prior to cooking.

Dark and light miso

DARK MISO

Dark miso includes two- and three-year misos made with rice (red, kome, genmai, or brown rice miso), barley (mugi miso), soybeans (hatcho miso), or buckwheat (soba miso), with colors ranging from russet red to deep brown. Proportions used to make dark miso are largely the opposite of those used in light miso, with a lower percentage of koji, more soybeans, and more salt (ranging from 10 to 12 percent). Fermented longer, and richer in flavor, dark miso is more warming to the body and is therefore more appropriate for colder seasons and climates. In addition to complementing hearty root vegetables, onions, winter squash, nuts, and nut butters, dark miso provides an excellent foundation for cooked beans, stews, tomato sauces, and soup of all varieties, not just miso soup. Miso tahini sauce is a classic and delicious all-purpose sauce. To make it, combine one part red miso with four parts tahini in a saucepan and thin with broth or water, adjusting the amount of water depending on whether you'd like to make a spread or a sauce. Stir constantly over low heat for 2 to 3 minutes before serving; don't allow the mixture to boil. It's even better topped with a bit of grated fresh ginger or freshly chopped parsley.

COOKING WITH MISO

Miso is high in sodium, so it can be used to replace salt. In general, 1 teaspoon of dark miso is approximately equivalent to 1½ to 2 teaspoons of light miso, which, in turn, is equivalent to about ⅛ teaspoon of salt. A good rule of thumb is to use no more than ½ to 1 teaspoon of dark miso or 1 to 2 teaspoons of light miso per serving. For extra depth of flavor and an interesting interplay of sweet and salty, miso can be used instead of salt when making desserts, or can be added to oatmeal and other hot cereals just before serving, substituting about 1 tablespoon of light miso or 2 teaspoons of dark miso for ¼ teaspoon of salt.

For best results, mix miso in a small amount of broth or water and stir it to form a paste before adding it to soups, sauces, or other dishes. Adding it just three or four minutes before serving will activate its beneficial bacteria and enzymes, but to avoid destroying those beneficial components, only add miso to foods when their temperature is far below a boil. In spreads, dips, and salad dressings, miso is primarily used for flavor, so the heat activation step isn't necessary; however, many of the other health benefits of miso will still be available.

To protect its taste, color, and texture, store miso in the refrigerator, preferably in a tightly sealed glass jar, although a plastic container with a snug lid will work well, too. When properly stored in the refrigerator, miso can last for many years, in part due to its high concentration of salt.

Naturally Brewed Soy Sauce

Like miso, naturally brewed soy sauce is another key condiment that provides the taste of umami. There are a couple of reasons for this. First, soy sauce's ancient Chinese origins are linked directly with miso production. And because the modern manufacturing process still involves several months of fermentation, microbial enzymes have time to free up amino acids, including glutamic acid, from the proteins in soy, setting the stage for soy sauce's ability to blend and intensify the flavors in food. While soy sauce is the generic term applied to all forms of this liquid condiment, the three main categories it encompasses—tamari, shoyu, and nonbrewed chemically hydrolyzed soy sauce—are actually very different from each other, not only in how they are produced but also in how they are used.

Unless specifically labeled as naturally brewed or traditionally brewed, much of the soy sauce commonly available in grocery stores and restaurants is nothing more than a chemically hydrolyzed liquid seasoning initiated by treating soybeans with hydrochloric acid. The liquid is then neutralized and filtered, and caramel color, salt, and corn syrup are added to provide color and some flavor. Preservatives are added as the final step. Although expedient and inexpensive, this process yields a harsh, salty, one-dimensional flavor enhancer, and food seasoned with chemically hydrolyzed soy sauce will be dull, lacking vibrancy and flavor.

In contrast, naturally brewed or traditionally brewed soy sauces rely on natural enzymes and several months of fermentation to break down the soybean protein into its flavorful constituents.

TAMARI AND SHOYU

Originating as a by-product of soy-based miso production in China twenty-five hundred years ago, tamari (which translates as "that which accumulates") was the rich liquid that naturally accumulated in the wooden miso kegs. Many years later, in the seventh century CE, Japan was introduced to miso and, consequently, tamari. Tamari soon became as appreciated and sought after as the miso itself. However, since it takes more than two thousand pounds of miso to yield only about five gallons of tamari, enterprising producers eventually developed a way to make tamari directly from soybeans without going through all of the stages of miso manufacture. The solution was a higher ratio of brine to solids in the fermentation mash.

Japanese tamari makers went a step further in the seventeenth century. They began adding wheat to the fermentation mix to create a soy sauce with a naturally sweeter taste, a seasoning they called shoyu. Fermentation naturally transforms the sugars in wheat starch into alcohol, creating the unique aromatic characteristics responsible for shoyu's flavor profile, which is so different than that of tamari.

HOW TAMARI AND SHOYU ARE MADE

Similar to the process for making miso, both tamari and shoyu are made by first combining cooked soybeans (and roasted wheat if making shoyu) with *Aspergillus oryzae*, the mold commonly used in Japan and China to start the fermentation process in food. After an incubation period of about three days, the mixture, known as koji, is transferred to fermentation tanks where it is combined with salt and water. The salt helps control the lactic acid and

yeast activity during the fermentation process and also acts as a natural preservative. During the five- to six-month fermentation period, the soy proteins are broken down into individual amino acids, including the all-important glutamic acid, and many complex flavors and fragrances develop. Thanks to the conversion of wheat into sugars and alcohol, shoyu develops different flavors and fragrances. The koji and brine mixture (called moromi) ultimately transforms into a reddish brown, semiliquid mash. Next, the moromi is pressed to yield liquid tamari or shoyu, which is strained, pasteurized, and, finally, bottled.

Pasteurization is done for a couple of reasons. In addition to improving the stability of the product by inactivating most of the enzymes and creating acids that inhibit the growth of microorganisms, the brief heat that occurs during pasteurization further develops compounds that contribute additional flavors and aromas. Although shoyu and most tamari brands are pasteurized, both should still be refrigerated after opening to protect their color and flavor.

A small amount of ethanol develops naturally in the process of making shoyu. Nonetheless, food-grade grain alcohol is usually added to virtually all brands of tamari and shoyu during the bottling process to provide extra protection against spoilage as well as help retain good flavor. Despite pasteurization and the addition of alcohol, some brands still include preservatives—an unnecessary additive, especially if these products are refrigerated after opening—so check ingredient labels before purchase and opt for preservative-free brands.

VARIETIES OF TAMARI AND SHOYU

Tamari and shoyu can range from thin to thick and from light to dark in color, and have complex flavors that range from mild to rich, and from salty to slightly sweet. Authentic tamari produced as a by-product of miso manufacture is occasionally available. Lighter in color, sweeter in flavor, and lower in salt content, it is ready to use as a seasoning, essentially as a kind of liquid miso. Typically left unpasteurized, miso tamari is generally sold in the refrigerated section. However, just like centuries ago, its availability remains limited, as removing too much tamari from the miso could adversely affect the flavor and character of the miso.

Japan actually recognizes five main traditional types of soy sauce. The first three—shiro, tamari, and koikuchi—differ from one another in color and flavor based on their specific ratio of wheat to soybeans, including the use of little or no wheat. The other two kinds of Japanese soy sauce have stronger flavors. Saishikomi soy sauce is fermented twice and is dark, and usukuchi, which is made with added amasake (a fermented beverage made from sweet rice), is salty and has a light color.

Chinese soy sauce is made primarily from soybeans, more in line with the original way tamari was made. Light Chinese soy sauce, made from the first pressing of the moromi mash, is a premium seasoning that is both saltier and lighter in color than the thicker, brownish black dark Chinese soy sauce, which is aged longer and has added molasses for a distinctive look.

However, the main difference among all of them comes down to whether the product is considered tamari or shoyu. Choosing between tamari and shoyu is not actually an either-or decision. Instead, it is matter of being aware of which type of soy sauce is best to use at various stages of cooking or as a condiment at the table.

Tamari is the kind to use when cooking food such as sauces (especially tomato-based sauces), soups, stews, stir-fries, and casseroles and other baked dishes. It's also best for roasting and grilling. Unlike shoyu, which contains more aromatic flavors that burn off at high temperatures, tamari has a deeper, stronger flavor that holds up better under higher heat and longer cooking. Tamari is also a better flavor enhancer. Because it is made only from high-protein soybeans, tamari contains over one-third more glutamic acid than shoyu does. Because it doesn't contain wheat, which causes alcohol to

develop, the flavor of tamari is smoother, richer, and more complex. Its color is a deeper brown than that of shoyu, and its consistency is somewhat thicker.

Shoyu, on the other hand, is best used at the table as a condiment or dipping sauce and in marinades and salad dressings. Its toasty, caramel-like, sweeter flavor is the result of the breakdown of wheat starch into different natural sugars. Like a fine wine, shoyu also provides a rich aroma and enticing, robust bouquet.

SODIUM IN TAMARI AND SHOYU

With just slightly less than 1,000 milligrams of sodium per tablespoon for both tamari and shoyu, it's best to use them with a light hand. Like miso, tamari and shoyu are meant to enhance, not overwhelm. Low-sodium versions of shoyu are also available, from which salt is removed after the fermentation process. This allows the complexity of flavor to develop as much as possible before the sodium is removed using an ion exchange process; in this method, the salt precipitates out onto two electrically charged plates from the shoyu between them. These low-sodium forms should be used just as you would use regular tamari and shoyu.

Umeboshi Plums

Umeboshi plums are made from sour, unripe fruits of the ume tree, which is native to China. Though they're called plums, they're actually more closely related to apricots. To make umeboshi plums, the fruits are pickled with sea salt for about a month and then removed from the brine to dry in the sun. In the meantime, dark red shiso leaves, also known as beefsteak leaves, are placed in the brine, both for their natural preservative qualities and for the benefit of their natural red dye. The dried fruits are returned to the now red brine to soak for several days, which changes their color from green to red. They are then removed from the brine once again and aged in barrels for around a year. When ready, umeboshi plums are sold in the whole pickled plum form as well as a convenient paste form, with the pits removed. The red brine drawn off of the pickled umeboshi plums and shiso leaves is sold as **umeboshi vinegar**, even though it isn't a true vinegar. With its unique, salty, tangy flavor, umeboshi vinegar is an all-purpose seasoning, delicious in salad dressings, dips, and marinades, or used as a condiment and splashed on vegetables, beans, and grains.

The distinctive sour and salty flavor of umeboshi plums is most commonly associated with nori rolls and rice balls. However, dips, spreads, salad dressings, sauces, broths, cooked grains, and vegetable dishes are all enhanced by a dab of umeboshi. Try it spread lightly on cooked corn on the cob instead of butter. Because umeboshi plums are high in citric acid and are a good source of potassium and iron, they've also served as a traditional remedy relative to their digestive and natural antibacterial effects.

Umeboshi plums and umeboshi vinegar

Sea Vegetables

A beautiful and extraordinary universe of plants lies just beneath the surface of the ocean, and people living in proximity to the coast have harvested and eaten many of these plants since ancient times. It's a shame they aren't better understood or more widely used in our modern Western world, as they're a valuable source of nutrients and can impart complex and unusual flavors to food. Although they are commonly called seaweeds, edible versions are often referred to as sea vegetables, a moniker that attempts to restore them to a position of esteem.

Throughout the world, both traditional and modern recipes use sea vegetables as a delicious addition to soups, sauces, salads, side dishes, snacks, and garnishes. They are found in recipes from Japan, China, Ireland, Scotland, England, Wales, Russia, Canada, Iceland, Norway, Sweden, Africa, Australia, New Zealand, Hawaii, the Pacific Islands, and the northeastern and northwestern coastal areas of the United States. Because they are a source of umami, the fifth taste that helps pull together and expand the flavors in a dish synergistically, the continued widespread use of seaweeds is no wonder. While research on umami was originally conducted on kombu, other sea vegetables also contain varying levels of glutamic acid, the amino acid responsible for their ability to enhance other flavors. And since they grow and reproduce within salty waters, minerals found in the sea, especially sodium, are also abundant in seaweeds, providing another aspect of seasoning that further explains their ability to accentuate flavors. Sea vegetables also play another, less apparent role in foods and cooking. Some, like Irish moss (carrageenan), contain gelatinous carbohydrates, making them a useful ingredient in food processing in the form of stabilizers, thickeners, emulsifiers, and suspending agents.

GETTING TO KNOW SEA VEGETABLES

Classified as marine algae, seaweeds are chlorophyll-containing plants without true stems, roots, or leaves that live in the sea or brackish water, often attached to rocks or other surfaces. Successful and resilient species, they've been around for more than two billion years. Most seaweeds are photosynthetic, relying on sunlight as an energy source from which to produce food. Although all have chlorophyll, many also contain other pigments in order to better absorb various wavelengths of light and capture more of the sun's energy. As a result, they occur in three main color groups—red, green, and brown—which is a handy way of classifying them.

Green seaweeds, such as sea lettuce, mainly contain chlorophyll, similar to their land-based brethren. **Red seaweeds**, which include dulse, laver, nori, agar, and Irish moss, primarily have red pigments, although they can look purple as well as a whole range of other related colors depending on the specific kinds of carotene pigments present. Because this class of pigments can be water soluble and heat sensitive, seaweed that looks red when uncooked may change to a dark green after cooking. **Brown seaweeds**, such as kelp, kombu, alaria, arame, wakame, sea palm, and hijiki, depend on brown pigments from other carotenoid pigments, fucoxanthin in particular. Although chlorophyll is also a component of brown seaweeds, its green color is masked by the brown.

NUTRITIONAL AND MEDICINAL ATTRIBUTES

Seaweeds have long been known for their nutritional attributes. Traditional Chinese medicinal texts as far back as 2700 BCE mention seaweed's medicinal qualities, including reference to its ability to reduce goiter. The Ebers Papyrus, the ancient Egyptian dissertation on medical care thought to have been written in 1550 BCE, also specifically includes the therapeutic use of seaweeds, as do Ayurvedic medicinal texts from the fourth century CE.

Current scientific research has keyed in on the phytonutrients in seaweeds, including lignans that may help prevent certain forms of cancer, including breast cancer. Tumor reduction, inhibition of cancer cell proliferation, free radical scavenging,

and significant antioxidant activity have also been exhibited by red and brown seaweeds. In addition, sulfated polysaccharides, a type of carbohydrate found in some of the brown seaweeds, are being explored as antiviral agents and as aids in preventing blood clots. Studies exploring polysaccharides in bladderwrack and kelp have also shown them to be a highly effective agent for reducing the effects of radiation toxicity.

With their ocean origins, sea vegetables are a valuable source of a wide array of trace minerals and, depending on the variety, small amounts of calcium, magnesium, and potassium. Sodium and iodine are the most predominant, and it is iodine that's responsible for the long history of use of seaweeds to treat goiter, even though this element was not identified and isolated until fairly recently. Iodine was discovered by accident in 1811 and isolated as a specific component of seaweed when Bernard Courtois, a manufacturer of saltpeter (potassium nitrate), was in the process of making gunpowder for France. Rather than using wood ashes, as he usually did, to extract sodium carbonate, a necessary component when making saltpeter, he decided to use burned kelp instead. When the characteristic violet-colored vapors we now know to be iodine rose from the mixture, he quit the saltpeter industry and spent several months investigating the chemical reactions and properties of the newly discovered element.

Most of the iodine used commercially is obtained as a by-product of various mining operations because this is an inexpensive source, but seaweeds are still noted as the most concentrated food source of the mineral, and they have the benefit of providing an array of nutrients beyond iodine itself. The amount of iodine in different types of sea vegetables varies, depending on the age and condition of the plant, season and geographic location of harvest, the part of the plant consumed, how it is prepared, and how the seaweed is stored.

While iodine is an extremely important nutrient, it is possible to get too much if excessive amounts of seaweed are consumed. This can have disruptive effects on the thyroid and cause a host of other problems. Recommended daily iodine intake for most healthy adults with normal thyroid function aged nineteen years and older is 150 micrograms, and the upper limit for this group of people is 1,100 micrograms. Recommended daily amounts and tolerable upper intake levels for children and adolescents are lower and vary depending on age group. Within these ranges, the amount that's safe to ingest depends on the individual. Some people are very sensitive to iodine and need to keep their daily intake on the low side. On the other hand, in some cultures where sea vegetables are a consistent part of the everyday diet, people may have adapted, making them able to tolerate higher levels.

As a class, red varieties of sea vegetables are consistently much lower in iodine than are brown ones, with nori containing the least (around 16 micrograms per gram), in contrast with brown varieties, of which kelp and kombu contain the most iodine (averaging 1300 to 1500 micrograms per gram, although sometimes as much as 2500 micrograms per gram). Even within the brown varieties, there is a wide range of iodine content, with alaria as low as 110 micrograms per gram, a marked contrast to the much higher levels found in kelp.

All in all, a little seaweed goes a long way, especially the brown varieties because of their higher iodine levels. Use common sense and moderation in deciding how much to eat and how frequently, and also be aware that how they are cooked and what is also included in the meal can affect the amount of iodine ingested. The iodine in sea vegetables is mostly water soluble, which means that boiling them in water will result in much of the iodine being extracted into the cooking water. The roasting method appears to release the least amount of iodine, while steaming and frying may release moderate amounts.

Eating sea vegetables in a meal that also includes goitrogenic foods may also help to lessen the effects of their high iodine content. Goitrogenic foods are those that contain substances that interfere with the thyroid gland's uptake and utilization of iodine, which is necessary for thyroid hormone production. They include soybeans (and products made from them), millet, peanuts, and cruciferous vegetables, such as broccoli, cauliflower, bok choy, brussels sprouts, rutabaga, turnips, and cabbage. For most people with healthy thyroid function, the potential negative effect of these foods is of no concern unless excessive amounts are consumed. Although some of the goitrogenic compounds in these foods may also be deactivated when they're cooked, eating goitrogenic foods with seaweeds not only provides a tasty combination but may help provide a healthy balance in terms of iodine as well.

Sea vegetables can be quite high in sodium, not surprising given that they grow in seawater. Excess salt can be removed by rinsing them with water. When you use them in a dish, you can reduce the amount of other salty seasonings or forgo them altogether.

Seaweed can also contain heavy metals, such as lead, arsenic, mercury, and cadmium, which are unhealthful to the human body at certain levels. Given that these heavy metals occur naturally worldwide because they may be leached from bedrock, sea vegetables often contain at least trace amounts. But to minimize your exposure, it's important to buy sea vegetables only from areas unpolluted by industrial waste. Good sea vegetable companies are very particular about where and how their seaweed is harvested, dried, and stored and test it regularly for heavy metals, as well as herbicides, pesticides, and microbial contaminants. Always purchase sea vegetables from companies that have a commitment to providing a high-quality product.

COOKING AND STORING SEA VEGETABLES
Adding small amounts of sea vegetables to soups, stews, or beans is a good way to start experiencing their unique flavors, textures, and colors. The mild flavors of nori, dulse, sea palm, and arame make them good choices to start with. Seaweeds are especially good cooked with grains, beans, and most root vegetables.

Since seaweeds can expand in volume up to sevenfold when rehydrated, only a small amount of dried seaweed is usually required. Most should be quickly rinsed with water to remove any surface dust, sand, or excess naturally occurring sea salt. Depending on the variety, they should then be briefly soaked before cooking in any quickly prepared dish. No soaking is needed when they're simmered in soups and stews for a long period of time.

Dried sea vegetables will keep indefinitely if stored in a tightly sealed container in a cool, dark place, such as a cupboard or pantry away from the stove. Cooked sea vegetables will keep for four to five days refrigerated.

AGAR

Agar is made from several varieties of red algae processed into lightweight, translucent bars which may be further processed into flakes or powder. The primary use of agar is as a gelling agent to make vegetarian gelatin-like desserts, vegetable aspics, puddings, and pie fillings.

The name *agar* is derived from a Malaysian word that means "seaweed." Using a traditional process that dates back to the seventeenth century, the red seaweeds used to make agar are harvested in autumn and sun dried. During the winter, they are transported to the mountains, cooked into a thick mixture, poured into trays, and cut into bars after the mixture has gelled. The bars are then put outside on suspended bamboo mats, where they undergo a repeated freeze-and-thaw process for ten days, freezing solid during the night and thawing during the day. As a result, water and other impurities are removed, leaving the bars of agar nearly white.

To make agar flakes and powder, the bars are simply crushed. Quicker to use, the flakes and powder are also less expensive and yield a harder gel than the more traditional agar bars. Check the ingredient label and avoid any agar in which sulfuric acid is used as a softening agent or inorganic bleaches or dyes are used to whiten and chemically deodorize the agar.

Cooking Guidelines

To gel 2 cups of liquid, use 3 to 4 tablespoons of agar flakes, 2 teaspoons of agar powder, or 1 agar bar. Agar flakes and powder do not have to be soaked prior to use. When using an agar bar as a thickening agent as an alternative to gelatin for making gelled desserts, first break it into pieces and soak them for 30 minutes, or until spongy. Squeeze out the excess water before using. Whatever form of agar you use, add the amount indicated above to 2 cups juice, broth, or water. Bring to a boil, lower the heat, and simmer for 10 minutes, stirring to thoroughly dissolve the agar. Transfer the liquid to a heatproof mold or glass baking dish and allow it to set. Agar will set at room temperature, but the gelling process is much quicker in the refrigerator, taking only about 45 to 60 minutes. Agar can also be used when making pie fillings, jellies and preserves, aspics, and puddings.

Clockwise from top: (1) Kelp, (2) arame, (3) laver, (4) dulse, (5) agar, (6) wakame, (7) nori, (8) kombu, (9) sea palm

ALARIA

Alaria is a North American variety of wakame that grows off the northeastern coast. Golden brown when fresh, it is very dark green, really almost black, once dried. Alaria has a taste similar to, but more delicate and slightly wilder than, Asian types of wakame, to which it is related. Like wakame, alaria is delicious in salads, miso soups, and stews, as well as cooked with grains. It requires a longer cooking time than wakame.

Cooking Guidelines

In soup, use about a 5-inch-long strip of alaria per quart of liquid. To bring out its sweet, mild taste and soft, chewy texture, alaria should be simmered for at least 10 minutes or pressure-cooked for 5 to 6 minutes. In salads, use alaria that has already been cooked or soak it in water or diluted lemon juice for 12 hours. For a salty snack or condiment, roast alaria in a 300°F oven for 3 to 5 minutes or pan-fry it in a well-oiled skillet over medium-high heat until crisp.

ARAME

Arame is a branched, feathery brown seaweed. Once the fronds are harvested, they're steamed and left to soak in the cooking water for up to twelve hours to make the arame more tender. The arame is then drained, shredded into long black strands, and sun dried. Although it looks somewhat like hijiki, its flavor is milder and sweeter and its texture softer. Arame is especially good in vegetable sautés, salads, and casseroles.

Cooking Guidelines

Before using arame, rinse it and soak for about 15 minutes. Once soaked and cooked, arame doubles in volume. Always cook arame before adding it to salads or casseroles. As an excellent introduction to arame, soak 2 cups of arame, drain, and sauté it with onions and carrots over low heat for about 30 minutes, mixing in a couple of tablespoons of sesame tahini diluted with equal amounts of water or mirin (sweet rice wine) during the last 5 minutes

of cooking. Serve as a vegetable side dish or use it as the filling for a savory vegetable strudel.

DULSE

Dulse is a reddish purple sea vegetable harvested from North Atlantic coastlines. Highly valued as a traditional staple in Ireland, Scotland, Wales, coastal Canada, and parts of the northeastern United States, it can be eaten raw as a tangy, salty, soft but chewy snack, or it may be cooked. Rinsing will make dulse tender, less salty, and milder in flavor. Because its red pigments are water soluble, dulse will become dark green during cooking. It will become more tender as it cooks and may dissolve with longer cooking times.

Cooking Guidelines

To reduce its natural sodium content before adding it to sandwiches or salads, briefly rinse dulse or soak it for up to 5 minutes then squeeze out the salty water. When cooking, add dulse about 5 minutes before the dish is done. To dry-roast dulse, place it in a skillet over medium-high heat or in a 300°F oven until the leaves turn greenish and crisp but not black. For richer flavor, pan-fry in a well-oiled skillet.

Dulse is delicious in sandwiches (though it may seem odd, try it with peanut butter), playing a dual role as both vegetable and tangy seasoning. When dry roasted and crumbled, dulse can be used as a salty, savory condiment to sprinkle over soups, salads, pasta, popcorn, and cooked grains. Pan-frying dulse in a well-oiled skillet gives it a delicious, baconlike flavor. Prepared in this way, it can be sprinkled on pizza, stirred into scrambled eggs or tofu, or used to make a vegetarian version of a bacon, lettuce, and tomato sandwich. When cooked in chowders, stews, and grains, especially oatmeal, dulse provides a pleasant seafoodlike flavor.

HIJIKI

Traditionally, hijiki (sometimes called hiziki) was considered a good food for helping maintain better-looking hair and skin. In fact, its Japanese name is translated as "bearer of wealth and beauty." The plant is also said to resemble strands of hair, due to its many branches, and the best hijiki is harvested from the tiny, thick curls that grow on the smaller branches near the surface of the water. Somewhat resembling a chubby version of arame, hijiki has a more pronounced flavor and tougher texture. In order to soften it, hijiki is washed after harvest, sun dried, steamed for four hours, and left to cool and dry again. It is then soaked in the juice of cooked arame to enhance its black color.

Unfortunately, because samples of hijiki have shown inorganic arsenic beyond typical regulatory limits of 1 milligram per kilogram, a level that may present health risks, many countries have advised consumers to avoid regular consumption of this sea vegetable. Arsenic is a semimetallic element that occurs in nature mainly in combination with other minerals. The inorganic form of arsenic, found in combination with one or more other elements such as oxygen, chlorine, and sulfur, can increase the risk of cancer if regularly consumed. Gastrointestinal problems, anemia, and liver damage are other possible effects. Only consume hijiki if you're sure its inorganic arsenic level has been tested to be significantly below 1 milligram per kilogram or the current regulatory level set by governmental food safety regulatory authorities.

Cooking Guidelines

Before cooking hijiki, rinse it thoroughly and soak it in water for about 15 minutes. Then discard the soaking water and simmer the hijiki for 30 to 40 minutes. If hijiki will be added to a recipe that requires further cooking, the initial simmering of hijiki can be reduced by about 10 minutes. Hijiki expands fourfold after soaking and cooking. Like arame, hijiki is delicious cooked with sweet vegetables, tahini sauces, tofu, and tempeh. It is also a good addition to casseroles, salads, noodle dishes, cooked rice, soups, and stews.

IRISH MOSS

Irish moss, a red variety of seaweed, is the primary source of carrageenan, a gelatinous polysaccharide used in commercial food production as a thickener or stabilizer. The term *carrageenan* is from the Irish word *carrigín*, which means "moss of the rock," and in Ireland, the gelling properties of this seaweed have been utilized since at least 1810. Not surprisingly, Irish moss grows in rocky areas along the Atlantic coast of Ireland, as well as in other parts of Europe and in North America. When fresh, it has a greenish yellow to dark purple color and a soft texture, albeit tough and flexible in nature. When sun dried, it is yellow and translucent and has a hard, smooth, hornlike consistency.

Cooking Guidelines

Unlike most sea vegetables, Irish moss is often used in its fresh form, cooked just after harvest. When soaked in lemon juice or water and chilled for a couple of hours, it forms a gel similar to what's achieved with agar. The gel can be cut into cubes and used as a refreshing ingredient in salads. If cooked with sugar, it can be made into Irish moss jelly. Fresh Irish moss can also be cooked in water as a thick, hot soup stock or to use in its gelled form once cooled.

To reconstitute dried Irish moss, first rinse it in warm water. Then soak it for 10 minutes, at which point it's ready to add to broth, juice, or milk as a thickening aid. Use about ½ ounce of dried Irish moss to thicken about 3 cups of liquid. Combine the soaked Irish moss and liquid, bring to a boil, then lower the heat and simmer for 15 to 20 minutes. Strain the liquid through a fine-mesh strainer to remove the carrageenan. At this point, other ingredients or flavorings can be added to the liquid. Pour the mixture into a dish or mold and refrigerate until set.

KELP

Also called Atlantic kelp or Atlantic kombu, kelp is harvested from North Atlantic waters. Although its thinner fronds give it a somewhat different appearance than Japanese kombu, the two can be used interchangeably in most recipes. Like kombu, Atlantic kelp is naturally high in glutamic acid, so it functions as a natural tenderizer and flavor enhancer. However, it is much more tender than Japanese kombu, and will actually dissolve if allowed to cook for more than 20 minutes.

Cooking Guidelines

When using Atlantic kelp as a flavoring agent for a broth or sauce or adding it to recipes, first rinse it quickly under cold running water to remove excess salt. For a light-flavored broth, add a small piece, about 5 inches in length, to water, place over medium heat, and remove the kelp just before the water comes to a boil. For a moderate amount of flavor, allow the kelp to simmer for 10 minutes before removing, and for even richer flavor, leave it for the full duration of cooking, letting it fully dissolve into the broth. To use Atlantic kelp while cooking beans, add a small piece, about 5 inches long, to the cooking water and leave it in the pot. In addition to enhancing flavor and tenderizing the beans, the kelp will also slightly thicken the broth.

Atlantic kelp is best simmered for 15 to 20 minutes or pressure-cooked for 5 minutes. For use as a condiment, dry-roast kelp for 3 to 4 minutes in a 300°F oven or pan-fry it in a well-oiled skillet for 4 to 5 minutes, until crisp. Because it isn't rinsed prior to dry-roasting or pan-frying, it will be too salty to use as a snack. Any white powder on the dried kelp is merely natural salts and sugars that may have precipitated from the seaweed during storage. Expect Atlantic kelp to expand up to 40 percent when rehydrated or cooked in water.

KOMBU

Kombu, one of the mainstays of Japanese cooking, is the key ingredient in dashi, the all-important broth used as a stock for soups and noodle dishes. Stiff, dark green, broad, and flat when dried, kombu is harvested from large, thick, leafy fronds that grow off the southeastern coast of Hokkaido, Japan's northernmost island. After harvest, the fronds are washed, folded, and sun dried before they are cut and packaged. What makes kombu so unique and invaluable is its naturally high level of glutamic acid, which accounts for its ability to enhance the flavor of other foods. Unlike MSG, kombu is a safe and nutritious flavor enhancer.

Cooking Guidelines

When using kombu as a flavoring agent for a broth or sauce or before adding it to recipes that include a moderate to high amount of liquid, rinse it quickly under cold running water or wipe it with a clean, damp cloth to remove the excess salt. For a light-flavored broth, add a small piece of kombu, about 3 inches long, to water, place over medium heat, and remove the kombu just before the water comes to a boil. The longer the kombu remains in the cooking water, the stronger the broth will be.

When preparing kombu as a cooked side dish or condiment, presoak it in cold water for 3 to

From top: (1) wakame, (2) two types of dulse, (3) kelp

5 minutes prior to cooking. If you soak it much longer, the kombu can become very slippery and hard to cut. When gauging how much to use, keep in mind that kombu doubles or triples in size after soaking or cooking. For use as a salty condiment or snack, dry-roast kombu in a 300°F oven for 3 to 4 minutes; grind it after roasting if you wish to use it as a condiment.

Like its cousin Atlantic kelp, Japanese kombu is an excellent addition to soup stocks, broths, and vegetable dishes. Beans are especially delicious when cooked with a small piece of kombu, about 2 or 3 inches long. It can also be used as a featured ingredient in side dishes, condiments, and candies.

LAVER

Consider laver to be the wild North Atlantic version of nori. Both are derived from the same species of red seaweed. Purple to black in color, laver is a traditional food in Scotland, Wales, and Ireland, where it is harvested in the winter from rocks, piers, and other vertical surfaces. Unlike cultivated Japanese nori, laver is left whole and not processed into sheets.

Cooking Guidelines

Traditionally, laver is slowly simmered for many hours into a thick, gelatinous puree and then eaten as a side dish, often served with butter. It is also used as the basis for laverbread, a recipe with a four-to-one ratio of laver to finely cut whole oats; the mixture is formed into patties and fried. To make a salty condiment with a nutty flavor, dry laver in a 300°F oven for 5 to 8 minutes until crisp, then crumble it over soup, salad, pasta, stir-fries, potatoes, or popcorn. Dried laver can also be eaten without further cooking, although it will be quite chewy in this state. To use it in salads, marinate it in salad dressing for at least 18 hours to tenderize it. The laver can then be left whole and added to the salad along with its marinade. Alternatively, you can discard the marinade and chop the laver before adding it.

NORI

Nori, the familiar wrapping used when making sushi and nori maki, is the cultivated form of laver grown in coastal areas of Japan, Korea, and northern China on nets suspended at the surface of the ocean. After harvest, it is washed and then, either manually or by machine, shredded and pressed between woven reed mats, drying it into the distinctive paper-thin sheets. Good-quality sheets of nori have a dark greenish black color with a somewhat iridescent sheen. Flavor and digestibility improve if the raw nori sheets are toasted. Large sheets of nori made specifically for preparing sushi have typically been toasted before packaging.

Cooking Guidelines

To toast nori, simply hold it about 10 inches above the flame of a gas stove burner—or, in a pinch, above a candle flame—for about 20 seconds. It will change from greenish black to a more vibrant green and become crisp. Use it to make rice balls or sushi, or crumble it or cut it into strips for use as a garnish for soups, salads, grain dishes, noodles, casseroles, and popcorn. A rich-tasting condiment for grains and beans can be made by cooking nori with a small amount of water and tamari until the water evaporates and the mixture becomes a thick paste.

SEA BEANS

Sea beans are collected fresh during the summer in salt marshes and tidal waters along the Pacific and Atlantic coasts. Also known as glasswort and marsh samphire, sea beans have crisp "branches" and stems that look like very thin, miniature cacti. Typically cooked, pickled, or used raw as a garnish, they retain a briny flavor that brings the ocean to mind.

Cooking Guidelines

To cook sea beans, first wash them thoroughly, then boil in unsalted water for 5 to 15 minutes, until the thin branches can easily be removed from the stalks with your fingers. Drain and serve the succulent green stems warm with butter or vinegar. This method makes a wonderfully complementary side dish for seafood.

SEA LETTUCE

One of the few sea vegetables in the green category, sea lettuce looks like its land-based namesake when fresh, consisting primarily of bright green, crumpled, extremely thin fronds. It grows along rocky or sandy coasts, often attaching itself to rocks and shells but sometimes floating freely.

Cooking Guidelines

When fresh, sea lettuce can be eaten raw in salads. For cooking, it's best to combine it with other ingredients to minimize its slightly bitter taste. Dried sea lettuce makes a nice addition to soups.

SEA PALM

A sea vegetable unique to the North Pacific Coast, sea palm has a delicious, subtly sweet flavor that makes it a favorite even among those who are otherwise reluctant to try edible seaweeds. While growing, sea palm looks remarkably like a miniature palm tree, complete with a hollow, trunklike structure flexible enough to withstand the waves and leaflike blades at the top.

Cooking Guidelines

Sea palm is generally available only in dried form. For use in salads, soak sea palm in water for 1 hour prior to use. Alternatively, simmer it in water for 5 minutes, then cool and add it to other salad ingredients. (It complements avocado nicely.) For soup, soak it first for 10 minutes before proceeding with the recipe. Sea palm is good in vegetable sautés, too. After a 10-minute presoak, cook the sea palm until tender, about 30 minutes, before adding it to the sauté.

WAKAME

Wakame is a common ingredient in miso soup and a tasty addition to vegetable dishes and salads. This member of the brown seaweed category is harvested along the coasts of Korea, China, and Japan using long poles with blades to cut off the long dark green fronds, which are then allowed to float to the surface. The fresh wakame is taken to shore, dried, trimmed, graded, and packaged. Like kombu and Atlantic kelp, wakame is high in glutamic acid, making it a good flavor enhancer and tenderizing agent. Instant wakame is made by a process of washing the wakame, simmering it very briefly in salted water for less than 1 minute, and then rinsing it several times to reduce the salt content. The tougher main rib and leaf tips are then trimmed away and the tender fronds are air-dried into the tight curls characteristic of instant wakame.

Cooking Guidelines

Wakame is one of the most tender sea vegetables, so only minimal soaking and cooking are needed for any recipe. Before using wakame uncooked or as an ingredient in cooked soups or foods, rinse it first to remove surface dirt. Presoak it for 3 to 5 minutes, and then squeeze out the excess water. Don't soak it longer, as it will become too slippery. After its tough ribs are trimmed away, wakame can be added to salads or cooked for at least 5 minutes in soups, stews, or with veggies. Two must-have classics are miso soup with wakame and cucumber wakame salad. When using instant wakame in soups, broths, and stews, no presoaking is necessary; just add it to the cooking water. Presoak instant wakame for 2 to 3 minutes before using it in salads. When rehydrated, wakame can expand up to seven times its original volume.

Sweeteners

There's no denying that sometimes nothing hits the spot more than something really sweet. Blame it on our genes. Since poisonous plants generally contain bitter alkaloids, scientists speculate this penchant for sweets may have evolved as a protective mechanism to ensure that our early ancestors ate enough high-calorie but nontoxic foods to survive through times of scarcity. However, in these days of plenty, the challenge is to choose sugars wisely and consume them in moderation to maintain a healthy weight. Because sugars contain so few nutrients in relation to their calories, minimizing their intake also helps ensure your diet is comprised of a high percentage of nourishing foods that contribute to optimal health and well-being.

The rate at which sugars are digested and the effects sugar has on the body both vary widely depending on the sweetener used and which types of sugar it contains in what proportions. The most nutritious sugars are those that remain in whole food form, in fresh and dried fruits, vegetables, milk (lactose), and grains (especially when sprouted). As a component of a whole food that also contains protein, fat, starchy carbohydrates, dietary fiber, vitamins, and minerals, these natural sugars are broken down more slowly and enter the bloodstream at a steady rate, providing the glucose the body needs for fuel in an optimal manner.

Scientifically speaking, sugars are categorized as monosaccharides (single sugar molecules), which include glucose, fructose, and galactose; and disaccharides (sugars in which two monosaccharides are linked together), such as sucrose, maltose, and lactose. Because glucose is already in the form used by the body, it's absorbed most quickly, requiring insulin to keep blood sugar levels in balance. In contrast, fructose and galactose must first be transported to the liver to be converted into glucose before they can be used as an energy source for the cells. Not only is the metabolism of fructose slower than that of glucose, but it also doesn't require insulin in the process, so it causes little fluctuation in blood glucose levels.

Sucrose, or table sugar, is hydrolyzed by enzymes in the digestive tract into its equal proportions of glucose and fructose. An enzyme called invertase accomplishes this, and the sugars that result are known as invert sugars. The glucose portion of invert sugars is absorbed quite rapidly, again requiring insulin. Because the primary sugar in maple syrup is sucrose, it affects the body in much the same manner. While fructose tastes sweeter, it metabolizes more slowly than glucose and sucrose do. Grain-based sweeteners, including barley malt syrup and brown rice syrup, contain varying proportions of glucose and maltose, but because they also contain a high level of more complex glucose chains called polysaccharides, which take longer to digest, they have a less pronounced effect on blood sugar levels.

Choosing among the Sweeteners

So which sweeteners are the best to use? Tried-and-true plant-derived sweeteners, as minimally processed as possible, are the best choice. They have proven to be exceptional in flavor and extremely effective in cooking and baking, not to mention safe and nontoxic. These natural sweeteners include familiar ingredients such as maple syrup, molasses, and natural sugar from sugarcane or beets, as well as some options that may be less familiar to you, such as agave nectar and stevia. Choosing among these many options comes down to how the sweetener will be used, as each type has distinctive flavors and functional properties, such as color, texture, and viscosity, all of which affect cooking and baking outcomes. For example, fructose is hygroscopic, meaning it readily takes up and retains moisture, therefore yielding baked goods that are softer and moister.

Organic versions of many sweeteners are widely available. This doesn't imply that they confer any health benefits beyond those usually associated with organic foods; it simply means that they have been produced from certified organically grown ingredients and processed in certified organic manufacturing plants. But because agriculture of crops grown for sugar can have substantial negative environmental impacts, purchasing organic sweeteners is good for the environment and is a good way to support sound farming and processing methods. It also helps you avoid potentially toxic chemicals and genetically engineered ingredients.

Because many of the sugars commonly consumed are the most unhealthful types, it will be useful to understand why they are best avoided before we explore the minimally processed natural choices that are preferable when using sweeteners at home or when looking at product labels.

Nonnutritive Artificial Sweeteners

Artificial and synthetic sweeteners have undergone chemical manipulation to dramatically alter the sweetener's sugar profile or to prevent the body from metabolizing the sweetener. Since artificial sweeteners are many magnitudes sweeter than table sugar, only a tiny amount is needed to sweeten foods, which means they contribute virtually no calories. As such, they are classified as nonnutritive sweeteners. They also don't affect blood sugar levels. Because such a small amount of artificial sweetener is needed to provide a sweetening effect, they are typically combined with dextrose or maltodextrin, which serve as carriers and also provide some bulk, making them easier to use.

These purely synthetic compounds are produced through complex chemical processes, and because they have no counterparts in nature, our bodies are ill equipped to deal with them. Although considerable time and effort have been devoted to developing sweeteners, chemists have never succeeded in duplicating important qualities of sugars, such as their complex, nuanced flavors and their wide range of functionality—qualities that cooks and bakers appreciate from experience. In addition, synthetic products can't provide the full range of nutrients found within natural products.

The artificial sugar craze started with saccharin, and since then a variety of sugar substitutes have been developed, including cyclamates, aspartame, acesulfame-K, sucralose, and neotame, each taking the spotlight for a while before being surrounded by controversy and concerns about negative health impacts. Although research results have been mixed, some studies do support these concerns, as do consumer reports of adverse effects.

Unlike other sugars, artificial sweeteners are devoid of functional properties that contribute flavor, texture, and other attributes to the foods they're combined with. The only thing they deliver on their own is a sweet flavor, and even that isn't done very well. Their sweetness doesn't have the clean taste found in granulated sugar and other natural sweeteners, and they often have a disagreeable aftertaste. Many of them aren't stable at a wide range of temperatures, which can also contribute to off flavors.

Even the weight-loss claims associated with artificial sweeteners are dubious. Artificial sweeteners perpetuate the myth that people can eat all the sweet foods they want and still lose weight. However, products made with nonnutritive artificial sweeteners still contain calories from the other ingredients, and some of these products contain just as many calories as those made with natural sweeteners. Even when they contain fewer calories, people may feel they can eat additional amounts, with the end result that they're consuming just as many calories overall; perhaps even more.

Highly Processed Sweeteners

Ironically, many highly processed sweeteners are classified as nutritive. Rest assured, they are categorized as nutritive simply because they provide calories, which gives them a defining contrast to artificial sweeteners (which are also very highly processed). In fact, as highly processed sweeteners, they are treated significantly beyond the basic procedures needed to concentrate sugar from a food. They may also be specially formulated to reduce effects on blood sugar or be manufactured or isolated from different food sources than those where the sweetening agent would naturally occur. Corn syrup, high-fructose corn syrup, crystalline fructose, and polyols are classic examples. Other highly processed sweeteners derived from foods will no doubt continue to flood the market, given all the research energy expended on trying to find the perfect "natural" sugar substitute in terms of both flavor and functionality. When it comes down to it, highly processed, nonnutritive sweeteners are considered safe, though not necessarily healthful. And they are certainly better alternatives than artificial sweeteners. However, for optimal flavor and digestibility, minimally processed natural sweeteners remain the better option.

CORN SYRUP

Although corn syrup is developed from corn, a natural product, the extent to which it is processed puts it in a completely different realm than minimally processed natural sweeteners, whose sugars are more simply extracted and concentrated. Corn syrup is produced from cornstarch using enzymes to hydrolyze, or break apart, long-chain starch molecules into shorter lengths. Specific proportions of glucose, maltose, and glucose polysaccharides (the remaining longer chains of glucose that account for corn syrup's thick viscosity) are created to match its intended application. The more cornstarch is hydrolyzed, the higher the corn syrup's percentage of glucose in relation to maltose, and the more quickly it metabolizes within the body. Manufacturers like corn syrup not just because it's cheap, but also because it helps retain moisture in baked goods, increase browning of foods, and control crystallization in candies and the formation of ice crystals in ice cream. It also contributes more viscosity to condiments and salad dressings.

Corn syrup for home use is generally made from a blend of ingredients rather than just corn syrup. Light corn syrup has some high-fructose syrup to increase sweetness and to reduce viscosity so it's easier to use. Salt and vanilla are also added to enhance flavor. Dark corn syrup typically contains golden syrup (also known as refiner's syrup), caramel flavor and color, salt, and sodium benzoate (a preservative), creating a product with a stronger flavor and darker color. While corn syrup is often depended upon when making pecan pies and candies, look for newer recipes that use less processed natural sweeteners, such as cane syrup or sorghum syrup.

HIGH-FRUCTOSE CORN SYRUP

Like regular corn syrup, high-fructose corn syrup is created by treating cornstarch with acids and/or enzymes to convert the starch into sugars. In regular corn syrup, which is only moderately sweet, this process, which is called hydrolysis, ends when a particular proportion of glucose and maltose is achieved. But in high-fructose corn syrup, production starts with a version of corn syrup that is already quite high in glucose. From there, additional enzymes are used to transform some of the corn's glucose molecules into the sweeter basic sugar, fructose—a sugar not naturally found in corn. Two varieties of high-fructose corn syrup (HFCS) are manufactured: HFCS-42 (42 percent fructose and 53 percent glucose) and HFCS-55 (55 percent fructose and 42 percent glucose). Complex sugars called oligosaccharides make up the remaining percentage of sugars to add up to 100 percent.

Although HFCS has the same sweetness level as refined sugar, which is composed of 50 percent glucose and 50 percent fructose, there is a very important difference between the two. The simple sugars in refined sugar are chemically bonded to each other in the disaccharide sucrose molecule, whereas in HFCS, the sugars exist as free, unbound monosaccharides. Therefore, despite what its name may imply, high-fructose corn syrup requires more insulin for its metabolism than fructose does. This difference is especially important for those with diabetes or who have difficulties with metabolizing sugars.

When it comes to health, HFCS is often blamed for the current epidemic of obesity and diabetes, as rates of both began increasing at just about the time HFCS appeared on the market. Food manufacturers like high-fructose corn syrup because it is much less expensive than refined sugar and extends shelf life. It also provides better browning in baked goods and softer textures in cookies and snack bars, and it's easier to blend into beverages. As a result, it is ubiquitous, making an appearance in a long list of foods to which it contributes unnecessary and unwanted extra calories and sugars: breakfast cereals, soft drinks, fruit drinks and juices, jams, jellies, soups, sauces, salad dressings, marinades, crackers, potato chips, pretzels, granola bars, energy bars, syrups, dessert toppings, meat products (bacon, ham, and deli meats), peanut butter, condiments (ketchup, mustard, mayonnaise, pickles, and pickle relish), and dairy products (ice cream, yogurt, and cheese spreads). HFCS-55 is used to sweeten carbonated soft drinks, and HFCS-42 is used in sports drinks, noncarbonated fruit-flavored beverages, and food products. The bottom line is, you can do better than HFCS.

CRYSTALLINE FRUCTOSE

Crystalline fructose is commercially produced from cornstarch that is treated with enzymes to create corn syrup with a minimum of 99.5 percent fructose, which is then allowed to crystallize. Since crystalline fructose is about 60 percent sweeter than sugar, only one-half to two-thirds as much is needed to achieve the same sweetening power, which means fewer calories are needed for the same level of sweetness, especially in cold foods. Fructose is used by food manufacturers to boost fruit and chocolate flavors, help keep foods softer and more pliable, and enhance colors and flavors in baked goods due to the increased browning provided by the addition of fructose.

For many years, crystalline fructose was thought to be nutritionally superior because it is metabolized in the body more slowly than glucose and sucrose. First absorbed in the small intestine, it is transported to the liver, where it is converted into glucose. As no insulin is needed in the process, little fluctuation in blood sugar levels occurs.

Now, however, pure fructose has lost some of its luster. Research has shown that too much fructose in the diet may lead to elevated triglyceride levels in the blood, increasing the risk of arteriosclerosis, or hardening of the arteries. The American Diabetes Association now recommends that people with diabetes avoid fructose unless it is naturally occurring in fruits, vegetables, and other whole foods. In other words, their advice is to avoid crystalline fructose. This is good advice for all of us. Foods naturally high in fructose contain other important nutrients not found in crystalline fructose, and they'll also have less impact on your blood sugar level than foods high in glucose. Stick with fructose as found naturally in fruits and other minimally processed natural sweeteners such as agave nectar, fruit-based sweeteners, and honey.

POLYOLS (SUGAR ALCOHOLS)

While not a familiar term to most, polyols, or sugar alcohols, are a class of carbohydrates that include erythritol, hydrogenated starch hydrolysates, isomalt, lactitol, maltitol, mannitol, sorbitol, and xylitol. Polyols are currently marketed to the general public as reduced-calorie sweeteners and promoted to manufacturers for their beneficial properties in food production. These often make an appearance in foods labeled as "lower carbohydrate," "low glycemic," "low calorie," and "sugar free," including chewing gum, candies, baked goods, jams, and preserves. Manufacturers also like them as they can help extend shelf life, promote product stability, boost moisture retention, and help reduce caramelization and browning of foods.

Although their chemical structure is partially similar to that of sugar and partially similar to that of alcohol, they don't actually contain alcohol as we typically think of it in beer, wine, and other alcoholic beverages. In comparison to white sugar, polyols can be anywhere from 50 to 90 percent

as sweet. Because polyols are metabolized differently than true sugars, they don't raise blood sugar and insulin levels to the same degree. Nor do they promote tooth decay, since they aren't as readily metabolized by bacteria in the mouth as with most sugars. They also typically provide about half the amount of calories as other sugars, with the exact amount depending on the specific polyol.

Sorbitol, one of the first polyols used commercially, often appears as an ingredient in candies for people with diabetes. Currently, however, the American Diabetes Association says that, while polyols are safe, they don't necessarily advocate them over other sugars because there's no evidence that they can have significant positive impacts on blood sugar fluctuations given the amounts in which they're usually consumed. Plus, people who need to manage their blood sugar levels must still factor in polyols as containing at least some carbohydrates.

Digestion is another important detail. Since intestinal microbes metabolize a portion of the polyols a person consumes, these sugar alcohols have the potential to cause diarrhea, gas, or nausea in sensitive individuals or when polyols are consumed in large quantities. It is an effect similar to that of prunes, which, interestingly, have the highest amount of sorbitol of any kind of fruit.

Although sorbitol is naturally found in prunes and other foods, for commercial use, sorbitol and other polyols are extracted from substances where they wouldn't be found in nature. For example, erythritol, hydrogenated starch hydrolysates, maltitol, and mannitol are all obtained from cornstarch. Isomalt is obtained from sugar, and xylitol from corncobs, birch wood waste, and sugarcane bagasse (the plant residues remaining after sugar is extracted). An exception is lactitol, which is made by hydrogenating lactose obtained from whey—certainly nothing you could make in your own kitchen!

Exploring Natural Sweeteners

Your best bet is to minimize your intake of sugars overall and, when buying or making something that would typically include a sweetener, choose one from the long list of minimally processed natural sweeteners described below.

AGAVE NECTAR

Agave nectar is derived from sap extracted from the pineapple-shaped core, called the pina, of the agave plant, a desert succulent that is native to Mexico. Out of the many varieties of agave, there are two that can be used for human consumption, *Agave tequilana*, and *Agave salmiana*. Although *Agave tequilana*, also known as blue agave, is well known as the source from which tequila is made, the juice expressed from the crushed pina, full of a carbohydrate rich dietary fiber called inulin, can also be used to make a delicious, sweet syrup. Only minimal processing is required to transform the inulin into sweet agave nectar that is naturally high in fructose. This is achieved by breaking down the bonds in its complex carbohydrates through thermal hydrolysis (a fancy term for heating it at different levels of heat) or hydrolyzing it with natural enzymes. Raw blue agave is processed under lower temperatures for a longer time to transform the agave's inulin into fructose. The juices are then concentrated into a thicker syrup, evaporating out excess liquid. Both light and dark varieties of agave nectar are available. Because it's only lightly filtered to remove extraneous materials, dark agave nectar is amber colored and has a subtle molasses-like flavor and a higher mineral content. Use it as a sweetener for baking and in sauces, and as a syrup or topping. Lighter agave nectar is more filtered for a milder flavor, allowing it to provide sweetness without adding flavor of its own, making it more multipurpose. It's also a good choice for sweetening beverages (both hot and cold) and fruit salads where a sweetener is desired.

Being high in fructose, consisting of 75 percent fructose, 20 percent glucose, and small amounts of inulin and mannitol, it has minimal effects on blood sugar; that is, it's low glycemic. Its high fructose content also makes it a good natural alternative to high fructose corn syrup as well as crystalline fructose processed from cornstarch.

Storage and Cooking Guidelines

Store agave nectar in a cool, dry area. Unlike honey, it won't crystallize or solidify when cold.

Although agave nectar is less viscous than honey, it can be used in most recipes that call for honey, thus providing an alternative acceptable to vegans. Substitute it for honey on a one-to-one basis. Also akin to honey, agave nectar contributes a moist texture to baked goods due to its high fructose content. Agave nectar is therefore most suitable for recipes designed to create soft cookies and baked goods, rather than crispy ones. As agave is 25 percent sweeter than sugar, when using agave nectar to replace conventional sugar, for each cup of sugar use ¾ cup of agave nectar and reduce the liquid by ⅓ cup. Lower the oven temperature by 25°F.

AMASAKE

Amasake, sometimes spelled amazake, is a creamy, rich beverage that, if left undiluted, doubles as a sweetener. A cultured food hailing from Japan, amasake is traditionally made by inoculating cooked sweet rice with koji, rice that has itself been inoculated with spores of the mold *Aspergillus oryzae*. In fact, its name means "sweet sake" in Japanese, and if the sake-making process were halted after its first fermentation stage, amasake would be the result. After an incubation period of six to ten hours, the koji starter transforms the grain's starch into maltose and glucose.

Because it is a fermented food and based on whole grains, amasake is easy to digest. Artisan amasake producers continue to make amasake by the traditional koji method and sell it fresh in stores or as a concentrate in shelf-stable pouches. Dried rice koji starter is readily available online or through mail order, so you can easily make amasake at home, too;

it's not unlike making yogurt. Either way, the whole-someness, flavor, and thick, puddinglike texture of traditionally made amasake is unsurpassed.

Enzyme-cultured amasake is also available; it's made by replacing part or all of the koji with enzymes made from sprouted grain, specially grown and isolated to create a specific sugar profile, flavor, and texture. This kind of amasake is milder in flavor and smoother in texture, characteristics that make it useful as a thick, ready-to-drink maltlike beverage or a milk substitute to pour over breakfast cereals. The different brands of amasake vary in sweetness as well as consistency, with some resembling a thin gruel and others skim milk. To create a smoother texture, some are thickened with xanthan gum.

Storage and Cooking Guidelines

Fresh, undiluted amasake can keep for up to ten days refrigerated. Diluted, enzyme-cultured ama-sake should be used within a week or by the date indicated on the product.

When using amasake in a recipe that specifically includes it as an ingredient, be sure to check whether the recipe calls for a traditional, thick type of ama-sake or the diluted variety made with enzymes. When using thick amasake in a recipe, process it in a blender if you prefer a smoother texture.

Traditional amasake can be eaten as is, like a pud-ding. Diluted with at least an equal amount of water, it can be chilled to drink as a smoothie or warmed for a hot, satisfying drink that is typically served with a pinch of grated ginger. In baked goods, it's a subtle sweetener that will also contribute some degree of leavening and moistness. Because enzyme-cultured amasake is already diluted, it can be substituted for some or all of the liquid in a sweet bread, muffin, or dessert recipe. Or you can thicken it with old-fashioned tapioca or agar flakes and serve it as a pudding or use it as a pie filling. When using it to replace conventional sugar, for each cup of sugar substitute 1¾ cups amasake and reduce the liquid by ½ cup. Some adjustments may also be required for the dry ingredients in the recipe.

BARLEY MALT SYRUP

Barley malt syrup is a thick, sticky, dark-colored sweetener with a distinctively malty, molasses-like flavor. It is made from sprouted barley that is dried and mixed with water and cooked grains, such as barley, rice, or wheat. The natural enzymes in the sprouted barley digest the cooked grain to create a sweet, thick mixture. Additional water is added to the slurry and the liquid is then cooked slowly to produce a concentrated syrup.

Barley malt is considered one of the better whole food–based sweeteners around. The sprouting pro-cess naturally transforms the grain's starch into a sweetener, creating a sugar profile with a high per-centage of maltose, along with lesser amounts of glucose and polysaccharides, longer chains of sug-ars that are digested more slowly. This allows for a more steady release of glucose into the blood and thus less fluctuation in blood sugar levels.

In contrast, **barley malt extract** is made with-out added cooked grains, which creates a stronger flavor. Malt extract with active enzymes (diastatic malt) is often used as an ingredient in bread baking, as it provides alpha-amylase enzymes that enhance the dough's fermentation rate. Products labeled as "nondiastatic barley malt" have been dried at high temperatures to retain the malt flavor but inactivate the enzymes.

Storage and Cooking Guidelines

Refrigerate barley malt syrup during warmer months to prevent fermentation.

Barley malt syrup is less sweet than sugar or honey and has a lighter, milder flavor than molas-ses. It can be substituted for cane syrup or sorghum syrup using equal measures. It also helps retain moisture in baked goods and contributes a dark, rich color. It's best in foods that take well to stronger flavors, such as baked beans, cookies, muffins, and some cakes. It is particularly good combined with ginger, chocolate, or carob. When using it to replace conventional sugar, for each cup of sugar substitute 1⅓ cups of barley malt syrup and reduce the liquid by ¼ cup. Add ¼ teaspoon of baking soda for a lighter texture in baked goods.

BIRCH SYRUP

Birch syrup, a sweetener concentrated from the sap of birch trees, has a caramel-like, slightly spicy flavor. In comparison to maple syrup, birch syrup is richer and more complex. The predominant sugars in birch syrup are fructose and glucose, whereas maple syrup is high in sucrose.

The flavor and color of birch syrup depends on the variety of birch tree, the minerals in the soil, and production methods. Most commercial birch syrup comes from Alaska, where three varieties of paper birch (*Betula papyrifera*) are used for sugar making, each conferring distinctive flavor and color characteristics. These qualities are further differentiated by the skill of the producer and the year the trees are tapped.

Although birch syrup is produced in generally the same manner as maple syrup, there are several factors that account for the higher cost of birch syrup. Time is the first factor. While the sap run from maple trees usually lasts four to six weeks, with birch trees it is typically only two to three weeks. The sugar content of birch sap is also much lower. It takes about 100 gallons of birch sap to make 1 gallon of birch syrup, in contrast to the 40 gallons of maple sap needed, on average, to make 1 gallon of maple syrup. This means there is a significantly higher percentage of liquid to solids in birch syrup, and as a result, 99 percent of the water content of the birch sap must be removed. To save time and fuel, most commercial birch syrup producers begin processing by using a reverse osmosis machine to remove about 70 percent of the water, rather than just boiling down the sap as is done with maple syrup. The resulting liquid is further concentrated using a low-temperature evaporator designed to help prevent scorching, an increased risk with birch syrup due to its high fructose content.

The color of birch syrup can range from light amber to deep reddish brown depending on when

Clockwise from top left: (1) Sorghum syrup, (2) brown rice syrup, (3) barley malt syrup, (4) cane syrup

the sap was tapped, the pH of the sap (which varies depending on the type of birch tree), and the temperature and time of cooking down the sap. Lighter syrups, from sap early in the season, are subtler in flavor. They are a good choice as a table sweetener to top pancakes, waffles, oatmeal, yogurt, and ice cream, as well as for cooking and baking when a more delicate flavor is desired. The darker-colored syrups have a more full-bodied, caramel-like taste that works well in all-purpose cooking and baking, including barbeque sauces, breads, granola, and cookies. They can also be used at the table as a more robust-flavored topping.

Products labeled "Alaskan birch syrup" are required to be made and produced in Alaska from Alaska paper birch sap. To use the term "pure birch syrup," the syrup must be from 100 percent Alaska paper birch sap concentrated to at least 66 percent but not more than 78 percent dissolved solids by weight (this is known as the Brix value) and free of any additional nutrients, additives, or chemicals, whether added intentionally or inadvertently.

Products simply labeled as "birch syrup," sometimes called breakfast-style birch syrup, are less expensive, milder, and sweeter because they're stabilized with added fructose. Labeling requirements stipulate that these syrups must contain a majority (51 percent by weight) of condensed Alaska paper birch sap, and no additives beyond fructose are allowed.

Storage and Cooking Guidelines

Store birch syrup in the refrigerator and use it within six months.

Birch syrup works best in recipes that call for liquid sweeteners with a high fructose content, such as agave nectar, concentrated fruit juice, and honey. When using it to replace conventional sugar, use an equal amount of birch syrup and decrease liquids by ¼ cup per each cup of birch syrup. Because of the high fructose content of birch syrup, baked goods will be moister, so cookies made with birch syrup will turn out soft rather than crisp. Baked goods will also be darker in color, as fructose-rich birch syrup caramelizes at a lower temperature than do sweeteners that consist primarily of sucrose. For a milder flavor or to extend its use, birch syrup can be blended with other sweeteners in recipes.

BROWN RICE SYRUP

Brown rice syrup, like barley malt syrup, is relatively rich in complex carbohydrates, so its sugars are released into the bloodstream more slowly. Based on whole or partially polished brown rice, its finished consistency is also similar to that of barley malt syrup.

The flavor of brown rice syrup is caramel-like, with the intensity depending on how it's produced.

The traditional way to make brown rice syrup is to add a small amount of sprouted barley (or occasionally sprouted rice) to cooked brown rice. The diastatic enzymes from the sprouted barley break down the starches of the rice into about 45 percent

maltose, 3 percent glucose, and 50 percent complex carbohydrates. It is then strained and cooked to yield a mildly sweet, golden syrup. Traditionally made rice syrup can be identified by the term "sprouted barley," "malted barley," "sprouted rice," or "malted rice" on the ingredient label. It is less sweet than table sugar or honey.

However, many varieties of brown rice syrup now on the market are made by using enzymes isolated from sprouted barley rather than sprouted barley itself. This allows manufacturers to control the amount and varieties of enzymes so, as with corn syrup, different types of rice syrup can be created depending on the intended use. In general, rice syrup made using isolated enzymes is sweeter than varieties made using traditional methods. While the extent of processing and the proportion of sugars will not be indicated on a label, these varieties generally contain 20 to 40 percent maltose, 20 to 35 percent glucose, and 30 to 40 percent complex carbohydrates. This type of rice syrup can be identified by the term "cereal enzymes" on the ingredient label, or they may simply say "brown rice, barley, water" or "brown rice, water."

The differences between traditional malted rice syrup and enzyme-treated rice syrup are apparent in baking. Enzyme-treated rice syrup will be higher in invert sugar (sucrose broken down into its glucose and fructose components) than traditional malted rice syrup, which means crystallization of sugars during baking will be hampered, making enzyme-treated rice syrup inappropriate for some applications. For example, cakes and muffins that are leavened with baking powder or baking soda should always be sweetened with traditional malted rice syrup. Those made with enzyme-treated rice syrups will tend to remain fairly flat and be goopy on the inside. Likewise, sweet-and-sour sauces or puddings thickened with arrowroot or kudzu are best sweetened with malted rice syrup.

On the other hand, because cookies are purposely low in moisture and aren't expected to rise to a large extent, they can be sweetened with either malted rice syrup or enzyme-treated rice syrup; they'll develop a crisp texture in either case. Marinades, salad dressings, toppings, and spreads that don't depend on added starch to create their texture or consistency can also be made with either malted rice syrup or enzyme-treated rice syrup.

Storage and Cooking Guidelines

Brown rice syrup can be stored at room temperature, but keeping it cool will reduce the tendency for mold to grow on the surface if condensation takes place in the jar. When using rice syrup to replace conventional sugar, for each cup of sugar use 1 to 1¼ cups of rice syrup, reduce the liquid by 3 tablespoons, and add about ⅛ to ¼ teaspoon of baking soda. Even though rice syrup is much less sweet than honey or corn syrup, experiment with using equal proportions of rice syrup when substituting for any of these more intense sweeteners. In time, you may find you prefer foods that are less sweet.

CANE SYRUP

Cane syrup is a traditional sweetener that was commonly made right on the farm in many rural areas of the southern United States. Although production of cane syrup declined as the number of family farms went down and other sweeteners became more inexpensive, now there's a resurgence of interest in cane syrup, in part due to the increased appreciation for local and regional foods.

Cane syrup is made from sugarcane, which is crushed to extract the juice. In a process not unlike cooking down sap to make maple syrup, the juice is boiled down and impurities that rise to the top are skimmed off. After the juice has evaporated into a thick syrup, it is strained and bottled. It takes 7 to 10 gallons of cane juice to make 1 gallon of cane syrup.

About half of the sugars in cane syrup are invert sugars (fructose and glucose), which help keep the cane syrup from crystallizing, along with about 25 to 30 percent sucrose. The long cooking time involved in the traditional method naturally caused some of the sucrose to convert to fructose and glucose. These days, some producers add an acid or invertase enzyme so they have better control of the process. In addition to reducing cooking time, this helps mellow out the flavor.

Storage and Cooking Guidelines

Unopened cane syrup can be stored up to two years. Once it's opened, refrigerate it to retard mold growth and use it within one year. Any crystals that form within the syrup during storage can easily be dissolved through placing the container in warm water.

Golden to medium-brown in color, cane syrup has a mild but rich flavor with hints of butterscotch and a thick consistency. Drizzle it over hot biscuits or pancakes or use it as a sweetener for baked goods and general cooking. Substitute cane syrup for light molasses or sorghum syrup using equal measures. When using cane syrup to replace conventional sugar, for each cup of sugar use 1⅓ cups cane syrup and decrease the amount of liquid by ⅓ cup.

COCONUT PALM SUGAR

Coconut palm sugar is a traditional sweetener in South and Southeast Asian regions where coconut palm trees are found; the trees can be tapped for their sap for twenty-five to forty years. Despite what its name may imply, because the sap is collected from the flowers or buds of the coconut palm before they would otherwise mature into coconuts, coconut palm sugar does not have a coconut flavor. In fact, its caramel, maplelike flavor is similar to that of brown sugar. And it can be used similarly in cooking, baking, in beverages, and as a sweet topping for oatmeal and other hot cereals, and, of course, cinnamon toast. However, unlike brown sugar, which is a product of refinement from sugar cane, coconut palm sugar gets the prize as a whole, unrefined sweetener that is also a good source of minerals and other nutrients.

Its production is very simple. After the whitish, translucent sap is collected from the cut flower buds of coconuts from the coconut palm tree, the sap is evaporated into a thick syrup to reduce its high water content. The evaporation process continues until the concentrated nectar crystallizes into a rich, moist sugar.

Storage and Cooking Guidelines

As it as just as sweet, coconut palm sugar can be substituted one to one in any recipe calling for brown or white sugar. Both regular brown coconut sugar, which tastes like brown sugar, and a "blonde" version that is slightly lighter in color and milder in flavor are available. Store in a cool dry place.

DATE SUGAR

Date sugar is made from dates first dehydrated to a 35 percent moisture level and then ground into a coarse, granular sugar. Its delicious, mild date flavor works well in recipes, contributing flavor and color somewhat similar to those of brown sugar. Compared to conventional sugar, date sugar is about two-thirds as sweet.

In addition to its natural sugars, date sugar retains many of the nutrients found in dried dates, most notably fiber and minerals. The specific proportions of sucrose, glucose, and fructose depends on the type of date, but the variety of date used to make the sugar is rarely revealed on the package. In general, glucose and fructose are the primary sugars found in most dates at the stage at which they're consumed, the result of action by the natural enzyme invertase, which breaks down much of the sucrose in the dates into its constituents, glucose and fructose. Known technically as invert sugars, these help enhance flavors and resist crystallization. As a result, they accelerate browning, help retain moisture, and contribute to a chewier, rather than crispy, texture.

The deglet noor variety of date is an exception, as the inversion process in this kind of date will be only partially complete at commercial maturity, leaving its sugar profile at nearly 50 percent sucrose and 25 percent each of glucose and fructose. Therefore, sugar made from deglet noor dates is higher in sucrose, which means it will perform more like conventional sugar in baked goods and yield somewhat crispier cookies.

Storage and Cooking Guidelines

Store date sugar tightly wrapped in the refrigerator or freezer to help prevent it from hardening. Many brands of date sugar contain a bit of oat flour to help prevent clumping.

Use date sugar as you would brown sugar, as a sweetener on both hot cereals and yogurt. It can be used for streusel-like toppings, but to prevent burning, this should be done near the end of the baking time. Brush the top of the baked good with oil or melted butter, sprinkle on the date sugar, and return it the oven for just 2 or 3 minutes. Date sugar can substituted for either brown or white sugar on a one-to-one basis in recipes for pancakes, cookies, breads, and muffins. Take a hint from the relative moisture inherent in brown sugar and emulate this characteristic when baking instead with date sugar by moistening it with some of the oil, melted butter, or other liquid ingredients in a recipe. When substituting for honey, use ½ cup of date sugar to equal ⅓ of cup honey. Trial and error will determine whether you need to add an extra couple of tablespoons of liquid to compensate for the reduced liquid in the recipe.

FRUIT-BASED SWEETENERS

Nothing beats the natural sweetness from fresh fruit picked at its peak of flavor. Whether fresh fruit is eaten as a snack, included in a meal, or served as a dessert, it's the pinnacle of the concept "naturally sweetened." Accordingly, it would seem to make sense that fruit would be the optimal choice as an added sweetener. However, its overall nutrient value and impact on metabolism depends on how far removed the fruit-derived sweetener is from fresh fruit. Freshly cut fruit, unsweetened fruit sauces and purees, and cooked dried fruit are the most healthful sweeteners because they retain most of the nutrients and fiber naturally found within the fruit. When used to sweeten a recipe, they can also replace some or all of the liquid ingredients. Additional concentrated sweetness can be achieved with uncooked dried fruit, which helps account for the frequent use of dried fruit in all kinds of baking and cooking.

Using these forms of whole fruits as sweetening agents contributes functional benefits beyond sweetening that aren't provided by other, more processed fruit-based sweeteners. They help maintain freshness and moisture within the final product and also provide extra texture and bulk; for example, raisin puree will help soften the crumb in baked products. And the pectin in applesauce and plum or prune puree emulates some of the qualities of fat, so these fruit sweeteners can also be used to replace some of the fat in a recipe.

The next best kind of fruit-based sweetener is **single-strength juices** extracted from whole fruit. To better appreciate how concentrated the sugars are in single-strength juice, keep in mind that few people could eat as much fruit in one sitting as it would take to make the amount of juice typically served. Juice can do an effective job as a subtle sweetener if it's used to replace some or all of the liquid in cooked hot cereals and baked goods. Juice can also be used instead of granulated sugar to create a delicious base and caramelized glaze when baking fresh fruit. However, the sugar content of single-strength fruit juice may be too low to achieve the level of sweetening typically desired in baked goods unless extra dried fruit or a boost from a more concentrated sweetener is added.

Concentrated forms of juice, such as **juice concentrates** (typically in frozen form), can do a better job as a sole sweetening agent. Juice concentrates are made by simply evaporating most of the water from the juice, concentrating the natural sugars (primarily fructose) with only a minimal loss of nutrients. To keep the aroma and flavor of the original fruit, the essence of the fruit is captured from the water vapor during manufacture and restored to the concentrate. Some brands also retain some of the fruit's pulp and fiber. Any flavor of fruit juice concentrate can be used

as a sweetener, but apple and pear have the most neutral flavors. As any juice concentrate will also provide some color, lighter-colored versions are appropriate for lighter-colored dishes and baked goods.

The sweetening power of fruit juice concentrate can be further heightened by evaporating even more of its liquid, yielding a syrupy sweetener that is about one and a half times sweeter than white sugar. Although a ready-made **extra-reduced fruit juice concentrate** made from pear, peach, and pineapple juices is generally available at natural foods stores and specialty grocers, you can easily make a similar product at home using any flavor of juice concentrate. Bring it to a boil, then lower the heat and simmer for 10 minutes until about as thick as honey. This is similar to the process of boiling maple sap to make maple syrup, concentrating the sugars and transforming the concentrate into an intense sweetener high in fructose. This extra-reduced fruit juice concentrate is a very concentrated sweetener on par with both honey and maple syrup and should be used accordingly.

Both fruit juice concentrate and the extra-reduced version are naturally high in fructose, so when either is used as a sweetener or simply as an ingredient, it will help retain moisture in the finished product. For example, cookies will turn out moist and chewy rather than crisp.

But just because an ingredient is made with fruit doesn't make it good. At the other end of the spectrum are highly processed, decharacterized fruit juice concentrates often used by manufacturers to sweeten cookies and other baked goods, as well as jellies, syrups, beverages, and cereals. These specialized fruit juice concentrates are processed to heighten their sweetening power and for a neutral flavor, rather than to retain any characteristics of the original juice. They are ultraclarified through heat, enzyme processing, and filtration to remove all natural color, flavor, fiber, and nutrients from the juice, so that only the sugars stay behind. As a result, these decharacterized fruit juice concentrates affect the body like high-fructose corn syrup (HFCS) does.

When it comes to sweetening foods with fruit-based ingredients, your best bet is fresh or cooked fruit, dried fruit, single-strength juice, or minimally processed fruit juice concentrates.

Storage and Cooking Guidelines

All thawed frozen juice concentrates should be kept refrigerated and used within two weeks.

Experiment by substituting unsweetened fruit juice or fruit juice concentrates for part or all the liquids called for in a recipe in place of sugar, but avoid fruit juice that is too acidic in yeasted breads, as it can interfere with the action of yeast. Try using up to ½ cup of dried fruit per loaf of bread or muffin recipe to provide added sweetness.

When substituting fruit juice concentrate for granulated sugar in recipes, use an equal amount and reduce the amount of liquids by ⅓ cup for each cup of sugar replaced. On the other hand, when substituting extra-reduced fruit juice concentrate for conventional sugar, use ½ to ⅔ cup per cup of granulated sugar and reduce the amount of liquid by approximately ⅓ cup for each cup of sugar replaced. In most recipes, extra-reduced juice concentrate can be substituted for agave nectar on a one-to-one basis. To prevent the acidity of fruit juice or any form of concentrated fruit juice from affecting the leavening process, add ¼ teaspoon of baking soda per recipe when making cookies, pancakes, muffins, and quick breads. Whenever substituting fruit juice (in any form) for sugar, lower the oven temperature by 25°F.

HONEY

Honey is extracted from honeycombs, where bees store the results of endless hours of labor. Created through quite an elaborate process, honey comes to us already concentrated and ready to use, with no additional processing required.

The process begins when bees collect flower nectar and put it into their internal storage area, the honey sac, to transport it back to the hive. At the hive, the nectar is transferred by mouth from the field bees to house worker bees as it continues its transformation into honey. The recipient bee ingests the newly obtained nectar, mixing it with enzymes produced from its mouth and honey stomach to both to break down the nectar's natural sucrose into glucose and fructose and to prevent fermentation, helping make honey's long shelf life possible. After being deposited in the hexagonal cylinders of the honeycomb, which is built from wax secreted from the glands of worker bees inside the hive, the honey is further evaporated through the action of bees fanning their wings; this gets the honey to the point that it can be stored without crystallizing. When a honeycomb cell is filled to capacity, it is capped with more wax. Considering that one pound of honey represents nectar collected from about two million flowers, it is a very valuable sweetener, indeed. Not only that, but it is relatively inexpensive, is widely available, and tastes great.

When beekeepers are ready to extract the honey, they remove the honeycomb and pack it in one of three ways: in smaller pieces as comb honey; as chunk honey, in which a piece of comb honey is covered with liquid honey; or as straight liquid honey, derived by spinning the honeycomb in a centrifuge to separate out the wax. Liquid honey may undergo an optional heat and pasteurization treatment at temperatures that range from 140°F to 170°F, depending on the method used to delay crystallization and prevent fermentation. Honey is sometimes filtered to remove pollen grains and small air bubbles that could cause cloudiness. However, the many beekeepers who prefer to retain all the natural flavor and nutritional properties of honey intact simply strain it to remove any wax and other extraneous particles, then let it settle to take care of any air bubbles naturally. As heat can adversely affect the finer, subtler attributes of honey, the less processing, the better.

Creamed or whipped honey has purposely been crystallized, using a controlled process to create a smooth, easily spreadable consistency rather than the coarse, grainy texture that occurs when honey

Honey

The color of honey is associated with the specific flower and the mineral content of the nectar. In general, the darker the color is, the bolder the flavor. For example, dark honeys such as buckwheat or heather are much stronger in flavor than light-colored orange blossom and clover honeys. Basswood, with its nearly translucent white color and strong, somewhat biting flavor, is an exception. Due in part to their higher protein content, darker-colored honeys promote surface browning of products that are baked, cooked, and roasted. Accordingly, choose lighter-colored honey when sweetening foods and beverages, where its golden hue is more appropriate. White honey is ideal when no additional color is desired.

The sugar profile of honey also affects its flavor and function. The predominant sugar in honey is fructose, followed by glucose, some maltose, and only a minute percentage of sucrose. Like other sweeteners high in fructose, honey tastes sweeter than granulated sugar, as much as one and a half times as sweet. There will be some variations in perceived sweetness among the many varieties of honey due to differences in the ratio of fructose to glucose among the floral sources. Honeys higher in fructose, such as tupelo and black button sage, will taste very sweet, while those with a higher percentage of glucose will taste less sweet in comparison. Honeys with a higher fructose content also tend to resist crystallization, whereas those with higher levels of glucose, such as **lavender**, **lehua**, and **Tasmanian leatherwood**, will crystallize quickly.

Beyond Sweetening

Like most highly concentrated sweeteners, honey can act as a preservative. It also has antimicrobial and antioxidant properties, both of which are beneficial to human health and a clear indication that there is more to honey than its sweetening powers. Recognized for centuries as an agent that can discourage the growth and persistence of microorganisms, honey was commonly used medicinally when dressing wounds. In fact, the antimicrobial properties of some varieties of honey can actually

crystallizes spontaneously. In this process, honey is heated twice, once to 120°F and then to 150°F, and then seeded with dried, finely ground honey to start and end the crystallization process under controlled conditions.

Honey can be packed as a varietal, a specific type of honey created by focusing the bees on one kind of flower, or as a combination of two or more kinds of honey selected to create a specific blend. Common varietals include **clover**, **orange blossom**, **buckwheat**, **alfalfa**, **fireweed**, and **basswood**, but there are thousands of other types reflecting the plants that grow or are cultivated in specific regions. The color, aroma, flavor, and composition of honey depend on the flowers from which the bees extracted the nectar.

There are an estimated three thousand honey varietals worldwide, including three hundred in the United States alone, each with unique characteristics: colors ranging from white to dark amber; aromas and flavors that can be subtle or bold; and viscosities ranging from very thin to very thick.

be so potent as to make them unsuitable for baking, because they can kill yeast and preventing leavening. However, this is the exception rather than the rule, especially as honeys with very high antimicrobial activity would generally be too expensive or too strongly flavored to be used as an ingredient. Nonetheless, to play it safe, some bread bakers stick with milder flavored honey, such as clover honey.

Darker honeys also tend to contain more antioxidants, in the form of the phytonutrients known as polyphenols. Because these compounds can slow oxidation in foods, including rancidity, adding honey to foods serves as a natural alternative to chemical antioxidant preservatives, such as BHT and BHA, which are also phenols. And, since honey supplies dietary antioxidants, it has the unique potential, even when heated or used in cooking, to help retard chemical reactions within the body that have been linked to many chronic diseases.

Some people also swear by using honey extracted from hives in their region as a way to boost tolerance to local pollens. Though this hasn't been proven by scientific studies, it's a widespread belief, and there's certainly no harm in the practice.

Given all of these potential health benefits, honey may be among the best sweeteners for contributing not just flavor but also well-being. However, it should *never* be given to a child under the age of one in any form, including via pacifiers, as a sweetener in beverages, or in food. Infant botulism is a rare but serious paralytic disease caused by the microorganism *Clostridium botulinum*, which may be present in honey in the form of spores. In infants whose intestinal microflora is still underdeveloped, the spores can germinate and grow in the lower bowel. Symptoms of infant botulism include constipation, lethargy, a weak cry, feeble sucking, and general muscular weakness. If any of these symptoms are present, the infant should be taken to a doctor immediately.

Storage and Cooking Guidelines

Store honey tightly sealed at room temperature. For optimal flavor and to prevent unwanted crystallization, raw honey should be stored at or below 50°F. Honey that has been pasteurized or heat-processed can be stored between 64°F and 75°F. Honey can be held at higher temperatures for brief periods of time, but avoid storing it near heat sources, such as a stove or oven. Honey that does crystallize can be used as such, or you can restore it to a liquid state by placing the jar in lukewarm water.

As a flavor enhancer, honey not only intensifies sweetness, but also decreases the perception of sourness (think yogurt or sour cream), bitterness (think chocolate or coffee), and saltiness (think cheese or salted nuts), further explaining its wide use in cooking and baking and as a condiment and topping. Since honey typically has higher levels of fructose, it has humectant qualities, so baked goods sweetened with honey retain moisture and stay fresher longer, and cookies made with honey have with a softer, rather than crispier, texture. Likewise, as fructose caramelizes at lower temperatures than sucrose, honey helps enhance browning.

If substituting honey for conventional sugar, use ½ to ¾ cup of honey per cup of sugar. Reduce the liquid by about ¼ cup for each cup of honey used. For improved volume and color in baked goods, add ¼ teaspoon of baking soda per cup of honey to neutralize its acidity. Since honey caramelizes at lower temperatures, reduce the oven temperature by 25°F. Honey can be substituted for birch syrup using the same amount indicated in the recipe. If replacing date sugar in a recipe, use ⅓ cup of honey as a substitute for ½ cup of date sugar, reducing dry ingredients as needed to compensate for the increased moisture added to the recipe from the honey.

MAPLE SYRUP AND MAPLE SUGAR

Maple syrup is a natural sweetener wrapped in tradition. Native Americans taught early settlers the technique for concentrating the sap that flows from sugar maples in the early spring, and although the process has been updated since that time, festivities associated with the annual ritual of maple sugaring exist to this day.

Of all the varieties of maple, the sugar maple (*Acer saccharum*), also known as hard maple, produces the best sap. Most of the world's maple syrup is produced in eastern Canada, followed by the northeastern United States, where sugar maples are abundant and weather conditions are optimal for maple sap flow. In fact, the maple tree is so significant to Canada that in 1965 the country adopted the now-familiar flag, which features the outline of a maple leaf.

Maple sugaring starts as spring approaches and temperatures begin to fluctuate, with nights below freezing and warmer days above freezing. The frozen sap, stored in the tree during the previous growing season, begins to thaw, creating internal pressure within the tree and causing the sap to flow out of any wound on the tree. Maple sugar producers capitalize on this phenomenon by purposely creating tap holes in the trees to capture the flow. The alternating freeze-thaw process during the four- to six-week tapping window causes the trees to take up water from the soil, which replenishes the sap so it will flow again the next day, when it's warm. The flow stops when the leaf buds begin to emerge and the freeze-and-thaw weather pattern ends. In the past, some producers put paraformaldehyde pellets into tap holes to boost production, but this is now illegal.

Each day the sap is collected, and it must be boiled down as soon as possible to ensure good quality and taste. The watery sap only has about 2 percent sucrose, so it must be evaporated until it's concentrated to about 65 percent sucrose, with a Brix level (a measure of the density of syrup), between 66 and 67 percent—high enough to prevent potential fermentation but low enough to avoid crystallization of the sugars.

The traditional method of evaporating the sap is to boil it for many hours, but to save energy and time, reverse osmosis devices are now often used to remove 75 percent of the water without heat.

The evaporation process is then completed by boiling the condensed sap, which develops the characteristic flavors and color of maple syrup. Minute amounts of a fatty substance, usually vegetable oil or a commercial defoamer made from vegetable fat, are sometimes added to help keep excessive foam from boiling over during the procedure. Some smaller producers might still use butter or whole milk, which are more traditional. When used in small quantities, defoamers will evaporate, not leaving a noticeable trace in the syrup. The syrup is then filtered to remove any gritty minerals (referred to as "sugar sand") and any other solids.

Maple Syrup Grading Systems

The grading of maple syrup is based on color and flavor, which are dependent on when during the maple syrup season the sap was obtained, the weather during the sugaring period, and the skill of the producer. In general, lighter-colored, more delicately flavored syrups are produced in the earlier stages of the sap run. Syrups that are darker and more concentrated are from later in the season. As the weather warms and the tree goes from winter dormancy into springtime mode, the mineral content of the sap increases and other metabolic changes occur that result in syrups with a deeper, more caramelized flavor.

There are three grading systems used for maple syrup intended for retail sale. The grades they denote are roughly equivalent, with the main difference being in the terms used. The US Department of Agriculture standards are a voluntary system developed to allow for standardized inspection and grading system of maple syrup in the United States. Vermont's quality standards, in place before the USDA standards were created, are required for syrup labeled as "Vermont maple syrup." In Canada, federally mandated standards govern strict labeling and grading requirements for all maple syrup produced in and exported from Canada. Thanks to strict laws in both the United States and Canada, it is easy to distinguish imitation maple products from

Guide to Maple Syrup Grades

- **US Grade A Light Amber, Vermont Fancy, or Canadian No. 1 Extra Light:** These syrups, made from first sap flows of the season, have a delicate maple flavor and are best for table use.
- **US and Vermont Grade A Medium Amber or Canadian No. 1 Light Grade A:** This is the most popular grade for pancakes. Generally made from the midseason sap run, it has a slightly darker, amber color and a gentle but more pronounced flavor. It's great for table use and good for cooking and baking.
- **US and Vermont Grade A Dark Amber or Canadian No. 1 Medium Grade A:** Generally made later in the season, this grade is darkly colored and richly flavored. It's great for table use and good for cooking and baking.
- **US Grade B, Vermont Grade B, Canadian No. 2 Amber:** Even darker in color and stronger in flavor, this grade is generally the last produced in the season. It's best for cooking and baking and good for table use.

the real thing. Neither country allows the terms *maple syrup* or *maple sugar* to appear on products that aren't pure. Instead, phrases such as "pancake syrup with artificial maple flavor" or "artificial maple flavor sweetener" are required to ensure consumers are not misled.

The high sucrose content of maple syrup also means that maple products will metabolize similarly to conventional sugars. However, they are preferable in terms of nutrient content, most notably calcium and potassium, along with smaller amounts of manganese, magnesium, phosphorus, iron, zinc, and the B vitamins pantothenic acid and niacin. That said, maple syrup, like any sweetener, should be used in moderation.

Other Maple Products

Maple cream is made by further boiling maple syrup to remove more moisture, stirring it as it cools so the crystals essentially become undetectable, leaving a creamy consistency. It is always created from the equivalent of US Grade A Light Amber syrup (Vermont Fancy, Canadian No.1 Extra Light), as it has the lowest amount of invert sugars. Because the fructose component of invert sugars is hygroscopic,

using maple syrup that contains too much invert sugar could cause excess moisture to be retained, interfering with the level of crystallization needed to create maple cream. Use maple cream as a topping for toast, pancakes, or muffins, or mix it with butter for a frosting.

Granulated maple sugar, the crystallized form of maple syrup, can be used just like conventional granulated sugar. Heating maple syrup to about 252°F to 257°F, which causes it to crystallize as it cools, makes maple sugar. After it's transferred to a flat pan to quickly cool, the maple syrup is stirred until crystallization occurs and then put through a screen to achieve uniform granule size. Like maple syrup, its sugar is primarily sucrose, although there is some amount of invert sugar as a consequence of the heating process. In a pinch, maple sugar could be cooked back into syrup by combining it with a small amount of water until the desired consistency is achieved.

Storage

Even though maple syrup purchased in metal tins or cans may have a quaint, old-fashioned feel, these can give the syrup a metallic flavor. Your best bet is to buy maple syrup in a glass container or transfer any maple syrup purchased in a can into a sterilized glass container. Maple syrup can be stored in a food-grade plastic container for three to six months, but since plastic is porous, changes in both flavor and color may occur. Nonporous plastic jugs are preferable, as they will keep out oxygen, which can negatively affect the syrup.

The shelf life of unopened containers of maple syrup stored at room temperature is about six to eight months. However, storing it in the freezer will help retain its flavor and quality indefinitely. If properly manufactured, maple syrup will not freeze, and after only an hour at room temperature, it will be of a suitable pouring consistency. It's most practical to store a smaller amount in the refrigerator so it's ready for use. At a minimum, all opened maple syrup should be stored in the refrigerator and used within six months. The cool temperatures will slow fermentation and prevent mold formation. Any crystals that form can be dissolved by gently warming the syrup.

Any syrup that develops an off flavor should be discarded. Technically, any mold that forms on top can be skimmed off. However, after doing so, reheat the syrup to around 190°F or to a slight boil, filter it, then transfer it to a sterilized container. If the syrup still has an off flavor, it should be discarded.

Granulated maple sugar has a shelf life of ten to twelve months when stored in a cool, dry place. Maple cream can be kept for up to two weeks in the refrigerator. For longer periods, it should be stored in the freezer and brought to room temperature before use.

Cooking Guidelines

In baking and cooking, the functionality of maple syrup relates to the fact that its predominant sugar is sucrose (88 to 99 percent). During processing, a small amount of the sucrose may be converted into fructose and glucose, especially in darker syrups. This may explain why different textures, although slight, may occur in baked goods depending on

Grade A maple syrup (left) and Grade B maple syrup

the grade of syrup used. When it comes to baking cookies, maple syrup will produce a crisp texture similar to that produced by other sweeteners that are also high in sucrose, such as conventional sugar. In fact, granulated maple sugar can be substituted for conventional granulated sugar on a one-to-one basis in recipes and give similar results. The only downside is its higher price.

Besides topping pancakes and hot cereals, maple syrup can be used to sweeten cookies, cakes, muffins, and granola. When using it to replace conventional sugar, for each cup of sugar use ¾ cup of maple syrup and decrease the liquid by 3 tablespoons. Add ¼ teaspoon of baking soda per cup of maple syrup to counter its acidity. Maple syrup can be substituted for honey on a one-to-one basis, but it will change the texture of the finished product.

MOLASSES

Molasses is essentially a thick syrup made from sugarcane juice. It was the primary, all-purpose sweetener in colonial America for baking, spreading on breads, making candy, and flavoring meat, and it remained popular until just after World War I, when granulated sugar became more affordable and took the lead. Ranging from golden brown and sweet to brownish black and somewhat bitter, the various colors, flavors, and grades of molasses reflect how the molasses was processed, whether as a direct reduction from the sugarcane juice or as a by-product from one of the stages of the sugar-making process. Sugarcane is always the source for molasses for human consumption. Molasses made from sugar beets has a strong fishy odor due to several inherent mineral salts, so it is added into cattle feed and also used for the production of yeast and citric acid.

Molasses is often touted as a good food source of iron, calcium, potassium, and magnesium, with blackstrap molasses considered the best. In fact, its calcium content explains why molasses is often added to baked bean recipes; it helps the beans retain their shape during the long cooking process. Even though the amounts of these nutrients are fairly small per tablespoon, any extra nutrients found in concentrated sugars is always a plus. Still, it is best to treat it as you would any other sweetener, using it in moderation rather than eating it by the spoonful as a dietary supplement.

Although most molasses sold to consumers is unsulfured, look for the term *unsulfured* on the label to be sure that's what you're getting. Molasses processed with sulfur dioxide is significantly inferior in flavor. If manufacturers use mature raw materials and clarify the juice during processing, sulfur dioxide is entirely unnecessary in the refining process.

Varieties of Molasses

Fancy molasses, sometimes referred to as original molasses, is the highest grade of molasses and the best tasting. It's made from sugarcane juice from which the sugar has not been extracted, which is filtered and slowly boiled down into syrup. The term Barbados is still often used to denote this high-quality molasses, originally used in reference to the island of Barbados, which was noted for its exceptional fancy molasses, not to mention its rum. Fancy molasses has a sweet, mild, light flavor and a rich amber color. Use it as a table syrup to top pancakes, biscuits, bread, and hot cereals and as a sweetener for baked goods. It is also good in marinades and sauces.

Molasses produced as a by-product of sugar refining will have a look and taste that reflects the particular stages of the sugar crystallization process from which it is derived. The later in the process the molasses is extracted, the darker, more strongly flavored, and less sweet it will be.

Dark or **cooking molasses** may be a by-product from the second stage of sugar crystallization or a blend of fancy molasses for sweetness and thinner consistency and blackstrap molasses for robust flavor. Darker in color and having a more pronounced flavor, these types of molasses are best for general cooking, flavoring, and baking rather than as a table syrup. Foods made with dark or cooking molasses will be less sweet and darker in color than those made with fancy molasses.

Blackstrap molasses is the final syrup left after crystallizing the conventional sugar from sugarcane. Its dark color is due to caramelization that occurs during repeated boiling during processing. It is slightly bitter or tart—a combined effect of its concentrated mineral content and the various chemical reactions that occur during the repeated boiling. Blackstrap molasses can be used in baking when a stronger flavor is desired. Alternatively, it could be blended with other types of molasses or other sweeteners to mellow its punch.

The functionality of each type of molasses depends on its sugar profile, which, like color and taste, is also determined by how the molasses was produced. All molasses will contain sucrose from the sugarcane as well as some invert sugars (fructose and glucose) depending on the temperatures and

Sugar Substitution Guide

Here are some handy guidelines for substituting alternative sweeteners for conventional granulated or brown sugar. For each cup of sugar, make the following adjustments to amounts of ingredients:

Type	Substitute per 1 Cup Sugar	Liquids in Recipe	Other Modifications
Agave nectar	¾ cup	Decrease ⅓ cup	Lower oven by 25°F
Amasake	1¾ cups	Decrease ½ cup	May require adjustments to dry ingredients
Barley malt syrup	1⅓ cups	Decrease ¼ cup	Add ¼ tsp. baking soda
Birch syrup	1 cup	Decrease ¼ cup	
Brown rice syrup	1–1¼ cup	Decrease 3 tbsp.	Add ⅛–¼ tsp. baking soda
Cane syrup	1⅓ cups	Decrease ⅓ cup	
Coconut palm sugar	1 cup	Equal amount	
Corn syrup	¾ cup	Decrease 3 tbsp.	
Date sugar	1 cup		Substitute for brown sugar
Fruit juice concentrate (thawed)	1 cup	Decrease ⅓ cup	Add ¼ tsp. baking soda. Lower oven by 25°
Fruit juice concentrate (extra reduced)	½–¾ cup	Decrease ⅓ cup	Add ¼ tsp. baking soda. Lower oven by 25°F
Honey	½–¾ cup	Decrease 2–3 tbsp.	Add ¼ tsp. baking soda
Maple sugar	1 cup		
Maple syrup	¾ cup	Decrease 3 tbsp.	Add ¼ tsp. baking soda
Molasses	1⅓ cup	Decrease ⅓ cup	Add scant ½ tsp. baking soda. Lower oven by 25°F
Sorghum syrup	1⅓ cup	Decrease ⅓ cup	
Stevia	1 cup (sweetener baking blends), 1 teaspoon (powdered and liquid extract)	See manufacturer's recommendations	See manufacturer's recommendations

length of time in the evaporation process. Fancy molasses, the least processed, will have the highest sucrose content and lower amounts of both invert sugars and minerals. At the other end of the spectrum, blackstrap molasses will have the least amount of sucrose and more invert sugars and minerals. Dark or cooking molasses will be in the middle. The higher the level of invert sugars, the more the molasses will help retain moisture in baked goods and the less likely it will be to crystallize.

Storage and Cooking Guidelines

Store molasses in a dry, cool area away from heat and humidity. Both fancy and dark molasses can be kept for one to two years, while three months or less is optimum for blackstrap molasses.

Molasses can be substituted equally for cane syrup and sorghum syrup. When using molasses to replace conventional sugar, for each cup of sugar use 1⅓ cups of molasses and decrease the liquid by ⅓ cup. Since baked goods sweetened with molasses tend to darken more quickly, reduce the oven temperature by 25°F. It's a good idea to add ½ teaspoon of baking soda per cup of molasses in recipes for baked goods to counteract its acidity; this will result in improved leavening.

SORGHUM SYRUP

Sorghum syrup is the concentrated juice of the sweet sorghum plant. A plant that looks similar to millet, this grain with sweet juicy stems is grown specifically for the production of syrup, especially in the southeastern United States. In contrast, sorghum varieties that have a lower sugar content are used primarily as livestock feed, and also as a food grain for humans in some countries. Though it was quite popular in years past, use of sorghum syrup declined as the price of sugar decreased and corn syrup became more widely available. However, it is still produced and is especially appreciated in southern states, where this regional product is traditionally poured on hot biscuits and pancakes or used as a sweetener in breads.

It takes about 6 to 12 gallons of sweet sorghum juice to make 1 gallon of sorghum syrup. After the juice is extracted from the sorghum by crushing the stalks, it is filtered to remove any stalk fragments and other impurities. The juice is then allowed to settle for a few hours to minimize any potential starch development that could cause the syrup to gel. Depending on the season and variety of sweet sorghum grown, the enzyme amylase (also called malt diastase) is occasionally added to help break down excessive starch into sugars.

The sorghum juice is then evaporated by heat in open pans, and skimmed continuously to remove proteins and starches that float to the top. The enzyme invertase may be added at this point to convert some of the sucrose into glucose and fructose so the syrup is easier to cook and less likely to crystallize in the process. The syrup is done when it has been concentrated into a clear, amber-colored, mildly sweet, sometimes tangy syrup that has a Brix level of 78 to 80 percent. In the process, sorghum syrup's natural mineral content, including

potassium, calcium, magnesium, zinc, and iron, is also further concentrated. The finished syrup is quickly cooled to retain as much of its natural color as possible, strained, and then sterilized by boiling before it's packed into containers.

The sugar profile of sorghum syrup is mostly invert sugars (with slightly more glucose than fructose), with about 25 to 30 percent sucrose and a very small amount of maltose. In addition to helping it resist crystallization, the high levels of invert sugars means it helps retain moisture in baked goods, creates softer textures in cookies, and, in general, functions similarly to other liquid sweeteners, such as molasses, cane syrup, and honey.

Storage and Cooking Guidelines

Unopened sorghum syrup can be stored for up to two years. Once opened, it should be refrigerated to retard mold growth and be used within one year. Discard the syrup if any mold develops. Any crystallization is easily remedied by placing the jar in warm water.

When using sorghum syrup to replace conventional sugar, for each cup of sugar use 1⅓ cups of sorghum syrup and decrease the liquids by ⅓ cup. An equal amount of sorghum syrup can be used to replace barley malt syrup, cane syrup, and light molasses in most recipes, with the exception of cookies and cakes that use baking powder. In contrast, recipes that use baking soda rather than baking powder will work well.

STEVIA

Native people in Paraguay and Brazil have used *Stevia rebaudiana*, a plant indigenous in these areas, as a sweetener for hundreds of years. Its sweet taste, two hundred times sweeter than sucrose, is from two primary constituents in the leaves, stevioside and rebaudioside, the latter being less bitter and astringent. In contrast to artificial sweeteners marketed as no-calorie alternatives to sugar, stevia has the merit of being a natural, plant-based substance. Because stevia's sweetness is from glycosides that the human body can't completely metabolize, it is also free of calories and, unlike many artificial sweeteners, its sweetness remains stable under heat.

Stevia has a long history of use as a sweetener in South America and has also been used for many years in Japan, China, and Central America. Sweet, purified extracts from stevia are allowed to be used and marketed as sweeteners within the United States, Europe, Australia, and New Zealand. In the United States, stevia's whole plant form can only be marketed as a dietary supplement. As of 2012, in Canada, fresh or dried stevia leaf can only be sold to consumers for personal culinary use, as long as no health claims are included on the product. Foods containing stevia leaf or its extract are not approved for sale in Canada although they are allowed within specific guidelines as ingredients in dietary supplement-based natural health products.

Storage and Cooking Guidelines

Store in a cool dry place. Stevia can be used in place of artificial sweeteners in hot and cold beverages or as a tabletop sweetener. It is available in liquid form for adding directly to a beverage or food, or in powdered form in individual packets and boxes; the powder uses either agave inulin or erythritol (a polyol) as a carrier for stevia extract. See the manufacturer's information for its equivalent in teaspoons of sugar and suggested recipes. Sweetener baking blends formulated for cup-for-cup sugar substitution using stevia leaf extract as a component are also available.

SUGARCANE AND BEET SUGARS

Although all forms of sweeteners consist of concentrated sugars, when the general term *sugar* is used, it commonly refers to the granulated sweetener extracted from sugarcane or sugar beets. In addition to adding sweetness and enhancing flavor, as all sweeteners do, the high sucrose content of granulated sugar provides unique texture and other characteristics when used in baking and cooking. Most cookies made with granular sugar have a crisp,

Clockwise, from top left: (1) Maple sugar, (2) muscovado sugar, (3) demerara sugar, (4) dark coconut palm sugar, (5) light coconut palm sugar, (6) turbinado sugar, (7) date sugar, (8) sucanat

almost crystalline texture upon cooling. The more molasses retained in the sugar during processing, the softer the baked goods made with it will be. Sugar's contribution to the color of baked goods also often depends on the level of refinement: the less refined the sugar, the darker the baked good. When granulated sugar and fat are creamed together, it incorporates air into the batter, producing exceptionally light and tender baked goods, a quality that's accentuated by sugar's tendency to inhibit gluten formation.

Despite praise for both its sweetness and its functional attributes in food, sugar has also been maligned for much of its history because of its degree of refinement and the accompanying reduction in nutrients. Nonetheless, it is, indeed, a naturally derived sweetener, and, as such, will always be a significantly better option than other more highly processed nutritive and artificial sweeteners.

And because of the wide range of sugar products representing varying degrees of refinement, there's usually a sugar available that can fit most any need.

The refining process generally starts with juice pressed from crushed sugarcane or a solution derived from soaking sugar beets in hot water to extract their sugar. In both cases, the liquid is then put through a series of steps, including purification, filtration, evaporation, crystallization, and centrifuging, to produce, at the far end of the process, white crystalline sugar.

Varieties of Refined Sugar

Although evaporated cane juice, milled golden cane sugar, and golden castor sugar, considered first-crystallization sugars, don't undergo all of the stages of refinement because they're finely granulated, they still function much like white sugar rather than darker first-crystallization sugars, like turbinado and demerara. The subtle taste and slight golden or tan color of evaporated cane juice and milled golden cane sugar reflect the fact that more molasses was removed during the process of centrifuging them. Both can be used interchangeably with white sugar in most recipes.

Light, Dark, and Specialty Brown Sugars

There are many varieties of brown sugar: the common light and dark varieties of soft brown sugar, as well as specialty brown sugars such as Sucanat, turbinado, amber crystal, demerara, and muscovado. Although they could be used interchangeably, each has a unique level of moisture and different quality of sugar crystal. Experiment to see which varieties you prefer for different uses or to figure out how the recipes should be adjusted for best results.

Sucanat, a registered trademark, is an acronym for *sugar cane natural*. This type of sugar is also referred to as "dehydrated cane juice." Its porous, dark granules are derived before the first crystallization process, resulting in a rich molasses flavor. Sucanat is good for baking, sauces, and sweetening beverages.

Turbinado is a light golden brown sugar from the first crystallization process with a mild molasses flavor and medium-size granules. It's a good all-purpose brown sugar for baking, sweetening beverages, sprinkling on hot cereals and fruit, and using in toppings, rubs, and sauces.

Amber crystal, known as coffee sugar in the United Kingdom, is a coarsely granulated, light golden brown sugar from the first crystallization process. It's especially good in coffee due to its texture.

Demerara is a crunchy, slightly sticky, coarsely granulated, light golden brown sugar from the first crystallization process. It has a mild molasses flavor and is good for sweetening beverages, sprinkling on hot cereals and fruits, and using in crunchy toppings on cookies, cakes, muffins, and desserts.

Light muscovado is a moist, fine-grained, light brown sugar with a butterscotch flavor. It's good for cookies, cakes, puddings, and sauces. **Dark muscovado** is an extra-moist, sticky, fine-grained dark brown sugar with a rich toffee flavor and more molasses than is in light muscovado sugar. (Molasses sugar is dark muscovado sugar that contains extra molasses.) It is good for cookies, chocolate cakes, fruitcakes, puddings, and sauces.

Storage Guidelines

Granulated refined sugar has a virtually indefinite shelf life if stored in a cool, dry place within a tightly closed container.

Light, dark, and specialty brown sugars stored unrefrigerated in a tightly closed container at temperatures between 65 to 95°F will maintain their quality for more than a year. To soften brown sugar that has gotten hard, place it in a bowl or, if easier, keep it in the bag and cover the brown sugar with a damp paper towel for 6 to 8 hours or overnight so it can reabsorb moisture and soften.

Suggested Reading

Aggarwal, B. B., and D. Yost. *Healing Spices*. New York: Sterling Publishing, 2011.

Albala, K. *Beans: A History*. New York: Berg, 2007.

Appleby, M. C., J. A. Mench, and B. O. Hughes. *Poultry Behavior and Welfare*. Cambridge, MA: CABI Publishing, 2004.

Bastianich, L. M. *Lidia's Italian-American Kitchen*. New York: Alfred A. Knopf, 2004.

Bastianich, L. M. *Lidia's Italian Table*. New York: William Morrow, 1998.

Belitz, H. D., W. Grosch, and P. Schieberle. *Food Chemistry*, 3rd revised edition. Berlin: Springer, 2004.

Belleme, J., and J. Belleme. *Cooking with Japanese Foods*. Garden City Park, NY: Avery Publishing Group, 1993.

Beranbaum, R. L. *The Bread Bible*. New York: W. W. Norton, 2003.

Berry, E., and F. Fabricant. *The Great Bean Book*. Berkeley, CA: Ten Speed Press, 1999.

Buhmann, S., with B. Repplier. *Letters from the Hive*. New York: Bantam Book, 2005.

Cheese Board Collective. *The Cheese Board Collective Works*. Berkeley, CA: Ten Speed Press, 2003.

Cheney, S. J. *Breadtime*. Berkeley, CA: Ten Speed Press, 1998.

Colbin, A. *Food and Healing*. New York: Ballantine Books, 1996.

Cook's Illustrated editors. *The Complete Book of Pasta and Noodles*. New York: Clarkson Potter, 2000.

Corriher, S. *CookWise: The Secrets of Cooking Revealed*. New York: William Morrow, 1997.

Creasy, R. *The Edible Flower Garden*. Singapore: Periplus, 1999.

Creasy, R. *The Edible Herb Garden*. Singapore: Periplus, 1999.

Dietary Guidelines Advisory Committee. *Report of the Dietary Guidelines Advisory Committee on the Dietary Guidelines for Americans, 2010*. Washington, DC: U.S. Department of Agriculture, 2010.

Divina, F., and M. Divina. *Foods of the Americas: Native Recipes and Traditions*. Berkeley, CA: Ten Speed Press, 2004.

Edwards, K. A. "Daily Life in Medieval Europe." In *World Eras: Medieval Europe, 814–1350*. Ed. by J. Hackett. Farmington Hills, MI: Thomson Gale, 2001.

Egan, T. *The Worst Hard Time*. Boston: Houghton Mifflin, 2005.

Fenster, C. *Gluten-Free Baking*. Centennial, CO: Savory Palate, 2004.

Fenster, C. *Gluten-Free 101: Easy, Basic Dishes without Wheat*, 4th edition. Centennial, CO: Savory Palate, 2003.

Freeland-Graves, J. H., and G. C. Peckham. *Foundations of Food Preparation*, 6th edition. Englewood Cliffs, NJ: Prentice-Hall, 1996.

Fuhrman, J. *Super Immunity*. New York: HarperOne, 2011.

Grandin, T., and C. Johnson. *Animals in Translation*. New York: Scribner, 2004.

Green, A. *Field Guide to Produce*. Philadelphia: Quirk Books, 2004.

Grigson, S. with W. Black. *Fish*. London: Headline Book Publishing, 1998.

Hagman, B. *The Gluten-Free Gourmet Bakes Bread*. New York: Henry Holt, 1999.

Heaton, D. D. *A Produce Reference Guide to Fruits and Vegetables from Around the World*. Binghamton, NY: Food Products Press, 1997.

Hensperger, B., and J. Kaufmann. *Not Your Mother's Slow Cooker Cookbook*. Boston: Harvard Common Press, 2005.

Hensperger, B., and J. Kaufmann. *The Ultimate Rice Cooker Cookbook*. Boston: Harvard Common Press, 2002.

Janick, J., and J. E. Simon. *Advances in New Crops*. Portland, OR: Timber Press, 1990.

Janick, J., and J. E. Simon. *New Crops*. New York: Wiley, 1993.

Janick, J. *Prospectives on New Crops and New Uses*. Alexandria, VA: ASHS Press, 1999.

Jenkins, S. *Cheese Primer*. New York: Workman Publishing, 1996.

King Arthur Flour. *King Arthur Flour Baker's Companion*. Woodstock, VT: Countryman Press, 2003.

Kiple, K. F., and K. C. Ornelas, eds. *The Cambridge World History of Food*. Cambridge: Cambridge University Press, 2000.

Kurlansky, M. *Cod: A Biography of the Fish That Changed the World*. New York: Penguin Books, 1997.

Kurlansky, M. *Salt: A World History*. New York: Penguin Books, 2002.

Kushi, A., with A. Jack. *Aveline Kushi's Complete Guide to Macrobiotic Cooking*. New York: Warner Books, 1985.

Leader, D., and J. Blahnik. *Bread Alone*. New York: William Morrow, 1993.

Loha-Unchit, K. *Dancing Shrimp: Favorite Thai Recipes for Seafood*. New York: Simon and Schuster, 2000.

Loha-Unchit, K. *It Rains Fishes*. Rohnert Park, CA: Pomegranate Communications, 1995.

Mann, Charles C. *1493: Uncovering the New World Columbus Created*. New York: Knopf, 2011.

Matterer, J. L. *A Boke of Gode Cookery, vol. 1*. Princes Risborough, Buckinghamshire, UK: Shire Publications, 2000.

McCalman, M., and D. Gibbons. *The Cheese Plate*. New York: Clarkson Potter, 2002.

McGee, H. *On Food and Cooking: The Science and Lore of the Kitchen*. New York: Scribner, 2004.

Nabhan, G. *Renewing America's Food Traditions*. White River Junction, VT: Chelsea Green Publishing, 2008.

Nestle, M. *What to Eat*. New York: North Point Press, 2006.

Niman, B., and J. Fletcher. *The Niman Ranch Cookbook*. Berkeley, CA: Ten Speed Press, 2005.

Opton, G. H., and N. Hughes. *Honey: A Connoisseur's Guide with Recipes*. Berkeley, CA: Ten Speed Press, 2000.

Ortiz, J. *The Village Baker*. Berkeley, CA: Ten Speed Press, 1993.

Pitchford, P. *Healing with Whole Foods*. Berkeley, CA: North Atlantic Books, 2002.

Rayner, L. *Wild Bread*. Flagstaff, AZ: Lifeweaver LLC, 2009.

Reinhart, P. *Artisan Breads Every Day*. Berkeley, CA: Ten Speed Press, 2009.

Reinhart, P. *Crust and Crumb*. Berkeley, CA: Ten Speed Press, 1998.

Reinhart, P. *The Bread Baker's Apprentice*. Berkeley, CA: Ten Speed Press, 2001.

Reinhart, P. *Whole Grain Breads*. Berkeley, CA: Ten Speed Press, 2007.

Robertson, L., with C. Flinders and B. Godfrey. *The Laurel's Kitchen Bread Book*. New York: Random House, 2003.

Robertson, R. *Fresh from the Vegetarian Slow Cooker*. Boston: Harvard Common Press, 2004.

Rögnvaldardóttir, N. *Cool Cuisine*. Reykjavik, Iceland: Vaka-Helgafell, 2004.

Rögnvaldardóttir, N. *Icelandic Food and Cookery*. New York: Hippocrene Books, 2002.

Saltman, J. *Amazing Grains*. Tiburon, CA: H. J. Kramer, 1990.

Sando, S., and V. Barrington. *Heirloom Beans*. San Francisco: Chronicle Books, 2008.

Sass, L. J. *Pressure Perfect*. New York: William Morrow, 2004.

Schneider, E. *The Essential Reference: Vegetables from Amaranth to Zucchini*. New York: William Morrow, 2001.

Schneider, E. *Uncommon Fruits and Vegetables: A Commonsense Guide*. New York: William Morrow, 1986.

Shurtleff, W., and A. Aoyagi. *The Book of Tofu*. New York, NY: Ballantine Books, 1979.

Shurtleff, W., and A. Aoyagi. *Tofu and Soymilk Production: The Book of Tofu, 2nd edition*. Lafayette, CA: Soyfoods Center, 1990.

Smith, M. *Your Backyard Herb Garden*. Emmaus, PA: Rodale Press, 1997.

Solomon, C. *Encyclopedia of Asian Food*. Hong Kong: Periplus Editions, 1998.

Thomas, C. *Melissa's Great Book of Produce*. Hoboken, NJ: John Wiley & Sons, 2006.

Weil, A. *Eating Well for Optimum Health*. New York: Alfred A. Knopf, 2000.

Weinzweig, A. *Zingerman's Guide to Good Eating*. New York: Houghton Mifflin, 2003.

Werlin, L. *The New American Cheese*. New York: Stewart, Tabori & Chang, 2000.

Willett, W. C. *Eat, Drink, and Be Healthy*. New York: Free Press, 2001.

Wood, E. *Classic Sourdoughs*. Berkeley, CA: Ten Speed Press, 2001.

Wood, R. *The Splendid Grain*. New York: William Morrow, 1997.

Wright, J. *Pasta*. London: Lorenz Books, 2003.

DISCARD